Social class and the division of labour

Ilya Neustadt

Social class and the division of labour

Essays in honour of
Ilya Neustadt

edited by

ANTHONY GIDDENS
Fellow of King's College, Cambridge

GAVIN MACKENZIE
Fellow of Jesus College, Cambridge

CAMBRIDGE UNIVERSITY PRESS
Cambridge
London   New York   New Rochelle
Melbourne   Sydney

Published by the Press Syndicate of the University of Cambridge
The Pitt Building, Trumpington Street, Cambridge CB2 1RP
32 East 57th Street, New York, NY 10022, USA
296 Beaconsfield Parade, Middle Park, Melbourne 3206, Australia

© Cambridge University Press 1982

First published 1982

Printed in the United States of America

Library of Congress catalogue card number: 82-4275

British Library Cataloguing in Publication Data

Social class and the division of labour
1. Neustadt, Ilya   2. Social class
—Addresses, essays, lectures
I. Giddens, Anthony   II. Mackenzie, Gavin
III. Neustadt, Ilya
305.5'1   HT609

ISBN 0 521 24597 4 hardcovers
ISBN 0 521 28809 6 paperback

Contents

Contents

Contributors

SHEILA ALLEN. Lecturer in Sociology, University of Leicester, 1961–65. Senior Lecturer in Sociology, University of Bradford, 1966–71, Reader 1971–72, Professor of Sociology since 1972.
President, British Sociological Association, 1975–77.
Author of: *New Minorities, Old Conflicts* (1971); (co-author), *Work, Race and Immigration* (1977); (co-editor), *Sexual Divisions and Society* (1976), and *Dependence and Exploitation in Work and Marriage* (1976); and numerous articles.

TOM BOTTOMORE. Lecturer/Reader in Sociology, London School of Economics, 1952–64. Professor and Head of Department of Political Science, Sociology and Anthropology, Simon Fraser University, Vancouver, Canada, 1965–67. Professor of Sociology, University of Sussex, since 1968.
President, British Sociological Association, 1969–71. President, International Sociological Association, 1974–78.
Author of: *Classes in Modern Society* (1965); *Elites and Society* (1964); (ed., with Robert Nisbet), *A History of Sociological Analysis* (1979); *Political Sociology* (1979) and other books and articles.

RICHARD K. BROWN. Research Officer in Sociology, University of Leicester, 1959–60. Assistant Lecturer and (from 1962) Lecturer in Sociology, University of Leicester, 1960–66. Lecturer, Senior Lecturer, and (from 1974) Reader in Sociology, University of Durham, 1966– .
Co-author, *The Sociology of Industry* (1981); (ed.), *Knowledge, Education and Cultural Change* (1973); and of numerous articles in the sociology of work and industry.

ELY CHINOY (1921–75). Assistant Professor, Associate Professor, Professor of Sociology, Smith College, 1951–69; The Mary Huggins Gam-

Contributors

ble Professor of Sociology, Smith College, 1969–75. Visiting Professor of Sociology, University of Leicester, 1963–64.
Author of: *Automobile Workers and the American Dream* (1955); *The Sociological Perspective* (1954); *Society* (1961); (ed.), *The Urban Future* (1973) and numerous articles.

ANTHONY GIDDENS. Lecturer, University of Leicester, 1963–70. Lecturer, University of Cambridge, since 1970.
Author of: *Capitalism and Modern Social Theory, The Class Structure of the Advanced Societies, Central Problems in Social Theory, A Contemporary Critique of Historical Materialism* vol. I.

JOHN GOLDTHORPE. Assistant Lecturer in Sociology, University of Leicester, 1957–60. Fellow of King's College, Cambridge, 1960–69 and Lecturer in the Faculty of Economics, Cambridge, 1962–69. Official Fellow, Nuffield College, Oxford, since 1969.
Author of: (with David Lockwood *et al.*), *The Affluent Worker* series 1968–69; *Social Mobility and Class Structure in Modern Britain* (1981) and other monographs and numerous articles.

PAUL HIRST. BA, University of Leicester, 1968. Lecturer in Sociology, Birkbeck College, University of London, 1969–78; Reader in Social Theory, Birkbeck College, since 1978.
Author of: *Durkheim, Bernard and Epistemology* (1975); *Social Evolution and Sociological Categories* (1976); *On Law and Ideology* (1979); (with B. Hindess), *Pre-Capitalist Modes of Production* (1975); *Mode of Production and Social Formation* (1977); (with A. J. Cutler *et al.*), *Marx's Capital and Capitalism Today* (2 vols. 1977 and 1978); (with P. Woolley), *Social Relations and Human Attributes* (London, 1982).

GEOFFREY INGHAM. BA, University of Leicester, 1964. Lecturer in Sociology, University of Leicester, 1969–71. University Assistant Lecturer and Lecturer, University of Cambridge, 1971–   ; Fellow of Christ's College, Cambridge, 1972–   .
Author of: *Size of Industrial Organization and Worker Behaviour* (1970); *Strikes and Industrial Conflict* (1974) and articles in the fields of social class, industrial conflict, etc.

TERRY JOHNSON. BA, University of Leicester, 1963. Lecturer in Sociology, University of Leicester, 1964–69. Research Fellow, Institute of Commonwealth Studies, 1969–72; Senior Lecturer in Sociology, University of Leicester since 1973. Joint Editor of *Economy and Society* since its foundation.
Author of: *Professions and Power* and numerous articles on the professions.

viii

DAVID LOCKWOOD. FBA 1976. Assistant Lecturer (1953–58) and Lecturer (1958–60) in Sociology, London School of Economics. University Lecturer in the Faculty of Economics, and Fellow of St John's College, Cambridge, 1960–68. Professor of Sociology, University of Essex, since 1968. Member of the Social Science Research Council and Chairman of the Sociology and Social Administration Committee, 1973–75.
Author of: *The Blackcoated Worker: A Study in Class Consciousness* (1958); (joint-author), *The Affluent Worker* (3 vols. 1968–69); numerous articles in journals and symposia.

GAVIN MACKENZIE. BA, University of Leicester, 1964. Lecturer in Sociology, University of Leicester, 1968–70. Fellow and (from 1982) Senior Tutor of Jesus College, Cambridge since 1970; Assistant Lecturer and (from 1972) Lecturer in Sociology, University of Cambridge since 1970.
Author of: *The Aristocracy of Labour: The Position of Skilled Craftsmen in the American Class Structure* (1973) and numerous articles. General Editor of Fontana New Sociology.

T. H. MARSHALL (1893–1981). Hon.D.Litt., Leicester, 1970; Hon.D.Litt., Cambridge, 1978. Lecturer in Social Administration, London School of Economics, 1925–30; Reader in Sociology, London School of Economics, 1930–39; Head of the Department of Social Science, London School of Economics, 1944–50; The Martin White Professor of Sociology, London School of Economics, 1954–56.
President of the International Sociological Association, 1959–62.
Author of: *James Watt* (1925); (ed.), *Class Conflict and Social Stratification* (1938); (ed.), *The Population Problem* (1938); *Citizenship and Social Class* (1950); *Sociology at the Crossroads* (1963); *Social Policy* (1965) and numerous articles.

ALI RATTANSI. Lecturer in Sociology, University of Leicester School of Education, since 1976.
Author of: *Marx and the Division of Labour* (1982) and several articles.

GRAEME SALAMAN. BA, University of Leicester, 1965. Lecturer in Sociology, Open University, 1971–79; Senior Lecturer since 1979.
Author of: *Community and Occupation* (1974); *Work Organisations, Resistance and Control* (1979); *Class and the Corporation* (1981); editor of numerous anthologies, including (with David Dunkerley), *The International Yearbook of Organisation Studies* (1979–   ) and author of numerous articles.

Contributors

RICHARD SCASE. BA, and MA, University of Leicester, 1964 and 1965. Reader in Sociology at the University of Kent at Canterbury.
Author of: *Social Democracy in Capitalist Society* (1977); (co-author, with Robert Goffee), *The Real World of the Small Business Owner* (1980) and *The Entrepreneurial Middle Class* (1982); (ed.), *Readings in the Swedish Class Structure* (1976), *Industrial Society: Class, Cleavage and Control* (1977), and *The State in Western Europe* (1980); also of various articles within the general areas of political behaviour, social stratification and industrial organisation.

JOHN SCOTT. Lecturer in Sociology, University of Strathclyde, 1972–76. Lecturer in Sociology, University of Leicester since 1976.
Author of: *Corporations, Classes and Capitalism* (1979); (with M. Hughes), *The Anatomy of Scottish Capital* (1980); *The Upper Classes: Property and Privilege in Britain* (1982).

Foreword

T. H. MARSHALL

Ilya Neustadt was born on 21 November 1915 in Southern Russia, near Odessa. At a very early age his family migrated to Bessarabia, where he went to school. The curriculum appears to have been a comprehensive one including elements both of the social and of the natural sciences. It was largely his wish to develop the latter that led him to embark on a year's course of medicine in Bucharest. It gave him, he says, a lasting interest in biology, but he was not tempted to adopt a medical career. He decided instead to move to the Liège School of Economics, where he obtained his doctorate in 1939 for a thesis on 'International Organisation in Central Europe'.[1] The thesis, a substantial work in diplomatic and legal history, ending with a passionate denunciation of 'the German avalanche', is dismissed by Neustadt today as 'not really sociological'. The most serious rival to the social sciences in his interests at this juncture was music. He was a very promising violinist and for one whole year he combined a full programme at the Conservatoire with the continuation of his political studies. But, although music might well have become his chosen career, he decided otherwise.

It was almost by accident that he turned from politics to sociology. After escaping from Belgium to London, his first intention was to enrol as a graduate student under Harold Laski at the London School of Economics. It so happened that Laski was not available and he was referred instead to Morris Ginsberg, and thus was led to adopt the subject which remained with him throughout his academic career. The thesis for which he was awarded the PhD degree was entitled 'Some Aspects of the Social Structure of Belgium' and was concerned in particular with the distinction between the 'old' and the 'new'

Final corrections were made to this preface on 27 October 1981. With deep regret we have to record that Tom Marshall died shortly afterwards, on 29 November 1981. We should like this book to serve also as a memorial to him.

middle classes.[2] There followed an interlude in which his most important assignment was to assemble a collection of Russian books in the LSE Library. He remained there until he went as lecturer to Leicester, where his sociological future was finally established.

Neustadt took up his appointment as Lecturer in Sociology in the Department of Economics in Leicester in 1949. His assignment was to teach the sociology special subject of the London External Degree of BSc(Econ). For some three years he discharged these functions single handed, until help came with the arrival of Joe Banks as Assistant Lecturer (who has since returned as Professor) and some three years later with the attachment to the Department of the distinguished German scholar, Norbert Elias. But in these first few years, Neustadt's greatest asset was without doubt the strong support given him by Arthur Pool, the Professor of Economics and Head of the Department to which sociology was attached. The warm welcome he gave to the new arrival helped to win for Neustadt a reaction of benevolent curiosity rather than of suspicion. 'He immediately intrigued us', says Bryan Wilson, one of his first and most distinguished students, 'as much by his own exotic origins as by the mysteries of the subject he was to teach.' He was quite unlike any other member of the faculty. 'He was,' says Wilson, 'by turns highly critical, endlessly timetaking, charming, amusing and irascible.' A tutorial might continue for two or three hours, without regard to the lecturer waiting for a classroom, and studies might be pursued on the lawn, in the pub or in the street. He was always 'exploring ideas, ruminating, in a sense teaching'. Lectures in these early days were a bit unpredictable; a successful lecture was a thrill, both for him and for his audience. It gave full scope to his very individual style in which there was, as he freely admits, more than a touch of the theatrical. The Neustadt image undoubtedly owed a lot to his 'exotic origins', but it would be erroneous to describe him as a 'foreigner'; he was – and at heart still is – a cosmopolitan. This showed itself most obviously in his effortless command of languages. The story is told that once, when somebody asked whether anyone present had read the whole of *'Das Kapital'*, Ilya answered quietly: 'I have; in French.' 'Why in French?' 'Because I couldn't find it in Russian.'

If not a 'foreigner', was he an 'eccentric'? In that respect, too, the image is misleading. Eccentricity does not match with the purposeful dedication to a cause that Neustadt exhibited from the first. And you do not lift a university department from the level of nought to a shade short of thirty by eccentricity alone. It requires shrewd, unremitting and determined attention to business of a very practical kind, as Vice-

Chancellors who have worked with him are willing to testify. In the competition for scarce resources, says Sir Charles Wilson, 'Ilya managed to get at least his share and sometimes more', thanks to 'a useful combination of obsessive determination and charm in his approach to colleagues'. Or, as Sir Fraser Noble put it, 'he encouraged the really bright young people, and he nursed the weaker brothers and sisters and fought like a tiger for their interests'. This might become exasperating at times for a wholly sympathetic Chairman with other matters to attend to. The game was played – and it did have something of the flavour of a game – without malice.

Much of what I have just said applies in particular to the period after which Neustadt had been given the official title of Head of Department (in 1959) and still more so when he became Professor in 1962. It is significant that Neustadt should have chosen 'Teaching Sociology' as the title of his Inaugural Lecture[3] – not the most usual angle from which to launch a professorial dissertation. But he had good grounds for doing so. For teaching was not only something that he did supremely well, but it was also, as used by him, the best way of explaining how the most fundamental principles of his subject could be imparted to his students. John Goldthorpe, seeking to discover the special quality of Neustadt's teaching style, suggests that it might be described as 'sociological good taste'; nothing slovenly, nothing makeshift, no cutting of corners, no jumping ahead before the foundations have been thoroughly grasped. It is probably in the seminar or small group that this method of teaching is most clearly exemplified, by relentless probing and Socratic questioning until in the end out of the teaching of sociology there emerge the principles of sociology, not incidentally but explicitly. Neustadt himself contributed richly to these probing questions, and not only in the classroom. At breakfast, in the garden or out walking, the familiar voice could be heard saying: 'I have a sociological problem.' Never just 'a problem'; always a 'sociological' one, which should imply that he is prepared to say what sociology is and what it is not: it is identifiable.

There is much talk in the Inaugural Lecture about science and its attributes, but it is not suggested that sociology is 'a science' and it would indeed be foolish to start that particular hare. The phrase which seems to me most accurately to express Neustadt's meaning is 'a scientific discipline', and it is precisely in the context of the teaching of sociology that he uses it. It may be said that medicine is not 'a science' but it is scientific, by virtue of being a 'discipline'. What this conveys is well suggested in a phrase used by Elias when he speaks of 'the highly specialised training embodied in the conceptual tools, the basic assumptions, the method of speaking and thinking which scientists use'.[4] A discipline of this kind is a means of extending the area of 'detachment' as against the area of 'involvement' (the terms used by Elias in this article), and thus of increasing the possibility of preserving standards of objectivity and scientific integrity in a field in which it is particularly difficult to do so without jeopardising the freedom of the sociological imagination. Neustadt insists on the importance of objectivity, but the last thing he would want to do would be to achieve it by putting his students into an intellectual strait-jacket. His approach to the subject is discriminating. He is the implacable enemy not only of the prostitution of a cheap kind of 'popular sociology' to the advancement of political ends; he is also insistent in warning against other kinds of lapse from true objectivity which, though meritorious in intention, can be dangerous in practice. He cites as one example sociologically oriented fiction, which can be very illuminating if properly reassessed, and as another, the impetuous assaults made on social problems by eager students in their desire to find quick and easy solutions.

It is not surprising that Neustadt should pick on Comte to provide a key to the essential substance of sociology, since Comte is probably the writer into whose works Neustadt has delved most deeply. He found it in the passage in which Comte urges us always to keep in mind the need for 'des conceptions et des études d'ensembles'.[5] Neustadt applies this principle at all levels, wherever it is possible to trace the interdependence of social factors and thus to proceed from analysis to synthesis. The 'wholes' revealed by these studies may be elements in the social structure or they may be taken at the macrosociological level, as by Comte himself, to refer to total societies or cultures. The approach is further elaborated by a passage in the Inaugural Lecture which shows how closely the substance of sociology is linked with the method. Neustadt writes: 'Among the main methodological tools of sociologists are comparisons of societies, past and present, at different stages of development, and in Leicester, particularly, teaching is centred on such comparisons.'[6] Comparison for Neustadt was not only a method of scientific procedure; it was an all-pervasive style of thought, and an element in his cosmopolitan character.

Nothing can better illustrate the significance of these approaches to sociology, as I have attempted briefly to set them out, than Neustadt's experiences in Africa. They began in 1957 when he was invited to spend a year as visiting professor in Ghana, where the teaching of sociology for the London External Degree was already in train. It was while he was there that he conceived the idea of promoting a survey of the economy and the social structure, for which the Census projected for 1960 – the first since independence – was expected to provide invaluable material. Neustadt returned in 1960 and 1962 to join with Walter Birmingham, an economist, and E. N. Omaboe, a Ghanaian demographer, to complete the planning, execution and editing of the research. It was published in two volumes in 1966 and 1967.[7] Neustadt was deeply involved in the whole enterprise and this experience, combined with the effect of living and working in the country and among the people of Ghana, was one by which he was both moved and excited. In addition, he was able to visit other parts of Africa, including an assignment by Unesco to Sierra Leone. Neustadt found in Africa a ready-made sociological laboratory. It was, he has said, as if the processes of social evolution described by Durkheim and Weber were being enacted under one's eyes, but with the motions accelerated. The immediacy of change was, he thought, something that most anthropologists missed, because they had too static a conception of social structure. Neustadt started from change and went on to find out how social institutions and individual personalities could be adjusted to it. As a young man said to him in Accra, when the talk was all about 'political emancipation' and 'responsible citizenship', 'we also want to be *subjectively* independent'.

The outstanding feature of what may be called the legacy of Leicester is undoubtedly the remarkably high proportion of teachers of sociology in British universities whose careers in sociology began in Neustadt's Department in Leicester. This is not just something one can find out if one troubles to look up the figures; it is a familiar part of the academic landscape, and it was achieved in just over 30 years, starting from scratch. The reputation of the department has been not only a British one, but an international one. This is evinced in two ways. First, by its recognition as a port of call for visiting sociologists from abroad; and secondly, by the international flavour of the staff. It is said that there was a period during which the British-born members of the department were in a minority. Neustadt was not – and would never claim to be – the sole source of this reputation, but he was the impresario who made it all happen. And he made a very definite and powerful personal contribution to the teaching of the subject. I am told that once, when asked what kind of sociology was taught in Leicester, he replied: 'There are only two kinds of sociology – good sociology and bad sociology. We teach good sociology.' I take this to mean that if a subject is really well taught, it cannot long remain a 'bad' subject. Good teaching will either expose it or refine it. Whereas it is all too easy for a 'good' subject to be badly taught. This is the measure of the teacher's power.

The book to which this memoir provides an introduction has been compiled by a selection of writers all of whom may be said to have participated in some way, as colleagues, students or associates, in what I have called the 'legacy of Leicester', and in this spirit it is dedicated to Ilya Neustadt and his Department. The theme chosen to bring the articles together – class and the division of labour – expresses one of his most central interests. At a time when sociology was dominated by the concept of 'social differentiation', Neustadt stressed the importance of the role of the division of labour in social analysis. This approach has the effect of throwing into relief the asymmetrical relations of power in the institutions of industrialised society and thus helps to amplify the treatment of social division as a sociological problem. The subject of the book is therefore both highly relevant to current sociological thinking and wholly suitable to serve as a tribute to Ilya Neustadt and his work.

Introduction

A concern with class analysis has long been one of the main preoccupations of British sociology. Certainly this is an area to which sociologists working in this country have made some of their most notable contributions. In recent years, however, reflecting in some degree changes that have been taking place within sociology as a whole, a fresh wave of research into problems of class inequalities and conflicts has been produced. Of particular importance, of course, is the fact that the past decade or so has seen a major revival of Marxist thought, in various forms; and this inevitably has made a deep imprint upon debates in class theory. Furthermore, in the postpositivist phase of the reconstruction of social thought, certain other issues have come to the fore that also have a direct bearing upon class analysis. These issues include basic problems about how human action should be conceptualised, and what relation should be supposed to exist between action and the 'structural' components of social institutions. In some part as a result of these developments, which indicate that all the social sciences share a common core of problems, the boundaries between sociology and other fields of social science have become much less impermeable than they used to be. The concept of the division of labour itself has once again become a unifying notion connecting the writings of sociologists and economists. A resurgence of interest in the state among sociological writers has helped to efface some of the barriers that used to separate sociology and political science. Not least important, at the same time as sociologists have recovered the importance of history, historians have been making increasing use of sociological methods and insights, thus creating a further *rapprochement* between previously distinct forms of intellectual endeavour.

The results of all this have by no means been wholly edifying. In social theory, much effort has been expended upon programmatic statements which promise a great deal but whose yield, especially in respect of generating substantive research, has been rather less than impressive. Something similar is true in the more limited confines of the study of class. There is certainly no shortage of abstract discussions of the concept of 'class' and related issues, often involving complicated formal categories which are at best remote from concrete problems of class analysis, at worst vacuous. We have tried to avoid such discussions in the articles collected together in this volume. Most of the contributors show themselves to be aware of current developments in social theory, but they have sought to draw upon these developments in a critical vein, and in the context of analysing quite concrete issues. The result, we think, is a book which provides an excellent introduction to contemporary work in class analysis, but which at the same time represents an important contribution to the existing literature in its own right.

Many of those who have contributed to this book, including its editors, were educated at a time at which sociology was (for the most part) dominated by 'structural-functionalism', and by a scorn for the historical study of long-term processes of social development. The influence of Ilya Neustadt over those who were his students or colleagues – together with the formidable impact made during his years at Leicester by Norbert Elias – ensured that few succumbed to these then prevalent ideas or tendencies. The work of Elias is now generally available in English, and no one today can doubt the significance of his achievements in sociology. In his teaching at Leicester, Elias attuned a whole generation of students to his ideas – which at the time remained largely unknown to those who did not enjoy personal contact with him. Neustadt wrote less than Elias, but his influence, in teaching and other contexts, was equally strong. In respect of the work incorporated in this book, Neustadt's approach was particularly important. As T. H. Marshall notes at the conclusion of his portrayal of Neustadt's career, Neustadt insisted upon the significance of the concept of the division of labour at a time when the more bland and diffuse notion of 'social differentiation' had very largely displaced it. Moreover, he emphasised forcibly that class divisions and class conflict could only be satisfactorily theorised in conjunction with an elaborated analysis of the division of labour.

What was then a heretical view has today become generally recognised to be of central importance. The 'division of labour' has become a respectable concept again – one which in the recent literature has received a considerable amount of attention. Several of the papers in this book focus directly upon the division of labour, considering especially Marxist views of its relation to class domination. Rattansi offers a discussion of this issue at source, in Marx's writings. His main thesis, interestingly and originally argued, is that the theme of the transcendence of the division of labour in Marx is by no means the utopian conception it has appeared to many of Marx's critics. In his early writings, Rattansi argues, Marx tended to merge the concepts of 'class' and 'the division of labour'. Hence he wrote as though the disappearance of classes, in a socialist society, would *ipso facto* entail the dissolution of the division of labour such as it is found in capitalism. Later he progressively abandoned such a view, as he came to see that large-scale industrial production imposes exigencies that are not simply and solely the outcome of class domination. He continued to accentuate the idea of the transcendence of the division of labour, but his emphasis shifted to the narrower issue of overcoming the division between mental and manual labour.

Rattansi's discussion forms a useful complement to those papers in the book which concern themselves with the division of labour as it currently exists in capitalist production. Recent analysis has been strongly influenced by Braverman's *Labor and Monopoly Capital*. This work deservedly ranks as one of the most notable contributions to the discussion of the division of labour within Marxist traditions. However, over the seven or eight years since the book first appeared, its limitations have become more and more apparent. The articles by Giddens, Salaman and Mackenzie focus upon some of these limitations, in the course of discussing various problems of class theory. Giddens connects a discussion of the relation between action and structure to a critical commentary upon Braverman's work, coupled to themes drawn from Max Weber's classical interpretation of bureaucracy. He points out that, although written from a Marxist standpoint, Braverman's conception of the fragmentation of the labour process in capitalism leads to conclusions not dissimilar to those of Weber, in respect of the inevitability of the concentration of power in the hands of the few. These conclusions, according to Giddens, are mistaken; they derive in some part from a failure to consider the 'dialectic of control' that operates in all organisations, in which shifting imbalances of power chronically occur.

In similar vein, both Salaman and Mackenzie emphasise the invigorating effect which Braverman's work has produced – stimulating a wealth of new studies of the labour process in different contexts of capitalist development. Among the most important of Braverman's claims (although it remains a controversial one) is that class domination enters into the very nature of industrial technology, especially

3

in relation to the mental/manual labour division. Braverman's book has also served to reopen questions of the character and origins of managerial control of the labour force. Accepting the significance of these contributions, like Giddens, Salaman finds their actual analysis by Braverman wanting. 'Management' is regarded as a passive category, not as a creative process involving knowledgeable agents. Moreover, position in the division of labour should be regarded as only one dimension of the structuration of class relationships, which also has to have reference to phenomena outside the industrial enterprise itself.

Mackenzie's article focusses on overlapping issues. In particular he is concerned with the issue of how 'class boundaries' should be conceptualised. Where the boundaries between classes lie, and how the delineation of different class groupings should be formulated, are major problems left by the legacy of Marx. These problems do not just concern the differentiation of 'capital' and 'wage-labour' as organised classes – 'bourgeoisie' and 'proletariat' – but bear particularly upon intermediate classes. Within the past few years several Marxist authors, including Poulantzas, Wright and Carchedi, have made attempts to identify the character of such intermediate classes in relation to capital and wage-labour. The value of their work, according to Mackenzie, is compromised by its formal, descriptive character. But rather than being dismissed, this work needs to be conjoined precisely to the sort of literature dealing with the dynamics of the labour process stimulated by Braverman and his critics. An historical approach is essential to this endeavour.

The direct study of varying forms of labour, especially in respect of assembly-line production, was, throughout his intellectual career, the prime concern of the late Ely Chinoy (the only American contributor to this volume). His discussion combines closely with those just referred to, although it is not explicitly concerned with Braverman's ideas. Chinoy concentrates particularly upon the application of the principles of 'scientific management' in the Ford Motor Company in the early part of this century. More recently management has made a series of efforts to synchronise the production line, using computers to assist in the coordination of workers and machines. But managers have come to recognise that speed and technical efficiency of production have to take second place to the quality of the end-product. Quality control cannot be built in to the production line by purely technical coordination, but depends upon securing the active involvement of the labour force with the work they do. Here lies one of the major sources of tension in assembly-line manufacture. For workers have abandoned 'craft values' in a context in which their labour has become increasingly routinised and mechanical.

Chinoy's discussion broaches questions of workers' attitudes to their labour, and wider issues of class consciousness. Several other papers in this book also explore facets of these problems. Lockwood's analysis, although couched in fairly general terms, provides a framework for exploring modes of compliance to the directives of those in authority. His argument has affinities with that of Michael Mann's characterisation of the legitimacy of authority in *Consciousness and Action among the Western Working Class*. This latter author emphasises that the compliance of workers to managerial authority in industry does not necessarily, or even generally, rest upon consensually shared goals. Rather, workers adopt 'pragmatic' attitudes towards their participation in industrial labour, seeing it in large degree as inevitable if not desirable. But at the same time they do not, for the most part, have an articulated conception of how things could be different. Lockwood similarly attacks 'consensus' theories of compliance to authority, developing a characteristically innovative interpretation of the neglected type in Durkheim's categorisation of forms of suicide: fatalism. 'Fatalism', Lockwood suggests, may be a concept capable of much broader application than Durkheim accords it. Chronic poverty, or fixity of status, in traditional societies may be accepted because these are seen as governed by forces over which those subject to them have no control. Much the same may be the case for those who carry out dull or oppressive work, or suffer long-standing unemployment, in capitalist societies. Fatalistic attitudes do not imply a heavy measure of direct coercion, but rather that the social circumstances in which individuals exist are seen as unchanging and unchangeable. Such a 'fatalism of belief', as Lockwood calls it, might be common in contemporary capitalist societies. Nonetheless it is to be distinguished from 'fatalistic ideologies' as such, the sort of 'ethics of fatalism' found for instance in the Indian caste system.

In spite of the now generally agreed necessity of incorporating an historical dimension into sociological analysis, many studies of class and class consciousness continue to imply that social life exists in a timeless vacuum. One of the important features of Richard Brown's paper is that he seeks to show how important work histories are in the detailed analysis of occupational categories. The notion of 'occupation' has been used by virtually all scholars who have written about the division of labour, but there are manifest inadequacies in the concept as it is ordinarily applied. Many accounts – one might again here instance the work of Poulantzas, Wright and Carchedi – tend to consider occupations only at one point in time. They neglect the temporal development of 'careers', which both intersect with, and help to constitute, broader institutional changes in class relationships over time. A single individual, for example, may occupy a succession of different positions in the division of labour in the course of his or her life-cycle. The study of work histories, Brown shows, is important both for explicating changes in class structure and in understanding forms of class consciousness. For the past and potential future 'work biographies' of individuals are likely to be the grounding for their attitudes towards work, and their more general consciousness, views and actions.

These considerations are germane to the analysis of relations between class, gender and the division of labour. For as Brown points out, undue focus upon the notion of occupation has obscured the significance of the labour of those who do not work in 'gainfully paid' jobs – particularly 'housewives'. Allen shows in her paper how commonly women have been ignored in class theory, and in research into class relationships. Recent work has done something to remedy this deficiency, but a great deal more is still needed. Work-history research is certainly crucial to understanding the intersection between sexual and class divisions in society. The 'interruption' of women's careers by the birth and bringing up of children, for example, is – both materially and ideologically – a major factor confining women to underprivileged sectors of segmented labour markets.

In referring to Mackenzie's paper, we have already mentioned the burgeoning literature concerned with re-examining the position of 'intermediate strata' in contemporary capitalist societies. Three articles in this volume, which complement each other rather neatly, concentrate directly upon these categories or groupings. Scase's discussion reiterates some of the points made by Giddens, Salaman and Mackenzie in criticism of the 'functionalist Marxism' of Poulantzas *et al.* But Scase is explicitly concerned with the petty bourgeoisie in the traditional sense of the term: that is to say, Poulantzas's 'old petty bourgeoisie'. The approach of the 'functionalist Marxists' is castigated because, in placing an overwhelming emphasis upon class 'positions' or 'places', they ignore the modes in which actors are able to organise their careers so as to influence what those positions or places actually *are*. The petty bourgeoisie, Scase claims, retain an important role in class relations in the capitalist societies today. In this respect he diverges from Marx's empirical prognosis of capitalist development, just as he differs from the theoretical standpoint of some of Marx's recent professed followers. Marx argued that the petty bourgeoisie would dwindle away with the maturation of capitalism, since large capital ousts small capital from more and more spheres of production. But small business, in various forms, continues to survive. Its continued existence, Scase reasons, is not to be understood solely as an archaic remnant of the early phases of capitalist development. Small business provides a potential avenue of upward mobility for those who lack the educational or technical qualifications to move up within larger organisations. Moreover, large firms are often dependent upon goods or services provided through subcontracting in areas of the economy – including the 'black economy' – where large-scale enterprise is neither feasible nor profitable.

In contrast, Goldthorpe and Johnson are both concerned with sectors of the 'new petty bourgeoisie' – or 'new middle class'. Goldthorpe, however, offers yet another term, borrowed from Renner: that of 'service class'. The service class, in Goldthorpe's analysis, consists of professional, administrative and managerial employees. In common with Mackenzie, he draws attention to the difficulties which Marx and subsequent Marxists have experienced in coping conceptually with such groupings; and he too is dissatisfied with the views expressed by 'functionalist Marxists'. But he also provides an incisive critical review of other perspectives from inside and outside Marxist thought. The idea of a service class, appropriately explicated, he concludes, is the most fruitful way of grasping the connections between structural components of the class position of higher white-collar workers and their typical conduct and beliefs. The 'code of service' which tends to govern the conditions of employment of such workers, which involves a certain moral quality, differentiates them from the single-stranded economic labour contract entered into by the working class and by lower-level office employees. Those in the service class are delegated with areas of responsibility in exchange for making a moral commitment to the enterprise within which they work. This both tends to give them interests different from those who are not delegated with such responsibilities, and stimulates different forms of socio-political action. In analysing these, Goldthorpe again places some considerable emphasis upon the importance of incorporating a time-dimension that allows for the study of overlapping career histories.

Johnson's discussion of the professions concentrates not upon the incorporation of professional employees within delegated authority systems inside organisations, but rather upon the relation between professions and the state. He sets out to criticise, on the basis of empirical evidence, the conventional thesis that 'state intervention' and 'professional autonomy' are opposed processes. The normal view in the sociological literature on the professions – one commonly shared by professionals themselves – is that the intrusion of the state into areas of economic organisation, the law or medicine compromises the autonomy required for the exercise of professional expertise. The 'delegated authority' that thereby results (and which Goldthorpe regards as the basis of the existence of the service class) has here normally been portrayed as the transforming of professionals into mere functionaries. Johnson has various objections to raise. For one thing, this view regards the state as a pre-formed phenomenon, which then 'intervenes' into various areas of professional competence. But this is obviously a misleading stance, since such 'intervention' is part and parcel of the very institutions that comprise 'the state'. State formation and professionalisation have in fact from the start been interrelated processes. It is a myth to suppose that professional autonomy can be found within 'professionalism' itself; such autonomy exists only in and through the articulation of the state and the professions. In the case of Britain, the imperial extension of state power has been particularly important in influencing the growth of the professions.

Furthermore Johnson goes on to suggest that some of the characteristics which have frequently been attributed to 'professionals' in general may rest upon mistaken generalisations from Britain to other societies. The 'British case', in this context as in others, might be the exception rather than the rule. The peculiarities of the British also form the main theme of Ingham's article, one of two contributions which discuss the top echelons of the class structure. Ingham develops a novel approach to a problem which has received relatively little attention from either sociologists or historians, in spite of its obvious importance to the study of contemporary British society: the relation between 'the City' and industry. Those who have written on the issue have almost uniformly stressed that the ascendancy of the City – the financial sectors of the economy centred in 'London – over industry has given a particular stamp to class rule in Britain. Ingham accepts the general tenor of this argument, but criticises the way in which it has been formulated, particularly by Nairn and Longstreth. These authors fail adequately to say what they mean by 'the City', or use ambiguous formulations; and they mistakenly identify the role of City institutions with finance capital as traditionally conceptualised in Marxism. Partly criticising Marx, but also drawing upon aspects of Marx's writings left undeveloped by Marx himself, Ingham argues that the principal operations of the City are concerned with commercial and banking capital. The commercial activities of the City have been essentially bound up with the international dimension of its involvements; but its privileged position has also been protected by 'internal' characteristics of the state.

Scott's discussion forms a helpful adjunct to that of Ingham, since he places his emphasis on the study of large industrial corporations. It is this, the 'propertied class', which is the subject-matter of his analysis and which consists of those who have 'effective possession' of capital. 'Effective possession' is defined not as simple legal ownership, but as the capacity to control the strategic deployment of capital. A distinctively privileged and powerful propertied class continues to exist in British society, as in other capitalist countries. According to Scott, the so-called 'managerial revolution' has altered the character of this class, but has certainly not led to its dissolution. Individual entrepreneurs no longer own and run the large corporations; but the industrial leadership continues to be drawn from a privileged class of propertied families. This is still a dominant class, not only in the sphere of economic power – which Scott discusses at length – but in other institutions also.

This collection of essays contains two which have a practical bent, in the sense that they are concerned with the possibilities of securing political change. Hirst's article focusses upon issues of current significance in Britain, although it has wider implications; Bottomore in contrast formulates a more embracing and comparative assessment of the possible future of socialist movements in Europe. Of significance is the fact that Hirst appears to react back against views expressed in his previous work. What have characteristically been seen by sociologists as 'structural' consequences of the division of labour, he contends, are in fact to be understood as the result of specific policies followed by different collectivities or organisations. He seeks to demonstrate this by studying incomes policy and forms of action devoted to implementing 'industrial democracy'. Neither the former nor the latter – including most notably the Bullock Report – have recognised the entrenched nature of differentials of interest and activity actively fought for by different groups within the working class as a whole. Hirst goes on to criticise those both on the Right and on the Left who hold that, in the long run at any rate, unions cannot significantly influence the overall distribution of income. They have done, and continue to do so. According to Hirst, however, the resistance which the union movement has put up against incomes policies is in some part misplaced. National incomes planning, he argues controversially, if it were established in an equitable fashion, rather than being used to hold down the wages of those least able to resist, should be endorsed by the unions. This must involve a 'socialist-egalitarian' incomes policy, something which Hirst believes would act to strengthen the power of the organised working class, not weaken it. But such a consolidation of working-class power would also require that workers be able to extend their capacities for control *inside* enterprises. The achievement of industrial democracy, even on the relatively limited scale proposed in the Bullock Report, Hirst says, would provide a stepping-stone for more radical change effected in a democratic fashion.

Finally, Bottomore discusses the prospects of political radicalism in the contemporary period against the backdrop of an earlier parallel analysis. Ten years ago, he writes, he proposed that a major turning-point had been reached in the political development of the Western European societies. The established parties, founded mainly on class lines, seemed to have reached an end-point in their development. On the Left, the existing socialist and communist parties were being outflanked by a new upsurge of revolt, in which student movements figured prominently. On the Right, conservative and liberal parties were being challenged by the rise of new technocratic elites, committed above all to rapid economic growth. To add to these tendencies, various forms of regionalism seemed to be gaining strength, although formed of uneasy alliances of groups drawn from different parts of the political spectrum. Today, Bottomore observes, much of this has changed. The radical movements on the Left have declined, and a new conservative mood has appeared in the context of world recession, 'stagflation' and a resumption of the arms race. At the same time, however, there has been a renewal of support for Left parties on a broad front in a variety of countries – Britain, as ever, being untypical in this respect. Many would see the policies of these parties, including established Communist parties, as reformist in character, and thus far from realising the emancipatory goals to which Marx anticipated that the labour movement would aspire. But Bottomore is more optimistic. Socialists, he argues, can no longer close their eyes to the glaring imperfections of the 'actually existing' socialist societies of Eastern Europe and elsewhere. Nonetheless there is a continuing vitality to democratic socialist movements in the West which, especially if they become conjoined to other radical forces that are now appearing, remains a major source of hope for the future.

In this brief introduction, we have tried to convey an indication of the contents of the volume which it prefaces. We believe that the book represents, as we have said, a significant addition to the existing literature concerned with class and the division of labour. As such, it is a fitting testimonial to the man to whom it is dedicated.

Marx and the abolition of the division of labour

ALI RATTANSI

Marx's early writings have a distinctly apocalyptical character and it is not difficult to understand why some critics have seen in his discourse a sort of disguised and secularised eschatology, an interpretation made much easier if his earlier and later texts are indiscriminately conflated to yield a unified doctrine.[1] The idea of the complete abolition of the division of labour, indeed the irrelevance of the category of division of labour to a future socialist order – explicitly announced for the first time in their writings by Marx and Engels in *The German Ideology* (1845–6) – appears to provide such critiques with easy and convincing support:

> in communist society, where nobody has one exclusive sphere of activity but each can become accomplished in any branch he wishes, society regulates the general production and thus makes it possible for me to do one thing today and another tomorrow, to hunt in the morning, fish in the afternoon, rear cattle in the evening, criticise after dinner, just as I have a mind, without ever becoming hunter, fisherman, shepherd or critic.[2]

The idea of the abolition of the division of labour goes hand in hand with the notion of the abolition of labour.[3] But did Marx continue to believe in this idyllic picture as a vision of socialism throughout his life? The suggestion that he may have altered his views – perhaps reluctantly – on the possibility of completely abolishing the division of labour is not unfounded. In the third volume of *Capital*, for example, Marx argues that the day-to-day labour necessary for individual and social survival will always remain unrewarding, the realm of freedom, creativity and fulfilment only being possible outside the sphere of material production:

> In fact, the realm of freedom actually begins only where labour which is determined by necessity and mundane considerations ceases; thus in the very nature of things it lies beyond the sphere of actual material production . . . Freedom in this field can only consist in socialized man, the associated

producers, rationally regulating their interchange with Nature . . . and achieving this with the least expenditure of energy . . . But it nonetheless still remains a realm of necessity. Beyond it begins that development of human energy which is an end in itself, the true realm of freedom, which, however, can blossom forth only with this realm of necessity as its basis. The shortening of the working day is its basic prerequisite.[4]

The publication of Marx's early works, the recent upsurge of interest in Marxism and the consequent publication of scholarly and critical studies on Marx of a very high order have, between them, failed to resolve this question in any decisive manner.[5] This paper, based on an exhaustive study undertaken elsewhere, attempts to shed new light on this complex but crucial issue.[6]

I

I shall argue that in his earlier writings Marx did believe in the possibility of the abolition of the division of labour *tout court* because at this stage of his formation he consistently conflated the concepts of 'class' and 'division of labour': this meant that the abolition of classes became synonymous with the abolition of the division of labour. As one aspect of this conceptual assimilation Marx conflated class with occupation such that the disappearance of classes automatically entailed the complete abolition of occupational specialisation, although it must be pointed out that Marx did not think of occupations *as* classes in the manner of some varieties of academic sociology. In his later writings, however, Marx's discourse displays the beginnings of a conceptual separation between class and division of labour, one implication of which is that the disappearance of classes with the emergence of a new mode of production does not automatically entail the complete abolition of occupational specialisation.

The modification in Marx's views, I shall suggest, was chiefly produced by a theoretical shift from *market* relations to relations of *production* as the basic starting point in his analysis; this led Marx to a recognition of organisational exigencies imposed by processes of material production as such, and especially large-scale industrial production, independent of deformations rooted in the existence of classes. Marx now came to believe that many aspects of the division of labour were unavoidable, and his main focus shifted to a concern with breaking down the barrier between mental and manual labour. This whole theoretical transformation is also related to Marx's more general attempt to break with a class-reductionist form of historical materialism and, in addition, to grasp the significance of possible 'natural' limits to social reorganisation.

Ali Rattansi

While any attempt to divide Marx's discourse into developmental stages inevitably encounters difficulties, a three-fold scheme probably constitutes the most adequate periodisation of his changing views on the division of labour. (1) The early writings, from the *Economic and Philosophic Manuscripts of 1844* to *The German Ideology;* at this stage Marx completely assimilates division of labour to class. (2) A transitional stage, chiefly represented by *The Poverty of Philosophy* (1847), in which Marx separates 'social division of labour' from the division of labour in manufacture; this period also contains some important political writings which register an attempt to detach the analysis of the state from a reduction to 'division of labour' *simpliciter.* (3) The mature texts, beginning with the *Grundrisse* (1857–8) in which Marx develops the theory of surplus value and begins to separate 'class' from 'division of labour'.

II

The conflation between class – defined in relation to the ownership and non-ownership of the means of production – and the division of labour is a pervasive feature of *The German Ideology;* it structures all aspects of the discourse, is boldly announced as a guiding principle almost at the beginning, and reappears at several other points in the text:

The various stages of development in the division of labour are just so many different forms of ownership, i.e. the existing stage in the division of labour determines also the relations of individuals to one another with reference to the material, instrument, and product of labour.[7]

Indeed, it is possible to observe in this text a quite remarkable extension of Marx's conceptualisation of the division of labour, and he places upon the notion a heavy descriptive and explanatory burden which threatens to strip it of any distinctive meaning. Almost any and every structural division, institutional separation and conflict of social or individual interest is either reduced to or seen as an aspect of the division of labour: town and country, capital and landed property, individual and society, men and women, mental and manual labour, craft and trade, industry, commerce and agriculture – all these social differentiations are seen as expressions of *the* division of labour, a form of theorisation crucially underpinned by a conflation between class and the division of labour.

One important dimension of Marx's analysis is the rise of the state and, in keeping with the discourse of the text, its morphology is explained as a direct outcome of the evolution of the division of

14

labour, seen as the true source of the 'contradiction between the interest of the individual and that of the community' which allows the state to appropriate an illusory communal and unifying role. Illusory, because in reality the state is always based on classes 'already determined by the division of labour, which in every such mass of men separate out, and of which one dominates all the others'.[8] Relations of exchange and market forces also have an important place in the theorisation: they are said to exacerbate the 'contradiction between the interest of the individual and the community' and serve to extend the loss of control over social processes and productive forces inherent in the division of labour. But the phenomenon of exchange is also assimilated to private property: the 'alien' power of the market, we are told in *The German Ideology*, will be dissolved 'by the communist revolution . . . and the abolition of private property'.[9]

Given the discursive structure of *The German Ideology*, it is not difficult to understand why the principle of the complete abolition of the division of labour (including occupational specialisation) is registered in this text without qualification. And although this principle is nowhere explicitly announced in the *Economic and Philosophic Manuscripts of 1844*, composed in response to Marx's first serious encounter with classical political economy, there is a direct line of continuity between the two texts: they share a reductionist theoretical structure in which private property, division of labour and exchange are woven into a seamless web such that the abolition of private property automatically entails the dissolution of the division of labour and relations of exchange. In the *1844 Manuscripts* this form of conceptual assimilation finds its discursive basis in Marx's remarkable analysis of the alienation of labour under capitalist conditions of production.

Marx identifies at least two key dimensions of alienation in the *1844 Manuscripts:* the *result,* and the *act* of production.[10] Or, as he makes abundantly clear, *class* and the *division of labour.* What Marx does here is to translate the insights gained from his reading of political economy into the vocabulary of alienation. The concept of alienation in the *1844 Manuscripts* is expressed in two different terms: *Entäusserung* (vb. *entäussern*) and *Entfremdung* (vb. *entfremden*). The first has strong associations with property, in the sense of either selling or renouncing it; the second emphasises a sense of distance in interpersonal relations or a feeling of something being strange and alien. Marx uses the two terms almost interchangeably, but this is hardly accidental for they are admirably suited to the two substantive propositions that Marx links in his discourse: alienation as class

15

relations, as propertylessness, and alienation as a feeling of painful strangeness imposed on the propertyless by the division of labour in capitalist factory production. Thus, in the language of political economy:

The accumulation of capital increases the division of labour . . . just as the division of labour increases the accumulation of capital. With this division of labour on the one hand and the accumulation of capital on the other, the worker becomes ever more exclusively dependent on labour, and on a particular, one-sided, machine-like labour at that . . . he is thus depressed spiritually and physically to the condition of a machine and from being a man becomes an abstract activity and a belly.[11]

Like other features of alienation, exchange also dehumanises: the worker, Marx points out, is reduced to the status of a commodity, is treated as an inanimate object by market forces, 'and it is a bit of luck for him if he can find a buyer'.[12] This is alienation as *Entäusserung*, a renunciation of man's essential powers to the inhuman forces of the market: 'Estrangement is manifested not only in the fact that my means of life belong to someone else, but also in the fact that . . . all is under the sway of inhuman power.'[13]

The concept of division of labour only emerges in Marx's theorisation in the *1844 Manuscripts*, and the distinctive role of the proletariat or propertyless as the vehicle of socialist revolution is also first announced in the same year, in the *Introduction* to the *Critique of Hegel's Philosophy of Right*. But the foundations of a discursive structure which theorised class, division of labour and exchange as inextricable elements of a web of oppression and exploitation can be identified earlier: they lie in the doctrine of total, universalistic emancipation, and in the critique of exchange relations and private property, both of which Marx had absorbed before he identified the proletariat as the agent of total emancipation or conceptualised the relation between his critique of exchange and private property and the effects of the division of labour in the factories of early industrial capitalism. In other words, the roots of the conflation between class and the division of labour that becomes evident in the *1844 Manuscripts* have to be sought in the conception of alienation that Marx had begun to fashion out of a curious amalgam of Hegelian and Young Hegelian ideas *before* his first serious encounter with political economy, and which is particularly clearly registered in *On the Jewish Question*, written in 1843.[14]

The argument of *On the Jewish Question* is simple but powerful: formal political freedom cannot be regarded as synonymous with total human emancipation, for the latter requires the abolition of *aliena-tion*, the transformation of social relations to conform to man's essential nature (or 'species-being') as a communal being.[15] In turn, this presupposes the abolition of both private property and exchange. The right of private property, Marx points out, is 'the right of self-interest', and thus the fundamental form of the alienation and separation of the individual from society. Symptomatic of this alienation is the overwhelming power of exchange over social relations. 'Selling', Marx says, 'is the practice of externalisation', while money 'is the alienated essence of man's labour and life'.[16]

The following year, impelled in part by his contact with French socialists in Paris, Marx identifies the proletariat or propertyless as the class 'that is the *complete* loss of humanity and can only redeem itself through the *total* redemption of humanity'.[17] The key role assigned to the proletariat, taken together with Marx's espousal of a view which postulated tight links between private property, exchange and alienation, make it possible to understand why, when Marx did finally incorporate the concept of division of labour into his analysis, he was able to assimilate it so closely to the concept of class: if complete human emancipation was only possible through the emancipation of the proletariat (or propertyless) as a class; if the *absence* of emancipation was therefore directly attributable to the existence of private property; and if – this being the crucial element Marx added *after* his reading of political economy – as a dimension of its 'universal suffering' the proletariat was subjected to the degradation of the division of labour in the factory, it logically followed that division of labour was indissolubly tied to class (or private property) and must necessarily disappear completely with the total abolition of classes and private property.

Insofar as Marx had already identified exchange relations as an essential dimension of alienation in bourgeois society, certain aspects of the concept of division of labour and its assimilation to class were implicit in his pre-1844 analysis. Given the double relationship of the concept of division of labour – that is, to exchange and to the differentiation of tasks – it reinforced the tendency to fuse occupational specialisation with class, a tendency already embedded in the reduction of all aspects of the proletariat's exploitation and oppression to its lack of property. As Marx put it in the *1844 Manuscripts*:

the emancipation of the workers contains universal human emancipation – and it contains this, because the whole of human servitude is involved in the relation of the worker to production, and *every relation of servitude is but a modification and consequence of this relation*.[18]

Ali Rattansi

It is the contention here that it was the sort of complex chain of rationalisation outlined above which resulted in Marx's fateful conceptual conflation between class and the division of labour.

III

The Poverty of Philosophy (1847), composed in opposition to Proudhon's *The Philosophy of Poverty*, registers a new element in Marx's conceptualisation of the division of labour: probably influenced by Babbage and Ure, Marx discriminates sharply between the division of labour in society and the division of labour in the factory. 'While inside the modern workshop the division of labour is meticulously regulated by the authority of the employer', Marx points out, 'modern society has no other rule, no other authority for the distribution of labour than free competition.'[19] Indeed, in *The Poverty of Philosophy* Marx abandons the gross over-extension of 'division of labour' that had characterised *The German Ideology*, and now criticises both Proudhon and Smith for their indiscriminate usage.[20]

Nevertheless, despite the absence in the text of any explicit argument about the *abolition* of the division of labour, it is possible to identify in this regard key elements of continuity between the discourse of *The Poverty of Philosophy* and *The German Ideology*. That is, they share a reductionist theoretical structure in which class and the division of labour are tightly interwoven, thus strongly implying that the abolition of private property would also entail the complete abolition of the division of labour. As Marx rhetorically asked in his letter to Annenkov prior to working on *The Poverty of Philosophy*, 'Is the whole inner organisation of nations, are all their international relations anything else than the expression of a particular division of labour?'[21] The same point is made in the text, but in relation to private property, for Marx argues here that 'to define bourgeois property is nothing else than to give an exposition of *all* the social relations of bourgeois production'.[22]

The period between *The Poverty of Philosophy* and the drafting of the *Grundrisse* (1857–8) may be regarded as a transitional one in Marx's theorisation of the division of labour, not merely because of the emergence of the distinction between the division of labour in society and in the workshop, but also because of modifications in Marx's conception of the state. Thus, while *The German Ideology* had theorised the state and its forms as yet another expression of the division of labour (and therefore as a simple reflection of prevailing relations of ownership), Marx's magnificent analyses of the revolutions of

18

1848–9 and the events in France leading up to Bonaparte's *coup d'état* of 1851 index an attempt to conceptualise state forms, and the political level more generally, in less reductionist terms.[23] For present purposes, the most important aspect of the new discourse is the idea of the necessity of 'smashing' the state as part of the process of transition to socialism.[24] That is, the abolition of the state is no longer assumed to be an automatic and unproblematic outcome of the abolition of classes and the division of labour: instead Marx recognises that it poses a political problem requiring a genuine resolution.at *that* level, for the state and its bureaucratic apparatuses possess a relative autonomy and an independent effectivity in relation to the economic level.

IV

Throughout the 1850s Marx continued his economic studies and it was during this period, in the winter of 1857–8, that he composed the draft of *Capital:* the massive *Grundrisse.* Both the *Grundrisse* and *Capital* register a profound theoretical break in Marx's economic discourse, and one which is closely bound up with the conceptual separation between class and the division of labour which marks his mature texts. The theoretical and methodological starting point of *Capital,* especially, differs significantly from that of previous writings.

Marx's pre-*Capital* economics centre around a theorisation and critique of the market as the fundamental institution of capitalism: unchecked competition is viewed as the basic driving force and the underlying cause of all other structural features of capitalism, and capitalism is indicted for the fact that even the labourer is turned into a commodity. However, in *Capital* Marx breaks fundamentally with this form of theorisation. The market is now regarded as a superficial and necessarily illusory representation of a much more essential, underlying process which contains the real clue to the operation of capitalism: its system of pumping out surplus value from workers in the process of *production.* The market represents the contract between capitalist and worker as an exchange of equivalents, thus masking the systematic asymmetry in the relationship, and Marx himself underlines this contrast in a revealing passage in *Capital:*

The consumption of labour power is completed, as in the case of every other commodity, *outside the limits of the market* . . . Accompanied by Mr Money-bags and by the possessor of labour power, we therefore take leave of this noisy sphere, where everything takes place on the surface . . . and follow

19

them into the hidden abode of *production* . . . there we shall see, not only how capital produces but how capital is produced. We shall at last force the secret of profit-making.[25]

Thus in the mature texts the critique of capitalism is based not on the dehumanisation inherent in labour-as-commodity, but on the extraction and appropriation of surplus value intrinsic to the process of capitalist production. However, this implies in turn the emergence of a new conception of 'relations of production' in Marx's discourse: the discontinuity between the earlier and mature theorisations of the relations of production lies primarily in the centrality of forms of the extraction and appropriation of surplus labour to the latter, and the retheorisation this entails for historical materialism more generally is indexed several times by Marx in *Capital*.[26]

The displacement of exchange and the theoretical shift to production, in the sense indicated above, represents a crucial stage in the disengagement of 'division of labour' from 'class' because it compelled Marx to rethink and reconstitute the category of production itself which, in one sense, had always been his point of departure. Especially, it led Marx to conclude that certain features of production were generic to it as a process and that it was to all intents and purposes futile to postulate their disappearance with changing social formations. But Marx's theorisation does not therefore become crudely ahistorical: it becomes, however, especially sensitive to the exigencies of large-scale industrial production, and this makes Marx much less sanguine about the possibility of completely dissolving the division of labour even in post-capitalist society.

In the *Introduction* which he composed just before writing the *Grundrisse* we can detect some of the first results of Marx's attempt to think through the exigencies of the production process abstracted from its conditions of existence in particular social formations:

Whenever we speak of production, then, what is meant is always production at a definite stage of social development . . . However, all epochs of production have certain common traits, common characteristics. Production in general is an abstraction, but a rational abstraction in so far as it really brings out and fixes the common element . . . the elements which are not general and common must be separated out from the determinations valid for production as such.[27]

Marx makes it perfectly clear in the *Introduction* that his object is not to produce a form of meta-historical analysis, for the general category of production 'is itself segmented many times over and splits into different determinations'.[28] In any particular instance, production is always carried out in a specific form and with its own determinations, as for example in agriculture or manufacture.[29]

There is, however, scant agreement about the significance of the *Introduction*, and there is some doubt surrounding Marx's own subsequent appraisal of it. In common with many others, Nicolaus concludes in his *Foreword* to the English edition of the *Grundrisse* that Marx had obviously decided that the 1857 *Introduction* represented a false start; henceforth, Nicolaus argues, Marx's starting point – as in *Capital* – lay in an analysis of the commodity, 'a compound, determinate, delimited and concrete whole'.[30] But this is to underestimate seriously the extent to which Marx continues to reflect on the problem of production in general, the structural consequences of particular types of production processes, and their articulation with the social relations of production, including exchange and distribution. This form of analysis necessarily plays a secondary role in *Capital*, for the explicit object of that work is the step by step demonstration of the theory of surplus value and thus the hidden mechanism of capitalist production.

Nevertheless, at several stages of the argument in *Capital* Marx's exposition proceeds by way of general remarks on various aspects of production as such, and includes a theorisation of the structural necessities imposed by particular processes of production on forms of social organisation including the division of labour. These remarks are scattered throughout the three volumes of *Capital* and the connection between them only becomes apparent when they are detached from the rest of this argument and made to run together as a single discourse. In *this* sense the starting point can be said to reside in Chapter VII on the labour-process, which Marx begins by underlining the centrality of conceptualising production 'independently of the form it assumes under given social conditions'.[31] In his chapter on 'Co-operation' as well Marx provides an abstract, formal definition of this form of production. Moreover, he immediately proceeds to analyse its general advantages regardless of the overall mode of production and class relations – for example, slave, feudal or capitalist – in which it is concretely realised.[32]

Elsewhere Marx focusses on the determinations implicit in the nature of mechanised production. Machinery, he argues, can only be operated by 'associated labour'; hence 'the co-operative character of the labour-process', Marx concludes, 'is a technical necessity dictated by the instrument of labour itself'.[33] Once established in any branch of industry, machine production forces related branches to mechanise, and the applied mechanical and chemical sciences are forced to innovate rapidly to prevent bottlenecks from crippling the overall production process.[34] The division of labour is also profoundly transformed: mechanisation creates 'new fields of labour' and 'carries the social division of labour immeasurably further'.[35]

V

The first sense in which the new discourse on production leads to a disengagement between class and the division of labour in Marx's mature texts is related to the distinction between division of labour at the level of *positions* and at the level of *agents*. While early texts like *The German Ideology* suggest that the very category of division of labour is irrelevant to future society, the later writings register the argument that at the level of *positions,* that is, at the level of productive tasks as such, the necessity for a determinate and structured division of labour cannot be done away with despite a change in the mode of production and the form of class relations. Thus in *Capital* Marx introduces a new term, 'division of labour in general', to conceptualise the differentiation of tasks at the level of positions, and this obviously derives from the discourse on *production* in general.[36] Marx sets out the logic of the new argument particularly clearly in a letter to Kugelmann written a year after the publication of *Capital:*

Every child knows . . . that the masses of products corresponding to the different needs require different and quantitatively determined masses of the total labour of society. That this *necessity* of the *distribution* of social labour in *definite* proportions cannot possibly be done away with by a particular *form* of social production but can only change the *mode* of its *appearance* is self-evident.[37]

This new form of theorisation provides the discursive basis for Marx's frequent, but relatively unnoticed argument on the functional exigencies of what he often calls 'large-scale' production; it also underpins his conception of the 'duality' of the capitalist production process, that is, on the one hand as a process for the production of use-values, and on the other as a process for the extraction and appropriation of surplus value. Each element of this duality, Marx argues, exercises an analytically distinct form of determination on the organisation and division of labour. This new standpoint is expressed in several passages in *Capital;* for present purposes it is sufficient to exhibit two of them.

All combined labour on a large scale requires, more or less, a directing authority, in order to secure the harmonious working of the individual activities, and to perform the general functions that have their origin in the action of the combined organism, as distinguished from the action of its separate organs . . . The work of directing, superintending, and adjusting, becomes one of the functions of capital, from the moment that the labour under the control of capital becomes co-operative. Once a function of capital it acquires special characteristics.[38]

The labour of supervision and management, arising as it does . . . out of the supremacy of capital over labour . . . is directly and inseparably connected, also under the capitalist system, with productive functions which all combined social labour assigns to individuals as their special tasks.[39]

Insofar as the labour of coordination and authoritative regulation of the production process had always been included in the concept of division of labour, Marx here is obviously detaching this element from the concept of class within which it had previously been completely submerged. At the same time the passage exemplifies the transformation in Marx's views on the *abolition* of the division of labour, for there is now a clear acknowledgement of the limits to this form of dissolution. Indeed, Marx argues that some determinate tasks would expand considerably under a system of collective production, book-keeping providing one important instance.[40]

While one of the passages cited above explicitly points to 'productive functions which all combined social labour assigns to individuals as their *special* tasks', it must be said that there are few other references in Marx's later writings to the continuing necessity for a determinate and structured division of labour at the level of *agents*, or what will henceforth be called the *social division of labour*. Nevertheless, it is the contention here that this proposition is implicitly supported by some of the arguments that Marx adopts in *Capital* and the other mature texts.

Note first of all that in *Capital* Marx actually displays a clear understanding of the geographical and environmental roots of specialisation: 'it is . . . the differentiation of the soil, the variety of its natural products, the changes of the seasons, which form the physical basis for the social division of labour'.[41] Indeed Marx even goes so far as to argue that the absence of fertility is vital in promoting economic development.[42] Elsewhere in *Capital* Marx notes the 'special advantages' that accrue from siting different forms of production in geographically appropriate areas, both nationally and internationally. The implication here is that there are 'natural' limits to the abolition of occupational specialisation insofar as particular types of occupation are tied to the existence of favourable environmental conditions. While the development of various forms of communication and transport may greatly enhance the possibilities for geographical

mobility and thus enlarge the opportunities for occupational variation for individuals, it is intrinsic to Marx's mature view that there
will continue to be a social division of labour both at a national and
an international level. As Schmidt observes, summarising Marx's
mature discourse on this subject: 'Men cannot in the last resort be
emancipated from the necessities imposed by nature.'[43]

Moreover, despite the fact that beginning with *The German Ideology* the concepts of 'Man' and 'human nature' as ahistorical essences
disappear from Marx's writings, this should not be taken to mean
that Marx fails to acknowledge that the fundamental physical constitution of human beings creates a basic, residual limitation to possible variations in the forms of labour and production.[44] Of course, if
we are to infer from this an argument concerning the limitations set
by 'human nature' to the complete abolition of occupational specialisation, we require a clear recognition on Marx's part that because
of the intrinsic human constitution, *individuals* will necessarily have
differing aptitudes and that a future socialist order would thus have
to take into account that not every individual is (even potentially)
capable of engaging in every type of work. This view is implied by
Marx in at least two separate places in the mature texts. In *Capital*
Marx refers not merely to the 'natural necessity' imposed by environmental circumstances, but also to the 'natural endowments' of individuals, a differentiation which he claims forms 'the foundation on
which the division of labour is built up' (and which is developed to
a perverse extreme in the capitalist factory).[45] In the 'Critique of the
Gotha Programme' (1875) he points out that 'one man is superior to
another physically or mentally and so supplies more labour in the
same time, or can labour for a longer time', and that the application
of the principle of equal remuneration for equal labour is bound to
lead to inequality because of the existence of 'unequal individual
endowment and thus productive capacity'.[46]

Although neither of these passages explicitly argues that differences in individual ability will prevent the complete abolition of
occupational specialisation, this point is intrinsic to the form of reasoning which characterises the later texts and serves to reinforce the
interpretation that there is in these writings a definite (if sometimes
implicit) separation between class and the division of labour. It is
thus not at all surprising that in their maturity both Marx and Engels
refer not to the abolition of the division of labour *simpliciter*, but talk
instead of the abolition of the *old* division of labour.[47]

However, if the break between the youthful and the later vision of
socialism in Marx's texts – as indexed, for example, in the two pas-

sages cited at the beginning of this paper – is to be properly understood, it is necessary to discuss the concept of 'scarcity' in his writings. The socialism of *The German Ideology* rests upon an 'absolute' conception of scarcity, thus presupposing the abolition of scarcity, and labour, as a result of the development of productive forces. This premise is particularly evident in the proposition that classes are the necessary outcome of 'restricted productive forces' and that without the 'universal' development of productive forces 'want is merely made general, and with destitution the struggle for necessities and all the old filthy business would necessarily be reproduced'.[48] This transhistorical conception of scarcity sits uneasily with the idea, registered in the same text, that the expansion of needs is inherent in productive activity: new forms and levels of production set new parameters for what are to count as the necessities of life.[49] It is this 'relative' conception of scarcity that achieves prominence in *Capital*, most especially in the argument that 'the number and extent' of the workers' 'necessary wants, as also the modes of satisfying them, are themselves the product of historical development, and depend therefore to a great extent on the degree of civilisation of a country'.[50] And instead of proclaiming the end of labour, as in *The German Ideology*, Marx now argues that 'labour . . . is a necessary condition, independent of *all* forms of society . . . it is an *external* nature-imposed necessity, without which there can be no material exchanges between man and Nature, and therefore no life'.[51]

Once the revision of the original scarcity thesis is set alongside the already discussed discursive changes and forms of argument evident in the mature texts, it is not difficult to understand why, in the passage from the third volume of *Capital* with which this paper began, Marx refers to the realm of freedom as a condition of existence that begins only where the realm of necessity ends. Indeed, the same point is also made in the first volume of *Capital* in a passage which underlines more clearly the significance of the 'relative' conception of scarcity.[52]

VI

If it is necessary now to acknowledge that the mature Marx does not believe in the complete abolition of the division of labour in future society, it is still unclear what forms he thinks the division of labour *will* take. Marx's reluctance to speculate about the precise character of a socialist reconstruction of the social order poses formidable problems of interpretation, and any attempt to provide an organisa-

25

tional sketch must be undertaken with some caution. Nevertheless, one broad theme consistently emerges in his mature discussions: the division between mental and manual labour and its connection with the problem of control over and participation in decision-making, both in the production process and outside it.

If anything can be confidently asserted about Marx's changing views on socialist society, it is that his attention shifts from a concern with the abolition of the division of labour as such (in the early writings) to an interest in overcoming the separation between intellectual and manual labour (in the mature period). It is this aspect of the capitalist labour process which emerges as the dominant theme in *Capital*, where Marx emphasises at several points that the most flagrant dis-memberment of the worker is accomplished by capital's continuous appropriation of the scientific knowledge and technical skills essential to the process of production. It is this process above all which turns the worker into a simple appendage of the machine, transforms labour into a mindless drudgery and allows capital to reproduce the conditions of existence of its domination.[53] Hence, too, the argument in the *Grundrisse* that labour concerned with material production can only have a 'free character' if it has 'a scientific character', thereby becoming 'the activity of a subject controlling all the forces of nature in the production process'. Marx's interest in overcoming the crippling effects of the division between mental and manual labour is also rooted in a more general prognosis of the increasing demands for variability in productive skills implicit in modern large-scale industry which, he argues, 'imposes the necessity of recognising as a fundamental law of production, variation of work, consequently fitness of the labourer for varied work, consequently the greatest possible development of his varied aptitudes'.[54]

To what extent did Marx believe in the possibility of completely abolishing the division between mental and manual labour? It is at least clear that the general cast of Marx's mature view goes against the idea that *every* worker could *individually* appropriate *every* possible form of scientific discipline and technical skill that is involved in diverse sectors of production in modern large-scale industry. The aim of socialism, given natural and technical imperatives, is not individual appropriation of all mental tasks, but *collective* appropriation such that, in relation to the means of production, 'the collective labourer, or social body of labour, appears as the dominant subject, and the mechanical automaton as the object'.[55] Even at the point where Marx discusses the urgent technical need for variability of skills, he does not suggest that every worker can acquire command over *every* skill: the aim is one of 'the greatest possible development of his varied aptitudes', whatever they might be.

Implicit in this injunction is the belief that every worker has the capacity to master both mental and manual skills and thus the ability to exercise some control over the production process. Hence Marx's keen interest in Owenite and other educational schemes which combined 'productive labour with instruction and gymnastics, not only as one of the methods of adding to the efficiency of production, but as the only method of producing fully developed human beings'.[56] The final result of this process, he adds, will be 'the abolition of the old division of labour . . . and the economic status of the labourer corresponding to that form'.[57]

Socialism for Marx meant above all the democratisation of all areas of social life, and collective participation in decision-making at the point of production constituted for him a fundamental index of the real development of a distinctly socialist labour process. Thus, when condemning the authority system of the capitalist factory as a 'caricature of that social regulation of the labour-process which becomes requisite in . . . the employment in common of instruments of labour and especially machinery', Marx mentions in particular the 'autocracy' of the capitalist and the absence of any 'division of responsibility' or 'representative system' to extend the area of control downwards to the worker.[58] This concern with accountability and its interpenetration with the notion of the abolition of the division of labour in the mature texts is also evident in Marx's writings on the Paris Commune of 1871. He welcomed the replacement of a standing army by the 'armed people', and favoured the amalgamation of legislative and executive structures so that executive functions could no longer remain 'the hidden attrributes of a trained caste', but had to be turned into roles that could be effectively performed by any ordinary citizen. In addition, Marx stressed the importance of the fact that all persons occupying positions of public authority – the police, magistrates, administrators and so on – were elected and instantly revocable agents, and were paid no more than other workers.[59]

It would be absurdly complacent to pretend that even Marx's mature conception of socialism can be accepted without qualification, for it contains several sets of propositions and presuppositions and implies many forms of practice that need reappraisal. This task I have undertaken elsewhere.[60] For the present it is sufficient to have demonstrated that those who present Marx's early vision of the abolition of the division of labour as Marxist socialism *tout court* do a grave injustice to Marx. Those Marxists who are convinced by the interpretation of Marx offered here will be able to shed a variety of beliefs which some of them have long been uncomfortable about defending, while those hostile to Marx will, I hope, find it more difficult to caricature and dismiss his thought as essentially eschatalogical and utopian.

Power, the dialectic of control and class structuration

ANTHONY GIDDENS

In this paper I shall seek to draw some connections between certain general problems of social theory and the analysis of class structure in capitalist societies. In a number of recent publications I have elaborated what I call the *theory of structuration* as a schema for coping with some of the most deeply embedded dilemmas of social theory.[1] The theory of structuration is based upon the following claims: that social theory (which I take to be relevant equally to each of the social scientific disciplines: sociology, anthropology, psychology and economics, as well as to history) should incorporate an understanding of human behaviour as *action;* that such an understanding has to be made compatible with a focus upon the *structural components* of social institutions or societies; and that notions of *power* and *domination* are logically, not just contingently, associated with the concepts of action and structure as I conceptualise them. I shall not be concerned to substantiate these claims in this discussion, but shall attempt rather to trace out a few of their implications for issues that I take to be important to class analysis.

Action, power and the concept of the dialectic of control

By emphasising that (the vast bulk of) human behaviour has to be treated as action, I mean principally two things. One I shall call the theorem of 'knowledgeability'; the second, that of 'capability'. Embodying a conception of action within social theory involves treating the human being as a knowledgeable and capable agent. By saying that human beings are knowledgeable agents, I mean that all of us know a great deal about why we behave as we do, and about the social conventions relevant to that behaviour. Philosophers are prone to talk of such knowledgeability in terms of the 'reasons' that individuals have for their conduct. However, this can be misleading, for it suggests that human conduct involves a string of discrete reasons aggregated together: and that every act has some definite reason attached to it. Rather than suggesting any such implication, I prefer to speak of the 'rationalisation' of human conduct as an inherent feature of human behaviour. I do not refer here to the Weberian sense of 'rationalisation', or to the Freudian: by the rationalisation of conduct I mean that human agents chronically, but for the most part tacitly, 'keep in touch' with the grounds of their activity, as a routine element of that activity. This 'reflexive self-monitoring' of activity is an integral element of all human social encounters. The knowledge-ability of human subjects, it is important to stress, is not limited to what people can *say*, if asked, about why they act as they do. This is the force of the adverb 'tacitly' in the sentence above. The specific contribution of phenomenological approaches to social theory has been to make clear that tacit awareness of conventions, anchored in, yet making possible the continuity of, social practices, is fundamental to the knowledgeability of human agents. Such tacit awareness is, in Wittgenstein's terms, knowledge of 'how to go on' in the contexts of practical day-to-day life: it is what I call 'practical consciousness'.[2]

By speaking of human agents as 'capable', I mean to refer to the philosophical theorem that action involves the possibility of 'doing otherwise'. Although such a notion is notoriously difficult to elucidate I take it to be an essential component of a theory of action.[3] To be able to 'do otherwise' is to be able to make a difference in the world, to influence a pre-existing course of events (either through actual behaviour or through refraining). I want to argue that this implies that the concept of action is logically involved with that of power: for power, in its broadest sense, is precisely the capability of 'making a difference' to a course of events. This is a theme I shall pursue at some length below. For the moment it is important to insist that action analysis must be complemented by institutional analysis in social theory; we have to acknowledge that the knowledgeability/capability of human agents is always *bounded*, or constrained by elements of the institutional contexts in which their action takes place. But it is a major error to treat the structural features of social systems as coterminous with such bounds. This is the characteristic view that has supported the dualism between action approaches and structural approaches, and that has been so entrenched in traditionally established forms of social theory. The structural properties of social systems should rather be seen as both constraining and enabling, in respect of human action; and the traditional dualism between action and structure has to be reinterpreted as a duality, in which structure is both the medium and outcome of knowledgeably sustained social practices. Again, I have detailed these ideas elsewhere.[4]

Let me pursue here the theme of the relation between action and power. I wish to distinguish two aspects of this issue: (1) the general implications of the logical relation between agency and power; (2) the mode in which power relations may be analysed as a chronically reproduced feature of social systems.

Of (1) we can say the following: to be a human agent is to have power, to be able to 'make a difference' in the world. This has direct consequences for (2), because it follows that, in any relationship which may be involved in a social system, the most seemingly 'powerless' individuals are able to mobilise resources whereby they carve out 'spaces of control' in respect of their day-to-day lives and in respect of the activities of the more powerful. One way of examining (1) is to consider instances which lie on the margins of action. These both help to explicate what it means to be an agent, and show how intimately this is related to power. But such examples also serve to demonstrate how closely (1) connects to (2), a connection which, I shall suggest, can best be handled by a concept of what I shall call the 'dialectic of control'.

Consider first an instance where A is injected with a drug by B, rendering A unconscious and immobile. Such a case clearly lies outside the scope of the agency/power relation: A ceases to be an agent, and while B potentially has power over A's fate, A has been rendered powerless. This apparently banal example is not without interest, however. If B can do more or less what he or she desires with A's body, including ending A's life altogether, it may appear that B's power over A is absolute or unconditional. And so in a sense it is, for A is incapable of resisting. Complete though it may be in one aspect, it is very limited in others. For by killing or immobilising A, B is necessarily deprived of whatever goods or services A might render within a continuing social relationship. The threat to do violence to another may be very often a major sanction helping to enforce modes of domination, but the actual destruction of one agent by another can hardly be regarded as the type case of the use of social power.

Consider a second example that one might suppose to be near the margins of whether or not a person remains an agent: someone in solitary confinement in a prison. Now it is clear that in such an instance the person does retain the capability of 'making a difference'. Such a capability includes not just the chance to invent modes of occupying the mind in circumstances of extreme tedium; the solitary prisoner normally possesses at least some resources that can be brought to bear against his or her captors. 'Dirty protests' or hunger strikes in Northern Ireland are familiar illustrations. There are many ways in which the seemingly powerless, in particular contexts, may be able to influence the activities of those who appear to hold complete power over them; or in which the weak are able to mobilise resources against the strong. There are few social relations, of course, which are as markedly imbalanced in respect of power as that between prisoners in solitary confinement and their jailors. But such examples serve to highlight the points I have in mind. These can be stated as follows. Anyone who participates in a social relationship, forming part of a social system produced and reproduced by its constituent actors over time, necessarily sustains some control over the character of that relationship or system. Power relations in social systems can be regarded as relations of autonomy and dependence; but no matter how imbalanced they may be in terms of power, actors in subordinate positions are never wholly dependent, and are often very adept at converting whatever resources they possess into some degree of control over the conditions of reproduction of the system. In all social systems there is a *dialectic of control,* such that there are normally continually shifting balances of resources, altering the overall distribution of power. While it is always an empirical question just what power relations pertain within a social system, the agency/power connection, as a connection of logical entailment, means that an agent who does not participate in the dialectic of control *ipso facto* ceases to *be* an agent.

I believe it true to say that in large areas of the social sciences – particularly (but not exclusively) in those dominated either by a general 'objectivist' position or more specifically by functionalism or by structuralism – human beings are not treated as knowledgeable, capable agents. This is perhaps most notoriously the case with Althusser's 'structuralist Marxism', and in the writings of those influenced by it: human agents are mere 'bearers of modes of production'. But, as I have argued elsewhere, a theory of action is also lacking in the functionalist sociology of Talcott Parsons, in spite of Parsons's labelling of his theoretical scheme as 'the action frame of reference'. Although Parsons may have moved towards a more objectivist stance in his later writings, as is often asserted, this was not a movement away from the concept of action as I have proposed it should be understood; for such a concept was not there in the first place. Garfinkel is quite right to say that in Parsons's theory human beings appear as 'cultural dopes', as impelled by 'internalised cultural values' that govern their activity.[5]

In the subsequent sections of the paper, I want to try to show that, however abstract they may appear, these general considerations have direct consequences for quite fundamental issues of class analysis. I shall not concern myself with either Althusser or Parsons, but rather with two authors, one 'classic' and one more recent, whose works have made a strong imprint upon the study of classes. First, Weber's discussion of the nature of bureaucratic organisation, and its association with the expansion of capitalism. The second is Braverman's investigation of the division of labour in his by now very well-known book, *Labor and Monopoly Capital*.[6] Although Weber's views are in certain key respects explicitly anti-Marxist, while Braverman claims to defend a Marxist standpoint, there are some major similarities between the conclusions which each author tends to reach. These similarities – or so I shall claim – derive in some substantial part from deficiencies which can be analysed in terms of the concept of the dialectic of control.

Weber: bureaucracy and capitalism

Marx and Weber are widely regarded as the two most pre-eminent contributors to general problems of class analysis. It is sometimes supposed that Weber's main divergence from Marx consists in expanding upon, and modifying, Marx's views by adding the concept of 'status group' or *Stand*, and that of 'party' to that of 'class'. Others point out that, by apparently identifying the notion of class with market relations, Weber fails to pursue the Marxian theme that class divisions are founded in the relations of production. But each of these comparisons is relatively superficial. Much more significant are the differences between Weber's conception of capitalism and that of Marx; the former's interpretation of bureaucratisation, of course, plays a pivotal role in these differences. When Marx wrote about 'bureaucracy' (in, for example, his early critical discussions of Hegel), he used the term in its traditional sense, to refer to the administrative apparatus of government. One of Weber's major theoretical innovations was to provide a compelling rationale for extending the notions of 'bureaucracy' and 'bureaucratisation' to a whole variety of social organisations. Lying behind this terminological difference, of course, is Weber's conviction that the 'steel-hard cage' of rational-legal organisation is a necessary feature of the expansion of capitalism – and that the bars of the cage would become even more confining were capitalism to be replaced by socialism.

Weber's portrayal of bureaucracy and bureaucratisation is so well known that it is necessary to give no more than the briefest presentation of it here. Weber sometimes uses the term 'bureaucracy' in the narrow sense I mentioned above; and he often also uses it as a general descriptive type (when talking of the traditional Chinese bureaucracy, etc.). But his most important formulation is as an 'ideal type': the more an organisation conforms to the features of the ideal type, the more 'bureaucratised' it can be said to be. The ideal type of bureaucratic organisation involves the following principal features: a formally delimited hierarchy, with the duties of distinct 'offices' being specified by written rules; staffing by means of full-time, salaried officials; and selection and allocation of officials by impersonal criteria, on the basis of 'qualifications'. 'Experience tends universally to show', Weber avers, that 'the purely bureaucratic type of administrative organisation . . . is, from a purely technical point of view, capable of attaining the highest degree of efficiency and is in this sense formally the most rational known means of exercising authority over human beings. It is superior to any other form in precision, in stability, in the stringency of its discipline, and in its reliability.'[7] But the 'technical effectiveness' of bureaucracy exacts a heavy price. It is the source of the alienated character of bureaucratic tasks. Weber's talk of 'precision', 'stability' and 'reliability' points to the direct connection between bureaucracy and mechanisation that he sometimes makes quite explicit. Bureaucracy, he says, is a 'human machine': the formal rationality of technique applies with equal relevance to human social organisation as to the control of the material world. A vital corollary to all this is the theme that, the more an organisation approaches the ideal type, the more it is the case that power becomes centralised in the hands of those at the apex of the organisation. The expropriation of the worker from control of the means of production (or 'the means of administration') is a process that inevitably and irreversibly accompanies the expansion of bureaucratisation. Although Weber did not coin the phrase 'the iron law of oligarchy', his ideas strongly influenced Michels and there is no doubt that the theorem 'bureaucracy means oligarchy' is fundamental to his writings.

Weber's specification of bureaucracy as an ideal type creates difficulties in assessing his views, since it seems to offer a mode of deflecting criticism. For if it is proposed that his conception of bureaucracy does not in fact provide a wholly valid or useful interpretation of the phenomena with which it is concerned, the response can be made that, as it is an ideal type, one should feel no particular qualms if it does not conform to social reality. Weber adds fuel to such a rejoinder when he comments that ideal types 'do not contain hypotheses', that they are no more than a 'one-sided accentuation' of reality.[8] I do not have the space here to discuss the notion of ideal types; but however it may be most aptly described, Weber's conception of bureaucracy certainly does contain hypotheses (concerning technical effectiveness, etc.) that can be adjudged in terms of how well they cope with the subject-matter they relate to.

Marxists have quite rightly regarded Weber's sombre projection of an increasingly bureaucratised social world – in which the alienation that Marx saw as involved for the wage-worker in the capitalist labour-process would become the ineluctable lot of everyone – as constituting a fundamental challenge to Marx's ideas. Marxist writers have attacked Weber's conceptions of capitalism and bureaucracy from various different angles. But most such attacks have converged upon a single standpoint: the traits that Weber attributed to an overall process of 'bureaucratisation' are in fact the specific outcome of capitalist class domination, and hence will be transcended with the advent of socialism.

I do not want to say that these critical views are without foundation, and shall later argue that Braverman's work contributes in an important fashion to them; but I do think they are seriously limited because they characteristically accept *too much* of what Weber has to say about the nature and consequences of bureaucratisation. That is to say, the common tendency among Weber's Marxist critics is to accept the essential elements of Weber's characterisation of bureaucracy, while declaring bureaucratic domination to be a specific outcome of the class system of capitalism. But Weber's conception of bureaucracy has to be confronted in a more direct way than this. There are four respects (among others which I shall not discuss here) in which the overall interpretation of bureaucracy that Weber offered has major weaknesses.

1. Weber seeks to draw a generalised contrast (in an 'ideal-typical' manner) between traditional and bureaucratic organisations, in which the 'steel-hard cage' of the latter denies to individuals the autonomy and spontaneity of behaviour possible in a non-bureaucratised social world. But this 'philosophy of history'[9] is surely not particularly convincing. Some forms of traditional organisation have scarcely allowed much autonomy of conduct to their members: not in spite of, but because of their nature as small, localised community forms. One can

readily detect in Weber's writing here the influence of a Romanticism that also resonates through Tönnies's opposition between *Gemeinschaft and Gesellschaft*.[10] In this regard, Weber's approach can usefully be balanced by Durkheim in the latter's discussion of so-called 'mechanical solidarity'.[11] Although communities dominated by mechanical solidarity offer the person a secure moral haven, the individual is nonetheless subject to what Durkheim refers to as the 'tyranny of the group'. The range of possible activities of the individual is severely curtailed by the norms of the collectivity, backed by 'repressive' sanctions. I am no more persuaded by Durkheim's account of the consequences of the expansion of the division of labour than I am by Weber's interpretation of bureaucratisation; but I think that the former author is correct in claiming that the movement away from *gemeinschaftlich* forms of organisation towards more large-scale, diversified ones, is frequently in some part a liberating phenomenon.

2. The 'iron law of oligarchy' is not a law at all; or rather it is a spurious one. The 'law' states that the increasing centralisation or coordination of activities that accompanies bureaucratisation necessarily means that power becomes more and more consolidated in the hands of a minority in an organisation. Stated as a universal tendency, however, such is simply not the case. It is easy enough to demonstrate this. The British economy today is considerably more highly centralised than was the case fifty years ago. But the very fact of such increased centralisation entails that certain nominally subordinate groupings of workers actually have more power now than they were able to wield previously. This is true, for example, of workers in public utilities, in the oil industry, etc. It is precisely *because* of the increased interdependence of everyone in a strongly centralised economic order that strategically placed categories of workers are able, through the threat of withdrawal of their labour, to increase their power. What applies within the economy, or the state as a whole, applies in more specific organisations also. An excellent illustration of this is work on a production line. What could be a better example of a highly 'formally rational' system, in which human beings and machines are strictly coordinated with one another? But again the strongly coordinated nature of such a production process, while it undeniably reduces labour to dull, repetitive tasks, in some respects increases rather than limits the power of workers involved in it. For a highly centralised production process tends to be much more vulnerable to disruption by small groups of workers than one in which labour tasks are less interdependent.

I do not mean to suggest by these illustrations that the centralisation involved in bureaucratisation leads to the opposite situation to that suggested by the 'iron law of oligarchy': i.e. that more centralisation entails the greater dependence of those in formal positions of authority upon their subordinates, and hence that the result is the diffusion of power downwards. Such a conclusion would, of course, be more fatuous than the famous 'iron law' itself. What I do mean to say is that there is no simple movement of power 'upwards' or 'downwards' with increasing bureaucratisation; normally there are various kinds of possible 'trade-offs' in the resources which can be actualised by groupings at different levels of an organisation.

3. The implications of point (2) are that bureaucratic organisations do not characteristically look much like Weber presents them in his 'ideal type'. As I have argued above, it is useless to respond to this by replying that ideal types by definition only approximate more or less closely to reality; the point at issue is how far Weber's formulation provides an apposite model for analysing contemporary forms of social organisation. And in fact there is good reason to suppose that, in modern bureaucratic systems, those in nominally subordinate positions usually have considerably greater control over the nature of their labour task than Weber allows. Although some of the work by Blau and others on the significance of 'informal relations' within bureaucratic hierarchies is worth mentioning here,[12] more directly relevant is that of Crozier.[13] As Crozier shows, the social (and often physical) distance between offices allows spaces of potential control for subordinates that are not available in smaller, more traditional communities. A formal authority system of an organisation that approaches the characteristics of Weber's 'ideal type', in fact, can often be more successfully circumvented or manipulated by subordinates than one in which those traits are less developed.[14] No doubt Weber was right to underscore the importance of written rules as a feature of bureaucracy. But the formal codification of procedures rarely conforms to actual practice; the 'rule-book' may be subject to divergent interpretations, and hence can be a focus for conflicts which subordinates may turn to their own advantage. The irony of the idea of 'working to rule' is certainly not lost upon those who invoke the practice as a strategy in the dialectic of control.

4. The above considerations place seriously in question Weber's theorem that the 'purely bureaucratic' type of organisation is the most 'formally rational' mode of exercising authority over human beings. This theorem is so important to Weber's association of bureaucracy with capitalism, and to his critique of socialism, that it is worthwhile

emphasising the point rather strongly. For it is the basis of Weber's cultural pessimism, and of his diagnosis of an antithesis between bureaucracy and democracy. Bureaucratic domination, in which the mass of the population are largely powerless to influence the decisions that govern the course of their day-to-day lives, is quite literally an irresistible force that sweeps us all along. Attempts to stem the tide merely succeed in giving it a greater force. But such pessimism is misplaced if Weber's characterisation of the main elements of bureaucracy is a misleading one. This should not in any way be taken to imply that the sorts of problems Weber connected to bureaucratic domination can be ignored. Quite the contrary. They remain of fundamental significance: but when we attempt to tackle them, on either a sociological or a political level, we have to disencumber ourselves from a good deal of what has become received Weberian wisdom.

How does such a critique of Weber's conception of bureaucracy connect with the methodological arguments I made in the opening section of the paper? For Weber was not by any streak of the imagination an 'objectivist'; rather, he stressed the 'subjective meaning' of human conduct as integral to social analysis. Without pursuing this issue in any detail, it can be said that, in respect of bureaucratic organisation, Weber associated 'meaning' with *legitimacy*. Consequently his account of bureaucracy is very much written 'from the top'; the ideal type of bureaucratic organisation is heavily weighted towards how the 'legitimate order of a rational-legal form' is sustained.

Braverman: class domination and capitalism

Braverman writes as a Marxist, and the starting-point of his analysis of capitalistic organisations is the sale of labour power as a commodity. In the sale of their labour power to the capitalist, workers cede control of the labour process; capitalists, for their part, seek to consolidate this control through 'management'. Workers have to be 'managed' without employers being able to rely either upon the moral ties of fealty involved in feudal class relations, or upon the use of physical force to make workers obey; their only real sanction is the economic constraint of the need of workers to find paid employment in order to make a living. The crux of Braverman's thesis is that managerial control is obtained above all via the effects of the division of labour. It is mistaken, Braverman argues, to talk about the division of labour in general. The 'social division of labour', which is found in all societies, has to be clearly distinguished from the 'technical division of labour', which is specific to capitalism. While the social division of labour involves the separation of tasks devoted to the making of whole products, the technical division of labour fragments the labour task into repetitive operations carried out by different individuals. The expansion of the technical division of labour, in Braverman's view, is the most basic element in extending managerial control over labour, because knowledge of and command over the labour process are thereby progressively 'expropriated' from workers. Braverman lays a great deal of stress upon the contribution of Taylorism, or 'scientific management', to this process. In Taylorism the operations carried out by the worker are integrated into the technical design of production as a whole. 'Scientific management' may seem in most countries to have made only a limited inroad into industry, and to have been generally superseded by the 'human relations' approach of Elton Mayo and his associates in the United States.[15] But Braverman claims that the impact of the 'human relations' view has been of relatively marginal significance. Taylorism serves as the chief set of organising principles of capitalist production.

Braverman's analysis, in my opinion, stands as a major corrective to some of the elements of Weber's account of bureaucratisation. Braverman shows that the rationality of technique in modern industrial enterprise is not neutral in respect of class domination. It would be difficult to exaggerate the significance of this. For if Braverman's argument is correct, industrial technique embodies the capital/wage-labour relation in its very form. Class domination appears as the absent centre of the linkage Weber drew between the rationality of technique and the rationality of the (formally) most 'technically effective' type of organisation, bureaucracy. It would follow that bureaucratic domination, and the concomitant powerlessness of workers, are not inevitable features of contemporary organisations; the transformation of the class relations incorporated within the 'technical division of labour' could in principle furnish the basis for the democratic reorganisation of the labour process. Braverman's work should therefore provide for a more optimistic assessment of the possibilities of unlocking Weber's 'steel-hard cage' than Weber's own gloomy vision of the future allows for. In fact, however, the process of the sieving-off of control of the labour process that Braverman describes appears to have just the same inevitable, irreversible character about it as the processes of bureaucratisation portrayed by Weber. The factors responsible for this, I want to argue, do in some respects have similarities to the shortcomings I have pointed to in Weber's treatment of bureaucracy; but this time they are very closely connected to an 'objectivist' methodological position that Braverman declaredly embraces towards the beginning of his book.

Labor and Monopoly Capital, he claims, is only concerned with the ' "objective" content of class', and not with the ' "subjective will" '.[16] The result is a work which, notwithstanding its self-professed Marxist standpoint, certainly drastically underestimates the knowledgeability and the capability of workers faced with a range of management imperatives. Braverman is mistaken to say that his work is unconcerned with 'subjective will': the 'subjective will' of *management,* as expressed in Taylorist strategies of control, is more than adequately represented in the book. What is lacking is an adequate discussion of the reactions of workers, as themselves knowledgeable and capable agents, to the technical division of labour and to Taylorism. Braverman bases his severance of the 'objective' from the 'subjective' components of class upon Marx's famous distinction between a class 'in itself' and a class 'for itself'. But it is important to see that this distinction conceals a possible ambiguity. For the differentiation could be taken to imply that 'class consciousness' can be equated with class 'for itself': and that therefore the 'objective' features of class can be examined without reference to consciousness (discursive or practical). This is evidently mistaken. All class relations obviously involve the conscious activity of human agents. But this is different from groups of individuals being conscious of being members of the same class, of having common class interests, and so on.[17] It is quite possible to conceive of circumstances in which individuals are not only not cognisant of being in a common class situation, but where they may actively deny the existence of classes – and where their attitudes and ideas can nevertheless be explained in terms of class relationships. Such is characteristically the case, as I have argued elsewhere,[18] with certain categories of white-collar workers.

Braverman's surprising disinclination to treat workers as knowledgeable and capable agents seriously compromises the validity of some of his conclusions. The implications of Braverman's analysis, which in emphasising the class character of managerial control begins from different premises to those of Weber, appear every bit as pessimistic as those of that author. For although Braverman's study is an explicitly Marxist one, there is no indication at all that the working class is likely to rise against its oppressors, or even that workers are able in some part to stem the advance of the processes that rob them of control over their labour. On the contrary, the spread of de-skilling, and the sieving-off of control over the labour task from the worker, appear to have much the same implacable force about them as the advance of bureaucracy depicted by Weber.

The revolution may be as far off as ever; but one can certainly doubt that the processes described by Braverman are either as clear-cut or categorical as his discussion suggests. One reason for this is that the technological changes constantly taking place in capitalist economies seem more complicated, in their effects upon the labour process, than Braverman allows. Certainly old craft skills are for the most part eliminated, but new types of skilled activity, albeit different in character, are continually created. Of course, what counts as 'skill' is a complicated matter, as Braverman and a host of subsequent commentators have recognised. But the factor of human knowledgeability again enters in here. For what counts as 'skilled work', or a 'skilled trade', depends in some substantial degree upon what can be *made* to count as such. There are many examples where workers have proved able to sustain the definition of themselves as 'skilled' in spite of changes in the nature of the labour task. A classic mode in which this has been achieved is via the 'balkanisation' of the labour market: where access to the occupation has been kept strictly limited by the union or workers' association.

Equally important are the various forms of worker resistance whereby workers have succeeded in maintaining a significant amount of control over the labour process itself. Historical studies of the American working class indicate not only that Taylorism had consistently less impact than Braverman claims, in large degree because of worker resistance, but that the expansion of 'human relations' ideology was partly due to working-class opposition to Taylorism.[19] It is perhaps worth adding that opposition to Taylorism was not confined to those most directly affected by it, the working class. Many employers and managers, in the USA and elsewhere (in contrast to the attitude of Lenin!) were either sceptical of scientific management or openly hostile to it, on a mixture of pragmatic and humanitarian grounds. In adopting such attitudes, even on purely practical grounds, managers were being quite realistic. For those who attempt to control a labour force are by no means impervious to understanding the Marxist adage that 'labour power is a commodity that refuses to be treated like any other commodity'.

This is where the point becomes particularly important that, in capitalistic economies, workers have to be 'managed', without the moral or military sanctions possessed by exploiting classes in prior types of society. In other types of class-divided society, the dominant class has normally had direct possession of the means of violence, and hence of disciplining recalcitrant labour where necessary. But in capitalism (a) regularised labour discipline is more integral to labour than in most contexts (especially that of the peasant producer) of production in earlier forms of society, and (b) the chief coercive sanction employers possess to ensure the compliance of the workforce is that the latter is propertyless, and hence compelled to find employment in order to make a living. It is quite right, I think, to argue that the significance of these phenomena can best be analysed in terms of the capitalist labour contract. But the contractual encounter between capital and wage-labour has to be seen as providing axes of chronic struggle in which the working class is by no means always and inevitably the loser.

There are, I consider, two connecting axes or 'sites' of class struggle in the capitalist societies. One is class struggle in the workplace, the main focus of Braverman's attention. As I have argued, I do not think Braverman adequately acknowledges the significance of such struggle on the level of day-to-day practices on the shopfloor. Braverman's work can here be usefully complemented by studies such as that of Friedman.[20] Friedman argues that not only Braverman but Marx himself, in anticipating the progressive homogenisation of labour through the undermining of skill differentials, fail to give sufficient weight to the influence of worker resistance at the level of the firm, and the need of employers or managers to incorporate the fact of such resistance into their own strategies. Friedman distinguishes two principal types of managerial strategy that are commonly used to control the labour force. One such strategy is that of 'responsible autonomy'.[21] Workers in these circumstances are allowed considerable independence of activity in the work situation, so that they are encouraged to cooperate in accepting technological changes in ways that conform to the overall aims of management. This can be contrasted with the strategy of 'direct control'. Such a strategy approximates to that which Braverman takes to be prevalent throughout industry. Here managers attempt to obtain the compliance of the labour force by close supervision of the labour process, and the sustaining of discipline by minimising worker responsibility through Taylorist techniques. Braverman, says Friedman, exaggerates the scope and the effectiveness of the second of these strategies. This overemphasis follows from 'a failure to appreciate the importance of worker resistance as a force provoking accommodating changes in the mode of production', a mistake which 'leads to a technological deterministic view of capitalist development'.[22] Part of the importance of distinguishing different types of managerial strategy in this way is that it becomes possible to connect the analysis to the study of dual or segmented labour markets. Those in weak positions in segmented labour markets are probably usually less able to resist incorporation within managerial strategies of 'direct control'. Such workers include particularly ethnic minorities – and women.

The second site of class struggle involves the pitting of labour movements against the organised power of employers and of the state. Here we have a prime example of the operation of the dialectic of control. In the early years of the development of capitalism, as Marx showed, the capitalist labour contract was a medium of bolstering the power of the emerging entrepreneurial class. By dissolving feudal bonds of fealty and obligation, the capitalist labour contract allowed for the 'freedom' of employers to buy, and workers to sell, labour power, at its exchange value. By making the relation between employers and workers a purely economic one, abstract 'political' rights were confined to a separate sphere of the polity, a separation first of all supported by property qualifications on the franchise. The capitalist labour contract, however, in the context of parliamentary government, allowed the creation of labour movements based upon the power generated by the threat or actuality of the withdrawal of labour. In my opinion, the struggles of labour movements to improve the general economic conditions of the working class, and to realise what T. H. Marshall calls 'citizenship rights', have helped profoundly to alter the characteristics of the capitalist societies of the West. Braverman is not directly concerned with such issues in his book, but again I do not believe they can be wholly separated from the problems he discusses. For the achievements of Western labour movements have undoubtedly acted to counter the kind of monolithic triumph of capitalism suggested by the style of analysis Braverman develops. Just as Braverman underestimates the significance of worker resistance in the workplace, many other Marxists have been dismissive of the part played by labour movements in transforming what C. B. Macpherson calls the 'liberal' state of the nineteenth century into the 'liberal democratic' state of the twentieth.[23] The worst of these analyses incorporate the flaws of both 'objectivistic' social science and of functionalism:[24] whatever citizenship rights the working class may have obtained are the result of 'adjustments' of the capitalist system protecting its source of labour supply. Consider the judgement of Müller and Neusüss on the welfare state: 'By establishing a minimum subsistence level (through workmen's protection and social security systems) the material existence of wage-labourers is ensured during the times when they cannot sell their labour-power on the market (sickness, old age, unemployment).'[25] Such assessments not only ignore the long-term battles workers have had to conduct in most countries to attain political and welfare rights, but once more treat workers as mere dupes of the system. Evaluations of such a kind have about as much validity as contrary assertions of the sort often heard from conservative sectors of the British press, that 'the country is run by the unions'. At least this second viewpoint does accept that the organised working class has achieved a considerable measure of power in the liberal democratic state, even if it wildly exaggerates the scope of such power.

Conclusion: agency and alienation

In this paper I have concentrated upon indicating that abstract issues of social theory do have a definite bearing upon concrete problems of social analysis. In emphasising the notion of the dialectic of control, I do not mean to imply that those in subordinate positions in social systems are chronically driven to, or are able to, overthrow those who dominate them. I am not suggesting some sort of revised version of Hegel's master–slave dialectic. But I do think the critique of Weber's interpretation of the expansion of bureaucracy (directed against Marxist class analysis) and of works such as that of Braverman (written supposedly precisely from a standpoint of Marxist class analysis) allow a more satisfactory understanding of issues of the relation between class domination and authority systems than their writings provide.[26] In concluding this brief discussion, however, I want to return to a more philosophical plane.

If my arguments about human agency and power in the opening part of the paper are correct, they can be related, I think, to Marx's discussion of the alienated character of capitalist production. To be an agent is to have the capability of 'making a difference', of intervening in the world so as to influence events which occur in that world. To be a *human* agent is to be a highly knowledgeable and skilled individual, who applies that knowledgeability in securing autonomy of action in the course of day-to-day life. By 'alienated labour' Marx refers to work situations in which the worker becomes an appendage of a machine – Braverman's study is about 'alienated labour' in this sense, although he barely mentions the term itself. In my terminology the connection of alienation with the 'human-ness' of man's 'species-being' can be expressed simply and coherently in a single sentence. The more a worker comes close to being an 'appendage of a machine', the more he or she ceases to be a human agent. As Marx puts it, 'The animal becomes human and the human becomes animal.'[27] The interest of this analysis for a philosophical anthropology of labour, however, should not make us forget that, precisely because they are not machines, wherever they can do so human actors devise ways of avoiding being treated as such.

Managing the frontier of control

GRAEME SALAMAN

Recent theories of the labour process, influenced by Braverman's *Labor and Monopoly Capital*, have revived interest in a sociology of management both as an integral part of the revival of interest in all aspects of the differentiation and coordination of labour within the capitalist enterprise, and as an element in the capitalist domination of the modern enterprise. Recent theories of the labour process depend upon the assertion of the crucial functions of management. Yet within such theories this category of employee, and the functions they are asserted to serve, remain underdeveloped and unexplored. This essay considers the manner in which management is theorised in the writings of Braverman and recent writers, relates this analysis to that advanced within recent class theory, and attempts to explain the shared weaknesses of these conceptions of management.[1]

The focus on conceptions of management within Braverman's writings is justifiable for three reasons. First, *Labor and Monopoly Capital* is a seminal work which has done much to establish the direction and parameters of recent discussions of the labour process. Since it is so influential, it is important to assess the value of that influence. Second, at least as far as the theorising of management is concerned, many post-Braverman writings adopt a broadly similar line to that of Braverman. Edwards and Friedman, for example, share Braverman's insistence that work design and control systems are structured by management in the light of the requirements of capitalist imperatives. In other words, management plays a crucial, if largely unexplored, role in all recent theories of the labour process. Finally, Braverman's analysis of management also relates closely to recent attempts by writers such as Carchedi, Wright and Poulantzas to establish the class position of intermediate class groups, including management. Despite their important differences, these writers, like Braverman, seek to establish class boundaries, and hence class locations, in terms of the functions performed by a class for capital.

Until recently the sociology of management has been vitiated by uncertainty not only about what managers did but, more importantly, the significance of what they did.[2] Pre-Braverman, sociological interest in management seemed to be interested in everything about management, and managers, except the nature and origins of management functions and management power, and their possible class basis. It is possible that this reflects an acceptance of the arguments, propagated by writers such as Kerr *et al.*[3] and other Industrial Society theorists, that organisational structure and the nature and allocation of differentiated functions were inevitable correlates of the application of neutral and societally desirable technology. According to such a view, management activity as an entirely technical matter, executing the neutral demands of the organisational system, is of no sociological concern or interest. But it also reflected the status of various forms of competing sociological theory, particularly the relative ascendancy of varieties of interactionism, and the relative lack of interest in forms of Marxist theory. Even as late as 1977, in a third edition of a popular text book in industrial sociology, a chapter on management could open thus: 'It has become accepted in recent years that management can make an important contribution to economic prosperity, and there has consequently been a growing interest in management education.'[4] The chapter continues by isolating three perspectives on management: a view of management as an economic resource, performing a set of technical administrative functions; as a professional corps, or as a system of power and authority 'within which different personal and group interests are pursued'.[5] Only in the third perspective is the possibility of management as a system of power considered, and even here the idea that such power may be related to the pursuit of sectional (or class) goals is only entertained with reference to conflicts *within* the management function.

Braverman radically changed all this. The main thrust of his analysis overall, and of his analysis of management in particular, is the relationship between the organisation of enterprise and the requirements of capitalism. The organisation of the enterprise reflects the problems of employing alienated and recalcitrant labour for the achievement of profit within the constraints and imperatives of a particular stage in the development of capitalism. Braverman thus de-mystifies management functions – and all aspects of organisational structure – by defining them as class functions.

Braverman's analysis of management operates at two levels. First he presents a highly detailed analysis of specific management functions and traces their connections to problems of the typical large-scale enterprise in monopoly capitalism. This aspect of the analysis starts with the separation, under scientific management, of mental from manual work – design, planning, accountancy and record-keeping from the de-skilled physical processes of production. 'The production units operate like a hand, watched, corrected and controlled by a distant brain.'[6] Concurrent with this process of separation, the expansion of the typical enterprise required an increase in a specialised management staff. While, as Braverman admits, top levels of management may be drawn from the same class as the owners of the enterprise, the 'direct and personal unity' between ownership and control is ruptured. Capital is now institutionalised in the elaborate structure of specialisms that constitutes modern management systems. Within the modern corporation not only are the functions of the original owner-manager now differentiated among a large group of expert managers, but these functions themselves have grown greatly with the development of new specialities and the increasing complexity of traditional ones. Braverman places particular emphasis on the development of two management functions, engineering and marketing. The latter, which subsumes its own myriad specialities, grows as an attempt to internalise, and thus to control, market determination of product demand. Braverman echoes Chandler's argument that the development of the large-scale modern enterprise depended upon the development of an administrative component which was able to coordinate internally the activities of numerous diversified business units.[7] The 'visible hand' of management is more efficient than the invisible hand of market forces.

But Braverman adds an important emphasis. The new, expert, and crucial management function not only attempted to reduce the uncertainties of the enterprise's external environment – particularly the market. It was also concerned to monitor and control the activities and efficiency of internal processes. Management, he writes, 'is a labor process conducted for the purpose of control within the corporation'.[8] In other words, management represents a distinct class (capitalist) interest, serves explicit class functions, and constitutes a major element in the oppression of working-class employees.

The second level of Braverman's analysis of management functions is less detailed and empirical. Indeed in a sense it does not occur, explicitly, at all, but must be inferred from his discussion of the nature of the connection between aspects and stages of capitalism, the internal organisation of the labour process, the role of scientific management in this relationship, and the analysis of class.

Braverman's examination of the labour process under monopoly capitalism reflects Marx's description of the transition from the formal subordination of labour – where the labour process occurs much as it did prior to the development of capitalism, but under the control and organisation of the capitalist – to the real subordination of labour, where production is transformed and differentiated by the application of science and technology. This transition is associated in Marxist analysis with two forms of subordination: absolute, from the prolongation of the working day; relative, from the increased productivity of labour.

The organisation and design of work under monopoly capitalism is characterised by the real subordination of labour and the constant and active pursuit of relative surplus value. These processes are stimulated by competition between firms, and the requirements of accumulation. This is revealed in the increasing application of scientific management, which represents the ideal method of work design under modern forms of capitalism because of its utility in the achievement of control. Control is defined in terms of the removal of any possibility of worker intervention in decision-making, and the increasingly thorough and detailed imposition of prescriptions and standards designed elsewhere. Scientific management thus represents a de-skilling of workers as part of an effort to reduce worker discretion and to impose management demands, standards, and production targets.

This argument has obvious implications for the development and role of management. Management is not only created by the requirements of capitalism, but once established in the early phases of monopoly capitalism, *it plays a major part in devising and/or installing the principles of work design which constitute the strategies of control* required to achieve greater profitability. It is management which 'de-skills' workers.

There is, however, a central ambiguity in the argument. Recent theories of the labour process, while they may show awareness of the differentiation and complexity of management functions and specialities, actually employ in their argument a very simplified conception of management. This not only vitiates their analyses of management – it also undermines their argument as a whole.

In what follows a number of criticisms of this approach will be developed. In the main these criticisms centre on the difficulties which accompany a form of analysis which takes as its starting point the functions (for, and within capitalism) of management. Such an approach, while in its own terms plausible, stops short of the consideration of how, when and under what conditions, the functions of managers serve as an actual basis for their sense of identification, consciousness, their conception of their interests and their definition of their professional function.

Management's role in the determination of new work forms

A simplistic notion of management results from conceptions of the causal mechanism which connects the development of capitalism to the internal organisation of the enterprise. Three arguments can be discerned: a form of functionalism, the assertion of an omniscient, purposive and conspiratorial management, and a form of reductionism.

The functionalist argument asserts that, in view of the competitive pressures on the modern enterprise, the requirement to accumulate creates a need constantly to transform the organisation of work so as to achieve ever greater levels of relative surplus value. Production must be made constantly more productive, if the firm is to survive. This pressure is translated into certain work forms whose application is required by the pressures to accumulate, i.e. to be competitive. Thus the imposition of scientific management principles becomes an *evolutionary necessity*. The alternative version accepts that the development of specific work forms is a consequence not simply of evolutionary necessity, but of management guile. The requirements of capitalism continue to supply the background to management efforts to transform the design of work in order to increase the achievement of relative surplus value and to counter, or to evade, varieties of worker resistance. The success of such efforts is rewarded by competitive advantage.

According to this first, functionalist, form of argument, management's role is simply to comply with the necessary historical process of the development of work forms under capitalism. Management simply represents a stage in the argument, a step in the unfolding of the historically necessary. Management is thus passive, reactive. According to the second form of argument, management, as the initiator of varieties of control strategy, is now active, but in an idealised and extravagant manner. Management is now omniscient, entirely concerned with, and accomplished at, devising new, more sophisticated strategies of design and control. Management restructures the enterprise to ensure its more profitable operation. Both of these arguments are, ultimately, reductionist. Both explain variations in the size, form and activity of management as responses to capitalism's imperatives. The relationship is regarded as automatic, unmediated, and unproblematic.

In short, it is a feature of recent theories of the labour process that management is regarded in a highly abstract and formalistic manner, either as an entirely passive category whose main responsibility is to grasp the advantages – the necessity for – scientific management and apply it, and in so doing to create a larger area of expert decision-making; or as an extraordinarily active category whose responsibility and achievement is to design more complex and successful forms of control. Both conceptions are inadequate, and this inadequacy casts doubts on the theories overall. Furthermore, both conceptions of management, despite their apparent differences, have much in common: in both cases, the actors themselves are omitted from the analysis. Their role is simply to conform with the demands of the organisation (the transformation of the labour process) and the requirements of the system (the imperatives of capitalist accumulation). As Giddens notes of this form of analysis: '. . . the teleology of the system either governs . . . or supplants . . . that of actors themselves'.[9] In this case in both forms of argument there is no allowance for actors' *active interventions*. The theoretically crucial relationship between form of economy and the internal organisation of the labour process occurs, in Giddens's phrase, 'behind the backs' of the actors whose conduct is central to the process itself. It is asserted as necessary, but the manner in which it might be achieved in practice is left unexplored.

The remainder of this essay will consider some problems which arise with these conceptions of management.

The determination of managers' class position by class function

In the late twentieth century it goes without saying that ownership or non-ownership of property is not in itself a sufficient basis for the allocation of *class boundaries*. If it were so, managers and others who receive preferential, privileged treatment within the modern enterprise must be regarded as members of the working class. As Parkin notes, such an inclusion would be extremely discomfiting since it is precisely this group which is most actively responsible for the oppression of shopfloor employees.[10] Braverman, like Poulantzas, Carchedi and Wright, finds this unacceptable. He insists that the term 'employee' is too gross to be useful. It must be differentiated.

Furthermore, like other writers, Braverman considers that the way to differentiate between propertyless employees is by reference to the functions they serve within the enterprise. Under monopoly capitalism, the nature of ownership itself becomes transformed and differentiated. With this differentiation, it is possible – indeed necessary – to move beyond the simple but now inadequate distinction between owners and non-owners, to a consideration of positions on a more complex structure of axes. The social relations of production are differentiated into two dimensions: economic ownership and possession, or, in Braverman's terms, the ownership of capital and the ownership of control within the enterprise.[11]

In this way capital itself is differentiated. And those who fulfil the functions of capital, also fill the place of capital. This means that it is now possible to belong to the capitalist class in two ways: '. . . by virtue of ownership of capital . . . (or) . . . as the direct organiser and manager of a capitalist enterprise'.[12] Furthermore, the class position of types of *all* employees is established by their function within the enterprise, since function is now an aspect of ownership. The major element in this functional differentiation, is position within the hierarchy of control. Braverman refers to '. . . the vesting of control in a specialised stratum of the capitalist class'.[13] Control itself, however, must also be differentiated, and again, like other recent writers, Braverman distinguishes between control over investment decisions and the allocation of resources, control over the production process itself (engineers), and control over labour. Using the criterion of function for capital within the differentiated enterprise, he argues that managers occupy an intermediate position between capital and labour: '. . . there is a range of intermediate categories, sharing the characteristics of worker on the one side and manager on the other in varying degrees. The gradations of position in the line of management may be seen chiefly in terms of authority.'[14] Braverman's theory of class is clearly related to the functionalism and reductionism of his overall argument. Indeed, it compounds some of the problems of that argument. In particular, it fails to '. . . consider the institutional "filters" which complicate the relationship between production methods, skill levels and class'.[15]

Braverman's class analysis is highly formal and abstract. It is concerned with the differentiation of system requirements within the enterprise. But it is not clear how far these differentiated functions relate to the development of real social groups. For classes to exist, it is necessary that they develop social organisation and culture. It is doubtful whether the position within the division of labour as described by Braverman constitutes a sufficient basis for the *structuration* of classes, although it may represent *one* element in such a structuration.[16] Certainly many writers are agreed that position within the division of labour and differences in location within the authority system of the enterprise, represent an important basis of class structuration. But the influence of these factors is greatly increased when they are allied to extra-organisational factors affecting the closure of these social groups (e.g. through structured variations in patterns and levels of mobility or in market capacity), and Braverman restricts his class analysis to internal organisational structure and functioning.

Secondly, Braverman's assessment of the basis of class location depends more on the variations in forms of control than on different positions within the hierarchy of control. Like other recent class theorists, Braverman regards certain sorts of control and decision-making as more closely connected to the bourgeoisie than other groups. Control over investments and financial decisions represents 'economic ownership'; control over labour and plant represents 'relations of possession'. Yet it is far from clear that this difference generates such differences in experience that managers executing these various decisions can be said to be part of, or see themselves as, identifiable social groupings. For Braverman's analysis of the class position of varieties of manager to be fully persuasive it is first necessary to assess how far the determinate dimensions he isolates are mediated so that they produce actual social groupings.

There is a third aspect to the problem. How far do the factors isolated by Braverman as the basis for the identification of class position actually represent a feasible basis of differences in interests? Clearly his analysis of the class position of managers and other intermediate categories is presented not as part of a theory of class, but as an integral part of a theory of labour within monopoly capitalism. The identification of the class position of managers and others with authority in the enterprise is a necessary part of the analysis, because, within this analysis, these employees act in certain predictable and crucial ways: to further the interest of capital. We may borrow Wright's query of Poulantzas's distinction between productive and unproductive labour: 'The key question . . . becomes whether this distinction represents a significant division of class interests.'[17]

These weaknesses manifest themselves empirically in a number of ways. First, how far do these functional differences coincide with those divisions within the class structure which research has frequently found to be most important and persistent? As Stephens notes, within recent theories of class which analyse class boundaries by reference to function, the manual/non-manual distinction loses its traditional importance, since, in itself, this is not regarded as coincident with the working class/non-working class distinction. Yet '. . . this division in the class structure is, or at least was, the most important dividing line in the collective political and social action of groups in capitalist society'.[18] Secondly, the allocation of class by organisational position creates very much the same problem as that faced by Weberian class analysis: namely, the criterion could well supply an enormous number of class positions differing from each other in degree of possession of the criterion. Where are the lines, the breaks, to be drawn? And can they be drawn by reference to organisational position alone? Thirdly, it must be remembered that, ultimately, theories of class involve theories of class *interests*. If the class positions identified by the use of the criteria offered by recent writers do not identify differences in interests then they are invalid, as Wright correctly emphasises. Yet it is far from clear that on their own, such criteria are useful in generating '. . . empirically identifiable divisions in the consciousness of people located in various positions in the class structure'.[19]

Interestingly, Braverman himself seems to lose confidence in the functional difference he describes, when it comes to considering this question of class interests, for he has recourse to more traditional determinants of class identification, namely factors remarkably similar to those described by Lockwood as 'market' and 'work' situation. Of managers he writes:

Their pay level is significant because beyond a certain point it, like the pay of commanders of the corporation, clearly represents not just the exchange of their labour power for money – a commodity exchange – but a *share in the surplus* produced in the corporation, and thus is intended to attach them to the success or failure of the corporation and give them a 'management stake' even if a small one. The same is true insofar as they share in a recognized guarantee of employment, in the semi-independence of their mode of labour within the production process, in authority over the labour of others, the right to hire and fire, and the other prerogatives of command.[20]

According to traditional sociological explorations of the determinants of class identifications and membership, this list of determinant factors is highly plausible. But Braverman, presumably, is arguing that variations in these key factors exactly mirror location within the differentiated functions of capital. However, the possibility must exist that members of the corporation may develop conceptions of their class interests which are at odds with their positions as ascribed by his analysis. Once this possibility is granted, then a further complication arises: namely that these groups may, as a result of these (misconceived) notions of interest, choose courses of action which could obstruct the connection between extra-organisational demands, and internal organisational structure and process.

Both logically and historically it seems most implausible that the division of capital's functions always and automatically produces variations in what we may call work and market situation. Rather, the evidence suggests that many of these variations are achieved by organisational groups as the outcome of sectional conflicts, professional strategies, internal bargaining, occupational closure, the 'negotiated order' of the enterprise. They are the result of differences in levels and forms of bargaining strength, levels of organisation, ability to deploy general ideologies of expertise, or skill. Braverman's argument here relies, as elsewhere, on a technicist notion of skill – skill, or organisational function, as a direct consequence of contribution to the requirements of capital. But he ignores the extent to which notions of skill, and of organisational power which accompany them, may be socially produced within the enterprise. Burawoy, in a pertinent comment on Braverman's inadequate notion of control, remarks that Braverman ignores the ways in which workers' interests are concretely produced and structured. He writes: '. . . the interests that organise the daily life of workers are not given irrevocably; they cannot be imputed; they are produced and reproduced in particular ways. To assume, (interests) . . . provides an excuse to ignore the ideological terrain where interests are organised'.[21] The same criticism can be applied to Braverman's consideration of management interests, and their origins: we cannot simply assume that these flow *automatically* from their position within the differentiated functions of capital.

Braverman's periodisation of capitalism

A further problem with Braverman's analysis is that it operates with an excessively rigid periodisation of capitalism. This has two aspects. First, he exaggerates the extent to which all capitalist economies can accurately be described as monopolistic. In the case of Britain, as Levine and Francis suggest, there is yet a considerable survival of forms of enterprise and control from earlier historical periods: i.e. the family-controlled firms.[22] Within such enterprises, selection of key, senior management figures, such as the chairman, is likely to be on non-meritocratic criteria. It is likely that the active survival of such non-rational values, and their influence on the rejection of professional management structures, will have implications for management's ability, or preparedness, to conform with its role as laid out by Braverman.

Secondly, Braverman's periodisation ignores the extent to which ideological and institutional aspects of one period may survive to exert influence on later periods. Francis, for example, reports that '. . . firms are not so tightly constrained by product and capital markets that those who control them have no discretion'.[23] Furthermore, Francis and other commentators have suggested that, in part, such discretion may be exercised in accordance with values developed in earlier periods. It is, for example, a common and probably well-founded diagnosis of the 'English condition' that modern capitalists are still influenced by the values and institutions of a landed past, showing a relative *lack* of interest in industrial activities, preferring to devote themselves to other pursuits: the land, property, politics. Again, if this diagnosis is correct it is likely to have implications for owners' preparedness – indeed their *capacity* – to recognise and act on the system requirements identified by Braverman.

In many ways the problem involves a restatement of the celebrated debate between Poulantzas and Miliband.[24] Poulantzas accuses Miliband of giving undue attention to the fact that capitalism does not depend upon personal motivations. Managers are important not because of their motivations, but because of their function for capital. Miliband accepts this but in turn replies that Poulantzas (and the same could be said of Braverman) overestimates the extent to which managers – or state bureaucrats – are constrained and determined solely by the 'objective relations' (of capital's requirements):

. . . the structural constraints of the system are so absolutely compelling as to turn those who run the state (or firm) into the merest functionaries and executants of policies imposed upon them 'by the system' . . . his analysis seems . . . to lead to a . . . structural super-determinism, which makes impossible a truly *realistic* consideration of the dialectical relationship between the state (or firm) and the system.[25]

In the case of Braverman's conception of management, and its place in his overall argument, this structural 'super-determination' is revealed in two ways: the assumption of management omniscience, and the lack of attention to the development of management preoccupations other than those specified by the system's requirements.

As we have seen, it is a necessary part of Braverman's argument that managers, as part of their execution of the differentiated tasks of capital, grasp the significance of scientific management and apply it as part of their responsibility to achieve control of the workforce. In the case of more recent writers, management's task is more complex:

to develop new strategies of control – bureaucratic, or responsible autonomy – as the deficiencies of 'direct', technical, control become apparent, or as the workforce develop counter-strategies. In both cases, it is necessary to the argument that managers achieve the same level of appreciation of the necessity for these strategies as that enjoyed by the ever vigilant sociologist. And in both cases it is necessary that they do not develop any alternative structures of knowledge, or perception, than that which is required to appreciate the benefits of these strategies of control.

There is considerable evidence that neither of these conditions can be assumed. Taylor himself complained of employers' unwillingness fully to implement his system. And Nadworny and other commentators have reported the extent of employers' resistance to, and suspicions of, scientific management.[26] Edwards reports that by the 1920s such enthusiasm as had ever existed for scientific management waned as corporate employers realised its limitations.[27] Such hesitation was even more marked in this country, where employers voiced concern at the inhumanitarian nature of Taylorism. Edward Cadbury, in an early assessment of Taylorism from the employers' point of view, writes: '. . . in the long run it will defeat itself for employers to consider a man as merely a tool . . . business efficiency and the welfare of employees are but different sides of the same problem'.[28]

It is not being argued here that it is impossible or improper to seek to uncover strategies of management control, or that such strategies do not show a broad, historical patterning of the sort described by Edwards. What is at issue, however, is the possibility of a number of important intermediate stages in the relationship between monopoly capitalism and the design of the labour process. Have managers an active role in this process, or does history reveal a process of necessary development which managers simply facilitate, but play no active part in? The latter seems to be the view of Braverman. Yet the evidence is that the development of strategies of control has been sporadic, muddled, and intermittent, with some periods of achievement, followed by others of failure, and with managers varying in their receptivity to new systems (managers in this country being notoriously slow at accepting the innovations of their North American counterparts). In addition, the whole process of managerial control and the relationship between this and the demands of monopoly capitalism is much more complex, contradictory and dialectical than envisaged by Braverman – not least because it takes place within the framework of class conflict and class relations, between constituted classes. To say this is not to argue the complete detachment of systems of work control from the pressures imposed under monopoly capitalism. But it is to argue that these work forms cannot be seen simply as a reflex of the system. The achievement of control is not only more multi-faceted than envisaged by Braverman, it is also more prone to contradiction, more autonomous.[29] Managers certainly are exposed to economic demands, and levels and forms of employee recalcitrance. But their responses will be mediated not only by ignorance, but by their own structures of knowledge and perception; their own sectional interests and objectives.[30]

Management professionalism, sectionalism and class functions

The mediation of managerial responses is accorded little recognition in recent theories of the labour process, although traditionally the sociology of management has been very concerned with the development of management not as a technical necessity within the large corporation, but as an identifiable social grouping. Braverman's analysis of management stops short of any consideration of how this category of employees might be transformed into a social grouping with a distinctive culture and identity. Presumably this was because he felt such interests to be dangerously close to the subjective preoccupations of much conventional sociology which he castigates early in the book. This omission is unfortunate because the way in which managers establish their shared identity, legitimise themselves to those they manage as well as to themselves, the ways in which they develop characteristic forms of organisation, recruitment, and ideology, or conceptions of interest and identity, are all important in influencing their interpretation of their role as described by Braverman, and in opening up the possibility of the sort of complex contradictory relationship between system and labour process which Braverman ignores.

Braverman's analysis of management functions allows that these range from positions very close to the senior executives, to others – the great number –which are close to the mass of labour. But how far do these variations –with respect to location within the hierarchy of command – constitute the sole, or even major, basis for the development of such recognisable and significant groupings? These are most usually established not on the basis of degree of authority within the organisational hierarchy, but on professional or occupational grounds. Once such groupings exist, furthermore, they become important as sources of group interest, organisation and culture. Evidence from numerous studies demonstrates their role in intra-organisational conflicts over decision-making, the distribution of resources, etc.[31] It is to be expected that the existence of such groupings within the management function will constitute an important mediating factor in the relationship between systems and labour process described by Braverman.

Similarly, ideologies and structures of perception developed as part of the structure of intra-organisational groupings (many of which will have strong relationships with their professional colleagues outside the enterprise) will cause members of such groups to develop conceptions of their responsibilities and priorities which may differ radically from those attributed to them by Braverman.[32] At issue here, in part, is the perennial problem of the implications of the employment of professionals within large-scale organisations. Certainly it would be unwise to assume that such institutional forms as professionalisation would not serve as an important 'filter' of the relationship between economic system and organisation of the labour process.[33] For example, as writers on management ideology have stressed, the first priority of the early managers was to establish the legitimacy of their position: that they had a job to do within the enterprise, and they were suited to it. Various ideas have been employed to achieve these ends.[34] These ideas, once incorporated into management organisation and thought, are capable of exerting some independent influence. Furthermore, some of these ideas were developed in response not to managers' organisational responsibilities, and the difficulties these raised, but in response to the strains of their organisational role – as employees intermediate between employers and workforce, as privileged but, apparently, non-productive employees, and so on. Typical ideological responses to these strains – such as to service to the community, or satisfaction of employees' needs – might also play a significant role in management intervention in the design and installation of systems of work design and control.[35]

We would therefore expect to find that professional ideologies, strategies and practices will, to the extent that they are successful, play an important part in resisting management efforts to 'decompose' professional tasks. Successful professional strategies, which retain the 'indeterminacy' of professional skills, will result in efforts towards incorporation. Unsuccessful strategies will permit proletarianisation. Market forces too will be of significance.

Graeme Salaman

Conclusion

It has been argued that Braverman's analysis of the relationship between forms of capitalism development and internal organisational work-control systems is flawed by an over-structured and incomplete conception of those members of the enterprise who are allocated, within his analysis, the role of mediating between economy and labour process. While managers are seen as reacting reflexively to system requirements, the possibility that they may not appreciate these requirements, or have some concern for aspects of their social predicament which flow from their intermediate, contradictory location, or professional membership are not included in the argument. Braverman's argument has no room for unanticipated consequences. It ignores the possibility that organisational categories need not find their defined interests solely in terms of their organisational function, but may develop sectional concerns, and sectional structures of knowledge through occupational and professional strategies.

These shortcomings in Braverman's analysis stem partly from his limited definition of control, which is defined simply in terms of work specification. His omission of the role and importance of management efforts to achieve some level of consent permits him to overlook the possibility of tension between aspects, as well as between forms and mechanisms, of consent.[36] But Braverman's preoccupation with the 'objective' content of class, '. . . the shape given to the working population by the capital accumulation process',[37] lies at the root of his analysis which, in reality, however, has less to do with the 'shape' given to the working population by the capital accumulation process, and more with an analysis of how this process itself occurs in monopoly capitalism. What is missing from Braverman's account is precisely how these processes impinge on the working population so as to generate identifiable structures of interest, consciousness and action. He simply assumes that to describe the process of accumulation with reference to the labour process, is to describe the structuration of classes. This essay has questioned this assumption. Furthermore, Braverman's conception is *functionalist* in that it seeks to explain the development, and consequent behaviour and thought, of a social category – managers – by reference to the requirements of the system. It is not clear how this analysis avoids the difficulties attributed to functionalist argument by Giddens.[38]

As a result of these difficulties, Braverman's analysis is over-determined and under-differentiated. It does not include the possibility of contradiction between management's role and management actions; it does not allow for unforeseen consequences, ignorance, sectionalism. While it insists on the importance of applying class analysis to management, and management action, it remains with an abstract, structural theory of classes which ignores both the fact and the manner of conflicts between constituted classes. Such struggles are important, because the development of the structure of the enterprise, and the design and control of the labour process take place within the context of struggle between classes and sections of classes. But such struggles are not necessarily, even usually, between classes as theorised by Braverman but between sections of classes. Furthermore, the arena of such struggles is by no means always the one recognised by Braverman, i.e. the sphere of production. These sectional struggles occur as much around questions of exchange relations or the market for labour.

Braverman's analysis of management, and of management's role in devising forms of work and control, is based on a conception of the capitalist class, and its functionaries, as fully conscious of its interests, organised to achieve them, united in its goals and values, and knowledgeable of the necessary techniques. A similar view of the working class is, however, notably absent from his analysis; the working class is seen as passive, cowed, acquiescent, though such acquiescence is left unexplained. The result is that Braverman's classes do not engage in class struggle; and the determinants of levels and forms of class relations, the factions between which these relations develop, and the role of such struggle in structuring class identifications and boundaries, are ignored. His view of the capitalist class inadequately theorises the relationship *within* this class; ignores the concrete, historical *process* by which classes – and fractions of classes – are formed; and overlooks the movable frontiers between and within classes. As Stark notes, an adequate analysis of the capitalist class and its role in the design of the labour process must depend on an analysis of the tensions, struggles and contradictions within and between factions as interests emerge, change, are supported or opposed.[39] One element of such a consideration would be a discussion of how aspects of the labour process impinge on educated, non-working class labour; how they affect professional aspirations and careers, middle-class values and expectations.[40]

To raise these criticisms is not, however, to dispute the seminal importance of Braverman's timely and influential work. It is simply to suggest that the questions Braverman raises are more important and useful than the answers he provides. As noted elsewhere, his analysis of labour processes within monopoly capitalism is excessively concerned with *one* structural solution to the problems of control and the intensification of efforts to increase relative surplus value.[41] And even his analysis of this strategy is weakened by a mechanistic conception of skill, control and class. Certainly Braverman has revived interest in a sociology of the labour process. But to advance, such an enquiry must replace assertion with investigation. What must be done is to research and debate the varieties of complex, sometimes contradictory ways in which economic system requirements structure workplace organisation and relations, within the context, not of abstract classification of classes, but of '. . . relations of conflict and alliance between and within the historically determined organisations which are constitutive of class formations across the various levels of social structure'.[42]

This essay has not argued for a return to those forms of managerialist theories which insist that an analysis of management, or of organisation, can only consist of an investigation of the motivation of managers, or employers. (Conventionally, of course, such insistence was tied to the assertion that management was now distinct from ownership, thus opening the way for the 'soulful corporation'.) Nor should this essay be taken to deny the centrality, to the organisation of the labour process, of the question framed by de Vroey: 'For which class interests are the corporation ruled?'[43] But the essay has suggested that the answers to de Vroey's question can only be achieved when the sociological study of the enterprise, and of managers (who must play an important part in 'ruling' the corporation), moves beyond the abstract statement of the differentiated functions and requirements of capital, to a consideration of how these are actually achieved, in the context of concrete mechanisms mediating between economy and work design. And such a consideration must bring to light the complexity, and contradictoriness, of a process which occurs constantly within the context of changing frontiers of control between classes, and fractions of classes.

Class boundaries and the labour process

GAVIN MACKENZIE

The legacy of Marx

Analysis of the 'boundary problem', as Poulantzas has recently characterised it, i.e. the *explanation* of the location of class boundaries, antedates the emergence of sociology as a distinct discipline. John Millar (who, it is often suggested, had a substantial influence on Marx) and Adam Ferguson, writing in the latter part of the eighteenth century, both saw classes as hierarchically arranged strata, ordered on the basis of wealth. Yet neither made any attempt to explain *why* the dividing lines between those strata fell *where* they did.

Half a century later Marx was quick to highlight this fundamental weakness. Only ' "vulgar" common sense turns class differences into differences in the size of one's purse'.[1] Furthermore, for Marx, the conflation of income categories with social classes obscured the fact that it is class struggle that is the motor of social change – a struggle which takes place between the *two* 'great classes', not the plethora of indeterminate groupings that can be identified from a perspective based on income categories. It is also, of course, to put the cart before the horse:

> The unequal distribution of economic wealth, goods and power, which forms the basis for a 'socio-economic' conception of 'social classes' is, for Marx, not the basis, but the *result* of the *prior* distribution of the agents of capitalist production into classes and class relations, and the prior distribution of the means of production as between its 'possessors' and its 'dispossessed'.[2]

In focussing upon the *mode of production* Marx puts forward an explicit *social structural* approach to the production and reproduction of social classes. This abstract or pure model of class structure is, of course, one which highlights the *exploitative* character of class (capitalist) society. This focus is rooted in the distinction between productive and unproductive labour, itself dependent on the labour theory of value in general and the concept of surplus value in particular. Thus the pure model points to the 'inner logic' or 'essential nature' of capitalism in general. However, as Marx was only too well aware, in specific societies at particular times that 'essential nature' will manifest itself in a wide variety of forms determined by a wide variety of factors.

> . . . in actual concrete, historical social formations, modes of production do not appear in their 'pure' state, on their own. They are always combined with and stand in a complex articulation to, other, previous or subordinate modes of production – and their corresponding political and ideological relations – which cross-cut and over-determine any tendency of 'pure' mode to produce a series of 'pure' classes.[3]

Hence, Marx discusses in a wide variety of contexts 'quasi class' groupings, such as the *Lumpenproletariat* ('this scum of depraved elements from all classes . . .'); the '. . . continual increase in numbers of the middle classes . . . situated midway between the workers on one side and the capitalists and landowners on the other' and the divisions *within* capital and labour where the 'two great interests into which the bourgeoisie is split – landed property and capital' are matched by the 'aristocratic attitude' with which skilled craftsmen treat the non-skilled sections of the proletariat.[4] But it is at this concrete level that the 'boundary problem' re-emerges with a vengeance. There can be no doubt that Marx was aware of these groupings that 'complicated' the underlying dichotomous class structure of capitalism; but nowhere does he attempt *to examine theoretically* the relationship between these groupings and the two 'great classes'. The 'boundary problem' goes unexamined and unresolved. Rather, intermediate classes are seen as 'transitional'. In the short run they might obscure or complicate the observed relation between capital and labour. In the longer term, however, the laws of motion of capitalism will simplify and clarify class relations so that intermediate groupings will become absorbed into one or the other of the two great classes, while *within* the proletariat '. . . machinery obliterates all distinctions of labour, and nearly everywhere reduces wages to the same low level . . .'.[5] This enables Marx to dismiss 'middle and intermediate strata' as being 'immaterial for our analysis'.[6]

This is not, of course, the view taken by Max Weber, for whom the analysis of class must be rooted in the analysis of the *market*. Class is a phenomenon of the distribution of *power* within a society, in particular the power to gain access to scarce goods and services in the market. Market power determines life chances, which determine class position. A class is then viewed as an aggregate of individuals who share a similar class position. Weber of course follows Marx in attributing crucial importance to private property in class formation: the possession of property is *the* basis of class division, because it confers advantage. But that advantage will depend upon the type and the amount of the property owned: so any given society might contain not a single ownership class but class*es*.

Most secondary discussions of Weber's analysis of social class view its major contribution as being the recognition of class differences (and therefore boundaries) *within* that segment of the population which is property*less*. The great mass of the population are 'negatively advantaged' in that they are forced to survive by the sale of their labour power on the market. But the skills, abilities and educational qualifications of people in this position will differ considerably and therefore, in simple terms of supply and demand, so will their degrees of market power. Of considerable importance here is Weber's recognition of the spread of bureaucratisation in all sectors of capitalism with the concomitant rise in the number of white-collar (middle-class) occupations.

In his focus upon power in the market, Weber thus fearlessly adopted an approach to the analysis of class that had earlier been explicitly rejected by Marx. Notwithstanding his recognition of the crucial importance of property, he views class distinctions as being reflected in 'differences in the size of one's purse'. And that is not only vulgar but it raises the possibility of there being an infinite number of classes corresponding to an infinite number of market (income) positions. In fact, however, Weber escapes this trap by arguing that *empirically* in early twentieth-century capitalism it was possible to discern only four 'social classes', groupings of individuals *within which* movement (social mobility) takes place freely. These four social classes are, of course, the dominant propertied and entrepreneurial groups, the 'propertyless white-collar intelligentsia', the petty bourgeoisie and the manual working class, within which there are divisions between the skilled, the semiskilled and the unskilled.

Academic sociologists have almost universally recommended Weber's approach as both appropriate and realistic for an understanding of the complexity of class differences to be found in late twentieth-century capitalist society. This has particularly been the case in the United States where, at least until recently, few observers would have disagreed with Page's observation that Weber's approach '. . . "fits" the realities of American social life more neatly than does what often seems to be the one-dimensional class approach of Marx and his followers'.[7] And in the last quarter of the twentieth century

65

such claims are not difficult to understand, given the steady increase in the proportion of the labour force engaged in white-collar employment, the steady rise (until recently, at least) in the standard of living, the expansion of the service sector and the increasing differentiation in the division of labour.

However, as a *theory* of class relations and, in particular, of class boundaries, Weber's approach is at best incomplete, at worst superficial; for at the end of the day, his identification of four social classes is merely descriptive. For example, his claim that a class boundary separates the manual working class from propertyless white-collar employees was, at least at that time, unobjectionable. But the crucial question is *why* the boundary fell *there* rather than, say, a bit 'higher up' or perhaps 'lower down'. And what other features of the institutional order of capitalist society, apart from market power, influence the formation of class boundaries? All of these questions must be addressed for even an adequate tilt at the boundary problem. Weber does not turn up for the tournament.

So the theorist of social class has been faced with a clear choice. On the one side is Marx's analysis: an abstract or pure model of class society focussing on the two great classes and inseparable from the concept of surplus value. Unfortunately the relationship between this abstract model and the realities of class inequality is, in theoretical terms, left undisturbed.[8] In contrast, Weber is concerned first and foremost with the 'complexity' of class inequality within twentieth-century capitalism – with the rise of the middle classes, with divisions within both capital and labour. But he forsakes explanation for description. The Weberian can tell us that class boundaries are located at certain points on the Market Power hierarchy. He cannot, alas, tell us *why*.[9]

Recently, however, the re-emergence of political economy generally has provoked renewed attempts to develop a theory of social class and class boundaries which specifically recognises the complexities of class inequality within late twentieth-century capitalism, but which also explicitly focusses on the *explanation* of these complexities. Some of the more significant of these attempts will be examined and found wanting. But, I shall go on to argue, these approaches have laid an extremely important groundwork, a groundwork which can be built upon by borrowing from a second corpus of contemporary writings – this time not only by sociologists, but also economists and historians. While these writings are not themselves directly concerned with the analysis of class boundaries, their focus on the accumulation and labour processes, managerial control and labour resistance, and finally the economic performance of monopoly capitalism are, I will argue, of central importance to this former concern.

Main currents of functionalist Marxism

Perhaps the most detailed and systematic recent contribution to the 'boundary problem' is that of Nicos Poulantzas. For this writer, classes comprise groups of individuals 'defined principally but not exclusively by their place in the production process . . .'.[10] This means that while economic criteria have the 'dominant role' in shaping class structure, *political* and *ideological* criteria are also important. Thus social classes are identified by their locations in the *social* (as opposed to merely *technical*) division of labour. The social division of labour within a particular social formation represents the interplay of economic, political and ideological factors. Furthermore, class locations within that social division of labour are objectively determined; they are '. . . independent of the will' of the individuals occupying those locations.

In this definition of the 'economic', the crucial distinction is between productive and unproductive labour. And by productive labour Poulantzas means labour that is *directly* involved in the material process of the production of wealth, i.e. commodity production. Therefore the economic criterion of social class revolves around the simple and basic relation of exploitation within capitalist society: the production or expropriation of surplus value. Classes are thus rooted in the *relations* of production: they have little to do with the size of one's purse or income, or whether one is a wage or a salary earner. This focus upon productive versus unproductive labour as the fundamental criterion underlying the relations of production requires Poulantzas, in a society where there is at least putative separation of ownership and control, to distinguish between three distinct forms or aspects of the relations of production: first, legal ownership, sanctioned by law; second, economic ownership, '. . . real economic control of the means of production, i.e. the power to assign the means of production to given uses and so to dispose of the products obtained'; third, economic possession, '. . . the capacity to put the means of production into operation', i.e. the actual physical control over the activity of production.[11] For example, under feudalism the serf was excluded from legal and economic ownership but retained economic possession over his parcel of land. In contrast, under advanced capitalist manufacture '. . . the direct producers (the working class) are completely dispossessed of their means of labour, of which the capitalists have the actual possession'.[12] The labourer becomes a 'mere appendage' of the machine.

As I have already indicated, for Poulantzas the economic criteria have a 'principal but not exclusive' role in the determination of social classes. Furthermore, he is at pains to stress that ideology and politics must not be viewed merely as systems of ideas but as 'ensembles of material practices'. Political practices are simply the relations of *domination* found at the place of production. In other words, the relations of control, of authority that typically characterise the manager–worker relationship are, for Poulantzas, political practices which reinforce/shape class boundaries. Finally, by ideological relations of domination Poulantzas is referring to the distinction between *mental* and *manual* labour. Mental labour is devoted to the planning, organisation and understanding of the production process, while manual labour is expended by the 'direct producers' who are themselves excluded from this 'secret knowledge'. And, of course, this exclusion is itself a *technique of control* found typically in the subordination of labour to capital.

Finally, it should be noted that Poulantzas explicitly rejects the distinction between a class *in* itself and a class *for* itself. '. . . Social classes do not firstly exist as such, and only then enter into a class struggle. Social classes coincide with class practices, i.e. the class struggle, and are only defined in their mutual opposition.'[13] In other words, classes cannot be understood independently of their relations with other classes: the position of the wrestler or lover locked in combat/embrace with his or her opposite number cannot be adequately understood if that opposite number is ignored. It takes two to tango.

On the basis of this theoretical framework, Poulantzas is able to identify three social classes within advanced capitalist societies: the bourgeoisie, the working class and the '. . . so-called "new middle strata" ', i.e. the petty bourgeoisie both traditional and new.

First, the working class is defined as comprising those individuals in the society engaged in productive labour, who are *directly* concerned with commodity production. This means, for example, that the lowly paid clerk whose function is to help capital minimise the cost of realising surplus value from the direct labourers is automatically excluded from membership in the working class. Politically, in terms of economic possession and legal and economic ownership (as defined above), the working class is uniformly and completely dispossessed, while in ideological terms it is excluded from all forms of 'secret knowledge'. This means that foremen – agents of the political domination of capital – are excluded from membership of the working class as are *all* white-collar workers, scientists or technicians insofar as they handle or manipulate knowledge, however insignificant, from which production workers are excluded. In short, the working class is viewed as that (small) proportion of the population which is engaged in (manual) productive work and which is dominated politically and ideologically.

In contrast the bourgeoisie is identified as that grouping within the class structure which dominates/controls both ideologically and politically, while its delimitation in economic terms is founded upon the distinction between economic possession and legal and economic ownership outlined above. Thus Poulantzas explicitly recognises the importance of the (putative) separation of ownership and control within monopoly capitalism, and he goes on to argue that *anyone* exercising physical control over the means of production (economic possession) or involved in discussions regarding, for example, what product to produce or how to distribute the wealth so obtained is fulfilling the functions of capital. By definition, therefore, such individuals are *bona fide* members of the bourgeoisie. This means, of course, that all managers enjoy membership of this class. Marx's distinction between 'capitalists without function' and 'functionaries without capital' is thus recognised. But, in contrast to Marx, Poulantzas does not see that the distinction has importance in the analysis of class boundaries.

Thus the boundary that separates the working class from the bourgeoisie is clearly delineated and explained. The next question to ask concerns the fortunes of the other 70% of the population. The answer is, of course, that they belong to the petty bourgeoisie or, more precisely, to the *'old'* or to the *'new'* petty bourgeoisie, a term adopted in preference to the more usual 'new middle class'. The old petty bourgeoisie, needless to say, is composed of (e.g.) self-employed skilled craftsmen, shop-keepers or independent farmers – individuals who neither control the labour of others nor are themselves controlled. This class has been shrinking in size as capitalism has developed. But, concomitantly, that development has given rise to the emergence, and rapid growth, of the 'new' petty bourgeoisie.

Economically, it is the distinction between productive and unproductive labour that clearly defines the class boundary between the new petty bourgeoisie and the working class. Being unproductive labourers (and thus not *directly* exploited), members of the new petty bourgeoisie lie *outside* the fundamental relationship of capitalism – that of capital and labour. Politically, too, this class occupies an ambiguous position. On the one hand, insofar as, for example, white-collar employees are engaged in aiding the extraction of surplus value from other (productive) workers, they clearly do not share a common class situation with such workers. However, on the other hand, insofar as these same white-collar employees are themselves dominated by capital, they cannot be viewed as *bona fide* members of the bourgeoisie either. It is this duality of domination and submission that is the defining characteristic of the new petty bourgeoisie. The same is true with regard to the ideological determinants of the class boundaries setting the new petty bourgeoisie apart from both the bourgeoisie and the proletariat. To be sure, members of the new petty bourgeoisie are distinct from the proletariat by virtue of their access to 'secret knowledge'. But insofar as that access is only partial and piecemeal, it does not serve as a qualification for gaining unquestioned entry to the bourgeoisie.

The petty bourgeoisie (old and new) within advanced capitalism is *in* but not *of* the fundamental class struggle between the bourgeoisie and the proletariat. As such, it cannot be viewed as possessing autonomous power – either in the short or in the long run. Ultimately, for Poulantzas it is a residual category dependent upon, rather than determining, the balance of forces between the two great classes.

In such a manner, therefore, the total population of any advanced capitalist society can be defined into one of three classes. There is an explicit attempt to recognise the importance of intermediate strata and to posit their relations with the old petty bourgeoisie. The analysis nonetheless contains at least three major weaknesses.[14] First, it is formalistic and mechanical to the point of aridity. Despite the fact that in the very first chapter Poulantzas reminds us that 'Social classes coincide with class practices, i.e. the class struggle', his parallel view that class locations are 'objectively determined' is the one that guides the analysis – which has therefore no place for discussion of conflict, resistance or indeed conscious actors of any shape or size. Second, and linked with the first weakness, is the fact that the schema is timeless, unchanging, ahistorical. To be sure there are references to other social formations, to the differentiation of the function of capital, to the decline of the traditional petty bourgeoisie, but there is no overall explanation of the historical processes which led to the existence of these three great classes or to the forces that might shape/change them in the future. At the end of the day, however, perhaps *the* flaw in Poulantzas's analysis is that it deeply offends common sense. As Wright has shown, the application of Poulantzas's schema to contemporary American society turns up the somewhat startling finding that only 19.7% of the population are in the working class. The new petty bourgeoisie, on the other hand, do rather better, laying claim to '. . . a mammoth 70% of the economically active population'.[15] That this class contains filing clerks, secretaries, some supervisors and the professions, does little to lower our eyebrows. In other words, Poulantzas's attempt to force or pigeonhole the population into one of three classes (boxes) according to the possession or non-possession of economic, political or ideological attributes is found lacking simply because it produces a picture of class structure which is unrealistic.

This weakness has recently been recognised by Wright, who has been at pains to argue that the analysis of class boundaries must recognise that many positions in the social division of labour, in class structure, *will be ambiguous.* To ignore this ambiguity, to claim that certain roles fall neatly (artificially) into certain classes because of a clear-cut conformity to or deviation from a single criterion (productive versus non-productive labour; mental versus manual labour) is to retreat rapidly from reality.

> An alternative way of dealing with such ambiguities in the class structure is to regard some positions as occupying *objectively contradictory locations within class relations.* Rather than eradicating these contradictions by artificially classifying every position within the social division of labour unambiguously into one class or another, contradictory locations need to be studied in their own right.[16] (italics in original)

In his analysis of contradictory class locations, Wright is concerned with looking at the ways in which the *development* of capitalism historically has *generated* a number of classes in 'contradictory locations' within the class structures of advanced capitalist societies. More precisely he focusses upon three interconnected structural changes: first, the progressive loss of control over the labour process by direct producers; second, the progressive differentiation of the functions of capital – this, of course, refers to the emergence and growth of the joint stock company and the separation of 'functionaries without capital' from 'capitalists without function'. Third, and following from the differentiation of the functions of capital, there occurs the development of 'complex hierarchies of control' within the business enterprise. These hierarchies emerge in connection with three components of the basic capital–labour dichotomy: control over the physical means of production (e.g. by managers); control over labour power (e.g. by foremen); control over investment/resource allocation (e.g. by directors). Needless to say, the division between the bourgeoisie and the proletariat involves polarisation on all three of these dimensions. The traditional petty bourgeoisie in contrast exercises control over the physical means of production and resource allocation but not, of course, over labour power.

As I have already indicated, however, the importance of Wright's analysis lies in the fact that he recognises that a huge segment (perhaps 50%) of the population of any advanced capitalist society cannot be slotted neatly into any of these three classes. Rather, they occupy positions in the social division of labour which can be defined by a contradictory combination of the three dimensions of control hierarchies outlined above. Thus between the bourgeoisie and the proletariat two distinct groupings can be identified. First are top and middle managers and technocrats who control the physical means of production and labour power but are largely excluded from control over investment and resources. 'Both middle managers and technocrats have . . . one foot in the bourgeoisie and one foot in the proletariat.'[17] The contradictory quality of this class location is thus particularly intense, not to say stretching. Second, lower-level managers and foremen exercise control only over the labour power of the proletariat. In addition, Wright recognises that the process of accumulation means that at any point in time there will exist a group of individuals who are moving away from the petty bourgeoisie, i.e. successful members of this class will expand their businesses, begin to employ others, and thus appropriate surplus value. Accordingly, between the bourgeoisie and the petty bourgeoisie is the contradictory class location of the 'small employer'.

Finally, and of particular importance, Wright draws attention to that large number of people between the proletariat and the petty bourgeoisie who, while enjoying partially self-employed status, are at the same time contributing to the self-expansion of capital. Essentially, their position lies *outside* the authority hierarchy associated with the production and distribution of wealth. Rather, they can be seen as '. . . occupying residual islands of petty bourgeois relations of production within the capitalist mode of production itself'.[18] Wright dubs individuals sharing this particular contradictory class location 'semi-autonomous employees'. Obvious examples include professionals, teachers, skilled craftsmen, or the owners of fast food franchises. For Wright, the contemporary American class structure can be fully schematised therefore in Figure 1.

It is important to note that Wright recognises Poulantzas's stricture that political and ideological criteria must be brought into the analysis of class boundaries. He wishes, quite properly, however, to maintain the primacy of economic relations and goes on to argue that '. . . the extent to which political and ideological relations enter into the

Figure 1. *The relationship of contradictory class locations to the basic class forces in capitalist society*

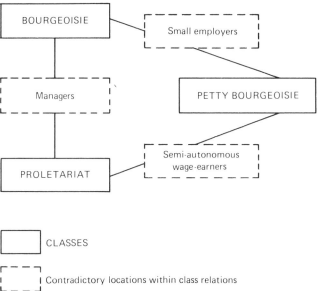

Source: E. O. Wright, 'Class Boundaries in Advanced Capitalist Societies', p. 27.

determination of class position is itself determined by the degree to which those positions occupy a contradictory location at the level of social relations of production'.[19] (italics in original) In other words, it is the *indeterminacy* of class formation/location in economic terms which 'allows' scope for the influence of political and ideological criteria/relations. Thus the mental–manual division may well reinforce the structural separation of (e.g.) technicians from the proletariat, while a strong trade union movement may contribute to the blurring of the line separating skilled craftsmen (semi-autonomous employees) from the proletariat.

There can be no doubt that Wright's analysis represents a significant advance upon that of Poulantzas. He recognises the *complexity* of class inequality in advanced capitalist society and he argues that that complexity can only be understood from a developmental, historical perspective. But in certain important respects it too is far from satisfactory. Space permits that I mention only three.

First, as in the case of Poulantzas, certain features of the schema offend against common sense. In particular, the contradictory class location of 'semi-autonomous employees' contains some particularly odd bedfellows – to regard skilled craftsmen, 'a professor in an elite university' and the 'owner of a gas station franchise' as members of the same class (or indeed class fraction) is silly, both theoretically and empirically. Second, the approach is again essentially mechanical – the population is neatly placed in boxes (albeit seven rather than three) according to a number of formal criteria. And although Wright is at pains to demonstrate the way in which the class structure as he portrays it has evolved, the *relations* between the classes seem curiously static. To be sure, he refers to 'tendencies', 'possibilities' and 'the dialectical relationship of class struggle'. But the overall schema is essentially piecemeal: 'Class struggle thus shapes the very contours of the class structure itself, which in turn influences the development of class struggle.'[20] An unobjectionable generality, but hardly one that aids our understanding of class structure, relations and processes *at the present time*. Finally, and linked to this second weakness, Wright shies away from relating his classificatory schema to the accumulation process, to the *development* of capitalist society. To be sure he lays stress on three 'interrelated structural changes' but largely in a descriptive manner: the *logic* of capitalism which might be seen as *explaining* these changes is not examined. There can be little doubt that Wright has gone beyond Poulantzas but, as it turns out, not terribly far.

At this point it is useful to refer briefly to the recent writings of Carchedi, despite the tortuous form these writings adopt.[21] The perspective adopted by Carchedi has much in common with that of Wright, including a reliance on a crude historical perspective.[22] That perspective leads Carchedi to focus on three distinct phases of capitalist development, culminating, of course, in monopoly capitalism. For Carchedi, class positions are determined by the interplay of three sets of factors: first 'ownership', i.e. real control (or not) of the means of production; second 'expropriation', the performance or expropriation of unpaid labour time; third the 'functional element'. This last is at the centre of his analysis and refers to the functions performed by capital and labour within the social relations of production. He traces the changes that have occurred in these functions during the three phases of capitalist development. In the third phase – that of monopoly capital – the functions can be divided into the 'global function of Capital' and the 'function of the collective worker'. Here production is no longer controlled by individual capitalists or their agents but by the 'global capitalist', i.e. capital organised on a global, differentiated and multi-national basis. And, for Carchedi, the essential role or function of global capital is the control and surveillance of the labour process. In contrast the function of the collective worker is the production of surplus labour or surplus value through his involvement in the detailed division of labour.

Focus upon 'ownership', 'expropriation' and the 'functional element' allows Carchedi to distinguish between the bourgeoisie and the proletariat in much the same way as Poulantzas and Wright. Similarly the middle classes comprise those individuals who participate in *both* the global function of capital *and* the function of the collective worker, i.e. *they occupy a contradictory position in the social relations of production.* In fact, Carchedi identifies three 'layers' of the middle class depending on whether the 'mix' is weighted in favour of capital or of labour.

As outlined so far, therefore, Carchedi has provided us with an analysis which has much in common with, although is certainly less refined than, that of Wright. But this lack of refinement is more than compensated for by Carchedi's explicit attempt to introduce a *dynamic* element into his formulations. Not only is he concerned with looking at the way the two great classes and the middle strata have evolved; he is also committed to understanding the forces within late capitalism which *continue* to influence class structure, relations and processes.

More precisely, for Carchedi the inner logic of advanced capitalism, the continuing drive to accumulate, *means* that capital will not only be attempting continually to increase productivity within the working class, it will *also* be constantly attempting to shift the balance between the global function of capital and that of the collective labourer found within the new middle classes. And that shift is, of course, in the direction of the proletariat. It involves, in other words, the proletarianisation of middle-class labour power. Needless to say, the main stimulus to such proletarianisation, i.e. changes in class boundaries, is the application of technology. To the extent, for example, that computerisation replaces or de-skills managers, then we have a clear example of the inner logic of capitalism *continuing* to influence the siting of class boundaries.

Why late capitalism should manifest this tendency towards the dequalification of middle-class skills and therefore class position is unclear. Of course, cost cutting may be an explanation. Alternatively, it is possible to suggest, as did Marx, that ultimately 'functionaries without capital' pose a threat to the system; their proletarianisation (or removal from the scene) could then be seen as a logical response on the part of capital. Furthermore, it is by no means empirically certain that Carchedi is correct in asserting that this tendency exists. For the present purposes, however, his arguments are important in that, to my knowledge, he remains the only structural Marxist who has made a genuine, if superficial and partial, attempt to provide a structural analysis of class boundaries that explicitly incorporates a recognition of *continued* development and change in class composition and structure.

Class relations in the labour process

Whatever their differences, all of these writers share a common concern with *control* rather than the formal ownership of productive property as the fundamental basis of class division. Gordon makes no bones about this: 'Capitalism has developed a production process which not only delivers the goods but also controls its workers.'[23] And, as more than one writer has pointed out, this common concern is one that does little to distinguish these Marxist writers from social theorists such as Giddens – or indeed Dahrendorf or Parkin. What is unique to the former group of writers, however, as I have already pointed out, is the historically inadequate, mechanical and largely static approach they take to the analysis of class boundaries. Of fundamental significance is the fact that control, both within and without the workplace, is seen as being timeless, uni-directional and stable. And such a retreat from reality is particularly puzzling at this time, given the joyful (re)discovery of the 'labour process' by economists, historians and sociologists in the latter half of the 1970s. Time dictates that I must leave it to others to speculate as to why and how these theorists of class boundaries have failed to notice that there is a noisy party going on next door. The important point now is that the people giving the party should be invited over for full and frank discussion.

The power of a *historical* approach to the analysis of class boundaries is perhaps most clearly illustrated by Braverman. In *Labor and Monopoly Capital* this author examines structural changes that have occurred in (American) capitalist society over the last hundred years. More precisely, he is concerned with two interlocking processes: first, the transformation of the labour process by monopoly capital; second, the consequences of this transformation for the class structure, i.e. class boundaries, of advanced capitalist society. In other words, and this is a step forward of the highest importance, Braverman is arguing that *the location of class boundaries can only be examined in terms of the organisation of the labour process.* Furthermore, although he is not so clear or explicit on this as one might wish, these transformations of the labour process and, thus of class boundaries, can only be seen as a direct consequence of the accumulation process – itself intrinsic to capitalism. 'In everything that follows, therefore, we shall be considering the manner in which the labour process is dominated and shaped by the accumulation of capital'.[24]

More precisely, Braverman is concerned with demonstrating how this 'shaping' of the labour process has meant on the one hand an ever increasing division of labour at the point of manufacture, and on the other hand the progressive *de-skilling* of the working class. Accumulation requires both processes for reasons adduced not only by Adam Smith but also by Thomas Babbage. However, both divided the de-skilled labour, coupled with the ever increasing concentration and centralisation of capital, brings to the fore the problem of the *coordination*, of the *management*, of the *control* of the individual corporation. 'It thus becomes essential for the capitalist that control over the labour process pass from the hands of the worker into his own.'[25] Needless to say this did not remain a problem for long but was 'solved' by capital by reference to two resources: the beliefs and dictates of scientific management; science and technology. The former provided capital or its agents with a theoretical basis upon which to wrest control of the labour process from the worker completely, while the latter provided the most important weapon with which this could be achieved. Not surprisingly, *Labor and Monopoly Capital* is subtitled *The Degradation of Work in the Twentieth Century.*

In a historical analysis which dovetails neatly with that of Braverman, Marglin has recently been concerned with the 'crucial characteristic', of the capitalist form of production, namely the gradual loss by the producer of all forms of control over the act of production.[26] There have been two main facets of this 'crucial characteristic': first, the development of the minute division of labour; second, the development of the centralised organisation that characterises the modern factory. And for Marglin the most important feature of these developments is that they have little to do with bland or class-neutral concepts of economic *'efficiency'* à la Adam Smith. Rather they facilitate the successful *control* and thus *exploitation* of one class by another, i.e. they facilitate the process of accumulation within capitalist society. Of crucial importance, therefore, is the fact that divided labour is conquered labour. Insofar as the accumulation process requires that capital or its agents successfully expropriates surplus value and/or labour, then this can best be achieved in a situation where the ability of labour to *resist* that expropriation is minimised. And, for Marglin, that situation is epitomised – the class boundary is maintained – when the labour force is fragmented and internally divided.

Similarly he questions the conventional wisdom which views the factory as more efficient in terms of technical superiority and/or in terms of economies of scale. The great advantage of the factory within class society is again one of control – one class can better discipline and supervise another in the factory environment than (e.g.) under the putting-out system. Under the factory system, therefore, the manager has greater power over the pace of work, its quality, the length of the work day and the prevention of pilfering.

In other words, the 'technical superiority' of divided labour and the factory is that they facilitate the exercise of class power, the pursuit of class interests, the maintenance of class boundaries. The issue is one of *class* rather than 'technical' or 'neutral' efficiency.

As I have already indicated, Braverman's concern is not only with documenting these changes in the labour process but also with examining their consequences for class boundaries and class structure. And these consequences must be seen as forceful and unambiguous. For the drive to accumulate, the doctrines of scientific management, and the inexorable push of mechanisation and automation have led to the emergence of a homogeneous and proletarianised working class in American society. This means that not only have old boundaries separating skilled from semiskilled from unskilled manual workers disappeared; so too have those that traditionally divided manual from non-manual employees. Indeed, Braverman's discussion of the proletarianisation of white-collar work is perhaps his most persuasive and dramatic. The mechanised or automated office is now merely concerned with processing a stream of paper – 'a stream of paper moreover, which is processed in a continuous flow like that of the cannery, the meat packing line, the car assembly conveyor, by workers organised in much the same way'.[27] If it is by now generally agreed that Mrs Worthington's daughter should reconsider the stage as a career, energies might now be directed towards disabusing her youngest child as to the joys, independence and creativity of white-collar work.

In short, adopting a historical perspective, Braverman has argued persuasively that the laws of motion of American capitalism have led to the breakdown of boundaries that previously separated white- from blue-collar worker, productive from non-productive, and skilled from non-skilled. In consequence, the American working class (which now, he argues, comprises some 69% of the total population) can now be seen as not only homogeneous but proletarianised. This is not the place for a discussion of the merits and demerits of Braverman's thesis. Such discussion is already on record.[28] The importance of his analysis for our purposes lies in the insights it provides regarding the power of a historical approach for the analysis of class boundaries, the inseparability of the analysis of the labour process and that of class boundaries, and the superiority of that approach to inadequately historical, mechanical formulations such as those of Poulantzas and Wright.

The dialectic of control and resistance

Powerful though the analyses of Braverman and Marglin are, they share the defect of determinism. Thus, although Braverman is at pains to recognise Marx's 'genius at dialectic', Sweezy captures the tenor of the book neatly when he describes it as looking at the '. . . consequences which . . . particular kinds of technological change . . . have had for the nature of work (and) the composition of the working class'.[29] Furthermore, this deterministic approach of Braverman's is itself linked with his puzzling claim that one can study the working class 'as it exists', i.e. without any resort to the analysis of working-class resistance, struggle or process. As I and others have argued elsewhere, the attempt to separate completely the analysis of a class *in* itself from a class *for* itself is to utilise a false dichotomy.[30]

This makes Gordon's recent distinction between *quantitative* efficiency and *qualitative* efficiency of particular importance for the historical and therefore *dynamic* analysis of class boundaries.[31] By quantitative efficiency, Gordon refers to the neo-classical view of economic efficiency, measurable in money terms and concerned with the achievement of the greatest possible physical output from a given set of physical inputs. In contrast qualitative efficiency refers to '. . . the ability of the ruling class to reproduce its domination of the social process of production and minimise producers' resistance to ruling class domination of the production process'.[32] In other words, Gordon wishes to stress firstly the fact that the *interests* of managers and workers are not identical, and that therefore secondly the cooperation/control of the workforce *has to be seen as problematic*. In other words, the explicit theme running throughout the work of Braverman and Marglin – that capitalists as managers can always successfully impose their will on their employees – is rejected. Rather, Gordon argues, worker resistance to the managerial prerogative must be regarded as normal and, indeed, potentially (partially) successful. And for our purposes, to the extent that worker resistance *is* successful then this will have important repercussions for the siting of class boundaries. Thus, for Gordon, the entrepreneur is continually being required to solve not one but two sets of imperatives. Indeed, 'Competition enforces capitalist concern with quantitative efficiency. Class struggle enforces capitalist concern with qualitative efficiency. The unity of production kneads together the two imperatives.'[33] The importance of this distinction for the purposes of the present essay lies in Gordon's suggestion that within late capitalism the requirements of quantitative and qualitative efficiency can undermine or contradict one another. 'Capitalists are forced, in other words, to accept sacrifices in potential physical output . . . in order to maintain worker discipline and reproduce their control over the means of production'.[34] Indeed, 'as capitalism develops and as workers continually develop their organised capacity to resist capitalist exploitation, it seems logical that . . . imperatives of quantitative efficiency will become increasingly determining'.[35] This means that certain crucial features of the class structure of advanced capitalist society can be seen in terms of the heightened importance of the imperative of qualitative efficiency – an importance which can only be understood in historical dialectical terms, i.e. an increase in the ability of the working class to *resist*. For example, Gordon argues that the continuing concentration and centralisation of the means of production within late capitalism (and therefore the growing homogenisation of the working class as detailed by Braverman) is quantitatively inefficient. Rather, 'capitalists may be continually driven . . . to increase the mass of "dead labour" confronting workers in order to minimise workers' resistance to their exploitation'.[36] Similarly, he argues, we can interpret the steady rise in unemployment within capitalist societies in recent years in similar vein. In terms of quantitative efficiency, this rapid expansion in the reserve army of labour might be expected to depress the market wage to a point when it is *cheaper* to employ men than machines. However, the entrepreneur may not make this choice on the grounds that the enhanced ability of the working class to disrupt or resist pushes the need for qualitative control to the fore. The disciplining effect of a high level of unemployment, with its consequences for class boundaries and class structure becomes, therefore, increasingly determining.

Richard Edwards has recently, and forcefully, questioned the assumption that worker resistance is something with which the student of class boundaries need not concern him or her self.

The labour process becomes an arena of class conflict and the workplace becomes a contested terrain. Faced with chronic resistance to their effort to compel production, employers over the years have attempted to resolve the matter by reorganising, indeed revolutionising, the labour process itself. That is, capitalists have attempted to organise production in such a way as to minimise workers' opportunities for resistance and even alter workers' perceptions of the desirability of opposition.[37]

More precisely, Edwards argues that three forms or systems of control can be identified within class-based societies.[38]

Simple control is found most typically in (small) firms ruled by a single entrepreneur. 'These bosses exercised power personally, intervening in the labour process often to exhort workers, bully and threaten them, reward good performance, hire and fire on the spot, favour loyal workers, and generally act as despots, benevolent or otherwise.'[39] In contrast, 'technical control' is actually embedded in the physical structure of the labour process – particularly the forms of technology utilised. The assembly line is the classical example. Finally, 'bureaucratic control' is exactly what it seems. 'The defining feature of bureaucratic control is the institutionalisation of hierarchical power.' Edwards's description of bureaucratic control bears a striking resemblance to that of Weber.

It is important to note that for Edwards each of the three forms of entrepreneurial control tends to correspond with particular stages in the development of (American) capitalism. Thus simple control characterised the small businesses of the nineteenth century – a form of control which became increasingly inappropriate (unsuccessful) in the large-scale corporations which emerged at the century's end. 'Pressure built up, making the old forms of control untenable.' Thus new (technical) systems of control were substituted.

As Gordon has emphasised, earlier production technologies differ in the possibilities they afford management for controlling the workforce – for exercising *qualitative* control – or as Edwards terms it, *technical* control. This simply involves placing control in the production technology itself, i.e. designing machinery and the flow of work so that the *technology itself* paces and controls the entire labour force. '. . . Control becomes truly structural'.

Not surprisingly, technology was first recognised as a basis for structural control in industries such as meat packing or auto manufacturing. The description of the organisation and pace of work in *The Jungle* is difficult to better as an example of the operation of technical control, although, of course, it is the Ford assembly line that usually comes to mind as the exemplar of a '. . . technically based

Gavin Mackenzie

and technologically repressive mechanism that kept workers at their tasks'.[40]

As before, however, this system of control quickly showed itself to contain contradictions; indeed, not only did technical control not remove conflict between capital and labour, by raising it to the level of the plant from that of the individual workplace it exacerbated it. As Kuhn and other earlier writers have shown, under systems of technical control, when workers on one part of the line bargain over a grievance or indeed withdraw their labour, *every* other worker is necessarily affected.[41] In other words, technical control systems provided exceptionally favourable milieux for the emergence and building of unions able and willing to exercise effective resistance. One of the most notorious recent examples of workers seizing the opportunities offered to them on a plate by a technical system of control is that of the Vega plant at Lordstown, Ohio. Indeed, for Edwards, '. . . Lordstown may have represented technical control's final gasp as an ascendent control system'.[42] To regain the ascendancy, capital has therefore once again been forced to search for ever more sophisticated (and effective) systems of control. The 'solution' has been found in *bureaucratic* control.

The most fundamental aspect of bureaucratic control is the institutionalisation of hierarchical power within the firm. And the bases of that power are *neutral, impersonal* 'company rules' and 'company policy'. '. . . Bureaucratic control is embedded in the social and organisational structure of the firm and is built into job categories, work rules, promotion procedures, discipline, wage scales, definitions of responsibilities and the like . . . all . . . depend upon established rules and procedures, elaborately and systematically laid out.'[43] These rules and procedures would, of course, be set by management. But once in force the expectation was that they would operate *in their own right*. In other words, the basic capital–labour relation disappeared from view. The lessons that have been learned from earlier (failed) modes of control are not difficult to spot.

A crucial feature of bureaucratic control is that it divides and stratifies the workforce, both vertically and horizontally; the ability of that workforce to resist is reduced accordingly and significantly. For example, in the Polaroid corporation, the plethora of job titles and pay schemes means that its 6,397 hourly workers are split into 2,100 different job classifications! And, Edwards is quick to point out, these classifications are not required by the dictates of 'technology'; rather they are social distinctions *imposed* on the workforce.

Perhaps equally important is the elaborate system introduced by bureaucratic control to *reward* cooperative behaviour on the part of individual workers. 'They function as an elaborate system of bribes, and like all successful bribes, they are attractive. But they are also corrupting.'[44] In particular of course, as others, particularly Marglin and Sweezy have argued, they divide and conquer the workforce.

Not surprisingly, however, bureaucratic control itself contains contradictions. 'Bureaucratic control threatens to become a pact with the devil that, while offering temporary respite from trouble, spells long term disaster.'[45] There are a number of reasons why this is so. First, bureaucratic control, with its complicated system of promotions and rewards assures long-term security of tenure for its employees. But such conditions for job security allow or give rise to a more fundamental questioning of the capitalist system *per se.* For 'Bureaucratic control has created among American workers vast discontent, dissatisfaction, resentment, frustration, and boredom with their work.'[46] There are at least two (interrelated) contradictory consequences of such discontent. First, reduced productivity, and second, demands for workplace democracy.

In this case, managers find themselves in a double bind. The lure of granting workplace democracy and thus increasing productivity is strong. But 'a little (democracy) is never enough'. Managers are well aware that if they succumb to the temptation of higher productivity they are at the same time undermining the very basis of their control.

A third contradiction of bureaucratic control is that a firm's wage bill becomes a fixed rather than a variable cost. As we have seen, for bureaucratic control to be effective, stability of tenure must operate. And yet a crucial requirement of the 'efficient' capitalist firm is that it be able to adjust the size of its workforce, particularly during downswings in the business cycle. 'Bureaucratic control is thus without contradiction only if capitalism itself is without crisis . . . The 1970's revealed the flow in that assumption.'[47]

The theme that Edwards most wishes to highlight in this analysis is continual *experimentation* on the part of management in labour organisation and control. 'Indeed the history of the labour process in the twentieth century is largely the story of how new contradictions emerged within large firms and how these corporations used their resources to resolve the contradictions.'[48] His approach is thus explicitly developmental *and* dynamic. And the new contradictions to which he refers in the quotation above all revolve around the 'general crisis of control within the firm' – a crisis which became both recurrent and visible as labour's organisation (and therefore ability to resist) slowly and inevitably improved. The implications of his

Gavin Mackenzie

analysis for the explanation of class boundaries – particularly, of course, divisions *within* the working class – are not difficult to see. This is also the case with regard to Edwards's discussion of the *labour market* (or, more accurately, labour markets) and the role it/they play (in concert with divisions in and patterns of control of the labour process) in determining class boundaries. (It is interesting to note the similarities between this discussion and Weber's earlier formulations.) In particular he argues that there exist in the US three distinct labour markets and that these play a crucial role in the creation and maintenance of divisions *within* the working class (which he regards as encompassing *all* employees – white- and blue-collar). The argument is simple: it is through labour market processes that workers are allocated to particular jobs. But as different groups in the labour market find themselves in very different positions (contrast the labour market for unskilled manual workers with that of physicians), then the *inequality* of labour markets has consequences for the inequality of social class.

These three labour markets work very differently for the people in them. More precisely, there exist three clusters of jobs with very different labour market outcomes and processes – wage rates, frequency of employment and so on – associated with each. First, the 'Secondary Market' is distinct in '. . . the casual nature of the employment. The work never requires previous training or education beyond basic literacy. Few skills are required and few can be learned. Such jobs offer low pay and virtually no job security. They are, in other words, typically dead end jobs . . .'[49] Invariably such jobs are non-unionised. Waiters and migrant agricultural workers fall clearly into the secondary market.

In contrast the 'Subordinate Primary Market' '. . . contains the jobs of the old industrial working class, reinforced by the lower-level jobs of unionised clerical employees'.[50] The presence of a union is important and is linked to the greater job security, higher wages, and opportunities for advancement (*within* the firm) that distinguish this labour market from the secondary market. To be sure, the work is often repetitive and routinised, but it is neither temporary nor casual. Lower-level clerical or railway employees are obvious examples of jobs in the subordinate primary market.

Finally, the 'Independent Primary Market' comprises three sets of jobs: 'middle layer' staff such as supervisors; skilled craftsmen; the professions. All require skills obtained in specialised education, benefit from career ladders, high income and security of tenure. 'Most strikingly, all independent primary jobs foster occupational consciousness; that is, they provide the basis for job-holders to define their own identities in terms of their particular occupation.'[51]

The importance of labour markets in the analysis of class boundaries is highlighted when one enquires as to the forces which segment the labour market in this way. Somewhat naïvely, Edwards rejects any explanation which has recourse to the *market power* of certain occupational groups. In his view, the existence of competition between workers makes the notion of 'worker-enforced segmentations' implausible. Rather, for Edwards, the fundamental basis for the segmented labour markets is to be found in the *workplace*. To be sure, labour-attributes such as education, experience or skill are associated with position in the labour market. But it is the system of control in the workplace that *creates the context* within which experience, training, ability, schooling, skills and other attributes assume their importance. Thus, for example, secondary work is organised in a way which does not require either education or experience, while subordinate primary work is structured so as to require them. *These segmented labour markets exist because segmented labour processes give rise to them.* In particular the secondary labour market results from the exercise of simple control in the workplace, the 'mixed' system of technical control and unions is the basis for the subordinate primary market while bureaucratically controlled labour processes give rise to the independent primary market. The three types of control thus give rise to three corresponding labour markets which in turn represent the fragmentation of the population in terms of social class. These fractions Edwards terms 'the working poor', the 'traditional proletariat' and the 'middle layers'.

As Edwards himself admits, his analysis is narrow and, particularly with regard to the 'middle layers', overly simplistic. For example, the interplay of labour process and labour market forces in influencing class boundaries will be very different in the cases of skilled craftsmen, supervisors and the professions – groupings which at present are conflated by Edwards into the 'Independent Primary Market'. But these weaknesses highlight rather than undermine the potential importance of the incorporation of the analysis of labour markets into that of class boundaries.

Conclusion

It is still early days. And in the last analysis, of course, the examination of class boundaries must be an empirical one. Nevertheless, the route to be taken is clear. The solution of the 'boundary problem' requires an approach which unambiguously regards the accumulation process as the bedrock of the analysis of class inequality.[52] This means that a developmental/historical perspective is essential as is the realisation that the *relations* between classes (or fractions of classes) are dynamic or dialectical. This means that, in contrast for example to the work of Poulantzas, the analysis of class boundaries must incorporate the action of actors at the same time as it pays primary heed to the forces of the organisation of production. Finally, the contemporary work of Edwards and others on the importance of labour markets indicates, as has happened before at another time and place, that the analysis of social class requires that we look beyond the factory gates.[53]

Control and resistance on the assembly line*

ELY CHINOY

'The net result of the application of these principles is the reduction of the necessity for thought on the part of the worker and the reduction of his movements to a minimum. He does as nearly as possible, only one thing with only one movement. . . I have not been able to discover that repetitive labor injures a man in any way.'

Henry Ford

In 1970, a Chrysler worker in Detroit pulled out a gun and went on a shooting spree that left two foremen and a job setter dead. A jury subsequently found him innocent because of temporary insanity. The defense had argued that he had been made temporarily insane by the strain of assembly line work. One juror is reported to have said, 'Did you see the cement room in that plant? Working there would drive anyone crazy.'[1]

Ever since it emerged, full-blown, in the Ford Motor Company plant in Highland Park, Michigan, in 1913, the automobile assembly line has been a dominating symbol of modern industrialism. Like all symbols, however, its meaning is complex and multi-faceted. On the one hand, the assembly line represents the fruitfulness and productivity of modern technology. 'Operation of the automobile assembly line,' says the *Encyclopedia Britannica*, 'epitomizes mass production.' Henry Ford once called it the 'new Messiah' because its productive capacity promised to make possible the satisfaction of human wants on an unprecedented scale. On the other hand, the authors of the report on *Work in America* prepared for the Department of Health, Education and Welfare in 1972 saw in the assembly line the 'quintessential embodiment' of 'dissatisfying work'. In *The Man on the*

*At the time of his tragic death, in an automobile accident on April 21, 1975, Ely Chinoy was writing up the results of a large-scale research project on the automobile assembly line. That research was supported by the Ford Foundation and had been carried out in the USA, the UK, France, Germany, Italy and Japan. Three chapters had been completed and there were extensive notes related to subsequent ones. The authors of the present volume have taken this essay from those materials.

87

Ely Chinoy

Assembly Line, the best available account of work on the line, Charles Walker and Robert Guest characterised the assembly line as 'the classic symbol of the subjection of man to the machine in our industrial age'. For Herbert Marcuse, 'the human degradation inherent in modern production finds its most brutal expression in the organization of the assembly line'.

What gave the assembly line its symbolic importance was its crucial role in the growth of a glamorous new industry. From its beginnings early in the twentieth century, the automobile industry expanded with extraordinary speed. In 1903, only 11,000 cars and trucks were built in the United States. In 1910, almost 200,000 were produced and the American love affair with the automobile was well under way. In 1913, the year the assembly line was fully developed, almost half a million cars and trucks were manufactured, 40% of them by Ford. The assembly line was both a response to the burgeoning demand for cars and a stimulus to that demand, for it helped to reduce costs and prices substantially. In 1910, the cheapest Ford cost $686.00, in 1914 only $390.00. In 1915, when well over 900,000 vehicles were produced, throngs crowded into a 'Palace of Transportation' in San Francisco to see a replica of the Highland Park assembly line that had so dramatically enlarged the possibilities of mass production.

Though essentially a product of the twentieth century, the assembly line rests upon familiar principles of production: the division of labour, the use of standardised interchangeable parts, and the utilisation of some sort of mechanical device to bring needed materials to the workers in order to minimise the time spent in moving from place to place. The contribution of Henry Ford and his co-workers was to combine these principles into an integrated system of production that also made use of new machines, new materials, and the refinements of scientific management. The ideal assembly line, according to Henry Ford, would carry the division of labour as far as it could go, reducing each worker's task to doing 'as nearly as possible one thing with only one movement'.

The first significant use of interchangeable parts is usually attributed to Eli Whitney in his Connecticut gun plant. As methods, materials, and tools improved, the use of standardised parts became widespread. By the end of the nineteenth century, precision engineering had already made possible quantity production of such things as telephones, bicycles, typewriters, and cash registers. The automobile industry was using standardised parts well before the introduction of the assembly line, as evident in Ford's advertising for its Model N in 1906:

88

We are making 40,000 cylinders, 10,000 engines, 40,000 wheels, 20,000 axles, 10,000 bodies, 10,000 of every part that goes into the car – think of it.

. . . For this car we buy 40,000 spark plugs, 10,000 spark coils, 40,000 tires, all *exactly alike*.[2]

Movement of materials mechanically through the production process also had significant antecedents. In 1784–5, Oliver Evans, an ingenious American mechanic, built a mill which turned grain into flour without human intervention. The grain was lifted to the top of the mill and was then moved mechanically downward through the various steps in the milling process, emerging as flour at the bottom. The British Victualling Office used a moving conveyor in the manufacture of ships' biscuits early in the nineteenth century, and other British manufacturers introduced various devices in their plants to move materials from place to place. Around 1870, meat-packing plants in Cincinnati installed a continuously moving line to speed up the 'disassembly' of hogs and cattle, a precedent acknowledged by Henry Ford in his reminiscences.

Use of the moving conveyor on the assembly process began in the Ford plant in the production of the flywheel-magneto. Prior to the introduction of the line, each worker had put together the whole unit, averaging about twenty minutes for each assembly. When the line was installed, the job was divided into 29 operations performed by 29 men; the time needed for each assembly was immediately cut to thirteen minutes and ten seconds. (Within a few years the time was further reduced to five minutes.) Before long the line was also being used for the assembly of motors and transmissions, with equally dramatic results.

So great was the volume of production on these three assembly lines that the final assembly line could not keep up with the flow of flywheels, engines, and transmissions; inventories of these parts grew rapidly. A moving line, initially kept in motion by a rope and windlass, was therefore installed to facilitate the assembly of the chassis and the completion of the car, thus reducing the man-hours required from an average of twelve and a half to five hours and fifty minutes. The rope and windlass were soon replaced by a mechanically powered chain. With the installation of the endlessly moving conveyor throughout the assembly process, the time needed to complete a car fell to one hour and thirty-three minutes.

The continuous rationalisation of automotive production, of which the assembly line was one result as well as a major stimulus to further progress, led eventually to what was once described as an almost totally 'kinetic' productive process. In the Ford plant, wrote Henry Ford in 1922,

Every piece of work . . . . . moves; it may move on hooks on overhead chains going to assembly in the exact order in which the parts are required; it may travel on a moving platform, or it may go by gravity, but the point is that there is no lifting or trucking of anything other than materials.[3]

So highly integrated was this system that an interruption at almost any point within it could rapidly slow down or even bring to a total halt the entire productive process. Not only did it therefore require careful planning to ensure an uninterrupted supply of parts, detailed scheduling to synchronise the flow of sub-assembly lines, and precise definition of jobs to make the most efficient use of labour, but it also generated intense pressure to keep things moving, men as well as materials. And it was this ceaseless pressure that was in large part responsible for the image of the assembly line as humanly destructive.

In addition to the body, trim, chassis, and final lines along which most of the assembly work is done, there are usually other lines on which components are put together. In one General Motors plant, for example, there were ten subsidiary lines, some of which even had smaller feeder lines of their own. Parts made on these lines, such as fuel tanks, steering columns, and seats and seat cushions, are fed into the assembly process at the points at which they are needed, usually carried there by a network of overhead conveyors that emphasise the incessant movement characteristic of automobile production. There are, to be sure, small sub-assemblies that may be done on benches or bucks adjacent to the line, though some plants make every effort to include them in the tasks assigned to assembly-line workers rather than freeing them from the demands of the line.

Throughout the entire assembly process, as well as on the final line, inspectors are at work checking on what is done and repairmen are available to eliminate any defects that may be found. If the deficiency is too substantial to allow for repairs to be made while assembly operations continue, the unit may be moved off the line to special areas where repairmen can do their work free from the pressures of the line.

To work effectively, this elaborate and complex system of production requires carefully timed and synchronised operations. The flow of parts and materials, whether from another department in the same plant or from a plant a hundred or thousand miles away, must be adjusted to the needs of the assembly line. If the flow is too great, costly and inconvenient inventories will accumulate. If delivery of any part slows down or ceases, the entire system will be affected. The assembly line will be forced to operate at a reduced tempo or stop entirely, while the production of other parts may have to be cut back or even stopped entirely in order to avoid excess accumulation of supplies and the clogging of the channels that feed the assembly line.

In addition to ensuring that the flow of parts and materials is not interrupted, it is also necessary to order carefully the precise sequence in which they are fed into the assembly process. The days of the highly standardised product epitomised in Henry Ford's policy, 'People can have the Model T in any color – so long as it's black', are long since gone, and many options are now available on any car recently begun. Scheduling of production has therefore become a complex process in which the various components ordered for each car must arrive at the assembly line just as they are needed. Seats with black upholstery ordered for a car with a white body must meet the trim line just as that body arrives at the spot where seats are installed. If a V-8 engine with automatic transmission has been ordered for that car, it must be fed onto the conveyor that carries engines to the chassis line so that it will be installed on the chassis to which the white body will eventually be joined. If wheels for that car are to have special hubcaps, those particular wheels must arrive at precisely the moment when the chassis reaches the place on the line for wheel mounting. And the white body must descend upon the specific chassis for which it is intended. If the next car on the line is to have a blue body with blue upholstery, a six-cylinder engine with standard transmission and standard hubcaps, then these components must follow those of the white car on the various feeder lines. Since these feeder lines vary in length and in the time required before they reach the assembly line, each component must start its journey at a different time in order to ensure assembly of the car with all the specified components. So complex has scheduling become that it is now computerised, with instructions fed from the central source to each feeder line or storage area specifying the timing and sequence of sub-assembly operations and the delivery of components to the appropriate assembly line.

Since the entire process is geared to the demands of the final assembly line, the *speed* at which the line runs in effect controls all the antecedent stages of production. And although the assignment of jobs and the speed of the line were initially determined by trial and error, systematic methods for deciding how fast the line should move and what each worker should do were soon developed. The principles of scientific management, including time and motion study, had already been enunciated by Frederick W. Taylor and were widely known when the assembly line was introduced, though much of what transpired in the automobile industry was the achievement of its own engineers and technicians. Taylor had lectured in Detroit to a group of automobile executives in 1909; his book, *The Principles of Scientific Management*, was published in 1911. Yet when he returned to Detroit in 1914 to lecture again, he remarked that the automobile industry provided 'almost the first instance in which a group of manufacturers had undertaken to install the principles of scientific management without the aid of experts'.

'Scientific' 'principles' continue to provide the basis for the setting of line speed. The total time required to assemble a car (or engine, transmission, body or any other component) is arrived at by a careful analysis of both the operations to be performed and the time needed for each, often measured in hundredths of a minute. Using one or another variant of time and motion study analysis, often referred to as MTM (Methods-Time Measurement, a system developed in the 1940s by three American engineers, H. B. Maynard, G. T. Stegemerten and J. L. Schwab, and widely adopted), each operation is broken down into the movements required and the time needed. Although this may entail close observation and timing of workers' actual performance, it also draws upon massive bodies of standardised data developed by industrial engineers. Operations are simplified as much as possible in order to achieve maximum economy of motion, thereby reducing the time required.

In determining the total time needed to complete the assembly operations, however, allowances of various kinds must be included. For example, in allocating tasks to individual workers, the foreman must somehow divide the multiplicity of operations so as to provide each one with tasks that will require the use of as much of the job cycle as possible. But it is often impossible to have each worker's timed operations equal the exact length of time available. Thus, instead of tasks that require, say, the full length of a 1.2 minute (72 second) job cycle, the worker may be assigned tasks requiring only 69 seconds, 'wasting' three seconds of each job cycle.

Determining total assembly time and the number of workers required is further complicated by both the great variety of options available on each car and the fact that several models may be assembled on a single line. The tasks to be performed may therefore vary from one car to the next, even in those plants in which only one model is being assembled. Window installations, for example, are not the same on a four-door sedan as on a station wagon or a two-door sedan. A radio with two speakers requires more elaborate wiring than a radio with only one speaker; power steering will necessitate operations not needed for regular steering. A worker may therefore need less than the full job cycle to complete his work on one car and more than the full job cycle to do his job on the next. A single General Motors line, for example, may assemble several different cars – Chevrolet, Pontiac, Oldsmobile and Buick, each with several models. It is therefore necessary to 'balance' the assembly line to ensure that each worker is neither pushed beyond the norm by a succession of cars requiring more than the available time nor left without anything to do for too long because of a series of cars on which his task can be completed in much less than the job cycle. (Like scheduling, this problem too has become so complex that it is now usually assigned to a computer.) As the head of the General Motors Assembly Division expressed it, 'Within reason and without endangering their health, if we can occupy a man for sixty minutes, we've got that right.' 'Reason' and 'right' are seen as perfectly legitimate terms to use in this context because, for this head, work standards are not arbitrary but are based upon a scientific analysis of the time required for each task. Characteristically, in a mimeographed statement about production and labour policies distributed by its public relations office, one European manufacturer observed:

Thus the assertion that the assembly line determines working speeds. This is completely false. As ever, on the assembly line as in all other production sections, job content and timing are determined according to time and motion methods.

Not all observers, however, view the findings and prescriptions of time and motion studies as being 'scientific', neutral or 'right'. Rather, they point out, the contract between capital and labour is like a rubber bag. How hard and well the seller of labour power will work will depend largely on the extent to which he can be *made* to. Thus the 'effort-bargain' – how much effort is expended by labour for a stipulated reward will depend on the extent to which management is able to impose its interests upon the workforce and the extent to which that workforce is able to resist. It is banal to remark that the interests of capital and labour are not identical. Equally it is naive to claim that a state of equipoise can be scientifically determined by management-inspired time and motion studies.

Given the fact that the relationship between managers and managed takes place on 'contested terrain',[4] the fact that *the line itself* acts 'as a "manager of men" which enforces a specific work pace and guarantees a predicted output'[5] is of particular importance. As one English observer remarked, in describing a plant in which efforts were being made to improve working conditions on the line,

> ... the line itself, with its complex tributaries of sub-lines, bringing up doors, body panels, and engines, all to be bolted on at just the right moment, imposes its own discipline, and the general effect, heightened by the unsmiling foremen surveying everything from their boxes, is reminiscent of an Egyptian engraving of a prince of the blood overseeing the construction of a never-ending pyramid, with clipboard rather than hawk or whip in hand.[6]

Before the recognition of unions which have imposed some restraint on management's power, workers were often undoubtedly pushed to the limit of their capacities. They were forced to work, often at relentless speed, for the full duration of every job cycle with no gap between the time required and the time available. It was because the assembly line's potential as an instrument for controlling the pace and tempo of work was ruthlessly exploited that the automobile industry acquired its harsh reputation with regard to the treatment of its workers and the speed-up became a perpetual source of contention between management and workers. In the days before there were contractual guarantees of relief time, one long-time worker reported, he had once been told by the foreman when he complained that he needed to go to the toilet, 'We don't regulate the line by your bowels, you regulate your bowels by the line.' Or nearly always: on one unusual occasion when the line on which I was working not only stopped but also backed up for a few feet, the faces of all the men around me were wreathed in smiles. The line, which had everyone in its grip, had not only forgotten to be itself, it was even contradicting its own logic.

Indeed, while the assembly line and the production techniques associated with it were quickly identified as the epitome of mass production technology and have retained this identification, the harsh realities of working on the line took somewhat longer to become widely apparent. Indeed, for a brief time after its introduction, the assembly line seemed to promise a new millennium for workers as well as increased production and extravagant profits for manufacturers. In 1914, Ford announced that the profitability of the enterprise made it possible to pay workers five dollars a day, almost double the going wages in the automobile industry and much more than wages in most other industries. Sceptics have argued that the real reason for this dramatic step, which made Henry Ford a national – even international – hero, was to be found in high labour turnover, a shortage of labour, or the threat of unionisation. Profits were so high that adding an estimated ten million dollars to the annual wage bill would not seriously reduce them, and there is little doubt that the high wage rate tied workers more closely to the company and rendered them more susceptible to the exigent demands of high-speed automotive production. Some years later Henry Ford himself described the five-dollar day as 'one of the finest cost-cutting moves I've ever made'.

With the announcement by Ford that 'the greatest and most successful' automobile company would 'inaugurate the greatest revolution in the matter of rewards for its workers ever known to the industrial world', Detroit became a Mecca for workers. The day after the announcement of the five-dollar day, ten thousand men besieged the Ford plant looking for jobs. Although few jobs were available at Ford and other manufacturers were slow to pay the same rates, thousands of workers were drawn to Detroit in search of the high wages presumably available there. Those who found jobs in the Ford plant held on to them (turnover dropped substantially) despite the fact that work there was becoming more and more routine and repetitive as the rationalisation of production continued.

Within a few years, however, the glamour and the promise had worn off. As wages rose everywhere, in part because of the impact of the First World War, the economic advantages of work on the line were counterbalanced, even outweighed, by the impact of the job itself upon the worker. The extraordinary economies inherent in assembly-line production were made possible in large measure by an elaborate division of labour that reduced most jobs to the endless repetition of simple tasks, and by the control over workers that the line allowed. Not only could fewer workers produce more cars, but those who remained could be made to work at higher levels of efficiency, their rhythm and speed determined by the speed of the line, their tasks rationalised by the application of modern techniques of time and motion study.

Because of its central role in the productive process, the assembly line soon affected all aspects of automotive production – the manufacture of parts, machining operations, forge and foundry, the flow of materials, inspection, maintenance, repair work. All had to be keyed to the requirements of the line and its endless movement. As the industry acquired a reputation for a hard-driving management that continuously exerted intense pressure for higher volume and lower costs, the assembly line became the central symbol of the human exploitativeness of modern mass production industry.

By the mid-twenties, the character of work on the assembly line was widely known and often commented on. A visiting German journalist summed up his impression of the assembly line as follows:

> The conveyor started as a simple means of carrying articles, but it became a tyrant dominating the workers. When the conveyor is speeded up, the workers are forced to follow its dictates, and to hurry with their jobs accordingly. The conveyor's speed invariably determines the worker's speed . . . If the management in a factory decides to increase its speed by ten per cent . . . tens of thousands of hands . . . must work ten per cent faster. The workers are bound to the conveyor the way the galley slaves were bound to the vessel.[7]

Perhaps not surprisingly, the second quarter of the twentieth century witnessed bitter struggles between workers and employers that erupted in the American automobile industry. Beginning in 1935 and with increasing momentum during succeeding years, automobile workers who were suffering, in the words of a report prepared for the National Recovery Administration, 'from insecurity, low annual earnings, inequitable hiring and rehiring methods, espionage, speedup and displacement of workers at an extremely early age', sought some measure of control over their jobs by joining a union that could bargain collectively with their employers. Managements that were intensely concerned with production and costs resisted vigorously any efforts to limit their control over their workers, using almost every device possible, including violence and labour spies, to forestall unionisation. Despite this resistance, the union, supported by a government that for the first time in American history was sympathetic to organised labour, eventually gained recognition from all the automobile producers and forced them to negotiate contracts that regulated wages, layoffs, and working conditions. The symbolic importance of the assembly line was thus reinforced by the fact that the automobile industry, which was so markedly identified with the line, had become one of the major battlegrounds in the war between management and labour. And although many changes have occurred in the automobile industry, which continually stresses its efforts to improve both production methods and the finished product, the assembly line remains much as it was and continues to set the tone and determine the rhythm and tempo of production – both as brute fact and strategic symbol.

During the past few years, the persisting problems of industrial work, and notably of assembly-line work, which for a time had seemed to be less pressing than they once were, have moved centre stage again. During the 1950s and 1960s, the problems of labour and of work, which had been so acute during the depression decade and in the years immediately after the Second World War, had receded into the background. Other problems – the Cold War, conformity during the 1950s, civil liberties, Vietnam, changing mores during the 1960s – preoccupied intellectuals, academics, politicians and the public. At the same time affluence and the promise of the automatic factory seemed to relegate work to a problem that the further evolution of industrial society would solve. Yet, as seems to happen so often, issues that once seemed on the way to interment came to life again.

Indeed the fact of worker resistance to managerial demands was vividly and publicly dramatised – by a widely reported strike at the Lordstown, Ohio, plant of General Motors when some 7,000 workers walked off their jobs in the spring of 1972. The Lordstown plant had been built in the mid-sixties and was retooled in 1970 to produce the widely heralded General Motors compact car, the Vega. The plant, according to General Motors, was the most modern automobile plant in the United States, its assembly lines capable of turning out 101 cars per hour. That there should be a bitter strike in which the major issues were how many men were needed on the line and how much each worker should do so soon after the plant went into operation seemed to raise again serious questions about the impact on workers of assembly-line technology and the managerial policies that went with it.

What actually caused the Lordstown strike became the focus of a bitter debate. Some critics emphasised the 36-second job cycle (the length of time within which each worker had to perform his task) on the Vega assembly line and the boredom and frustration to which it presumably gave rise. General Motors countered that all assignments on the line could be done in the time available and pointed out that strenuous efforts had been made in designing the plant to simplify jobs and make them easier to perform. Some observers argued that the youthful labour force (the average age was 24) would no longer tolerate dull, repetitive work on the line as readily as their elders had. Both labour and management spokesmen pointed out in response that there had been strikes at the same time at other General Motors plants in which the workforce was not as young as at Lordstown. Union leaders insisted that the strike was a result of management's efforts to speed up production rather than of lowered tolerance for routine jobs or increased boredom. In a sense, the company agreed with the union, for it claimed that it was merely trying to maintain production 'standards'. The strike, management asserted, was the result of a corporate reorganisation in which various operations were consolidated within the General Motors Assembly Division. GMAD, they noted, was simply trying to eliminate superfluous labour and maintain plant discipline. Strikes had occurred, they pointed out, in eight of the ten plants which had become part of the Assembly Division.[8]

The events at Lordstown and the subsequent debate placed the assembly line at the centre of the discussion of the relationship between capital and labour in the work situation. In the rash of newspaper and magazine articles on job satisfaction which appeared during 1972 and 1973, the assembly line was frequently used as the central example of oppressive and unsatisfying work. When a subcommittee of the Senate Committee on Labor and Public Welfare held hearings on 'Worker Alienation' in the summer of 1972, the first two witnesses were the President of the Lordstown local of the United Automobile Workers and an assembly-line worker from the plant. The report, *Work in America*, which appeared late in 1972 and received wide circulation, also found the '*locus classicus* of dissatisfying work' in the automobile industry, especially on the assembly line. In the article in *Fortune* which first publicised the 'blue-collar blues', Judson Gooding reported his observation that 'In some plants worker discontent has reached such a degree that . . . . . screws have been left in brake drums, tool handles welded into fender compartments (to cause mysterious, unfindable, and eternal rattles), paint scratched, and upholstery cut'.[9]

However, the most substantial evidence that there are serious conflicts inherent in assembly-line work can be found in the extent to which automobile producers have committed energies and resources to making work on the line easier to control, easier to accept. Saab and Volvo have received the greatest attention, but many other companies have also made some effort to improve morale and increase compliance among assembly-line workers – General Motors, Ford, and Chrysler in the United States, Fiat, Renault, Volkswagen, and Daimler-Benz in Europe. Thus schemes to 'enrich', rotate or 'enlarge' jobs have come and gone in a large number of instances. Saab-Scania and General Motors have both recently experimented with group assembly, while ergonomics has enjoyed a recent but brief return to the stage. Industrial democracy or co-determination has been put forward as a solution but, at least in the USA and UK, welcomed neither by the representatives of capital nor labour. And although some of the projects have been modest and explicitly experimental, others have required expenditures so substantial that it is unlikely that they would have been made had not management considered the problem serious and pressing.

It remains a fact, however, that the impediment to the adoption of many of these schemes is their negative impact on profitability. If an improvement in 'the quality of working life', in the compliance of assembly-line workers, raises production costs then such improvement can only be rejected by management. And this simple fact has increased in importance during the 1970s as the car-producers of the mature Western economies have increasingly failed to compete successfully with the Japanese.[10] As an American industry analyst explained it: '. . . you will have to demonstrate that it (an experiment) will pay and arguing in terms of human values is soft-headed from their (management's) point of view . . . If profits are to go down because of this, then obviously the decision will be against it'. Put simply, the condition of a profits-squeeze which has characterised car production in the West during recent years has pushed management not in the direction of 'humanistic' solutions to the problem of labour control but towards technological ones. The logic behind the decision of management to 'regain control' through the adoption of new technology is argued forcefully by the authors of *Work in America*:

Many industrial engineers feel that gains in productivity will come about mainly through the introduction of new technology. They feel that tapping the latent productivity of workers is a relatively unimportant part of the whole question of productivity. This was the attitude that was behind the construction of the General Motors auto plant in Lordstown, Ohio, the newest and most efficient auto plant in America . . . What does the employer gain by having a 'perfectly efficient' assembly-line if his workers are out on strike because of the oppressive and dehumanized experience of working on the 'perfect' line? As the costs of absenteeism, wildcat strikes, turnover, and industrial sabotage become an increasingly significant part of the cost of doing business, it is becoming clear that the current concepts of industrial efficiency conveniently but mistakenly ignore the social half of the equation (of production).[11]

At the present time it is in the area of body assembly that this new 'industrial efficiency' is most apparent. Virtually the entire body of

Ely Chinoy

the Volkswagen Beetle is put together automatically; the welding lines are capable of completing 3,000 bodies per day and require only 80 skilled workers whose task is to keep the machinery in working order. In the Lordstown plant, which can produce 101 Vegas per hour when the line is moving at full speed, 95% of the welding is now automated; on the Chevrolet Impala, which was assembled at Lordstown at the rate of 50 to 60 cars per hour before the plant was converted to the production of the Vega, only 20% of the welding was automated. After the welding is completed, whether by men or machines, the seams are usually soldered and polished in order to ensure a smooth joint. (In the Lordstown plant, these operations have now been virtually eliminated by redesigning the body panels.) Fiats, we are told, are 'handbuilt by robots', while a significant feature of British Leyland's 'fight back' involves the replacement of workers by Unimates to build Mini Metro bodies.

To be sure, organised workers in the mature capitalist economies have successfully developed strategies of resistance to the managerial prerogative, but at the cost of a growth in the reserve army of labour. The profit-making, efficient and humanised assembly line is indeed a contradiction in terms. And that contradiction could only be overcome by changes more widespread and far-reaching than those discussed above.[12] Indeed, as I have expressed it earlier:

If workers find it difficult to realise the values they have acquired from the larger culture, as they do in the case of success and advancement, then the solution to the problems of the meaning and purpose of their labour lies not merely in reorganisation of the job situation but in changes in the values of the larger society or in institutional changes which give them a greater degree of control over their fate.[13]

Fatalism: Durkheim's hidden theory of order

DAVID LOCKWOOD

I

The significance of Durkheim's concept of fatalism is wholly unappreciated. The idea is seldom discussed and then only in relation to the study of suicide.[1] Unlike anomie, it has had a most undistinguished sociological career. This is curious because if anomie can serve to illuminate in a quite general way the nature of social disorder, why should fatalism not be regarded as having the capacity to provide an explanation of order that is of equally wide scope? The aim of this essay is to show that hidden in the concept of fatalism there is indeed such a theory, though it bears little resemblance to what is taken to be Durkheim's major contribution to the analysis of social integration.

It is understandable that fatalism should have been neglected because Durkheim devotes no more than a few lines to the concept, and then only, it would seem, out of a logical instinct for symmetry. It appears as the opposite social state to anomie, which is a condition in which normative rules suddenly lose their power of regulating the wants of individuals. Consequently, fatalism is defined as 'excessive regulation', 'excessive physical or moral despotism', as a situation in which the future is 'pitilessly blocked and passions violently choked by oppressive discipline'. At one pole, then, there is an extraordinarily weak social regulation of wants, at the other an unusually stringent limitation of them. If anomie means that horizons become abruptly widened so that aspirations know no bounds, fatalism refers to hopes so narrowed and diminished that even life itself becomes a matter of indifference. As examples of the latter, Durkheim refers to suicides committed by slaves, and he concludes by saying that in order to 'bring out the ineluctable and inflexible nature of a rule against which there is no appeal, and in contrast with the expression

David Lockwood

"anomy" which has just been used, we might call it *fatalistic suicide'*.

As it stands, Durkheim's treatment of the concept hardly goes much beyond the dictionary definition of fatalism as 'submission to all that happens as inevitable', and the possibility of deriving a theory of social order from it would appear to be small. Nevertheless, a start can be made by considering the two main assumptions of his account. The first is that fatalism, like anomie, is a matter of degree. In characteristic fashion, he uses the term 'excessive' to describe both the fatalistic over-regulation of wants and their anomic de-regulation. It is reasonable then to suppose that fatalism is to be understood as varying according to the amount of 'oppressive discipline' involved. The second point is that there are two kinds of discipline; fatalism results from either 'physical or moral depotism'. In seeking the meanings that can be attached to these terms it is convenient to begin with physical despotism. The most obvious instance of this is coercion, and social organisations in which order is maintained by excessive and oppressive discipline of a direct and personal kind are all too familiar. These extreme cases, however, are of little relevance to an understanding of the more general problem of order because the degree of coercion required to ensure the compliance of inmates of organisations such as prisons and concentration camps is incapable of being reproduced as the sole or even as the major means of securing enduring social stability in a society of any size and complexity. The various arguments against a 'coercion theory' of social order have been well rehearsed[2] and it is no part of the present argument to reiterate or to challenge them. Moreover, to identify fatalistic order with a coercive regimen of this kind would be completely out of keeping with Durkheim's view that the coerciveness of society lies in its supra-individual nature. It has been argued on good grounds that in the course of his work Durkheim's idea of social constraint changed from a view of social facts as things, or conditions of social action, to a notion of social facts as moral forces which exert their influence by becoming internalised needs of the individual.[3] This distinction between social conditions and moral beliefs is indispensable to a closer understanding of fatalistic order.

The first conclusion that can be drawn from it is that 'despotism' presents itself most effectively not as direct personal oppression but in the form of impersonal social constraint. What are called the 'unintended consequences' of 'latent functions' of purposive social action belong to this category. These terms refer to the systematic effects of social interactions which appear not to be the outcome of human volition and which thus acquire the property of objective conditions.

102

In this way, massive unemployment or abject poverty have very often been experienced as unavoidable 'facts of life', privations that are due to anonymous forces over which no one has control. These conditions have the effects of narrowing people's horizons and inuring them to what seems to be part of the natural order of things. Students of the 'culture of poverty' have shown in some detail how such fatalistic attitudes are engendered and how they contribute to the maintenance of life styles which serve to accommodate people to conditions of adversity.[4] In a similar fashion, the structure of social organisation itself may take on the property of unalterability or inescapability. When Weber speaks of 'the iron cage' of bureaucracy, or Marx of the 'fetishism of commodities', it is presumably to this kind of social fact that they refer. In all these instances, what is especially conducive to a fatalistic attitude is not so much the degree of 'oppressive discipline' involved, but rather the fact that social constraint is experienced as an external, inevitable and impersonal condition. For however oppressive direct personal coercion may be, it can never produce the same kind of acquiescence as that which is born of social conditions that appear to be unattributable to, and thereby inconvertible by, human agency.

This kind of 'conditional fatalism' probably comes closer to Durkheim's notion of 'moral despotism'. Indeed, it may be all that he means by the latter term. 'Moral' has such a wide and uncertain significance in Durkheim's vocabulary that any further discussion of its association with fatalism is bound to be fairly speculative. Nonetheless, it is worth pursuing the idea that the meaning of moral despotism is not exhausted by the concept of conditional fatalism. The clue to what might further be implied by it is to be found in Durkheim's distinction between 'the spirit of discipline' and 'attachment to social groups'. Throughout his writings, these two 'elements of morality', which are fundamental to his explanations of social order and disequilibrium, simply appear in different guises (egoism versus anomie, ritual versus belief, organic versus mechanical solidarity, and so on). Now fatalism, like anomie, has to do with the way in which wants are disciplined, and for Durkheim the principal source of this regulation is the system of values and beliefs which makes up the collective conscience.[5] One entirely consistent interpretation of moral despotism, then, is that it refers to some aspect of the collective conscience which has the capacity to make individuals accept their life situation as unquestionable, because any alternative dispensation is, by virtue of the beliefs they hold, unthinkable. Here, by contrast with conditional fatalism, it is the constraint of a system of beliefs, rather than sheer force of circumstances, which is the key to social order. But if this interpretation is correct, it follows that moral despotism has its origin in precisely that aspect of the collective conscience which Durkheim deliberately excluded from his study of the religious life: namely, the 'confusing details' of the creeds and doctrines themselves. His silence on this subject is most remarkable. It is true that at one point in his writings, and in a manner not distinct from that of vulgar Marxism, he does appear to attribute to religious beliefs in general the capacity to induce a fatalistic ethos among believers.[6] But this passing remark goes very much against the grain of his conception of sociology as a subject concerned with the covariation of social facts; and the assumption that all religions and ideologies have the same social consequences affords no basis for the serious examination of moral despotism.[7] If fatalism and anomie are the limiting cases of moral discipline, and if the chief source of the last is 'religious' (in the widest, that is to say Durkheimian, sense of the term), then moral despotism must vary according to differences in the *structure* of religious beliefs. In short, certain types of beliefs must be assumed to be more conducive than others to what Mannheim has called the 'ethics of fatalism'.

Before attempting to substantiate this point, two further general implications of the concept of fatalism need to be brought out. The first concerns its consequences for the Durkheimian, and therefore for the normative functionalist, solution of the problem of order. The second has to do with the connection between fatalism and ritual, which for Durkheim is the core of the 'religious life'.

II

There can be no more firmly established canon of sociological orthodoxy than the belief that Durkheim's major contribution to the understanding of social integration consists in his discovery and elaboration of the concept of the collective conscience. Renamed the 'common value system', this idea became the lynchpin of normative functionalism, which, as the most influential school of neo-Durkheimian thought, took it as axiomatic that widespread consensus on ultimate values is not only a normal feature of stable societies but the single most important precondition of social order. From these assumptions it follows that the basic point of reference in the analysis of social integration are the processes by which values become internalised in actors, and that the conformity of actors with institutional norms must be understood first and foremost as the outcome of this commitment to values legitimating specific role obligations.[8] In this perspective, there is little room for explanations of order that emphasise the significance of either coerced compliance or the 'natural identity of interests'; explanations that are commonly believed to be the only possible alternatives to a 'consensus' theory of society. The last, as represented by normative functionalism, has been subject to much condign criticism, but attempts to displace it have resulted in little more than a regression towards some kind of equally unacceptable 'coercion' model of society. In this whole controversy, however, it has not been recognised that what is conventionally taken to be Durkheim's classical solution of the problem of order is not the only one that can be derived from his conceptual scheme. In the idea of fatalism there are the makings of an alternative explanation that depends neither on the assumptions of consensus theory nor on those of the latter's two chief rivals. Most importantly in the present context, the concept of fatalistic order can dispense with the view that widespread agreement on the ultimate values legitimating institutions is a prerequisite of social stability. A sufficient condition of order is simply that the structure of power, wealth and status is believed to be inevitable, or, as Durkheim says, ineluctable. The general point has been well made by Tumin in his review of the evidence concerning the characteristic modes of response of lower strata to their position in the social hierarchy:

The fact is that we have tended to infer, from the relative stability of caste positions and arrangements over time, that the denigrated and depreciated castes accept as legitimate and appropriate a status of denigration and depreciation. But this inference, taken from the absence of significant action designed to alter the situation, neglects the numerous other reasons for such inactivity by lower caste members or relatively deprived peoples all over the world. In the more general case, it is probably true that subordinate people's failure to improve their situation is as much due to their inability to conceive of a possible alternative, and/or when they do conceive and desire alternatives, to contrive ways to carry out these ideas. Only in a very restricted sense of the word can people under such circumstances be said to 'accept' their positions. And this degree of acceptance is a far cry from any acceptance of the legitimacy of the situation under which they live, if by legitimacy we mean more than nominal conformity to the dominant norms.[9]

This formulation, however, still leaves open the question of how the inability to conceive of an alternative state of affairs arises. For there is after all an important difference between fatalistic beliefs stemming from the individual's realisation that he is personally in the grip of circumstances over which he has no control and fatalistic beliefs resulting from his socialisation into an ideology that provides

David Lockwood

a comprehensive account of why circumstances are beyond his (or anyone else's) control. The distinction is important if only because equally adverse conditions do not always produce equally fatalistic beliefs or the same degree of acquiescence to adversity. This is another reason for thinking that it might be useful to view moral despotism as a system of 'oppressive' beliefs. But in this case, how does the explanation of order differ from that advanced by normative functionalism? Does it not also presuppose the existence of a common value system, of a moral consensus?

The difficulty here lies in a further ambiguity of the term 'moral', which Durkheim uses to refer not only to values or ethical standards but also to beliefs about the nature of the physical and social world. To speak of moral despotism is therefore to conflate two distinct elements that enter into any ideology and to treat as unproblematic the very connection between them which the idea of fatalism would seem to make questionable. The chief social fact that ideologies seek both to explain and to legitimate is human fortune and misfortune, and in particular inequalities of power, wealth and status. But they do so more or less successfully, depending on the extent to which the existential and moral beliefs of which they are composed are in harmony with one another; in this respect ideologies differ markedly in their 'closure' or 'exploitability'. They differ also in the degree to which it is the existential or the moral element which has the more extensive hold over the various groupings of society, and most importantly over its lowest strata.

These facts have not been sufficiently well recognised by normative functionalism, which has tended to treat values and beliefs as an integrated whole as far as the motivation of actors is concerned.[10] The main advantage of the concept of fatalism would seem to be that it leaves open the question of whether, and to what extent, beliefs in the inevitability of social structures are associated with beliefs in their justness and legitimacy. Indeed, by making it possible to ask whether institutions would continue to be supported in the event of the collapse of beliefs about their inevitability, the concept helps to provide a closer definition of solidarity. For it could hardly be denied that a society in which people continue to support central values and institutions, even though they can conceive of realistic alternatives to them, is in a real sense more solidary than a society whose members cannot make this comparison. Finally, the concept of fatalism has the merit of being able to explain those fairly common cases of societies undergoing a sudden discontinuity from order to disorder as a result of their members' exposure to new beliefs: for example, so-called 'revolutions of rising expectations'. The only way in which the value consensus theory of order could attempt to explain this kind of dis-continuity would be to assume that the pre-existing orderliness of such societies was really a condition of potential instability charac-terised by weak attachments to, or even alienation from, common values and beliefs. But since this type of theory rejects the argument that societies can be held together by expediency or coercion, it would still leave unexplained the sources of orderliness of a potentially unstable society. The concept of ideological fatalism involves no such dilemma.

The extent to which subordinate strata regard their positions as legitimate, as opposed to simply accepting them as unalterable, is a matter that is closely bound up with the question of whether social cohesion is based principally on beliefs or ritual. For while Dur-kheim defines a religious community by its adherents' shared beliefs and their participation in a common ritual, it is a frequently noted aspect of the variability of religious institutions that the strict obser-vance of ritual practice is by no means always associated with a strong commitment to the beliefs the ritual symbolises; indeed, very often the beliefs in question are no more than superficially understood. Robertson Smith, to whom Durkheim owed a great deal in forming his theory of the elementary religious life, drew a firm distinction between the external constraints of ritual in ancient religions and the internal constraints of conviction in modern religions:

It is of the first importance to realise clearly from the outset that ritual and practical usage were, strictly speaking, the sum-total of ancient religions. Religion in primitive times was not a fixed system of belief with practical applications; it was a body of fixed traditional practices to which every mem-ber of the society conformed as a matter of course. To us moderns, religion is above all a matter of conviction and reasoned belief, but to the ancients it was part of the citizen's public life, reduced to fixed forms, which he was not bound to understand and was not at liberty to criticise or neglect. Reli-gious nonconformity was an offence against the state; for if sacred tradition was tampered with the bases of society were undermined, and the favour of the gods was forfeited. But so long as the prescribed forms were duly observed, a man was recognised as truly pious, and no one asked how his religion was rooted in his heart or affected his reason. Like political duty, of which it was indeed a part, religion was entirely comprehended in the observance of certain fixed rules of outward conduct.[11]

Although the difference is certainly overdrawn, the point is an important one. It is exaggerated because the relative salience of ritual and belief varies with the rhythm of routinisation and renovation common to all sacerdotal institutions. Even so, societies can be graded

David Lockwood

according to the extent to which ritualisation is the predominant mode of religious integration, a tendency that is the more apparent the greater the intellectual gulf between the beliefs of dominant and subordinate strata. This is a line of analysis that Durkheim's theory excludes; or at least directs attention away from. It is true that he thought of ritual as the more fundamental aspect of the religious life, but it was also a mode of action that he considered to be inseparably connected with the reaffirmation and reinforcement of a common belief system. Ritualisation, which term may be used to refer to Robertson Smith's emphasis on the routinisation of religious conduct, thus differs markedly from the Durkheimian notion of ritual as an extraordinary moment of collective 'effervescence' in which a society undergoes a periodic act of moral communion and re-making. By concentrating on the 'elementary' case of a socially unstratified 'church', Durkheim was not led to consider the nature of religious integration in those far more numerous instances in which the refined soteriologies of the *Lehrstand* have at best only the most feeble and tenuous links with the substratum of folk magic. In such societies, the elementary fact of religious life is the chasm between elite and mass religiosity; and as a result the applicability of Durkheim's concept of the church as a morally unified community is severely limited. Under these conditions, ritualisation acquires its significance as the chief means by which the rudiments of the dominant belief system can be infused into the plebeian collective consciousness. But this superficial appropriation of popular beliefs is obtained only at the cost of the deformation and degeneration of elite ideology, through its embodiment in rituals whose symbolism has to accommodate religious needs that remain primarily oriented to magical solutions of everyday exigencies.

It is perhaps profitable, then, to think of ritual and belief as alternative and inversely related modes of religious, and hence, in Durkheim's understanding, of social integration. Ritual, or rather ritualisation, is likely to be the principal agency when the cultural stratification of society is profound. But it will be especially prominent if, in addition, widespread heterodoxy is freely tolerated or (and this might amount to the same thing) less easily manageable. Indian religion, for example, is characterised by just such an extensive ritualisation of conduct and by a correspondingly weak dogmatism.[12] At the opposite extreme (the case from which normative functionalism seems to have generalised its peculiar ethnocentric idea of social solidarity), is the kind of society in which dominant values and beliefs, principally those of 'secular' religions, are much more accessible to the masses; and in which therefore the problem of consensus, the legitimation and delegitimation of the centre, becomes of much more crucial importance. In this case, the need to secure social integration through pervasive ritualisation is less imperative, and the resort to manufactured ritual of a quasi-Durkheimian kind is occasioned less by the lack of a 'common' value system than by the tension between an overly articulate ideological promise and the evident faultiness of the reality it enshrines.[13]

The question of whether the mass of the population is integrated into a religious community through ritual rather than belief has a direct bearing on fatalism. The crux of the matter is that the concept of fatalism forces a distinction between a social order that is based on a commitment to ultimate values that legitimate it, and one that rests on the rather less secure foundation of beliefs in its unalterability. And ritualisation clearly approximates the latter case. For if the value and belief system communicated to the masses through ritual is remote from their understanding, then the question of its function in legitimating their life situation is otiose. Plamenatz makes this point well when he writes:

In the Middle Ages, most people who were called or who called themselves Christians were ignorant and illiterate; and it is impossible that many of them understood what the religion they adhered to was all about. They were churchgoers and participants in ceremonies rather than persons having definite beliefs. We ought to say of them, as of the illiterate peasants in the Balkans and the southern parts of Italy as late as our own century, that they did not challenge the doctrines of the Church, and not that they accepted them. Where orthodoxy is unchallenged nothing more is required of most people than outward conformity, and orthodoxy is never less challenged than when the vast majority are illiterate, or almost so, and are incapable of either accepting or rejecting the doctrines which are orthodox.[14]

Ritualisation has, then, a close affinity to fatalism; and there are several reasons why this should be so. When ritual symbolism provides the bridge between the disparate beliefs of higher and lower strata, it is in the nature of this syncretisation that the dominant belief system remains cognitively remote from the masses and is just as likely to be regarded as part of the same unalterable order of things as are the institutions it seeks to legitimate. Moreover, in having to meet the exigent, relatively crude, redemptory interests of the masses, this symbolism tends to reinforce fatalistic attitudes by parochialising the sense of injury, injustice and discontent, the more so when it is charged with magical significance. Fatalistic beliefs in chance and luck are very generally held by people who perceive their lives to be subject to supernatural forces that are only marginally within

David Lockwood

their control. And since magic operates within the interstices of the soteriology of the ruling stratum, far from weakening the ideological sanctioning of the existing social order, it buttresses it.[15] Ritualisation is not, however, the cause of fatalism. Rather, they are respec-tively practices and beliefs whose mutually reinforcing and socially stabilising effects are most evident in those societies in which the lower strata stand at such a great distance from the ideological centre that its constraint over them consists chiefly in its inscrutability.

But while this is perhaps one sense in which Durkheim's notion of moral depotism may be understood, it is very much a conceptual point of reference, a limiting case. In one form or another, the rudi-ments of the dominant ideology are conveyed to the masses through ritual symbolism and stand in varying degrees of integration with popular beliefs. Because of this, it is important to return to the prob-lem of what Mannheim has called the ethics of fatalism. For there is clearly a difference between the more general case of fatalism that is augmented by people's inability to question a remote and largely incomprehensible ideology, and fatalism that is grounded in their acceptance of a system of beliefs, which, however imperfectly it is understood, is, by virtue of its particular soteriology, an ideology *of* fatalism.

III

Probably the most thoroughgoing attempt to explain social order in terms of ideological fatalism is Weber's account of the Hindu doc-trine of *karma*, which is part of his wider thesis that the theodicies of 'Asiatic religion' precluded the development of an ethical interest in radical social transformation. A major starting point of his work on Indian religions is the problem of why rebellion against the caste system had not been more frequent and widespread.[16] In seeking to provide a solution of this problem primarily by reference to the basic presuppositions of Hindu soteriology, Weber was, it may be assumed, not oblivious of the political and economic conditions that would have placed obstacles in the path of any concerted 'class' action on the part of the most disadvantaged, and thus potentially revolution-ary, castes. What he wished to prove was that the goal of social rev-olution was unthinkable in the first place. His most categorical state-ment of this view is as follows: 'That these religions lack virtually any kind of social-revolutionary ethics can be explained by reference to their theodicy of "rebirth" according to which the caste system is eternal and absolutely just.'[17] The logic of *karma-samsara-moksha* did not, however, prevent inter-caste hostility; and what Weber has to say about it brings out once again the highly questionable sense in which a social order based on a system of fatalistic beliefs may be said to be 'legitimate'.

Estranged castes might stand beside one another with bitter hatred – for the idea that everyone had 'deserved' his own fate did not make the good fortune of the privileged more enjoyable to the underprivileged. So long as *karma* doctrine was unshaken, revolutionary ideas or progressivism were inconceivable. The lowest castes, furthermore, had the most to win through ritual correctness and were least tempted to innovations.[18]

Furthermore, this doctrine, 'the most consistent theodicy ever produced by history' and shared by all Hindus,[19] not only acted as an infallible prophylactic against lower-caste revolt, but decisively determined the other-worldly religious interests of the many sectarian movements that challenged Brahminical orthodoxy and found their adherents mainly among the middle and higher castes. As Weber puts it, 'An absolute presupposition of Hindu philosophy after the full development of the *karma* and *samsara* doctrines, was that escape from the wheel of rebirth could be the one and only conceivable function of a "salvation".'[20]

Since Brahmins awarded themselves the exclusive privilege of being able to seek release from the *karma* mechanism, it is understandable that there was a strong incentive to doctrinal innovation among those less fortunately placed. For example, heterodox sects, and in particular the Jains, appealed especially to relatively privileged groups whose positions in the secular and ritual hierarchies were incongruous,[21] just as the *bhakti* movements, promising redemption through ecstatic devotion to a saviour deity, recruited extensively from lower castes who were, according to orthodoxy, condemned to the torment of a virtually endless cycle of reincarnations.[22]

In general, the states and stages of salvation envisaged by Hindu philosophies were as myriad as the methods by which it was believed that they could be achieved. Weber's basic contention, however, is that although their specific goals and means might vary, all indigenous soteriologies were oriented to the same ultimate end, which Mrs Stevenson epitomises in the opening sentence of her book on Jainism: 'The desire of India is to be freed from the cycle of rebirths, and the dread of India is reincarnation.'[23] Whatever the preferred salvation technology (meditation, asceticism, orgiasticism, *bhakti*), a radical denial of the purpose of worldly redemption was common to both orthodoxy and heterodoxy. There were many movements that rejected Brahminical authority, it was not unusual that caste was

David Lockwood

regarded as irrelevant to salvation, and some sects, most notably the Lingayats, even dispensed with the doctrine of transmigration. Yet, given the direction of the basic religious interest, the goal of protest could not be to reconstitute society in accordance with some external ethical commandment, to replace caste by another form of social organisation. It was constrained rather to assume some form of what Dumont has called 'renunciation'.[24] On this point, Weber is unequivocal. As regards 'open-door castes', namely 'Jainism, Buddhism, some of the revivals of Vishnu faith in a redeemer, and the Shiva sect of Lingayat, all of which are considered absolutely heretical', his claim is that 'there is no basic difference between their sacred paths and those of orthodox Hinduism' and that none of them undermined the prestige of mystic contemplation as the highest holy path.[25] Finally, in Weber's estimation, these higher ethical currents scarcely touched the mass of the population who for the most part, as always, relied on what were essentially magical remedies against immediate distress.[26]

Although Weber's thesis of *karma*-induced fatalism has not escaped criticism, much of which concerns issues that he himself considered problematic, it is not easily dismissed as a major element in the explanation of the stability of the traditional caste system.[27] And while it is possible that the system was in certain respects more fluid than Weber thought, the results of recent anthropological and historical studies of social mobility have not removed the need to find an answer to his basic question of why the caste order remained so remarkably immune to rebellion. These studies show that, far from accepting their positions as unalterable, individuals and subcastes at most levels of the hierarchy consistently strove to elevate their ritual status, and that, where they achieved a dominant influence in terms of economic or other forms of power, such as numerical preponderance in a locality, they were generally successful in this endeavour. Although strict *karma* doctrine might have demanded undeviating conformity to the duties of immutable caste position, it is clear that aspirations for upward mobility were by no means limited to those that might legitimately be fulfilled in the next cycle of rebirth. Despite the spiritual penalty of demotion attaching to such conduct, it appears that status usurpation was endemic in the traditional caste order and, as in other systems of stratification, it was closely bound up with status incongruities stemming from shifts in the distribution of power.[28] Nevertheless, the fact remains that this mobility involved positional rather than structural change; it left the caste system intact, and was indeed a means of stabilising it.[29]

The same was true of radical sectarian protest movements that challenged orthodox beliefs and treated caste as irrelevant to salvation. Yet in this case, the way in which Weber seeks to explain how such movements were contained introduces an important qualification into his basic thesis that the stability of the social order was guaranteed by the fatalistic implications of *karma* doctrine alone. Virtually without exception, sects that sought to dissociate themselves from the caste system were, in one way or another, forced to accommodate to its boundary-maintaining ritual. Even movements that denied Brahminical authority, along with some of its most basic tenets, ended up by acquiring a quasi-caste status and undergoing internal differentiation that reproduced the main features of the wider ritual hierarchy. Of the Lingayat, which 'represented a type of particularly sharp and principled "protest" reaction to the Brahmans and the caste order', Weber notes tersely that it was 'pressed back into the caste order by the power of the environment. It did not escape again.'[30] Here Weber refers to constraints of a very different kind than those imposed by fatalistic beliefs.

When a principled anti-caste sect recruits former members of various Hindu castes and tears them away from the context of their former ritualistic duties, the caste responds by excommunicating all the sect's proselytes. Unless the sect is able to abolish the caste system altogether, instead of simply tearing away some of its members, it becomes, from the standpoint of the caste system, a quasi-guest folk, a kind of confessional guest community in an ambiguous position in the prevailing Hindu order.[31]

Generally speaking, this ambiguity was resolved, and the position of the sect determined, by the way in which its style of life accorded with orthodox ritual observances of the host society.

This line of argument raises certain doubts about the validity of Weber's basic thesis. First of all, inability 'to abolish the caste system altogether' is a very different matter from the inability to conceive of its rejection as a religiously meaningful objective. There are many reasons why the abolition of caste was not feasible, a major one being that the high degree of internal differentiation of the lower castes, together with their geographical dispersion and isolation in a myriad of what Bailey has called 'village microcosms', was a powerful obstacle to any concerted action.[32]

In posing the problem of why lower-caste rebellion was ostensibly so limited, and in seeking to explain this mainly by reference to religious factors, Weber must have assumed that the social and economic conditions impeding rebellion were not essentially different from those obtaining in other comparable societies that did experience frequent and widespread peasant revolt. But he never attempts to substantiate this very large assumption; and this omission is a serious weakness in his argument.

Another difficulty arises in connection with his claim, which is undeniable, that anti-caste movements were generally neutralised by the 'power of the environment', that is to say, by the constraint of ritual, which was the core of the religious order.[33] It is, however, essential to Weber's thesis that the observance of ritual duty was guaranteed principally through spiritual sanctions, by the beliefs in *karma* and *samsara*, 'the truly "dogmatic" doctrines of all Hinduism'.[34]

But whether radical secular protest by lower castes was stifled mainly because of their indoctrination into these beliefs is a question that is highly debatable and unlikely ever to be settled by appeal to historical evidence. To begin with, while Weber was aware that caste discipline was enforced by a whole range of material sanctions, it is possible that he underestimated the extent of their deployment, especially against the untouchables, who were in fact, if not in theory, integral to the system, and who must have formed a substantial part of those whom he considered as potentially rebellious. He probably also underestimated the extent to which economic and other forms of power not only decided ritual ranking but helped to maintain the caste system as a whole.[35] Quite apart from these considerations, it is quite impossible to know how far down the caste system the ideology of fatalism reached and with what practical effects. What slight evidence there is does not always sit easily with Weber's thesis. For example, it is by no means clear that the stability and rigidity of caste was always regularly associated with widespread belief in *karma* doctrine.[36] More importantly, the fact that anti-caste sects and movements recruited extensively from among lower castes shows that, even if *karma* doctrine was implanted in the minds of the masses, this did not make egalitarian ideas unattractive to them or prevent them from seeking to abandon their ritual duties.[37]

This last point, however, leads back once again to the strand of Weber's argument that is at once most crucial and most difficult to disprove. For if, as many experts believe, the *bhakti* movements were the major expression of lower-caste 'rebellion' against the Brahminical order, what was it that prevented them from carrying their anti-caste ideology into practice outside their own religious communities? Weber's answer is clear. What impeded them was not mainly their inability to mount a frontal attack on the caste system as a whole, or the 'power of the environment' which ritually encapsulated them.

What was decisive was that, especially insofar as these movements were anchored in, and constituted a reaction to, indigenous Hindu soteriology,[38] the nature of their rejection of caste had to be passive and accommodative, rather than active and social-revolutionary. In the last analysis, these movements were directed to the same kinds of other-worldly goals as those of the multi-faceted orthodoxy they attacked.

This, then, is Weber's 'anti-critical final word' on the Hindu ethic. From a social scientific point of view it may be less than satisfactory. In the end his thesis is not open to empirical refutation and is hedged in by many refined qualifications. Nevertheless, in its range and power, it is at the very least a theory of ideological fatalism that has no rival. And that is why so much attention has been devoted to it here.

IV

While Weber's attempt to explain the lack of revolutionary movements in traditional India must be regarded as inconclusive, it is necessary to recognise that his views on the fatalistic implications of 'Asiatic religion' relate also to China. And it is possible that the interpretations that have been put upon the significance of the Taiping rebellion provide much less unequivocal support of his thesis than any evidence that is likely to be forthcoming in the case of India. In Weber's estimation, the Taipings represented 'the most powerful and thoroughly hierocratic, politico-ethical rebellion against the Confucian administration and ethic which China had ever experienced'.[39] His opinion is shared by many contemporary Sinologists, and most emphatically by Levenson,[40] who consider that the Taipings represented a decisive break with the previous pattern of inveterate, though intra-systemic, rebelliousness.

The significance of the Taiping rebellion for Weber's thesis can only be appreciated in the context of his theory of the general nature of 'Asiatic' soteriology, the distinctive feature of which was that 'knowledge, be it literary knowledge or mystical gnosis, is finally the single absolute path to the highest holiness here and in the world beyond'.[41] The aim of this knowledge was the comprehension of an immanent and impersonal sacred order, and it generated a type of religious orientation that stood in fundamental contrast to the one that derived from the conception of a personal transcendental god whose ethical demands were in tension with the world and who had

115

David Lockwood

created man as his tool for fulfilling these demands. As Weber puts it,

None of these mass religions of Asia, however, provided the motives of orientations for a rationalized ethical patterning of the creaturely world in accordance with divine commandments. Rather, they all accepted the world as eternally given, and so the best of all possible worlds. The only choice open to the sages, who possessed the highest type of piety, was whether to accommodate themselves to the Tao, the impersonal order of the world and the only thing specifically divine, or to save themselves from the inexorable chain of causality by passing into the only eternal being, the dreamless sleep of Nirvana.[42]

This distinction is not only vital to the way in which Weber seeks to discriminate between Occidental and Asiatic soteriologies, which find their respective limits in inner-worldly asceticism and other-worldly mysticism; it also has a direct bearing upon the difference between rebellion and revolution. The usual distinction between revolutionary and rebellious movements (irrespective of their success) is that, whereas the former seek to change the entire structure of authority, the latter seek only to replace particular occupants of positions of authority.[43] If this distinction is accepted, then it is easy to see that there is a close relationship between fatalism, rebellion and the conception of the divine as an immanent principle of order. One way of defining an ideology of fatalism is to say that those who share it will be constrained to limit their social protest to rebellion. It is precisely this type of ideological constraint which Weber saw as inherent in the religions of India and China. There were differences, the most important one being that secular rebellion had a legitimate purpose within the Confucian world view, whereas in Hindu theodicy it was utterly meaningless and futile. But the revolutionary transformation of society was in both cases ruled out; it was, given the presuppositions of the belief systems, unthinkable.

The Chinese experience supports Weber's argument remarkably well. 'The Chinese have been called the most rebellious but the least revolutionary of peoples,' writes Marsh, 'even the overthrow of a dynasty did not legitimise a basic, revolutionary change in the system of stratification. It signalled, rather, a return to a traditional, ideal *status quo*, which had been outraged in the downward swing of the dynastic cycle.'[44] Moreover, what was crucial in legitimating, directing and limiting the traditional pattern of protest was the Confucian concept of 'Heaven', the impersonal and immanent cosmic order. According to Confucian orthodoxy, disturbances in this order were attributable to the rulers' ritual impropriety, and their loss of the 'mandate' of Heaven was a legitimate ground for rebellion, through which the intrinsically harmonious order could be restored. It is against this background that the Taiping revolt stands out as distinctive in its aims, and the explanation of their novelty is one that adds considerably to the credibility of Weber's thesis.

There is fairly general agreement that, in contrast with previous movements, which had pursued restorationary goals, the Taiping uprising was revolutionary. And even though it failed to put its ideas into practice, it is considered to have had a lasting and shattering effect on the structure of Confucian authority. As Levenson puts it: 'Proto-revolutionary Taiping rebels took the Confucian-imperial order out of the path of rebellions, and set it up for the unmistakable revolutionaries who were still to come.'[45] Whereas earlier rebellions had sought to replace emperors and ruling cliques through whose derelictions of ritual duty the natural social equilibrium had been disturbed, the Taipings envisaged a far-reaching transformation of social institutions, including the abolition of emperorship itself. In this way, it directly challenged the central Confucian doctrine of immanence,[46] which had hitherto survived any challenge from Taoist and Buddhist ideas that had provided fuel for rebelliousness. The source of the new, utopian element in Taiping ideology was undoubtedly exogenous, deriving from Christianity, with its conception of a personal, transcendental god and its millenary promise. Taiping ideology was naturally a syncretisation of indigenous justifications of rebellion and 'imported' Christian beliefs; but it was the latter which appear to have been decisive in switching the movement from a rebellious to a revolutionary track.[47]

This is all that Weber's thesis would require in the way of confirmation. It is therefore arguable that the nature of the entry of the Taipings into Chinese history provides much firmer evidence in support of his general theory of the religious determination of interests than any that is likely to emerge from the historical study of the caste system, or indeed from the protracted controversy over the 'protestant ethic' and the 'spirit of capitalism'. For what distinguished the Taiping uprising from previous ones was not so much a fundamental change in the social and economic setting of the movement as the extent of its ideological discontinuity. History is not a laboratory. It is, nevertheless, fairly safe to say that the social conditions that gave rise to the Taiping revolt were not basically different from those that were the occasion of previous rebellions.[48] And the obstacles to revolutionary change remained largely the same. Among them, probably the most important was the well nigh invincible position of the

David Lockwood

Confucian ruling class, who, as landlords, officials and scholars linked by extensive kinship networks, virtually monopolised major power resources.[49] In this respect, the fate of the Taipings was no different from that of any preceding rebellion. All of this, however, adds further support to Weber's thesis. He concluded that the Taiping revolt showed that 'it was not an insurmountable "natural disposition" that hindered the Chinese from producing religious structures comparable to those of the Occident'.[50] In the light of subsequent work, he might have concluded that, until the Taipings, what hindered the Chinese from producing revolutionary movements was an insurmountable system of fatalistic beliefs.

V

Weber's studies of Indian and Chinese religions come nowhere near providing incontrovertible proof that beliefs in the immanent nature of the sacred are sufficient to account for the peculiar structural stability of these societies and the distinctive forms of social protest they experienced. Such a conclusion would anyway be completely out of keeping with his general observations on the determination and effects of religious interests.[51] Nevertheless, his work still stands as the most thoroughgoing analysis of the 'ethics of fatalism'. It is ironic then that, although his studies of comparative religion are so highly esteemed by normative functionalists, their relevance to the Durkheimian theory of order has largely been ignored. For if the foregoing arguments have any substance, Weber's studies of 'Asiatic' religion provide grounds for thinking that the concept of fatalism, far from being an obscure afterthought deserving of no more than its relegation to a footnote of *Suicide,* is in fact the key to a completely different solution of the problem of order than the one Durkheim has been credited with. Most importantly, Weber's work shows that if any precise meaning is to be attached to the idea of moral despotism this can only be discovered through an analysis of the ideological constraints inherent in the structures of specific belief systems. This kind of enquiry has not been central in the theory of order and conflict propounded by Durkheim and elaborated by his successors. The neglect of it is one main reason why fatalism remains Durkheim's hidden theory of order.[52]

Work histories, career strategies and the class structure

RICHARD BROWN

Introduction

The division of labour is a central element in the social structure of any society.[1] In industrial societies like our own, discussion of the division of labour usually focusses on the occupational structure, and occupational categories of a more or less carefully demarcated kind are used as the basic building blocks both for the presentation of descriptive accounts of social conditions and for the analysis of such features of a society as class structure and social mobility. Such a focus is not entirely satisfactory; it tends, for example, to obscure the social function of those without a gainful occupation,[2] such as housewives and students, and to lead to the neglect of other basic components in any analysis of class situation, such as property ownership. Nevertheless the relative accessibility of occupational information, and the existence of well-known and widely accepted ways of classifying it, make possible a whole range of studies which would be much more complex to undertake without such a simplified basis for comparison.

Indeed the importance of occupation as a 'variable' derives from the fact that for the majority of the population in an industrial society their occupation (or the occupation of parent, spouse or some other source of material support) is the major determinant of their life chances. Class situation cannot be regarded as synonymous with occupation but analyses of class structure, from widely different theoretical perspectives, necessarily give occupation a central place. Similarly those who have attempted to investigate and analyse values and beliefs, 'world views', 'images of society' or class consciousness, have also tended to concentrate on comparisons of occupational categories.[3]

The inescapability of some use of occupational categories in a wide range of sociological work cannot conceal the far from unproblematic nature of such categories. This is reflected in the major changes in standard classifications of occupations for census purposes since 1951, and, with the exception of the 1980 classification, their incompatibility with the classification used for some other official purposes such as the New Earnings Survey. It is highly improbable that all of these changes are due to developments in the occupational structure itself. The problematic nature of occupational classifications is reflected even more clearly in the construction of quite separate original schemes for the social grading of occupations by three research groups working on social stratification and social mobility in Britain during the 1970s, and the further modification of one of those schemes by a fourth such group.[4]

In the light of these obvious difficulties and disagreements about how best to categorise occupations it might seem cavalier to raise further demands. Nevertheless, as some of those engaged in such research themselves have remarked, most analyses of the occupational structure are cross-sectional; they consider occupations at one point in time and take no account of the fact that any one individual may occupy a succession of positions in the division of labour – a succession which forms a 'work history' or, possibly, a 'career'. Any exploration of the concomitants and significance of occupational categories should therefore take into account the varying past and future work histories of those in the category at any one time if it is to be fully satisfactory. Such past and potential future work histories are likely to be particularly important for an understanding of the meaning of an occupation to its holder and of the influence of occupational position and milieu on values and beliefs.

The importance of 'work history'

The most obvious reason for considering work histories arises from the fact that in a significant number of cases employees may be in jobs which they do not regard as their 'real' occupation. As Bechhofer points out:

. . . workers in certain skilled trades will continue to refer to themselves as in the trade even when doing other work . . .

Clearly, the fact that a man continues to refer to himself by his original skill, even when employed in other work, is important because it says something about his 'self-image'. For some types of analysis the possession of a skill, even if it is not being used, may be more important than the performance of a particular job at the time of enquiry. For these reasons it may well be important to collect a job-history.[5]

And he wisely goes on to warn: 'analysing job histories is far from easy . . .'. Such a discrepancy between current occupations and what respondents regarded as their 'main' jobs was indeed apparent in research by the author and colleagues in three areas of Newcastle upon Tyne. Many men claimed a different 'main line of work' from their current occupation, and even more had experienced considerable job, occupational and industrial mobility.[6]

There are, however, more central reasons for investigating work histories, as two recent studies have stressed. In reporting what was essentially a cross-sectional study of social mobility, in which the collection of work history information had a subsidiary role, Goldthorpe also drew attention to the deficiencies of such a cross-sectional approach and the desirability of using work history data, and went on to suggest that certain types of work history may be discernible from such data.

> . . . adopting a diachronic or biographical perspective on mobility produces a very different picture from that derived from the synchronic, cross-sectional view of a conventional mobility table . . .
> Our work history data . . . show that a wide diversity exists in the actual routes and sequences of worklife movement that men have followed even between similar origins and destinations. Thus, these data must serve to undermine the idea of there being, as some writers have suggested, a 'normal career curve' by reference to which the interpretation of cross-sectional data might be aided. It is true that our findings would suggest that certain relatively well-defined types of worklife 'trajectory' could be specified; but whether it would be possible to assimilate the mobility experience of the population at large to some manageable number of such types is a question which here at least, we must leave in doubt.[7]

Goldthorpe emphasises particularly the importance of taking account of work histories in the case of those in 'intermediate class' positions, because 'men in such positions . . . have a relatively high propensity to be mobile from them'.[8] It was in conjunction with an examination of the class situation of one such intermediate-class grouping, clerical workers, that Stewart and his colleagues made what is perhaps the strongest assertion of the importance of work history data in research on stratification. They argued that 'Occupational categories, as conventionally defined, may contain people with a diversity of statuses', and went on to point out that 'people become clerks under diverse circumstances'. In analysing the occupational identities of clerks they found it necessary to distinguish between those who entered such employment relatively early in their working life, the majority of whom were in due course promoted, leaving a minority of relative failures; and those who entered white-collar work later,

Richard Brown

after considerable experience of manual work. The position of clerk has quite different significance for young clerks and the two types of older clerk. They argued, therefore, that it is necessary to 'separate individuals and jobs and give a more coherent account of the relationship between them', and suggested that 'the very question "what is the class position of clerks?" is invalid, because "clerks" does not define a meaningful reality in stratification terms'.[9]

Recent research, therefore, has given rise to influential voices calling attention to the importance of work history information. But the importance of recording and analysing 'work histories' or 'careers' for an understanding of the division of labour and the class structure in industrial societies has in fact been advocated over a long period. To take two examples: Form and Miller in a paper published in 1948 distinguished 'modal career patterns' and related them to both social origins and security and insecurity in employment;[10] and just over a decade later Wilensky lamented:

The volume of writing about careers is large. There is uncommon agreement that types and rate of mobility are crucial to an understanding of modern society. And there are hints that work-life mobility may be more fateful than intergeneration mobility. It is therefore remarkable that detailed work histories which cover a decade or more have been reported in only about a dozen studies, and have been related to other sociological variables in still fewer. Limited as the few systematic studies of job histories are, they leave no doubt that modern adult life imposes frequent shifts between jobs, occupations, employers and work-places, and that these moves involve status passage which is momentous for both the person and the social structure.[11]

The failure to respond to the pleas made so clearly for more than thirty years[12] may be partly explained by the very considerable practical difficulties of securing adequate work history information and the even more intractable conceptual and technical problems in analysing it when it has been collected. Even if the aim is the modest one of securing largely 'factual' information about the succession of occupations experienced by a sample of respondents, and (perhaps) also about some of the considerations and contingencies which influenced movement between occupational positions, the collection of such information can become very complex. A number of studies have shown, however, that with care such data collection problems can be overcome, and overcome for the relatively large sample sizes needed to accommodate the variety of occupational experiences which are a major reason why work history information is wanted in the first place.[13]

The more difficult problems relate to the analysis of such data. Certain uses are relatively straightforward: one can, for example, extract information about the first or previous jobs of those currently in clerical work, as Stewart and colleagues did, so as to distinguish different types within the category of clerk; or one can identify those cases where respondents had been out of work for more than a month during the previous year, whether or not this period was continuous, in order to distinguish the 'sub-employed' from the 'employed' and the 'long-term unemployed', as Norris did in a study which obtained work history information for the previous five years.[14] It is much more difficult to examine the work histories as wholes and to establish types of patterns, yet this is often desirable if full use is to be made of the information for the more general exploration and explanation of other characteristics such as attitudes and values, or occupational identities.

Carr-Hill and Macdonald have provided a very full and expert account of the problems and some possible solutions. Like a number of others they have used graphical techniques to display the incidence and range of occupational movement, over a given grading of occupations, related to age and/or calendar years. Such graphs can also be related to particular events in the lives of the subjects or in the wider society.[15] They reveal very vividly the varying degrees of 'order' or 'disorder' in the work histories of any sub-group selected for examination, but they do not answer the more basic questions of which sub-groups to select nor provide a clear indication of whether the whole range of work histories could be contained within a typology which could make the use of such information in subsequent analysis more easily possible.

In the remainder of this paper I shall suggest some considerations which might enter into the construction of such typologies, and attempt to show from the literature and from research in which I am currently involved, the value of studies of work history patterns.

Types of work history

So far the advocacy in this paper of the importance of work histories in a wide range of research has been largely in terms of their utility in understanding otherwise inexplicable empirical findings. There are, however, more fundamental reasons for considering work histories of importance and it is from these that one can derive a basis for devising an initial typology of work histories.

Work histories focus attention on one of the areas of social life where there is an interaction between individual decision and action and social structural opportunity and constraint; and where the outcome of such interaction has important consequences for both individual and society. 'Choice' or 'loss' of a job, for example, can radically affect individual identity; the movement of individuals into and between occupations has important consequences for employing organisations, occupational associations, and class formation.

This centrality of the notion of work history is clearly expressed in the well-known discussion by Goffman of the concept of career.

One value of the concept of career is its two-sidedness. One side is linked to internal matters held dearly and closely, such as image of self and felt identity; the other side concerns official position, jural relations, and style of life, and is part of a publicly accessible institutional complex. The concept of career, then, allows one to move back and forth between the personal and the public, between self and its significant society . . .[16]

In considering work histories as the outcome of such processes we must initially consider the *resources* which any individual brings to the world of work. Such considerations provide a clear link with conventional analyses of class structure.[17] Individuals may possess, or be able to acquire, material resources ('property') which enable them to avoid entering the labour market at all; their work history is that of the 'self-employed' (in its broadest sense), owning their means of production, however minimal, providing goods or services directly to customers, and perhaps employing others. Those who are propertyless, however, may nevertheless have resources which give them some greater or lesser 'market capacity' – educational qualifications, professional certification, manual work skills, valued work experience, and so on. Such capacities typically offer the prospect of more desirable work and generally of advancement in work to more skilled and/or responsible positions. Those with such skills can in principle be distinguished from those with nothing but their labour power to sell (though work histories show that that can, in practice, cover quite a wide range of differing 'resources' or 'market capacities' and consequently of opportunities for employment). Thus, in general, we would expect to find work histories differentiated as between the 'propertied' and the 'non-propertied', and within the latter, and very much larger, category, in terms of varying market capacities.

Resources may constrain choices and actions by individuals in seeking work but they do not necessarily determine them. An understanding of work histories involves also taking account of the predispositions, preferences and expectations of the individuals concerned, and such considerations provide a link with another body of literature, that concerned with such *orientations to work*.[18] Orientations to work have, of course, been categorised in a bewildering variety of ways. What is most important for present purposes are the expectations and preferences of the individual with reference to the succession of employment (or self-employment) over time. Such expectations and preferences will influence the *strategy* they adopt in the labour market, and may well lead to different strategies being pursued by those who have comparable resources.

A basic distinction must be between those who expect and seek some form of advancement during their working life, who are oriented towards a 'career', and those who have no such expectations. Neither category is necessarily homogeneous, however. Those oriented towards a career can be subdivided into those who seek and expect advancement within an employing organisation and therefore pursue an 'organisational' strategy, and those whose expectations of advancement depend on using their skills and qualifications to move from employer to employer and who therefore pursue an 'occupational' strategy. Such strategies are, of course, best considered as ideal types in terms of which a more varied pattern of work histories may be understood.

Such orientations and the strategies to which they give rise do not emerge independently of resources nor in isolation from the structure of opportunities. The links between them have been clearly established in Ashton's work on the development of different frames of reference among young male workers.[19] He has argued that children are allocated – primarily on the basis of supposed ability – to different streams or channels in the educational system. These channels offer differing possibilities of securing educational qualifications, resources which will provide access to jobs at different levels in the labour market. At the same time, in passing through these channels and acquiring these resources, the individuals concerned develop self-images and orientations to work which are appropriate for the eventual occupational opportunities to which the channels lead. Ashton distinguished three main types of opportunity, each with an appropriate frame of reference: 'middle-class careers' which 'provide the highest and most secure incomes as a reward for those who are successful in climbing a relatively lengthy career ladder'; 'working-class careers' which 'provide the possibility of training' in skilled manual work 'and of moving up one or two steps on the career ladder'; and careerless occupations which offer immediate rewards but little or no chance of promotion or advancement.[20] Such a typology was 'not intended to be exhaustive';[21] further types and subtypes may be discernible, but they too could be expected to reflect the ways in which self-images and orientations are acquired in the

Richard Brown

process of passing through the educational system and into work, and are influenced by available resources and opportunities.

On the basis of our consideration of differences between individuals in their resources and orientations we can suggest that there may be four ideal typical strategies underlying individual choices and actions in relation to work and employment: the 'entrepreneurial', where resources are such that self-employment is possible; the 'organisational' and the 'occupational', for those who seek a career with advancement in work on the basis of skills, qualifications and experience, but differ as to whether this is sought primarily within one employing organisation or by movement between them; and the 'careerless', for those expecting only or mainly immediate rewards from work, though their priorities as between different combinations of such immediate rewards may vary considerably. Such strategies, however, are not formulated in isolation from the *structure of opportunities*.[22]

In a society like our own the opportunities still exist to establish one's own business and thereby escape the status of employee altogether. It is conventionally agreed that such opportunities have been greatly reduced since earlier periods of capitalist development, because of the increasing domination of the economy by large corporations, the growth of the public sector, and so on. Indeed, in recent years there have been officially promoted efforts to reverse these trends and increase the opportunities for small business. Some such opportunities, however restricted, to establish or acquire one's own business, must exist for the entrepreneurial strategy to be possible.

The other strategies must be related to opportunities in the labour market. Labour markets are clearly fragmented and divided in various ways, but the most useful distinction for present purposes is that between 'internal' and 'external' labour markets.[23] The growth of large-scale organisations, in both the private and the public sector, which has restricted opportunities for 'entrepreneurs', has also provided the conditions for internal labour markets. Employees can be recruited through one or more entry points into the organisation and then offered the prospect of a career moving up the hierarchy to better rewarded and more prestigious positions. In the ideal typical case all such posts are filled by internal promotion, and employees are offered long-term security of employment even if not certain advancement. In contrast smaller employers, large organisations without such internal labour markets, and industries characterised by casual or fluctuating employment, recruit in some sector or sectors of the external labour market, do not necessarily offer long-term security, and do not prefer internal promotion over recruitment to higher status positions from outside the organisation. Clearly there is a congruence between an 'organisational' career strategy and the internal labour market, and an 'occupational' career strategy and the external labour market, though this should not be taken to imply that in practice the pursuit of such strategies will necessarily restrict individuals to considering only certain types of labour market opportunity.

The careerless are also faced by both internal and external labour markets, and as a result of their paucity of resources they may be in no position to choose what strategy to pursue. Certainly some workers become trapped within internal labour markets and are consequently 'employer dependent';[24] whilst others are unwillingly forced to seek work in the external labour market with increasing risks of sub-employment.[25] Chance and constraint play a larger part in the work histories of those without resources than for others. It is nevertheless possible to suggest that actual work histories for the 'careerless' do display differences which reflect choices as between stability of employment and the pursuit of opportunities in the external labour market; this will be explored further in the final section of the paper.

Types of middle-class careers

In the final sections of the paper I wish to discuss, first, how far the typology I have suggested is congruent with certain published studies which have developed comparable categories, and, secondly, whether it is helpful for the analysis and understanding of the work histories of manual workers, which have so far had far less attention. In assessing the utility of some such typology of work histories as the one I have outlined, it can be suggested that two related conditions should be met if a claim is to be sustained that investigating and analysing work histories is not only possible and interesting but also important: that those with similar occupational titles or in the same occupational category can be shown to differ in systematic ways with regard to their work histories; and that those in the same category who have such differences in their work histories also differ in other important respects, such as with regard to occupational identity, attitudes towards employer or union, or more generally in their images of society. Though the evidence is far from conclusive, it does provide some support for both parts of the claim.

All the empirical work I shall consider, both in published studies and from our own research, relates to men.[26] The majority of those

127

studies which have tried systematically to record and analyse work histories have been concerned with those who have, in some sense, pursued careers. One such grouping to attract a lot of attention is that of business leaders. Bendix, for example, distinguished three types of business leader in terms of their routes to the top: 'heirs . . . who have inherited considerable wealth and, hence, have come to control a firm either through direct legacy or through purchase'; 'entrepreneurs' 'who start firms of their own at some point in their careers'; and bureaucrats whose careers 'tend to show a succession of salaried jobs, which lead to an executive post'.[27] Erikson, in a study of 'industrialists' in the steel and hosiery industries, used a similar typology; she distinguished the 'independent' careers of those who founded or helped to found a firm; those whose major work was in their father's firm; 'salaried administrators' whose careers were primarily as employees and who reached the top by virtue of executive experience rather than investment; and those who had spent most of their lives practising an independent profession.[28]

These types do appear to coincide with those suggested in the previous section. 'Entrepreneurs' and 'independents', and those who inherit control of a business, have pursued an entrepreneurial strategy, though, as Bendix notes, such a strategy may be preceded by considerable periods of time as an employee when it is by no means certain that the career will eventually be that of an entrepreneur.[29] 'Bureaucrats' or 'salaried administrators' have pursued organisational career strategies, and 'professionals' occupational ones.

Career patterns and orientations have also been investigated in strata below the very top. Particularly influential has been Gouldner's analysis of the 'latent social roles' of 'cosmopolitans' and 'locals'; the former are 'low on loyalty to employing organisation, high on commitment to specialised role skills, and likely to use an outer reference group orientation', whilst the latter have the opposite set of attributes.[30] Cosmopolitans are oriented towards an occupational career strategy, and locals towards an organisational one. This or a closely parallel distinction underlies much of the discussion in the literature of the different relations to their employing organisations and different career lines, of bureaucrats and professionals, line and staff, managers and scientists.[31] The needs of large-scale organisations for expertise of various kinds create opportunities for those with the appropriate qualifications and abilities to pursue occupationally oriented career strategies which are different from those of 'organisation men' in that they have 'a labor-market status which applies to a wide range of organisations defended by professional associations, while bureaucrats are more oriented to particular organisations'.[32]

In many cases, of course, those pursuing organisationally oriented career strategies have different occupational titles from the professionals and 'experts', though they are generally placed within the same groupings once occupational categories are aggregated in any way. In some cases, however, those with the same fairly narrowly defined occupational title clearly have different orientations. Gouldner's cosmopolitans and locals, for example, were all teachers or administrators in a liberal arts college; and a study of scientists in or entering industry showed clear differences in orientations and career strategy between those who wished to pursue a career in scientific research and those who were using their scientific qualifications as the basis for an administrative career.[33]

The question of whether those who have reached positions of business leadership by different routes will have different values and goals has aroused considerable controversy. The argument for difference has been put most strongly by the 'managerialists', but this has been questioned, on both theoretical and empirical grounds.[34] More clearly established were the differences between cosmopolitans and locals with regard to both actions (participation) and attitudes (towards student behaviour), though a replication of the study in a British context was altogether more inconclusive.[35] The absence of more decisive findings relating career patterns to attitudes and values should not perhaps be found surprising in the light of the mixed results of similar studies of the socially mobile.[36]

The evidence from Stewart and his colleagues' discussion of the class situation of clerks is, however, rather more substantial. They differentiated types of career on a different basis from that suggested here. However, they were able to show that among clerks aged 35 and over there were significant differences in attitudes to management (the white-collar group who have failed to gain promotion have generally more aggressive attitudes towards their own management than the ex-manual workers), and in what they termed 'society unionateness' (the ex-manual workers were significantly more likely to identify with the working class.)[37] In this case, differences in work histories for those in the same occupation were clearly and meaningfully related to differences in attitudes and values.

Richard Brown

Working-class work histories

The majority of manual workers lack the resources and the opportunities to pursue a career. They are unlikely, therefore, to be concerned with strategies for advancement in work and to have such strategies reflected in the pattern of their work history; to a much greater extent their opportunities for employment are determined for them by others, rather than chosen by themselves (especially when overall levels of unemployment are high). Their work histories are in general rightly labelled 'careerless' and they frequently appear 'disorderly'. Nevertheless it is important to consider how far such work histories are patterned and may be considered as constituting distinct types; and to ask whether individuals with different resources and orientations do pursue differing strategies (perhaps giving priority to the more modest goals of stability and job security rather than to advancement).

Norris's work provides some important evidence.[38] He found that in Sunderland in 1972–3 those who were sub-employed (had experienced four weeks unemployment during the previous twelve months) could be divided into three main groups in terms of their work history over the previous five years. Nearly half of the sub-employed (but a majority of all workers) were *stable;* they tended to be older, to have experienced a single period of long-term unemployment, and to suffer from ill-health or disability; a (basically organisational) strategy of seeking work stability had been upset by job loss, and age and disability then made it difficult to obtain any sort of employment. Secondly, a small group of the sub-employed (and an even smaller proportion of all workers) were *employer changers;* they had remained in the same occupation but had changed their employers three or more times in five years. This represented a strategy of deliberate movement within a particular sector of the labour market seeking higher earnings and/or variety of work experience. Such an (essentially occupational) strategy becomes less successful with age and a decline in physical capacities, and with falling demands for their particular skill; and it is anyway subject to high risk of redundancy. Finally, a large minority of the sub-employed (but a smaller proportion of all workers) were *unstable,* changing occupation and employer. Their situation was not so much due to pursuing a labour market strategy which had failed as to being unable to pursue any coherent strategy at all because of the scarcity of secure jobs. Despite being younger, they had in particular been unable to obtain any foothold in employing organisations with internal labour markets, and displayed 'the almost "classic" symptoms of the dual labour market theorists' secondary workers; low pay, frequent job changing, no occupational or industrial identity, a high rate of redundancy, a high rate of recurrent unemployment and a high occurrence of erratic and downward skill mobility'.[39]

In the course of a survey of all the households in an inner city area in Newcastle upon Tyne carried out in 1977, a colleague and I obtained details of the work histories of 189 men, all of those interviewed who were economically active.[40] Information, as complete as possible, about each job and about periods of unemployment, as well as a great deal of other data, was obtained for the whole period from 1945, or the date of starting work if later. These data have been analysed using cluster analysis techniques to search for distinctive patterns of employment and labour market experience in the individual case records.[41] Clustering techniques permit a large number of separate attributes to be considered simultaneously and produce a varying number of more or less homogeneous clusters. Care has to be exercised in using such techniques, because the number of clusters chosen for examination is fairly arbitrary, and their nature and composition may not be stable. On the basis of several trials, however, each using different combinations of variables, certain clusters, each with the same core composition, could be clearly identified. These eight work history patterns covered the experience of just over half the men; the remaining men's work histories did not appear to fit neatly into any one of these patterns.

The first type consisted of those, all aged under 40, who had some sort of educational qualification, had left school (often a selective secondary school) after the minimum school leaving age, and who had a record of stable employment in most cases in routine white-collar work. This category of *stable white-collar workers* included about 6% of the respondents.

Secondly, there was a small number, also all aged under 40 and mostly with educational qualifications gained by staying on at school, who had had a relatively large number of short-term jobs in a wide variety of occupations and industries, including experience of routine white-collar work. This grouping of mostly *unstable white-collar workers* included less than 3% of the respondents and they had all had some experience of unemployment.

Thirdly, there were those, many but not all aged under 40, who had left non-selective schools at the minimum leaving age and without educational qualifications; they had a record of very stable employment in skilled manual work and in many cases qualifications derived from an apprenticeship. Their work experience had been solely confined to jobs, and in many cases the same occupation, in the Registrar-General's Socio-Economic Group 9 ('skilled manual work'), and within one or two industries. These *stable skilled manual workers* comprised 10% of respondents.

Fourthly, and in contrast to the third type, there was a smaller grouping of men, mostly aged less than 40, and mostly without any educational qualifications or advantages, who also had had a lot of experience of skilled manual work. In the case of this cluster, however, there had been frequent change of jobs, and to a lesser extent of industries and occupations; all of them had had work which could be classified in more than one socio-economic group; many of them had worked in the construction industry at some stage. In contrast to the first and third types, the men in this grouping of *unstable skilled manual workers*, which comprised 4% of all respondents, had experienced a good deal of unemployment, including long-term unemployment of more than six months.

The fifth and largest cluster consisted of older men, mostly over 40, whose distinguishing characteristic was their job stability. Typically they had three or four jobs involving two or three distinct occupations (and bringing them within two socio-economic groups) in two or three different industries; but in almost all cases they had remained in those jobs for five years or more on average. They had no apparent special skills or qualifications, but these *older stable non-skilled manual workers*, nearly 12% of those interviewed, had the lowest incidence of unemployment.

Sixthly, and in sharp contrast to the fifth type, there was a cluster of mostly older men whose distinguishing characteristic was their job, occupational and industrial instability: they had had more jobs, for shorter periods of time, involving three or more different industries. Although many of them had held jobs classified as skilled (S.E.G.9), they were without educational or any other qualifications. This grouping of *older unstable unskilled manual workers*, about 7% of the respondents, had also experienced relatively high rates of unemployment – including recurrent and long-term unemployment – of redundancy, of illness and of low paid work.

The seventh cluster also consisted of unstable men, but younger – mostly aged under 40, without qualifications of any kind, whose work experience included a great deal of mobility between jobs, occupations and industries, but very little experience of skilled manual work. This small grouping of *younger unskilled and unstable workers* (less than 3% of respondents) could be said to have the worst record so far as unemployment was concerned; all of them had had some experience of unemployment and the incidence of long-term unemployment was the highest of all for this group.

Finally, there were those, mostly still in their teens, whose employment record did not show any great degree of instability for the simple reason that they had either never been employed or had only had one or two jobs during their relatively short period in the labour market. All of these *teenage unemployed*, who comprised 8% of those interviewed, had some experience of unemployment, in many cases long term; a few had never worked at all.

The area within which this research project was carried out was chosen because it was known to be deprived, with a highly mobile population suffering from above-average levels of unemployment and low paid work. Our respondents, therefore, could be expected to have 'disorderly' work histories and the finding that certain types can nevertheless be distinguished adds support to the claim that working-class work histories can be seen to be patterned in meaningful ways. The types which have been outlined differ from each other in respect of two main considerations: their resources or 'market capacities' (educational qualifications and occupational skills), and the stability of their employment record. The first two clusters contain those with educational qualifications which appear to have been a basis for undertaking non-manual work; the next two contain those with qualifications or claims to perform skilled manual work; and the remaining four for the most part contain those with only their labour power to sell. The differences within these broad skill groupings are between those who have pursued (or been able to pursue) a labour market strategy which gave priority to job stability and those who did not. It is not possible to say, on the basis of evidence currently available, how far the unstable work histories resulted from 'choice' or from 'constraint'. In the case of the older unstable unskilled workers (group 6) there is some evidence in their experience of illness and redundancy that the pattern may have been forced on them rather than chosen. The clusters of unstable white-collar and skilled manual workers (2 and 4) on the other hand appear likely to contain some who, like the 'employer changers' distinguished by Norris, had chosen to move from job to job in search of higher pay or variety of work; and there is little doubt that the stable white-collar and skilled manual workers (1 and 3) could have changed jobs more frequently so that their relatively stable work histories must result from deliberate choice.

The types of work history related clearly to aspects of the respon-

Richard Brown

Table 1. *Class struggle?*

'Do you think that there is a class struggle in Britain at the present time?'

	N	Yes	No	Don't know
		%	%	%
Cluster				
1. Stable white-collar	12	33	50	17
2. Unstable white-collar	5	100	—	—
3. Stable skilled manual	19	37	42	21
4. Unstable skilled manual	8	63	13	25
5. Stable unskilled	22	32	45	23
6. Older unstable unskilled	13	69	31	—
7. Younger unskilled	5	80	20	—
8. Teenage unemployed	15	47	13	40
TOTAL	99	48	32	19

dents' then current employment situation. This is not surprising but nevertheless indicates how those who are nominally within the same occupational and 'class' groupings can be significantly differentiated in terms of their work histories. Current unemployment, for example, was highest for teenagers (8) and the younger unskilled and unstable workers (7) amounting to three quarters or more in the cluster in each case; in contrast only one or two of those in the three stable clusters (1, 3 and 5) were unemployed at the time of interview. Among those in work the incidence of low pay (having earnings in the lowest 10% of all earnings in the region at the time) was most frequent for the unstable unskilled workers, older and younger (6 and 7). These two groupings and the teenage unemployed also scored highest on a composite index of multiple deprivation which was developed during the project.

The interviews during which the work history data were obtained were not primarily intended to explore the attitudes or values of respondents. They did, however, include a few questions of this type and two of them provide some evidence of a relationship between work history patterns and attitudes. During a short series of questions on political and social issues respondents were asked to comment on 'Do you think there is a class struggle in Britain at the present time?' and their overall opinions are recorded in Table 1. Though the numbers are small it is clear that those with stable work history patterns whatever their skill level, were less likely than those with

Table 2. *The future?*

'Over the next five years would you expect things to be better, about the same, or worse?'

	N	Better	About the same	Worse	Don't know
		%	%	%	%
1. Stable white-collar	12	58	17	25	—
2. Unstable white-collar	5	100	—	—	—
3. Stable skilled manual	19	53	21	5	21
4. Unstable skilled manual	8	37½	12½	37½	12½
5. Stable unskilled	22	23	14	55	9
6. Older unstable unskilled	13	38	15	38	8
7. Younger unskilled	5	60	40	—	—
8. Teenage unemployed	15	40	20	33	7
TOTAL	99	44	17	29	9

unstable patterns to agree that there is 'a class struggle'; and this was not only the case overall but also for each of the first three pairs of clusters considered individually, pairs of clusters between which the skill level of work experience has been roughly comparable.

Earlier in the interview, in the context of questions about their standard of living, respondents were asked to assess their future over the next five years; the pattern of replies, shown in Table 2, was rather different. In the case of this question 'optimism' was associated with skill and younger age groups; indeed the most 'pessimistic' was the older group of 'stable unskilled', who were perhaps realistically aware that their strategy of pursuing job security would become increasingly difficult with advancing years.

Despite obvious weaknesses these findings provide grounds for thinking that further and more sensitive exploration of the relationship between work history patterns and attitudes and values could be rewarding. The types of work history make good intuitive sense; it would be desirable to develop techniques which retain more of the sequential relationship of the events which form the data for a work history; and, most important, more knowledge and understanding is needed of the actors' priorities and choices in the labour market as they saw them in retrospect if not at the time. In this connection, but of more general relevance too, it would be important to explore the nature of respondents' occupational identities and the way these change in the light of the intended and unintended features of their work histories. It will be possible to pursue some of these issues in our current research.

Conclusion

Changes in occupational structure are the subject of frequent comment and much scholarly attention. The literature on careers is extensive, though mostly relating to fairly narrow, organisationally or occupationally defined, milieux. Major recent contributions have greatly advanced our knowledge and understanding of social mobility, including work-life mobility. But a focus on work histories, in addition to rather than in place of these other types of enquiry, involves exploration of patterns of stability and movement within and between occupations, and between occupational, organisational or labour market settings, including movement which is not conventionally recorded as occupational or social mobility or regarded as a career. It also raises the question of the ways in which occupations and groupings of occupations are differentiated in terms of the typical work history patterns of those who fill them. And such a focus, I have suggested, necessarily draws on work on class situations, orientations to work and the labour market. It therefore contributes significantly to our understanding of two of the central theoretical issues in sociology: the articulation of social action and social structure, and the relationship between social location and social consciousness.

Gender inequality and class formation

SHEILA ALLEN

To write a paper on women and class structure raises many problems, not least of which is that it is likely to be so negative towards the discipline that for a convinced sociologist the experience is a particularly ambivalent one. The subject forces me to be very critical of the sociological endeavour, which Ilya Neustadt believes in so firmly and which he has done so much to promote among many generations of students and colleagues. In his elegantly constructed and presented Inaugural Lecture, *Teaching Sociology,* delivered in October 1964, he made many points, as pertinent today as they were then.[1] I shall select only one, in which he quotes Westermarck's observation made in 1907: 'Anyone who takes up the study of sociology must not expect to come to an exhibition, where every article may be had ready and finished. On the contrary, he will find that he has entered a workshop, where everything is in the making – and he will have to take part in the work.'[2]

Studies of class inequality and its relation to the division of labour have been central themes in Western sociology since Westermarck made this point, yet those who endeavour to analyse women's position in the class structure enter a workshop which is lamentably ill-equipped for the task. There are few tools but, more important, little recognition that the task requires even burnished tools let alone freshly fashioned ones. In other words, there is little acknowledgement in the literature about class structure that gender divisions have important consequences for class relations and class action.

Mainstream analyses of the class structure have been impervious to one of the major divisions of labour, that between men and women in respect of the rearing of children and the servicing of members of households. This division has until recently been accorded the status of a natural order, not to be questioned, rather than a socially constructed set of relations in need of investigation and explanation.

137

Following from this, stratification theories including theories of class (whatever other theoretical differences they incorporate) have been constructed in such a way as to treat as marginal over half the population, and failing even to recognise them when they belong to the wage-earning population. This neglect is an interesting sociological phenomenon in itself and one which has given rise to considerable comment over the last decade. But an explanation of it must await analyses which go beyond an acknowledgement of the subordination of one gender by the other, to the processes of social and class formation through which this subordination develops, varies historically and culturally and is perpetuated. In other words, the phenomenon itself must be treated sociologically.

During the last decade, however, there has grown a new awareness in sociology of the fact that women are part of social relations as well as men. There have been papers deploring their regular exclusion, both from theory and empirical work – highlighting the conceptual blindness of sociology which makes it inadequate to explain the ordering and changing of social relations. But the initial excitement has to some extent evaporated; the relatively naïve assumption of the middle seventies – that, having pointed out the gaps and some of the fundamental flaws of a sociology which 'forgot' gender divisions, moves would be made towards creating a paradigmatic shift – has proved to be largely groundless. A certain tedium now surrounds attempts to raise the question again, or to pursue it in one or other field of sociological enquiry. Teaching texts, research monographs and major analytical essays are still published which give little, if any, serious attention to the sociological questions raised by these challenges but which nonetheless claim to deal with the major concerns of contemporary sociology and society.[3]

This does not mean that nothing has been achieved. A great deal of work now exists about gender divisions, and in this one must include the work of anthropologists, social and economic historians, economists, and historical demographers, as well as sociologists, which has opened up, frequently in a challenging way, areas which were considered unproblematical in the sociology of ten or fifteen years ago. It is not possible in one short paper to review this literature or to tackle many of the aspects of class analysis upon which it has a bearing. I shall therefore discuss two problems. Both are crucial to our understanding of class relations, though they are treated within sociology largely as separate fields. This is because the development of the discipline has been located in an intellectual culture which characterises 'as general, universal, unrelated to a particular position or a particular sex as its source or standpoint, [what is] in fact partial, limited, located in a particular position and permeated by special interests and concerns'.[4]

The first of the two problems stems from the fact that class theory has been based on unexamined conceptions of the family which give rise to the interrelated assumptions that (a) the family is the unit of class and is therefore the most useful and adequate unit of analysis, (b) that women – particularly, but not only, married women – derive their class position (and their status) from their male kin, (c) that women are dependent in critical respects on men. A discussion of the adequacy of this conceptualisation must examine it in the light of the questions raised in recent work on the history and sociology of the family and the existing information on household composition and relations. This will enable us to evaluate the types of generalisation, perpetuated by theories based on these assumptions, which are incorporated into many aspects of sociology.

The second of the two problems is the use of occupation as the major index of class position. This raises theoretical questions of some significance in its own right. However, in this paper the main focus will be on the implications of such analyses for an understanding of the division of labour in relation to class, taking into account gender.

Households and marriage

The relations within households (families) and their articulation with the structuring of production relations, as well as those of distribution and exchange, are analytically some of the most difficult areas of contemporary sociology. They are also arguably the most significant in terms of relating gender and class. Certainly, the assumption that the family is the most appropriate unit for stratification analyses has been criticised in terms of status approaches, in terms of a feminist–materialist approach to class, and in terms of official statistics, among others.[5] But it remains one of the most resistant to change. If we are to include women, the relevance of family history to the social division of labour and to questions of class and status cannot be doubted. Specifically, it holds out an encouraging prospect for developing a more adequate understanding of the incorporation of gender divisions into the contemporary social and class formations.

The field of family history has grown remarkably over the past two decades and its challenge to many sociological generalisations about the relations between family forms and processes and the development of industrial society has been noted.[6] Yet this work on family

139

histories has so far not been incorporated into the principal class analyses. Nor, to any great extent, has use been made of the insights from historical and comparative work, which alert us, among other issues, to the distinctions between family and household. While the family, when used as the unit of class analysis, obscures and universalises relations between men and women, the issues become a great deal clearer if the household as a unit of shared productive, reproductive and consumption relations linking men and women into the 'external' social formations is considered.[7] For the forms which households take cannot be understood apart from both the ideological constructions of kinship and family, and in terms of the differential linkages of members to the broader socio-economic context. Undoubtedly, there are, certain problems with the data on contemporary households.[8] Nevertheless, the official picture is one in which the two parent two dependent children household represented only 30% of household forms in 1961 and only 26% in 1978. And even the household form of a married couple with dependent children constituted only 38% and 33% of all households in 1961 and 1978 respectively.[9]

The collection and processing of data on 'head of household' and 'main economic provider' complicate the picture still further if we wish to use official data to underpin the class theories so commonly used. 'All married couple households which depend chiefly on the economic contribution of the woman will, following the rules, be coded as possessing a male "chief economic provider".'[10] The division between men and women in terms of who is the economic provider or how this task is shared is not available from the official data. Consequently, the *assumption* of women's dependence on men is in question. Hilary Land's analyses of households concluded in the mid 1970s that '. . . at the very least, one in six of all households, *excluding* pensioner households, are substantially or completely dependent upon a woman's earnings or benefits and the *majority* of these households contain either children or adult dependents.'[11] Such data could perhaps be included in analyses which have assumed a particular form of family as the unit most appropriate to understanding class relations.

Through assumptions, both of sociologists and official statistics gatherers, we know all too little of actual household forms and the relations within them. But if we start from an assumption that household units are composed of a variety of adults, dependents and providers, together with, in a minority of cases, dependent children, we can then ask questions relevant to class structuration, and begin to

140

collect the necessary data. An important problem at the present time is clearly our sociological ignorance about how women, daughters, wives and mothers, relate to each other and to males within 'families' and households. Ideologically, the situation is simple; there is one breadwinner (male) to whom all the females and the male minors stand in relations of dependence and derived class. How far such dependency is a reality, what conditions or changes it, remain largely unexplored. In other words, the continuing acceptance of ideological constructions in respect of gender relations encourages a reluctance to examine the ways in which these constructions articulate with the actual relations between men and women at different points in the life-cycle. A good example of this reluctance is found in the recently published findings of the Oxford Mobility Survey.

Marriage patterns as demonstrated by the Survey show there is slightly more mobility upward and downward for women through marriage than for men through the labour market.[12] This marriage mobility is measured by comparing the man's (husband's) social class (occupational status) with that of his father-in-law when his wife was aged fourteen. It is claimed that a woman's 'class fate' is more loosely linked to her social origins than is a man's.[13] However, for those who are not convinced that marriage transforms the woman into the class or status position of the man she marries, there are problems with an approach which assumes a derived class position first as daughter and then as wife. Marriage contracts do not bestow educational or professional qualifications nor do they transfer, in any mechanical or permanent sense, social or politically powerful backgrounds or any of the other ascribed statuses to those who do not possess them in their own right. It remains to be determined how, and to what extent, marriage partners derive attributes from one another.

Materially, the wife may share fully in the life-style of her husband, though without more data on the distribution of economic resources between husbands and wives we need to be cautious about our assumptions.[14] For example, a downwardly mobile woman (in marriage terms) may have access to inherited capital or parents or kin economically better off than her husband, who support her and her children (and her husband) in a variety of crucial ways. On the other hand, an upwardly mobile woman (in marriage terms) is unlikely to have educational or occupational qualifications bestowed through marriage (though research into this phenomenon is lacking). The acid test may be the end of the marriage, through death or, more usually, divorce, although even this has problems since we do not know how far an independent income enables women to consider divorce to a greater extent than those who lack such an income. Delphy has argued that:

A large number of women who are divorced or about to be divorced come on the labour market in the worst possible conditions (as do widows) with no qualifications, no experience and no seniority. They find themselves relegated to the most poorly-paid jobs. This situation is often in contrast with the level of their education and the careers they envisaged or could have envisaged before their marriage, the social rank of their parents, and not only the initial social rank of their husbands but, more pertinently, the rank he has attained when they divorce, some five, ten or twenty years after the beginning of their marriage.[15]

Given patterns of the dissolution of marriage, the ex-wife, particularly the middle-aged one, is both in material and power terms a question mark as far as her class position is concerned. She may, where she has produced children, retain a vicarious connection with her acquired social status, but even this may be much reduced, and is by no means guaranteed.

It may be that woman's class fate *is* more loosely linked to her social origins than a man's. Such a claim can be made at present *only if particular kinds of statistical evidence are used which have been collected in ways which close off the very questions that need investigation.* Some check on the woman's (wife's) occupational position and educational level at the time of marriage would begin to give more indication of the processes involved. Data on the occupation and marketable qualifications of the women at the time their spouses are being surveyed would indicate whether or not the marriage, up or down, had conferred on the women (wife) a status similar to that of the husband. We need to ascertain whether working-class women (in terms of father's origin) remain potentially, and in the case of divorce or a wide variety of other situations actually, working class, whatever sort of man they marry. Do they move up and down, according to circumstances, their own as well as their spouses? Similarly, we need to ask if middle-class women (measured in terms of father's origin), without independent incomes or actual middle-class occupations, are potentially downwardly mobile, whatever class of man they marry.

In this connection it is important to note Anderson's argument, that interdependence between family members has been much reduced over the past fifty years.[16] If he is correct then the family unit cannot, without examination, be taken as the unit of class analysis. He does not, however, analyse the differential positions of wives and husbands in terms of this reduction of interdependence. Delphy has recently gone further, suggesting that 'The specific relations of production of married women . . . are characterised by dependence', and that this places husbands and wives in patriarchal and antagonistic classes which override the commonality of industrial class. But sociologists have obscured this relationship while using it 'to situate women within the classical system of stratification'.[17]

Clearly, substantial doubt can be cast on the simple assumptions about marriage and the family which continue to underlie mainstream sociological analyses. The way forward is to confront the questions of the marriage relationship, relations within households (and all they entail) and between these and the dominant mode of production and its multifarious sub-modes.

Occupation and class

The use of occupation as an index of class, whatever its inadequacies, has attained an influential position in the discussion of class theories relating to class situation and class consciousness. In empirical work it situates the discussion of many substantive issues. It is therefore necessary to examine it in relation to the question of women and class inequality. This particular form of analysis assumes that:

the nature of occupations themselves, their job characteristics, their non-pecuniary rewards, and so on, were crucial factors in shaping class attitudes and behaviour. In other words, it is within the division of labour, rather than in property relations, that the behaviourally relevant divisions of class were to be found. This proposition has reached its most formalised expression in the one model of social class which can claim to enjoy almost universal acceptance by Western sociologists; namely, the manual/non-manual model.[18]

There are two sets of questions. First, those that relate to how far a division between manual and non-manual occupations can be accepted as a class model. Some years ago, David Lockwood distinguished between the market, work and status positions of clerks and related it to the question of consciousness.[19] He concluded that, though sellers of labour, clerks occupied market, work and status positions objectively different from other groups of sellers of labour power (for example, industrial workers or agricultural workers) and that their class consciousness was related to their different class position, measured by these criteria. Since that time there has been an enormous expansion in white-collar occupations. Much of this has involved women, particularly in routine white-collar employment. There has also been a comparable expansion in the organisation of some white-collar workers into trade unions and remarkable displays of class consciousness which have blurred whatever distinctions existed between manual and non-manual categories.

Sociologists, nonetheless, have continued to treat the manual/non-manual divide as a crucial one and Marxist sociologists have been much engaged in debating questions of whether or not those in white-collar occupations were a new petty bourgeoisie or members of the working class. The evidence in Britain on the growth of white-collar trade unionism and the forms of industrial action they have adopted does not warrant many of the claims, in behavioural terms, of a petty bourgeoisie type of response. Such behaviour may relate predominantly to the public (state) sector of employment, though the growth of trade unionism in banking, finance and insurance, for instance, has also to be noted.

Many of these white-collar occupations in no way control the work of others, nor are they rewarded financially or in fringe benefit or status terms. There is the current example of some civil servants who are aware that they earn about two pounds more than unemployed social security claimants – they may be fortunate in having jobs, but they have no long-term security, no realistic prospects of promotion and their salaries do not pay their mortgages. How far is it the case that they see the differences between themselves and their 'clients' in class terms? In some areas, it is the unemployed manual trade unionists who are giving advice and aid to the striking civil servants. Such alliances may be temporary and in many sectors of the economy may not have been forged. What, however, is in question is the usefulness of the traditional distinction between manual and non-manual workers in which a difference or a conflict of interest has been assumed. Whether there are antagonistic divisions within the class composed of those who sell their labour power, and if there are, where these are located, are questions which remain open. A closer analysis of the routine non-manual work of women is imperative to the theoretical development of these questions.

But let us turn to the second set of questions relating to those approaches which take occupation as the index of class and mobility between classes. It is quite clear that such approaches have excluded the majority of women. This is because of the assumption that women, particularly married women, do not have occupations; if the woman *is* recognised as having an occupation, it is generally assumed that the occupation of the husband is the one that articulates with the class system. Furthermore, underlying the collection of many statistical data (currently as well as in the past) is the assumption that work is not only paid, but regular, full-time and single job only. Temporary, part-time, multiple jobs are less likely to be recorded or to be included in serious discussions of the relations between work and class relations. This is problematic for many reasons. This conception of work is so restrictive that it obscures as well as marginalises much production, consumption and exchange which may have a direct bearing on class structure and class relations. It does not separate women from men in any complete sense, but it marginalises women to a greater extent than men in relation to the class structure as conceptualised.

At the present, in Britain, the economic activity rate of men and women on leaving school is very high and very similar. The women's rate then diverges from the men's rate, showing considerable variation with age. The overall rate is estimated to be 51% with 70% economically active in the 35–54 age-group, the lowest rate being in the over-sixties and at age 30, when it is about 40%. The pattern for married and non-married women differs, the latter having rates between over 60 and over 90% for all ages between 16 and 60 years of age. Married women show a continuing drop until the age of 30 to an economic activity rate of 40% after which there is a steady rise to about 60%, until their late fifties, when the rate again begins to decline. The point to be made of course is that if occupation (employment) links men into the class structure, then women's occupations should be recorded in all sociological analyses of class inequality.

The industrial and occupational distribution of women is reasonably well known. They form half the labour force in clothing and footwear, professional and scientific services, distributive trades, insurance, banking, finance and business services and miscellaneous services, and under 10% in mining and quarrying, shipbuilding and construction. Among manual-working women, over half are in catering, cleaning, hairdressing or other services described as 'personal'. In non-manual work over 50% of them are in clerical and related occupations. Women make up 51% of all non-manual workers and 28% of all manual workers. There is a concentration, which should not be overlooked, of men in manual work, and within ten of the 28 industrial sectors they constitute over 80% of the workforce. These patterns have come to be described as segregated and segmented labour markets. This is one sense in which we can consider patterns of linkage between occupation and the class structure which have different implications for men and women. We cannot say a great deal about it in specific terms because the necessary investigations have not been carried out.

Nonetheless, in general terms, we can hypothesise about the different ways in which men and women articulate with the class structure in terms of their market and work situations. For instance, in terms of marketable skills, economic rewards, promotion and career prospects, and the internal situation of work groups and hierarchies, there are marked differences for men and women. We need to know a great deal more before we can draw conclusions about the extent to which gender gives rise to a specificity of class location which overrides cross-gender class interests.

Since it has been assumed in occupational analyses that *men's* jobs and employment patterns explain the class location of *families*, the necessary questions have not been asked, nor alternative interpretations of existing investigations considered. For example, if we accept a narrow and partial definition of work as paid regular employment, then we may have little difficulty in accepting, without qualification, the received wisdom that there has been an increase in married women working. In Britain the economic activity rate of women was as high in 1861 as in 1971, and for married women as high in 1851 as in 1951. However, the *extent* of any increase is open to question on technical grounds in terms of the changes in the ways such data are collected over time. Similarly, the base line chosen for comparison is crucial. Even if we restrict ourselves to the twentieth century we should be aware of the caution necessary in interpreting some of the data. 'It is not possible to gauge for the earlier censuses (1921, 1931, 1951) the extent to which people who had some part-time employment . . . were entered as having an occupation or being involved in "Home duties".'[20] The change in 1961 from 'normally occupied' to 'economically active' was an improvement; it includes those in employment at the time of the census and those out of employment but actively seeking work. It does not include those who were employed at other times (but not at times of census) or who do not define themselves as intending to get employment. This may partly explain why half a million women reported by the Ministry of Labour in 1961 to be in the labour force were not recorded as economically active in the census of that year.[21] It should be evident that those who argue that women were peripheral to the class structure because in the past they did not work are presenting a very partial and distorted picture of women's waged work and ignoring the pattern of waged working in the lives of many men.[22]

Conclusion

The argument is not that women are a separate class: such a proposition necessitates the denial of the centrality of divisions inherent in the relations of production, consumption and exchange which separate men from other men and women from other women. Rather, the argument is advanced that women, through the relations of production, consumption and exchange, are involved in the system of class relations *in their own right*. This argument changes not only our perception of women's position, but of class relations, introducing specifications and inconsistencies which remain uninvestigated for both women and men.

In commenting upon some of the recent work on social mobility, Heath summarises one position as follows: 'If there is sexism in sociology, then it is because it accurately reflects the sexism within the wider society.'[23] This may be a shorthand way of explaining much of the work on social mobility and social stratification, but it scarcely amounts to an argument for continuing to pursue such kinds of sociological analyses and using scarce social science resources to do so. The substitution of racism for sexism in the above quote will be sufficient to indicate that sociological analysis requires something more than a reflection of prevailing ideological relations. To limit sociology in this way impoverishes the scientific status of the discipline. A major shift of emphasis is required away from a limited intellectual discourse towards an attempt to represent more closely the experience and condition of class situations as these relate to men and women, either separately or in combination.

The petty bourgeoisie and modern capitalism: a consideration of recent theories*

RICHARD SCASE

This chapter reviews Marxist and non-Marxist theories of the petty bourgeoisie. Three separate approaches are identified and examined. Essentially, all of these fail to link satisfactorily the reproduction of the petty bourgeoisie to the general process of capitalist accumulation. In particular, an over-emphasis – particularly by Marxists – upon petty bourgeois *positions* has led to a neglect of the manner in which *actors* are able to create opportunities for small-scale capital accumulation and, hence, sustain the reproduction of *positions*. It is the contention of this essay that further research needs to focus upon these processes and, thereby, relate the analysis of the petty bourgeoisie – both in terms of its *positions* and *actors* – to the central dynamic of accumulation in capitalist society.

At the most general level, the petty bourgeoisie consists of a *mélange* of groupings which, nevertheless, share a common feature: their ownership of small-scale capital.[1] This is typically used for productive purposes in conjunction with the proprietors' and, often, others' labour.[2] However, the relative *mix* of capital and labour is highly variable. There can be instances when the proprietors' income is mainly derived from property ownership (as with small rentiers), when income is primarily acquired through the exercise of labour (as with craft workers and freelance professionals), and other cases when there is a 'mixture' of both resources (as with shopkeepers, small farmers and those engaged in the provision of many personal services). Since the petty bourgeoisie consists of proprietors who actively use their capital for a wide variety of purposes within different sectors of the economy, it is not surprising that their location within

*This essay is one of a number of joint publications stemming from an S.S.R.C. research project on the role of small businesses in a modern economy, undertaken in collaboration with Robert Goffee.

modern capitalist society has often been regarded as problematic. Indeed, it is possible to identify three distinct approaches to the study of the petty bourgeoisie. First, it is regarded as 'separate' and 'removed' from the two major classes of capitalist society. Secondly, it is seen as part-and-parcel of an emerging 'post-industrial' or 'service' class structure. Finally, from the Marxist perspective, it is interpreted as a legacy of an earlier pre-capitalist form of production.

The first approach regards the petty bourgeoisie as an independent 'stratum' which is separate from both the bourgeoisie and the proletariat. Bechhofer and his colleagues, for example, have argued that it represents a stratum which is 'in some sense marginal or detached from the major classes and interests of contemporary industrial societies'.[3] At one point, this leads to the suggestion that it is *'outside'* the class structure, whilst at another, it sits 'uneasily *between* the major classes' (emphasis added).[4] On the basis of their own empirical enquiry the authors conclude, 'In a very real sense the petite bourgeoisie is detached from the concerns of the working and middle classes. To a large extent the small businessman finds himself a mere spectator at the arena in which the forces of labour and big business confront each other.'[5] Notwithstanding this, Bechhofer and his colleagues regard the petty bourgeoisie as fulfilling important ideological functions within contemporary society if only because it is the custodians of certain 'core' capitalist values. They claim that an overriding value of many small-business owners is *independence;* the appeal is to be 'your own boss' and, thereby, avoid the constraints of employment associated with large-scale corporations. The strength of this appeal is sufficient to compensate for frequently long and arduous working hours; indeed, their 'autonomy' often turns into 'serfdom' such that 'theirs, it seems, is a freedom to establish an extraordinary form of self-exploitation'.[6] Despite this, most remain firmly committed to notions of 'individualism' and 'independence' and this is reflected in their attitudes, life-styles and patterns of consumption.[7] In sum, society is seen to be 'open' and it rewards those prepared to work hard and make the necessary self-sacrifice. To quote the authors they are,

. . . the repository of many of the traditional values upon which a capitalist social order was built. The shopkeepers' passionate individualism and the moral evaluation of work emerge clearly enough. So too does the vision of a *laissez-faire* economy in which men like themselves will prosper. Moreover, their belief that by hard work and wit you can succeed is crucial to the conception of ours as an open society. Thus, the symbolic significance of the stratum resides in the fact that, to many, their lives appear to demonstrate the possibility of individual mobility. Despite the modesty of their origins many have succeeded, that is, in terms quite fundamental to the capitalist society. They have won, albeit in small measure, property and autonomy.

Finally, we would argue that the significance of these central concerns in the political and social philosophy of the petty bourgeois is this: espousing an ideology of independence and hard work he is inclined to the belief that inequality is the result of the differential distribution of talent and effort. In doing so he buttresses the present system of inequality and offers it legitimation.[8]

Even though the development of large-scale corporations and the growth of the state has fundamentally altered the structure of the economy, such beliefs reinforce the desirability of capitalism as a socio-economic system. The persistence of small-scale enterprises – whether in farming, commerce or industry – preserves an image of competition which conceals the reality of domination by large-scale monopoly enterprises. Bechhofer and his colleagues summarise the economic position of small-business owners as follows,

Running their own enterprises, be they small workshops, or retail stores or service operations, they are forced into some awareness of their vulnerability to change, to the booms and recessions in the economy, to the fiscal and other measures of the state . . . The sense of precariousness, of contingency, leads to the awareness of life as 'struggle' and to ambiguity in their relationship to others in the major classes. Small capital is menaced from above and below . . . in all circumstances it is a dependent stratum, dependent first and foremost on the dominant economic groups and institutions. It is their decisions, their interests that do most to affect the size and circumstances of the stratum.[9]

If this view suggests that the petty bourgeoisie persists in a 'marginal' sense, the second approach argues that it will fulfil an increasingly important function in an emerging post-industrial society. Several factors are said to underlie this trend. Some writers have claimed that as a result of a growing concern with the 'quality of life' the number of independent small-scale enterprises is likely to expand.[10] Within this argument a heavy emphasis is placed upon the growing 'diseconomies' and 'dysfunctions' of large-scale bureaucratic organisations which are said to produce inferior quality goods under conditions that lead to work dissatisfaction amongst employees. Thus, 'small is beautiful' since it encourages the production of goods and services in the context of more 'meaningful', and, therefore, less alienating, work environments.[11] Boissevain has recently listed the various manifestations of this trend in the following terms,

First, increasing awareness of environmental pollution has furnished a niche for entrepreneurs able to provide natural products, whether for the stomach, the body or the mind . . . Secondly, both the increase of the size and the power of firms . . . has reduced the relative autonomy of managers . . . Many dissatisfied managers in large corporations strike out on their own . . . Thirdly, there is growing realisation that the quality of life in urbanizing Europe is adversely affected by the disappearance of neighbourhood shops offering varied products, repair services, flexible opening hours and credit facilities. Finally, . . . is the belief that a reduction in scale provides satisfaction. Many have stepped out and down.[12]

Employees who choose to set up their own businesses are helped, it has been argued, by recent technological developments which are encouraging the growth of the domestic economy. The micro-chip computer, for instance, allows relatively sophisticated software to be purchased cheaply and used in the home. This has led Martin and Norman to speculate that 'we may see a return to cottage industry, with the spinning wheel replaced by the computer terminal'.[13] If this proves to be correct, there could be potential for a considerable expansion of independent, small-scale production. Some commentators have argued that such opportunities will be increasingly exploited if only because of a marked decline in 'formal' employment which will force many to consider alternative ways of earning a living.[14] Consequently, the growth of 'informal' economic activity has attracted much attention and Pahl, for example, has claimed that 'the substitution of informal, household production of services for the purchase of services from the formal economy' could serve as the basis for an alternative means of income.[15] He continues,

Unemployment in the 1980's may, therefore, be a different kind of experience from that described for the period half a century ago. A man with his own tools, his own time and a long-stop income in the form of unemployment pay may not be in such a vulnerable position: his *work* identity can still be maintained even if his employment identity is in abeyance.[16]

If 'informal' work in the 'cash economy' is increasing while 'formal' employment declines, this could provide new avenues for small-business formation and growth.[17] It has been suggested that this trend is further encouraged by the increasing 'burden' of state regulations, controls and taxes. Thus, Boissevain has suggested that, 'the desire to avoid progressively heavier levels of taxation and contributions for social services has stimulated . . . people to start up on their own'.[18] Taken together, these changes are leading, so it is claimed, to a fundamental alteration in both the pattern and nature of economic activity within modern societies. As such, they constitute the basis for a regeneration of the petty bourgeoisie within a developing 'post-industrial' society.

Such a view stands in sharp contrast to the third perspective – the

151

Richard Scase

Marxist – which regards the petty bourgeoisie as the legacy of a pre-capitalist form of production which continues to persist within present-day capitalist society.[19] Essentially, this approach suggests that, in the long run, the development of capitalism will lead to the dissolution of the petty bourgeoisie within the bourgeoisie and the proletariat. As Marx claimed in the *Communist Manifesto*,

The lower strata of the middle-class – the small trades-people, shopkeepers and retired tradesmen generally, the handicraftsmen and peasants . . . sink gradually into the proletariat, partly because their diminutive capital does not suffice for the scale on which Modern Industry is carried on, and is swamped in the competition with the large capitalist, partly because their specialised skill is rendered worthless by new methods of production.[20]

This prediction is based upon an analysis of the capitalist mode of production which distinguishes the stages of Cooperation and Manufacture from Modern Industry.[21] Under conditions of Cooperation the worker is an autonomous craftsman, but with the development of capitalist Manufacture a division of labour emerges and he becomes a specialist in one rather than a number of activities. To quote Marx, 'each workman (becomes) exclusively assigned to a partial function, and that for the rest of his life, his labour power is turned into the organ of this detail function'.[22] With the development of Modern Industry, characterised by mechanised factory production, the worker 'becomes a mere appendage to an already existing material condition of production'.[23] As a 'machine minder' his conceptual capacity is further reduced whilst, at the same time, the amount of capital required for production becomes greater. Under these circumstances few workers will become capitalists and, furthermore, few small-scale producers will be able to compete with the production methods of Modern Industry which inevitably become 'the general, socially predominant form of production'.[24] Thus, 'the larger capitals beat the smaller' causing 'the ruin of many small capitalists, whose capitals partly pass into the hands of their conquerers, partly vanish'.[25] The growth of Modern Industry, then, restricts the opportunity for workers to function as independent tradesmen or to become business owners while, at the same time, it destroys the capital of existing small-scale producers and manufacturers.

Given these developments in the capitalist mode of production, the petty bourgeoisie is typically viewed by Marxists as the legacy of pre-capitalist simple commodity production. Thus, although the capitalist *mode* of production may be dominant in society, prior *forms* of non-capitalist production may persist within it. Similarly, the existence of large-scale capitalist enterprises in the present stage of 'monopoly' capitalism does not preclude the persistence of small-scale capital units characteristic of 'competitive' or 'private' capitalism. However, to claim that the petty bourgeoisie represents a legacy of declining importance does not explain *how* or *why* it is currently reproduced.

Poulantzas, for example, who defines the 'traditional' petty bourgeoisie as the self-employed and those *'not chiefly involved in exploiting wage labour'* (emphasis added)[26], merely states that 'the contemporary existence of the petty bourgeoisie in the developed capitalist formations . . . depends on the perpetration of this form in the extended reproduction of capitalism'.[27] This is cumbersome description rather than explanation, and is indicative of the fact that Poulantzas sees this class as a declining vestige of the simple commodity form 'which was historically the form of transition from the feudal to the capitalist mode'.[28] Similarly, Wright tends to ignore the actual mechanisms which account for the persistence of small-scale commodity production in contemporary society.[29] He defines the members of the petty bourgeoisie as *those who either work for themselves or, despite the employment of some labour, generate the bulk of surplus value.*[30] In a similar fashion to Poulantzas, he sees this form of production as subordinated to capitalism and yet fails to explore fully the implications. In his terms, the petty bourgeoisie have *full* economic ownership of the means of production and *full* control over the allocation of their resources and yet they control little or no labour power. As such, he regards their class position as unambiguous.[31] But obviously, if members of the petty bourgeoisie produce commodities they *are* affected by the conditions of the market as they exist under monopoly capitalism. Thus, the constraints exercised by, for example, financial institutions and large-scale capital enterprises may severely curtail the *real* control that 'independent' small-scale producers are able to exercise over the use of their investments and resources. If 'economic control' is diminished, on Wright's criteria, the class location of the petty bourgeoisie in contemporary capitalist society cannot be regarded as 'unambiguous'. Indeed there are severe limitations to any analysis which solely views petty commodity producers as representative of a surviving 'simple' or 'feudal' form which somehow persists within contemporary capitalism.

The Marxist interpretation of small-scale capitalists, however, is rather different. They, unlike the petty bourgeoisie, own and control larger capital assets and employ more sizeable workforces. They are, for example, the owners of family firms and of medium-sized, non-monopoly enterprises in general. According to Poulantzas, 'Non-monopoly capital is not a simple form that is preserved or conserved, as in the case of feudal forms surviving within capitalism, but a form reproduced under the domination of monopoly capital.'[32]

If this type of small-scale capital is representative of an earlier competitive stage of capitalism it is, nevertheless, seen to be shaped by the contemporary forces of monopoly capitalism. Consequently, Poulantzas suggests a number of functions which small enterprises fulfil in the modern economy. They often operate, for example, in sectors characterised by low profits and high risks, and those which 'service' large corporations. They may also function as a 'staging post in the process of subjecting labour-power to monopoly capital', and as a means whereby prices may be set at a level which allows monopoly capital larger profit margins because of its cheaper production costs.[33] Poulantzas further argues that the apparent independence of small-scale capital is constrained by monopoly standardisation of products, the patenting of technological innovations and the 'leonine controls' imposed by finance capital as a condition for extending credit.[34] Consequently, the *real* economic boundaries of small-scale, non-monopoly enterprises – so clearly defined in *legal* terms – become increasingly indeterminate. In contrast to the petty bourgeoisie, Poulantzas emphasises that 'the criteria by which non-monopoly capital is defined are always located in relation to monopoly capital . . . There is in no sense a simple "co-existence" of two separate watertight sectors.'[35] Thus, the relationship between the two forms of capital is variable and dependent upon 'the phase of monopoly capitalism and its concrete forms (branches, sectors, etc.) within a social formation'.[36] Despite the extent to which monopoly capital reduces the economic viability of small-scale enterprises, then, Poulantzas recognises their continuing functional importance and, hence, their persistence within contemporary capitalism. Similarly, Wright argues that 'small employers' are caught between simple commodity production and the capitalist mode of production in a 'contradictory class location'.[37] But although this implies that 'small employers' are partially integrated within the capitalist mode in a manner in which the traditional petty bourgeoisie are not, he does not elaborate upon this.

There is, among these Marxist writers, a neglect of the empirical dynamics whereby the petty bourgeoisie are reproduced under the conditions of monopoly capitalism. This would seem to be the result of excessively abstract analyses which focus exclusively upon positions rather than actors, that assume their progressive decline and which fail, therefore, to study empirically present-day processes. In fact, Westergaard claims to be 'both puzzled and disturbed by contemporary Western Marxist work in which the concrete differential impact of capitalist economic processes on people's lives and prospects . . . seems to recede into remote distance . . . or to be brought into the picture only in a context of abstraction which, untranslated, leave the reality of human experience difficult to recognise.'[38] Indeed, Poulantzas and Wright explicitly deny they are concerned with the human actors who occupy class places or positions which constitute the essential focus of their discussions. According to Poulantzas,

The principal aspect of an analysis of social classes is that of their places in the class struggle; it is not true of the agents that compose them. Social classes are not empirical groups of individuals . . . The class memberships of the various agents depends on the class places that they occupy; it is moreover distinct from the class origin, the social origin, of the agents.[39]

Even Wright, who is committed to the idea that 'Marxist theory should generate propositions about the real world which can be empirically studied',[40] and who attacks abstract class definitions which relegate the complexities of 'concrete social structures' to a secondary role, does not consider it necessary to 'discuss contradictory locations that occur because an *individual* simultaneously occupies two class positions within social relations of production' (emphasis added).[41] He argues that dual class membership, although of significance 'in certain historical circumstances', does not present 'the same kind of analytical problem as *positions* which are themselves located in a contradictory way within class relations' (emphasis added).[42] Once again, then, the discussion of class actors is deemed to be of less significance than that of abstractly-defined class locations. As Parkin has argued, this is because

Notions such as the mode of production make their claims to explanatory power precisely on the grounds of their indifference to the nature of the human material whose activities they determine. To introduce (such) questions . . . is to clutter up the analysis by laying stress upon the quality of *social actors,* a conception diametrically opposed to the notion of human agents as *Träger* or 'embodiments' of systemic forces.[43]

Clearly, the reproduction of the petty bourgeoisie within economies characterised by the dominance of large monopoly enterprises requires detailed empirical study. Abstract analyses that attribute priority to modes, forms and stages of production, and to class positions rather than to class actors fail to account sufficiently for the mechanisms whereby the petty bourgeoisie is reproduced in present-day society. If, as in most Marxist analyses, the distinction between actors and position is too sharply drawn, then areas of the class structure within which there is a significant degree of social

Richard Scase

mobility may be inadequately understood.[44] Poulantzas acknowledges that some manual workers and artisans become petty bourgeois producers but he overlooks the actual material processes which allow this mobility.[45] Although, therefore, at the theoretical level the simple commodity form *can* be distinguished from the pure capitalist mode of production, this type of analysis often detracts from the study of empirical relationships. Because the petty bourgeoisie is seen to be fairly 'insulated' from the capitalist mode of production, the concrete relationships between its members, small-scale capitalists and large-scale corporations have been relatively unexplored. Further, there have been hardly any sociological studies of the processes whereby actors can experience mobility into the petty bourgeoisie through the small-scale accumulation of capital.

In some ways it is surprising that contemporary Marxists have neglected the analysis of these processes, given the importance which both Marx and Lenin attributed to them. In their respective accounts of the development of capitalism in Britain and Russia, they recognised the continuing formation of small-scale petty commodity producers, despite long-term trends. Thus, Marx pointed out that,

. . . individual capitals, and with them the concentration of the means of production, increase in such proportion as they form aliquot parts of the total social capital. At the same time, portions of the original capitals disengage themselves and function as new independent capitals . . . Accumulation and the concentration accompanying it are, therefore, not only scattered over many points, but the increase of each functioning capital is thwarted by the formation of new and the sub-division of old capitals. Accumulation, therefore, presents itself on the one hand as increasing concentration of the means of production, and of the command over labour; on the other, as repulsion of many individual capitals one from another.[46]

Similarly, although Lenin asserted that 'the fundamental and principal trend of capitalism is the displacement of small-scale by large-scale production',[47] he emphasised the persistence of petty production which ensured the continuous formation of various intermediary strata,

In every capitalist country, side by side with the proletariat, there are always broad strata of the petty bourgeoisie, small proprietors. Capitalism arose and is constantly arising out of small production. A number of new 'middle strata' are inevitably brought into existence again and again by capitalism (appendages to the factory, work at home, small workshops scattered all over the country to meet the requirements of the big industries, such as the bicycle and automobile industries, etc.).[48]

Both Marx and Lenin, then, acknowledged the continuing reproduction of the petty bourgeoisie within capitalist society. Although

the development of capitalism would ultimately lead to their dissolution, the conditions which enabled their reproduction – although
on a more limited scale – persisted. What, then, is lacking in contemporary Marxist accounts are empirical analyses of the ways in which
this reproduction now takes place.[49] As Miller has pointed out, 'The
small business sector as a whole . . . is large and strong in most capitalist nations . . . (It) should not be regarded as an anachronism that
will surely and swiftly fade away as big enterprises grow.'[50] The
implications of this for class structure have been stressed by Mayer,

> The lower middle class was expected to shrink drastically in importance,
> perhaps even to sink altogether into the proletariat; but this expectation,
> which was so widely shared, has not been fulfilled. Even the old lower mid-
> dle class of petty independence has displayed an extraordinary longevity. To
> be sure, since the mid-nineteenth century the economic and numerical weight
> of small craftsmen, tradesmen, and peasants has declined strikingly. But this
> decline has been less rapid than commonly assumed. In fact, now and then
> the number of small shopkeepers and service operators actually increased,
> especially under conditions of acute economic distress.[51]

Consequently, a satisfactory analytical framework must take account
of the fact that the small-scale production of goods and services is
embedded within a general process of capital accumulation. Although
this assumption is explicit in, for example, Lenin's discussion of the
development of capitalism in Russia, it is largely absent in present-
day work.[52] Even though the possibilities for actors to become small-
scale proprietors may now be generally less than during earlier stages
of capitalism, they are certainly greater than many Marxists assume.
As such, they provide avenues for individual mobility of a 'non-
career' or 'non-meritocratic' kind. Whereas sociological studies of
upward mobility have focussed on the acquisition of educational and
technical qualifications and upon promotion within and between
hierarchically-organised large-scale corporations, little attention has
been devoted to petty capital accumulation as an alternative channel
for personal success.[53] Thus, managerial, professional and manual
employees can, in various ways and for different reasons, become
small-scale proprietors. As Mayer has argued, the petty bourgeoisie
functions as,

> A buffer between capital and labour . . . (and) as a bridge and mediator
> between them. Moreover, the petite bourgeoisie is the predominant channel
> for social mobility; skilled manual workers can and do move into it from
> below, while from within its bulging ranks it raises its own spiralists to
> higher rungs on the income and status ladder. This lower middle class also
> serves as a net that cushions the fall of the skidders and the superannuated
> of both the higher middle class and the grande bourgeoisie.[54]

In other words, the petty bourgeoisie offers opportunities for upward mobility for those who are unable to obtain entry into various salaried middle-class occupations. Several writers have emphasised the importance of self-employment and small-scale proprietorship as avenues of self-advancement for deprived and disadvantaged groups.[55] If, through lack of credentials or because of explicit/implicit discrimination, some individuals and groups are unable to compete equally with others for occupational preferment, the market provides an apparently 'open' career alternative. It offers the promise that personal success can be related to the producer's capacity to provide goods and services for an 'impersonal' market. Thus, members of minority groups who experience discrimination within the occupational structure often seek self-advancement through proprietorship.[56]

Similarly, managerial attempts to extend *real* control over the work process in large-scale capitalist enterprises can provoke *individual* as well as *collective* protest; in response to attempts by employers to increase the extraction of surplus value by curtailing worker autonomy, employees can individually 'opt out' of the capitalist work process by becoming small business proprietors.[57] This strategy, however, legitimates rather than challenges the capitalist order. Even though, subjectively, the self-employed and small employers may often express 'antagonistic' and even 'oppositional' sentiments, objectively they are attached to the logic of capital accumulation through the petty production of goods and services for the market.[58]

However, these 'escape' routes are more available in some sectors of the economy than others; where the work process is particularly labour-intensive as, for example, in personal services, the retail trades, hotel and catering, and in the building industry, conditions are particularly favourable for self-employment and small-scale business formation.[59] Similarly, the 'specialist' needs of large-scale capital, the growth of sub-contracting and the increasingly important 'black economy' provide contexts within which small business enterprises are likely to emerge. Consequently, many Marxist analyses, entwined as they are in debates about stages, forms and modes of production, have often overlooked these continuing empirical processes that lead to the persistence of the petty bourgeoisie. Of course, it must be accepted that modern societies are characterised by the growing domination of large-scale corporations that determine the parameters within which small-scale capital accumulation occurs. Nevertheless, there are still many social and economic processes conducive to the formation of small businesses and, hence, to the reproduction of the petty bourgeoisie.

Proprietorship, however, does not constitute an 'open' avenue for self-advancement; there are divisions that constitute substantial barriers to the process of mobility through capital accumulation. Indeed, there are a number of social as well as financial and market factors which limit small-scale capital growth.[60] Within the labour-intensive sectors of the economy, where most small businesses are formed, these surround the employment relationship. The self-employed, for example, trade with their labour and, as former employees, frequently lack the skills necessary for the supervision of labour. Similarly, small employers encounter problems in the employment of staff which limit their potential for, and predisposition to, business growth.

These problems can be attributed to three major factors. First, there is the proprietors' own occupational experience; many lack the 'technical' skills of management and only those who have previously been employed as managers possess the necessary expertise to cope with the large-scale employment of labour.[61] Secondly, one of the more important motives for proprietorship is the desire to escape from the constraints of the capitalist employment relationship. Thus, for the self-employed, work autonomy is a major goal; to employ labour not only creates problems of supervision but infringes upon this autonomy. Similarly, small employers are, in a sense, self-employed with employees. Essentially, they value productive work and can often only cope with the employment relationship by acting as fellow employees and cultivating a strategy of *fraternalism*.[62] Thirdly, the employment relationship can be an obstacle to business growth because it is shrouded in distrust.[63] There is a widespread view, shared by many proprietors, that the employment of labour inevitably creates managerial difficulties; consequently, they are often reluctant to expand their enterprises. Thus, increased production and additional profits may only be pursued if they do not require the recruitment of extra staff. It is for these reasons that sub-contracting is so attractive to many proprietors; in addition to 'off-loading' a number of administrative overheads and financial costs, it enables them to abdicate partially, if not wholly, many facets of the employer role.[64]

Nevertheless, some of the self-employed and small employers do overcome many of these obstacles and embark upon a sustained process of capital accumulation. Some become owner-controllers who, ceasing to work alongside their employees, become singularly and solely responsible for the supervision of their employees while others accumulate capital to an even greater extent and become owner-directors.[65] Thus, the scale of business activities becomes such that these owners can no longer personally perform all the functions of supervision and control and it is necessary for them to delegate and sub-divide these tasks through the creation of administrative structures. Consequently, we may regard owner-controllers and owner-directors as members of the bourgeoisie rather than of the petty bourgeoisie.[66]

In this way, the petty bourgeoisie sustains the more general process of capital accumulation. Petty commodity production not only offers an 'escape' from proletarian deprivations but also provides an avenue – albeit very limited – into the privileges of the bourgeoisie. However, it also legitimates the operation of the capitalist order in at least three further ways. First, and most importantly, it sustains private property ownership. It consists of proprietors who own varying amounts of capital assets; any upward mobility entails the further acquisition of assets through the accumulation process. Secondly, it legitimates the capitalist economy because proprietors use their assets for the purpose of producing commodities which are sold in the market. This material circumstance is reflected at an ideological level in the commitment to 'risk', 'chance', the virtues of 'free competition', and opposition to the growth of the state, trade unions and business monopolies; all of which are seen to challenge the market that is the basis of petty bourgeois existence.[67] Finally, the petty bourgeoisie sustains capitalism by providing a material basis for certain 'system-maintaining' values. Despite sources of differentiation, proprietors tend to emphasise the desirability of the market, personal ownership and profit as the major means whereby resources can be rationally distributed in society.[68] This is reflected at the political level by 'rightist' parties which, in turn, shape the parameters of political debate and, hence, core elements of the political culture.[69] Accordingly, forms of social democratic collectivism which may represent the interests of subordinate groups are often regarded as threats to individual rights and liberties.

To conclude, it is clear that the persistence of the petty bourgeoisie cannot solely be explained (and invariably dismissed) as a legacy of an earlier pre-capitalist form of production. Furthermore, it cannot simply be regarded as 'marginal' or 'outside' the capitalist accumulation process. On the contrary, it persists because of its material and ideological functions within contemporary capitalism.

Consequently, there is a need for more attention to be devoted to the empirical processes whereby the petty bourgeoisie is reproduced under the conditions of present-day capitalism rather than upon further theoretical discussion of the forces which may be conducive to its long-term decline. Such work should place less emphasis upon the distinction between actor and structural position since in the empirical analysis of the petty bourgeoisie this is often difficult to make; proprietorship is 'carved' out of a process of capital accumulation. Although, then, it is possible to conceptually differentiate between petty bourgeois actors and positions, this can detract from an understanding of the processes whereby actors, themselves, contribute to the reproduction of positions. It is only by recognising this, that the petty bourgeoisie – shaped as it is by the forces of modern capitalism – can be adequately understood.

On the service class, its formation and future

JOHN GOLDTHORPE

I

The rise of what will here be termed 'the service class' – the class of professional, administrative and managerial employees – is a development within the advanced societies of the West which has been a source of evident difficulty for social commentators and theorists. In particular, it has created problems for those for whom the prime function of sociological analysis is to offer some cognitive grasp on the future course of *political* change, and whose interests centre on the implications of such change for the stability, or otherwise, of the capitalist order.

Thus, for Marxists, the growing importance within the occupational division of labour of professionals, administrators and managers represents a further – but critical – evolution of the problem of 'intermediate strata', which of course extends back to Marx's own attempts to analyse the class structure of nineteenth-century capitalist society. Hitherto, the standard, and logically consistent, Marxist strategy in this respect has been to regard such strata as essentially temporary and epiphenomenal in relation to the basically dichotomous class structure proper to the capitalist economic system. The aim has then been to show how, through the dynamics of this system, the members of these strata are destined to become assimilated either into the working class via a process of 'proletarianisation' or conceivably, but to a far lesser extent, into the capitalist class via a process of 'incorporation'. However, while some degree of empirical respectability (if not cogency) may be given to arguments claiming the proletarianisation of, say, routine clerical or sales personnel, or the incorporation of senior business executives, there remains a large and growing range of the intermediate strata of the present day in regard to which such arguments can have no credible application.

Recognition of this fact has then led to Marxist analysts adopting a variety of other approaches to the problem – but not, it would seem, with any very satisfactory results.

For example, one attempt, originating with French Marxist writers of the 1960s, such as Belleville, Mallet and Gorz, treats expanding groupings of relatively well-qualified white-collar employees not as being proletarianised in any conventional sense, but rather as forming a key component of a 'new' working class.[1] In alliance with production workers in technologically advanced industries, these representatives of 'technical and scientific labour' are seen as having the capacity to revitalise the struggle for socialism by countering 'economistic' tendencies within the labour movement and by bringing issues of *control* to the centre of its concerns. However, the alliance envisaged has, so far at least, failed to develop, even in the French case which appeared especially favourable to it, and the thesis of the new working class would now in fact seem to be rather rapidly losing support.[2]

A rival thesis, first advanced in the United States in the 1970s by John and Barbara Ehrenreich, gives the impression of departing more sharply from Marxist orthodoxy in that it does not attempt to maintain the dichotomous model of class structure. Rather, it proposes a new 'Professional-Managerial Class' (PMC) as a formation specific to the monopoly stage of capitalism, and one which gives rise (somewhat remarkably) to a 'three-way polarisation'.[3] The PMC is characterised as a class of non-productive workers, made possible by the growth of the social surplus, whose function it is to ensure the 'reproduction' of class and cultural relations. As therefore the main agency of social control under monopoly capitalism, the PMS stands in evident opposition to the working class; but at the same time it is also seen as being in necessary opposition to the capitalist class over issues of ownership and control, and in fact as forming 'an enduring reservoir of radicalism'. It was from the PMS that the New Left was largely recruited and, although now in decline, this movement, it is argued, may be seen as the forerunner of more broadly-based and wider-ranging ones which the PMC has the potential to generate and which could, eventually, transcend its differences and conflicts with the working class. In the end, thus, it turns out that the PMC thesis is so developed as to permit the dichotomous model once more to impose itself. In the same way as with the 'new working class' thesis – and no more convincingly – an anti-capitalist alliance becomes crucial to the political scenario that is envisaged.

Finally, it may be noted that certain exponents of currently fashionable forms of 'structuralist' Marxism, such as Carchedi and Wright, have sought to deal with the analytical difficulties posed by the new intermediate strata by introducing the notion of 'contradictory' class locations. Under monopoly capitalism, it is held, many white-collar employees are in part engaged in performing functions of 'global capital', most notably, the surveillance and control of labour, but in part also perform tasks and roles that are those of the 'collective worker' as, for example, in coordinating the labour process or providing specialised knowledge and expertise. Thus, while a basically dichotomous class structure must be recognised, certain social groupings have to be seen as holding positions that are ambiguous in relation to this structure.[4] However, the rather evident weakness of this approach is that it does little more than restate the problem from which it began. Although developed by writers who are again expressly concerned with the possibilities for a political alliance between the working class and newly-emergent white-collar groupings, it conspicuously fails to offer any insight into the forms of collective action in which the latter might typically engage. This is so because the categories that are applied in the analysis of class locations simply do not map onto ones that are of any known value in explaining how such action is generated; and thus, in order to achieve any relevance for practice, structuralist analyses of the kind in question must always be supplemented by 'untheorised' – i.e. essentially *ad hoc* – appeals to the effects of specific political or ideological circumstances.[5]

So far at least, then, Marxist attempts to adapt class analysis to the expansion of higher-grade white-collar employment, and to achieve some understanding of the political implications of this expansion, can scarcely be regarded as successful. At the same time, though, it has also to be recognised that intellectual efforts made in similar directions but under the inspiration of political interests of a different character do not prove to be significantly more convincing.

For example, American writers of generally liberal persuasion were initially inclined to take a highly positive view of the progressive 'up-grading' of the occupational structure which accompanies economic growth. This process ensured that Marxist expectations of intensifying class polarisation would be disappointed, and that in fact modern society would become increasingly 'middle class'. Furthermore, the growing influence of the values of professionalism and managerialism were seen as crucial in shaping a new, 'post-capitalist' social order which would be both more efficient and also more humane and just than that which had preceded it.[6] However, such optimistic perspectives, characteristic of the 1950s and earlier 1960s, could not, it seems, be sustained as American liberalism was forced to come to terms with subsequent outbursts of cultural and political radicalism. For what was found most perplexing and disturbing about this radicalism was that it appeared to arise not primarily from among the more deprived and disadvantaged groups within American society, but rather from among members of the new middle strata whose emergence had been regarded as powerfully reinforcing social stability.

In response to this situation there has then been developed the theory – or rather a number of different theories – of what has for the most part been termed simply the 'new class'. The common ground here would seem to be that this is a class whose economic basis lies in its 'cultural capital' – that is, in its members' possession of relatively high levels of education and training – and whose interests can therefore be differentiated both from those of the owners of capital in the conventional sense and from those who have no more to offer on the market than their labour. But, beyond this, interpretations diverge in a way that evidently reflects the severe political strains to which American liberalism has been subjected.

On the one hand, for those commentators whose reaction to the radicalism of the late 1960s and 1970s was a shift towards 'neo-Conservatism' – for example, Moynihan, Kristol or Wildavsky – the motivation of the leaders of this radicalism is to be sought chiefly in their envy, frustrated ambition and self-seeking. Although holding materially and psychologically rewarding occupations, members of the new class, it is argued, still feel set apart, especially in terms of status and power, from those whose position in society is founded on substantial wealth. They are thus highly receptive to 'adversary culture' (which embodies a democratised version of the old aristocratic disdain for industry and commerce), and at the same time find in political activity, and especially in that directed towards increasing governmental intervention and control, a valuable counter-resource to wealth. While invoking the ideals of equality and collective concern for the under-privileged, they seek unremittingly to strengthen their own class position.[7] On the other hand, though, among liberals who have themselves become radicalised to some extent, the new class, as might be expected, is viewed in a less hostile, more hopeful, manner. Thus, for instance, Gouldner has argued that the new class has to be seen as 'morally ambivalent'. It undoubt-

John Goldthorpe

edly pursues its own elitist aspirations and cultivates its own class interests, but it *is* also capable of perceiving and representing the collective interest; and, moreover, chiefly in virtue of its distinctive 'culture of critical discourse', it has the potential to be a decisive emancipatory force against all forms of economic and political domination. Indeed, Gouldner would go so far as to claim that if a 'universal class' is to be recognised in modern society, this must now be the new class, however flawed, rather than the industrial proletariat whose potential is exhausted.[8]

The major difficulty of such theories of the new class is rather apparent, and may be regarded as in effect the converse of that found in the Marxist analyses previously outlined. The latter begin with attempts to determine the changing structure of class positions and formations, but the results of these theoretical endeavours do not relate satisfactorily to the observed pattern of socio-political action. In contrast, 'new class' theories have been directly prompted by an apparent shift in this pattern – an upsurge of radicalism within the middle strata – but the difficulty then is that of providing an adequate account of the structural location of the actors involved. In effect, a class analysis is being pursued in order to explain a phenomenon which – aside from appearing rather transient – has never been more than a minority one. The fact that certain expressions of radicalism can be predominantly associated with the new middle strata does not of course mean that these strata are predominantly radical, and 'new class' theories tend thus to be always in danger of over-explaining. Indeed, it would seem that their exponents are often uneasily aware of this danger; for, as their arguments develop, it is rather typically the case that their conceptions of the new class become in some way narrowed down, so that they would seem intended to apply in fact only to certain quite limited sections of the middle strata: for example, only to employees in the public or 'non-profit' sector, or to the 'scientific intelligentsia', or to those with a 'liberal arts background', or even just to 'intellectuals'. However, since such redefinitions are for the most part undertaken only implicitly or tacitly, they do little to help matters. While the diversity of new class theories is made still more apparent, it becomes hard to know in any particular instance exactly what is being claimed and, especially, exactly what connection is being proposed between a given class or occupational location and a propensity to radicalism.[9]

It can thus be said that a satisfactory account of the sociological and political significance of the expansion of higher-level white-collar employment is still to be provided. But the attempts reviewed above do at least have the value of pointing up the basic *desiderata* for such an account or at least for one which is to be offered in terms of class. First, it is of course necessary that good grounds should be given for treating the range of employment in question as bringing individuals into essentially similar class positions and relations; but, second, it is also necessary that the issue of how such structural analysis is to be linked to observed patterns of collective action should be explicitly faced. It is, then, the central purpose of this paper to argue that by developing the idea of the service class, and by allying this to the concept of class formation, the way can at least be indicated of meeting these *desiderata* somewhat more adequately than hitherto.

II

The idea of the service class originates with the Austro-Marxist, Karl Renner.[10] For Renner, the service class (*Dienstklasse*) comprised three main elements: employees in public – i.e. governmental – service (civil servants and other officials); employees in private economic service (business administrators, managers, technical experts, etc.); and employees in social services ('distributive agents of welfare'). Renner follows a fairly orthodox line of Marxist analysis in arguing that while these groupings do not share in the ownership of the means of production, they are still to be distinguished from the working class in that the labour they perform is non-productive: they are not themselves a source of surplus value but, rather, a charge on the surplus value which is extracted, directly or indirectly, from the working class. However, at the same time Renner seeks also to distinguish the service class from the working class in a way which is of far greater sociological interest and consequence: that is, by emphasising the extent to which the 'code of service' that regulates the employment relationship of service-class members differs in its implications from the 'labour contract' that applies in the case of the working class. Thus, starting, it would seem, from Max Weber's classic account of the position of the bureaucratic official, Renner points out that 'a salary differs fundamentally by its nature and in the way it is assessed from a wage'; and further that the salaried employee is set apart from the wage worker by both the relative security of his employment and by his prospects for material and status advancement. But what is of key importance is that Renner recognises, as underlying all these dif-

John Goldthorpe

ferences in conditions of employment, a more basic difference between the 'service relationship' and that of employer to wage worker which lies, one might say, in their moral quality: namely, that the former relationship, in contrast with the latter, necessarily involves an important measure of *trust*. It is, then, this insight of Renner's which may most usefully be exploited for present purposes: that is, in seeking to fill out the idea of the service class and to employ it in understanding the place of professional, administrative and managerial employees within the class structure of contemporary capitalist society.[11]

To begin with, it may be suggested that the requirement for trust in the employment relationship derives from two main exigencies that an employer, or employing organisation, may face: first, that which arises when authority must be delegated; and second, that which arises when specialist knowledge and expertise must be drawn upon. For what in both these cases is implied is that social control within the organisation must be weakened or at all events diffused; it can no longer be exerted directly and in a detailed fashion from a single source. Those employees to whom authority is delegated or to whom responsibility for specialist functions is assigned are *thereby* given some legitimate area of autonomy and discretion. And it must then *pro tanto* be a matter of trust that they will act – i.e. will make decisions, choices, judgements, etc. – in ways that are consistent with organisational goals and values. In other words, how well these employees perform from the standpoint of the organisation will in crucial respects depend on the degree of their moral commitment to the organisation, rather than on the efficacy of 'external' sanctions and rewards.[12]

However, this is not to say that no connection exists between the nature of these employees' work tasks and roles and the typical form of their conditions of employment. On the contrary, the conditions which in their case regularly apply – the conditions, in effect, of bureaucratic employment – are ones which clearly reflect, whether by design or evolution, the need for creating and sustaining an organisational commitment. Most obviously, perhaps, a broad tendency exists for the degree of discretion that an employee exercises to be associated with his level of remuneration. But of greater importance here are more qualitative features of the bureaucratic or service relationship through which its 'market' character is considerably modified. In the case of the wage-worker, the labour contract provides for more or less discrete amounts of labour to be exchanged for wages on a relatively short-term basis; but the service relationship is such that the exchange in which employer and employee are involved has to be defined in a much less specific and longer-term fashion and with far greater moral content. It is not so much that reward is being offered in return for work done, but rather 'compensation' and 'consideration' in return for the acceptance of an obligation to discharge trust 'faithfully'. This is then, as Renner implicitly suggests, the real significance of payment in the form of a salary rather than of wages, and likewise of the range of 'fringe benefits' with which the bureaucratic employee is usually provided. But what is yet more central to the logic of the service relationship, in regard to monitoring and maintaining the quality of service given, is the part played by rewards that are of an essentially *prospective* kind: that is, as embodied in understandings on salary increments, on security both in employment and after retirement and, above all, on career opportunities.

The argument for treating professional, administrative and managerial employees as holding basically similar class positions may therefore be put as follows. These employees, in being typically engaged in the exercise of delegated authority or in the application of specialist knowledge and expertise, operate in their work tasks and roles with a distinctive degree of autonomy and discretion; and in direct consequence of the element of trust that is thus necessarily involved in their relationship with their employing organisation, they are accorded conditions of employment which are also distinctive in both the level and kind of rewards that are involved. In other words, professional, administrative and managerial employees are in these ways typically differentiated from other grades of employee – and most obviously from wage-workers – in the character of both their work and their market situations. Given this conception of the basis of the service class, it then becomes possible in turn to treat fairly systematically various issues which arise concerning both its internal divisions and its 'boundaries' with other classes.

The objection which has perhaps most often been made to the idea of the service class as introduced by Renner and as previously developed (most notably by Dahrendorf)[13] is that it seeks to bring together two broad occupational groupings – professional employees, on the one hand, and administrators and managers, on the other – which in fact differ significantly in their position and function within the division of labour. Thus, for example, Giddens has contended that while individuals in these two groupings may have generally similar market situations, they are at the same time typically involved in quite different kinds of 'para-technical relations'.[14] However, in the conception of the service class that has been presented, no claim arises

169

that its constituent occupational groupings do share in similar 'para-technical relations'. The basic commonality in the work situations of members of these groupings, from which the similarity in their market situations in turn derives, is seen to lie rather at the more fundamental level of the degree of autonomy and discretion with which they necessarily operate – in response to the two organisational exigencies that were identified: the need to delegate authority (met chiefly via the administrative-managerial function) and the need to draw on specialised knowledge and expertise (met chiefly via the professional function). From this point of view, then, the occupational differences that have concerned Giddens and others may best be associated with *situs* divisions that can be traced *within* the service class, just as they can of course within other classes. And, it may be added, the service class, again like other classes, can also be seen as being sectorally divided – the public/private division as recognised by Renner being perhaps of major importance; and, further, as being internally stratified in terms of the levels of wealth, income, consumption standards, etc., of its constituent individuals and families.[15]

As regards the boundaries of the service class, there are two main issues that call for comment. First, since the service class, as conceptualised, is a class of employees who are appointed to the positions they hold, some higher agency is evidently presupposed, and the question thus arises of how this should be understood. The idea of a service class can, for example, be readily allied with that of a capitalist or ruling class, as indeed it was in Renner's initial account. However, to posit a superior *class* is not the only conceptual possibility. Alternatively, for example, control over the service class may be seen as exercised, with differing degrees of directness, by a number of elites with memberships of differing degrees of stability. Which of these models is generally the more valid for Western societies of the present day is, of course, a matter of major debate, and one which must be settled ultimately by means of relevant empirical enquiry. But, for present purposes, the important point which can in any event be made is that a crucial differentiating feature exists to mark off in principle – though borderline groupings will inevitably exist – the higher echelons of the service class from those who, so to speak, stand over them: namely, that the latter owe their positions not to processes of bureaucratic appointment and advancement but rather to their own *power*, whether the bases of this are economic, political, military or whatever.[16]

The second issue which arises also derives from the idea of the service class as a distinctive class of employees. The foregoing attempt to characterise the service class has proceeded largely on the basis of comparisons drawn between the work and market situations of professional, administrative and managerial employees and those of rank-and-file wage-workers. However, the question then presents itself of the position of various other, quite sizeable, groupings of employees that may be identified within modern societies: most notably, routine clerical and sales workers, technicians, foremen and other supervisory personnel. The line of division between these groupings and the lower levels of the service class may indeed be often difficult to establish in particular cases. But if the key analytical issue here is taken as that of the nature of the exchange involved in the employment relationship of individuals in these groupings, then it would appear that, for the most part, they must be placed outside the service class. For although usually accorded at least some aspects of 'salaried staff' status, what such employees most often, and most crucially, lack are the prospective rewards implicit in the service relationship in the form of security of status and recognised career lines. Occupational groupings of the kind in question, it may be argued, are the truly 'intermediate' ones within the class structure of modern capitalism. While set apart from rank-and-file labour in some cases by their function and more generally by their conditions of employment, they remain differentiated from those groupings that constitute the service class in being only imperfectly integrated into the bureaucratic structures of their employing organisations.[17]

III

Having set out the grounds on which professional, administrative and managerial employees may be regarded as occupying similar class positions, and ones which may be distinguished from those of other major groupings, the next step might appear to be that of specifying the interests that are associated with these positions and, on this basis, seeking to interpret the pattern of socio-political action displayed by service-class members. However, it is a central theoretical claim of this paper that in order to link satisfactorily the analysis of class positions to the understanding of collective action, a crucial intervening variable must be recognised: namely, that of processes of class formation. These processes may be divided into two main kinds: first, those associated with the extent to which classes acquire

John Goldthorpe

a demographic identity – that is, become identifiable as collectivities through the continuity with which individuals and families retain their class positions over time; and second, those associated with the extent to which classes acquire a socio-cultural identity – that is, become identifiable through the shared and distinctive life-styles of their members and their patterns of preferred association.

So far as the degree of formation of the present-day service class is concerned, a primary consideration must be the remarkable growth of this class in all Western societies in the course of recent decades. Time-series showing in detail the proportionate expansion of professional, administrative and managerial employment can be derived from national census statistics; but as a rough indication of the order of magnitude of the development in question, it may be said that while in the early twentieth century, professional, administrative and managerial employees accounted for only 5–10% of the active population in even the most economically advanced nations, by the present time they quite generally account in Western societies for 20–25%.

The more immediate causes of this expansion can be seen as ones which have created the organisational exigencies for the delegation of authority and the application of specialist knowledge and expertise in which, it has been argued, the *raison d'être* of the service relationship resides. Among these causes could be numbered, first, a growth in the scale of organisation – in government, business, social welfare, etc. – and in the range of functions pursued through such organisation; second, the steady advance in the technology thus employed; and, third, an increase in specialisation and so-called 'rationalisation', which in effect typically involves the removal of such discretion and autonomy in work as lower-level employees may possess and their concentration at higher levels, in professional, administrative or managerial hands.[18]

However, in regard to the formation of the service class, it is the *consequences* rather than the causes of its rapid rate of expansion that are of chief importance; and two in particular should be stressed. First, the pressure of demand for professional, administrative and managerial employees, at least over the period since the Second World War, has meant that the basis of recruitment to the service class has been remarkably wide. Results from national studies of social mobility regularly indicate that only a minority – usually between a quarter and a third – of men (and women) presently found in service-class positions are in fact the offspring of parents who held such positions.

172

Table 1. *Inter-generational recruitment of men, age 20–64, in service-class positions in three Western societies (early 1970s)*

	Service-class members in		
Class of origin	England (1972)	France (1970)	Sweden (1974)
	% by column		
Service class	31	31	24
Routine non-manual	10	12	6
Petty bourgeoisie	11	17	14
Farmers	3	10	14
Working class (including foremen and agricultural workers)	46	29	42
TOTAL	101	99	100
Service class as % of total male employed population	25	22	24

Source: Calculated from data presented in Robert Erikson, John H. Goldthorpe and Lucienne Portocarero, 'Intergenerational Class Mobility in Three Western European Societies', *British Journal of Sociology* vol. 30 (1979), *q.v.* for further details of data, categories, etc.

For example, recently assembled data for England, France and Sweden, in which a relatively high degree of comparability in class categories has been achieved, display the pattern of inter-generational recruitment of men to service-class positions that is presented in Table 1.[19] That this pattern does essentially derive from the expansion of the service class – rather than from some increase in the equality of class mobility chances – may be confirmed by further analyses of the data in question. These reveal that the *relative* chances of access to service-class positions of men of different class origins in fact change only slightly, if at all, across successive birth cohorts.[20]

Secondly, it is important to recognise that the extent of demand for service-class personnel has, in some instances, resulted in the recruitment of substantial numbers of individuals whose levels of education and formal qualification are rather surprisingly low. The British case provides perhaps the most striking illustration of this point, as is suggested by the data of Table 2. As might be expected, it is within the administrative and managerial situses rather than the professional one that the degree of evident 'under qualification' is

John Goldthorpe

Table 2. *Levels of education and qualification of men, age 20–64, in service-class positions, England and Wales, 1972*

| Occupational grouping | % having | | |
	Selective secondary education[a]	University degree[b]	No formal qualification of vocational relevance
Professionals (including higher-grade technical employees)	69	20	15
Administrators and officials	66	7	47
Industrial and business managers	65	5	40

Notes:
(a) I.e. at grammar, technical or independent school
(b) Including recognised equivalents such as Diplomas in Technology
Source: Oxford National Occupational Mobility Inquiry, 1972

most marked. Nonetheless, taken overall, these data still point up clearly enough the danger of seeking to characterise the groupings that have here been taken as constituting the service class in essentially 'supply-side' terms: that is, in terms of their distinctive possession of 'cultural capital' or of their 'command over theoretical knowledge'. In fact, the level of education and formal qualification within the present-day service class would appear to display a rather high degree of cross-national variation – depending chiefly on whether some movement towards the mass provision of 'tertiary' education was achieved before the period of rapid expansion of service-class occupations or, rather, as in the British case, only when this expansion was already well under way.[21]

As a result, therefore, of their wide basis of recruitment and the possibly very variable levels of education and training of their members, the service classes of present-day Western societies can be expected to have only a rather low degree of both demographic and socio-cultural identity. To the extent that the individuals occupying service-class positions are 'first-generation', with diverse social origins, backgrounds and biographies, they are likely in turn to fol-

low more diverse life-styles and to be involved in more socially het-
erogeneous patterns of association than would be characteristic of
members of a class at a relatively high level of formation. An illustration of the latter point can be provided by the data of Table 3. These
suggest that both the fact of being inter-generationally mobile into
the service class and also the mobility route followed – which is closely
linked with educational attainment – have an effect on the extent of
the individual's cross-class ties. Thus, it can be seen, those upwardly
mobile men who entered (higher-level) service-class positions only
some years after completing their full-time education have most cross-
class ties, and in fact draw only a little over half of their most frequent spare-time associates and of their other 'good friends' from
among other service-class members.

However, while the rapid growth of the service class has clearly
had consequences that have militated against a high degree of class
formation, it must also be recognised that, even within this period
of expansion, a number of countervailing tendencies are evident –
and ones which would seem likely to be of major significance for the
future. First, where data are available on patterns of class mobility or
immobility in *lifetime* perspective, it is regularly observed that men
who enter service-class occupations – from whatever origins and via
whatever route – have a very low probability of thereafter leaving
such occupations.[22] This finding, one would suggest, results in part
directly from the character of the service relationship. The understanding on security of employment and status, which was identified
as one of the key rewards held out by employing organisations to
motivate the faithful discharge of trust, is scarcely compatible with
the frequent practice of radical demotion. Thus, where service-class
personnel fall short of the expectations of their employers, the outcome tends to be – other than in the most extreme cases – not dis-
missal from or relegation within the bureaucratic hierarchy, such as
would imply a decisive *déclassement* of the individual, but rather an
absolute or relative lack of advancement within this hierarchy. However, from the present standpoint what is chiefly important is that
the continuity with which service-class positions are typically held
is a major factor in the formation of the expanding service class at the
level of demographic identity or, in other words, as a specific social
collectivity.[23]

Secondly, while national mobility studies regularly reveal a wide
basis of inter-generational recruitment to service-class positions, they
also reveal, with no less regularity, that expanding service classes

Table 3. Class distribution of most frequent spare-time associates and other 'good friends' for sub-samples of service-class members (males, age 25–49, England and Wales, 1974) selected by mobility pattern

Mobility pattern	Class distribution (%) of					
	Most frequent spare-time associates			Other 'good friends'		
	Service	Intermediate	Working	Service	Intermediate	Working
Inter-generationally stable in higher level of service class (N=75)	63	28	9	81	14	5
Directly mobile to higher level of service class (i.e. on completion of full-time education) from lower intermediate or working-class origins (N=100)	61	32	8	67	26	7
Indirectly mobile to higher level of service class from lower intermediate or working-class origins (N=151)	51	32	17	58	31	11

Source: Goldthorpe et al., Social Mobility and Class Structure, Table 7.1, 7.2, 7.7 and 7.8, q.v. for further details of data, categories, etc.

Table 4. *Class destinations of men of service-class origins by birth cohort in three Western societies (early 1970s)*

Country	Birth cohort	Class destination				
		Service class	Routine non-manual	Petty bourgeoisie and farmers	Working class (including foremen and agricultural workers)	Total
		per cent by row				
England	1908–22	58	11	8	22	99
	1923–27	64	7	8	20	99
France	1906–20	60	9	14	16	99
	1921–35	64	9	7	20	100
Sweden	1910–24	57	12	10	22	101
	1925–39	67	11	5	17	100

Source: Calculated from data presented in Robert Erikson, John H. Gold-thorpe and Lucienne Portocarero, 'Intergenerational Class Mobility in Three Western European Societies', *British Journal of Sociology* vol. 30 (1979), *q.v.* for further details of data, categories, etc.

preserve a high degree of inter-generational *stability*. Thus, the comparative class mobility data for England, France and Sweden that were previously drawn upon can be further used to show, as in Table 4, that in each country alike a majority of those men who were the sons of service-class fathers were themselves found in service-class positions; and that, again in each country, that proportion *rises* from the older to the younger of two successive birth cohorts.[24] Moreover, as earlier indicated, in no case do any sizeable shifts appear to have occurred over time in the – obviously very favourable – chances of men of service-class origins gaining access to service-class positions relative to the chances of men of other origins being mobile into the service class. Not only, then, do individuals, once established in the service class, tend to retain their positions, but a similar tendency may be said to apply in the case of families also; and the demographic identity of the service class is, of course, in this way further developed.

It has been sometimes claimed by Marxist authors that the growth of the service class is more apparent than real – reflecting to some

John Goldthorpe

substantial extent the 'dilution' of professional, administrative and managerial occupations either through actual processes of de-grading or alternatively through the spurious up-grading – or mere relabelling – of what are really only routine technical, clerical or supervisory jobs.[25] But this argument is difficult to reconcile with the evidence of the apparently undiminished capacity of the service class to 'reproduce' itself, even as its numbers have increased. To no less an extent than previously, members of present-day service classes would appear to be advantaged, in comparison with most other sections of the population, in terms of the resources, economic and otherwise, on which they are able to draw in order both to maintain their own positions and to further the life chances of their children. The impression that generally emerges from the relevant data is of a class which, far from being threatened with any kind of decomposition, is rather at one and the same time expanding *and* consolidating.

Finally in this connection it should also be noted that various indications exist that the growing demographic identity of the service class will in future tend to be accompanied by a parallel development of its socio-cultural identity. To begin with, although the social origins of present-day service-class members are indeed diverse, there seems little reason for supposing that any serious barriers exist to the socio-cultural assimilation even of those who have experienced mobility of a long-range kind. Thus, while the upwardly mobile sub-samples of service-class members represented in Table 3 are shown to have, overall, fewer spare-time associates and other 'good friends' from within the service class than do men inter-generationally stable in this class, it is also the case that only a smallish minority have *no* such ties of sociability with other service-class members: in fact, only 10% among those whose mobility was 'direct' and 20% among those whose mobility was 'indirect'.[26] And it is relevant here to add that the clear trend evident across birth cohorts of current members of the service class, in Britain and elsewhere, is for the 'direct' mobility route to become increasingly important.[27] Thus, it may be anticipated that differences in educational background, and hence in lifestyles, both among those mobile into the service class and between its mobile and stable components will steadily diminish.

Furthermore, it also seems unlikely that the situs divisions that have been recognised within the service class will prove a source of major socio-cultural differentiation. For one thing, mobility between these situses would appear to be fairly frequent, both in the course of working life and inter-generationally. In the former case, the most notable tendency is for professionals eventually to take up administrative and managerial positions; while conversely, in the latter, it is for the sons of administrators and managers to be, if anything, *more* likely to be found in professional occupations than in ones similar to their fathers'.[28] Then again, various kinds of evidence can be provided to suggest that men in different types of employment within the service class represent preferred associates for each other in sociable activities.[29] In sum, it may reasonably be supposed that a broad similarity in life-styles prevails from one situs to another, and that cross-situs social ties are quite extensive.

IV

From the foregoing discussion of the formation of the service class one conclusion regarding judgements of its socio-political potential may then rather readily be drawn: namely, that it could well be misleading to seek for indications of how this potential might subsequently develop in the pattern of socio-political action actually displayed by salaried employees to date. As was earlier remarked in criticism of 'new class' theorists, this pattern must be recognised as a far from uniform one, and indeed as one which, from a class perspective, appears more or less incoherent. Such a situation, it can now be seen, can scarcely be thought surprising, if for no other reason than on account of the rapid growth of the service class in the recent past and, in turn, its still relatively unformed state. In such circumstances it must always be problematic how far the socio-political orientations of class members can be related to the positions they hold in common, or have rather to be understood in terms of the very varied social trajectories that they will have followed in the course of reaching these positions.[30] It is in fact only as the tendencies that will serve to increase the demographic and cultural identity of the service class become further advanced that a more consistent pattern of action might be expected to emerge, and one that is more capable of being given a specifically 'class' interpretation.

One may thus further conclude that the best basis for informed speculation on the future of the service class as a socio-political force must at this stage lie in an analysis that proceeds from structural considerations. However, this will need to be one undertaken on significantly different lines from those followed in Marxist accounts of the new 'intermediate strata' of the kind that were earlier reviewed. That is to say, the concern must be not with class relationships defined abstractly, in terms of an economic theory from which no bridges to social action can be constructed, but rather with the actual, empirically determinable, social relations that prevail between service-class members and members of other classes. And in turn, class interests, rather than being dogmatically 'imputed', must be understood as arising directly out of these social relations and as having a subjectively meaningful connection with them for the actors involved. While no analysis of this kind can be developed in detail within the scope of the present paper, certain major outcomes may be anticipated and set in critical contrast with those of other accounts.

To begin with, from the conception of the service class that has been presented the clear expectation must be that this class, as it consolidates, will constitute an essentially *conservative* element within modern societies.[31] Although the service class is a class of employees who are subordinate to some form of higher agency, it is also the case that the employments in which its members are engaged are those which would be generally reckoned as most desirable in terms of both the intrinsic and extrinsic rewards that they afford. It has been taken as a defining characteristic of service-class occupations that they involve the exercise of authority and/or of specialised knowledge and expertise. And consequently, it has been argued, their incumbents perform their work tasks and roles with some significant degree of autonomy and discretion, and furthermore enjoy conditions of employment which are decidedly advantaged relative to those of other grades of employee, especially when viewed in lifetime perspective. From this standpoint, therefore, the service class appears as one which has a substantial stake in the *status quo*, and little structural basis is evident either for the Marxist concern with some possible alliance between the working class and groupings that have been here regarded as constituent of the service class, or for the preoccupation – whether in fear or hope – of 'new class' theorists with the potential of such groupings to generate new forms of cultural and political radicalism.

What would appear to be chiefly neglected by Marxist authors is the problem of how professional, administrative and managerial employees can come to see their interests as being served by the radically egalitarian elements which would, presumably, be central to a socialist political programme. The expectation must rather be – unless powerful countervailing influences can be identified – that these employees will in the main act in the way that is characteristic of members of privileged strata: that is, that they will seek to use the superior resources that they possess in order to *preserve* their positions of relative social power and advantage, for themselves and for their children. Indeed, it would already seem rather clear that the legitimatory ideology to which the service class will primarily resort in the context of distributional conflict is that of 'meritocracy' – with the definition and criteria of merit being so conceived as to maximise its members' competitive advantages. And the associated 'exclusionary strategy', to follow Parkin's recent analysis, is then that of 'credentialism' or, in other words, the use of formal qualifications as a means of controlling entry to – rather than of guaranteeing performance in – the more desirable locations within the division of labour.[32]

As was previously noted, the evidence on class mobility chances would indicate that even over the period of the rapid expansion of the service class, the favourable position of men of service-class origins, and especially relative to those of working-class origins, has been generally maintained. And there would seem little reason to suppose that as the degree of formation of the service class increases, it will become in any way less ready, or less able, to engage in distributional conflict – in which the working class could be reckoned as its major adversary. Indeed, a greater degree of stability and social homogeneity within the service class may be expected to provide a firmer basis for a tendency that is already clearly strengthening: that is, for service-class groupings to pursue further their material interests through organisation and various forms of 'trade-union' action. Such a strategy is, of course, of long standing in the case of many professional groupings but is at the present time being increasingly adopted by administrative and managerial employees. And rather than this being taken as indicative of proletarianisation – as in the more facile Marxist interpretations – it may on the contrary be far better seen as an attempt to prevent proletarianisation and to maintain favourable class differentials in pay and conditions and in life-chances generally.[33]

Moreover, even if attention is focussed more specifically, as Marxists might wish, on the sphere of production rather than of distribution, it would still seem that the service class and the working class are structurally oriented far more towards conflict than collaboration. It may be insisted that the members of these classes have in common the position of employees, excluded from the ownership or strategic control of the means of production; but over against the significance of this fact for social action must be set that of the major differences that exist between their characteristic work situations. Thus, it may be argued, any expectation – such as was held by 'new working-class' theorists – that a revival of *syndicalisme gestionnaire* might be spearheaded by groupings of professionals, technologists

John Goldthorpe

and other *cadres* is likely to be disappointed, in that the interests of these grades of employee in issues of control tend to be divergent from those of rank-and-file workers. It is in the nature of the work activities performed by members of the service class that they provide an area of autonomy and discretion; and a class interest may well exist in enlarging this area or, in other words, in reducing the degree of control exercised 'from above'. But any kind of generalised workplace democracy which would give greater decision-making and regulatory power to the rank-and-file could only be threatening to service-class employees in implying a greater degree of control 'from below' – what would in effect appear from their point of view as undue interference in their professional judgement and expertise or undue limitation of their administrative and managerial prerogatives. If meritocratic arguments will form the basis of the resistance of the service class to greater distributional equality, then technocratic ones, it may be expected, will be typically deployed against attempts to create more egalitarian relations in production.

From the standpoint of 'new class' theorists, a structural approach to the supposed radical potential of this class is clearly problematic, since their prime concern is to explain disaffection with the established order on the part of those who are recognised as occupying relatively privileged positions within it. Moreover, unlike Marxist authors, they do not wish to postulate any basic opposition of interest between the new class and a capitalist or ruling class standing over above it. In fact, 'new class' theorists appear generally to accept the view that the power to which new-class members are ultimately subordinate has by now become largely dispersed among a number of functionally differentiated elites. Consequently, the explanatory accounts to which they resort are forced onto essentially psychologistic lines, and centre on the *hostility* that is felt by the new class towards those who can outrank them on the basis of wealth and its attributes. It could further be said that the emphasis in these accounts often falls on factors that are more obviously related to the newness of the new class than to its 'classness' – for example, its members' experience of mobility, 'status inconsistency' or cultural discontinuity.[34] Where, then, 'new class' theorists would seem to be at their weakest is in failing to supply any good grounds for the expectation that the white-collar radicalism which has seized their attention will be sustained and generalised. In contrast, the argument that would follow from the conception of the service class here developed would rather be that while such radicalism may continue to erupt sporadically, the fact that it does indeed have no structural basis – such as a grounding in conflictual class relations – means that it is unlikely to result in any large-scale mobilisation against the *status quo*. Even as the service class reaches a higher level of formation, white-collar radicalism will remain minoritarian, intermittent and localised; and indeed, to the extent that recent manifestations *do* reflect, so to speak, the growing pains of this class, then, with its consolidations, a *decline* in radical impulses could be anticipated.[35]

Finally, some comment would seem necessary in one respect in which a degree of convergence does apparently occur between the analysis of the present paper and those of both Marxist and 'new class' theorists: that is, no reason emerges for supposing that the service class will have any particular commitment to capitalism *per se*. Insofar as its privileged position is one actually established within a capitalist social order, it is difficult to see the service class as providing the basis for a serious attack on this order. But if as a result of the functioning – or malfunctioning – of the capitalist economy, threats were to become evident to its privileged position, then, it could well be supposed, the service class would show more concern with the preservation of the latter than the former. The interests of bureaucratic employees have after all no intrinsic connection with the institutions of private property in production or the free-market system – as was indeed already noted with some foreboding by conservative commentators at the time when the numerical preponderance of such employees over independent businessmen and professionals was first becoming apparent.[36]

As, then, in recent years the performance of Western capitalist economies has evidently deteriorated, much interest has centred on the response of professionals, administrators and managers to the threats posed to them by unemployment and, more pervasively, by underemployment and the contraction of career opportunities. For a number of writers, pursuing both Marxist and 'new class' lines of analysis, the ending of the long boom of the post-war period clearly signals the emergence of objective conditions under which the radicalisation of higher-level white-collar employees may be envisaged on a far wider basis than hitherto.[37] However, several grounds for scepticism in this regard may be noted, consistently with the general argument that has been advanced on the essential conservatism of the service class.

First, although there can be no doubt that threats to the security and prospects of advancement of service-class members have increased, and may well increase further, it does not automatically follow that these difficulties will be interpreted in such a way that will lead to political dissidence.[38] Apart from anything else, it must be kept in mind that in times of economic contraction, class inequalities may well widen: the incidence of unemployment shows a marked class bias, being of course most severe among manual wage-workers and in turn serving generally to undermine their bargaining strength. Thus, a tendency for a period of deflation and recession to be viewed within the service class as some kind of economic – or political – necessity may be encouraged by the probability that the relative position of its members within the distributional struggle would be preserved or even improved. Secondly, if a strong political response were to be provoked, it is by no means assured that this would be one that would bring the service class together with other employee groupings in some kind of 'leftist' movement. And especially if the relative advantages of the service class *were* in some way being eroded, it might be thought at least as likely that any radical reaction would indeed occur in the opposite direction. It is here obviously worth recalling that in the inter-war years sociological interest in the 'new middle classes' came eventually to focus on their propensity to *resist* proletarianisation and, in some instances, to respond to threats to their class and status position by lending their support to authoritarian attempts at buttressing the capitalist order.

In the circumstances of the present day, it may be suggested, service-class disaffection is in fact most likely to be produced by crude neo-liberal policies which, in seeking to revive Western economies by reinforcing specifically capitalist disciplines and incentives, lead in effect to the depression of economic activity, and the severe restriction of public expenditure, on a *long-term* basis. But even then it may be doubted whether such disaffection would be associated with any substantial movement of service-class opinion in favour of trying to overcome current economic difficulties through distinctively left-wing measures – with their quite unwelcome egalitarian implications; and all the more so since from the standpoint of the service class other clearly more attractive political options may be identified. In particular, one may point here to the varieties of 'liberal' or 'bargained' corporatism which have emerged in the recent past out of largely pragmatic attempts to achieve a more comprehensively 'managed' capitalism. Within these forms of political economy, distributional processes, and pay determination especially, become subject to greater political control; and distributional outcomes thus reflect, over and above market power, the effectiveness with which collective interests receive organised representation. However, as was earlier remarked, an increasingly stable and socially homogeneous service class is unlikely to be at any disadvantage in this respect. And moreover, in corporatist institutions and procedures it may hope to achieve the yet more secure establishment of the principles of meritocracy and technocracy through which it seeks to give its privileged position a rational and moral basis.

The state and the professions: peculiarities of the British

TERRY JOHNSON

The central focus in what follows is a critique of the way in which sociologists have conventionally conceptualised the relationship between the state and the professions. In particular, it is an attack on the way in which the history of that relationship has been moulded by the concepts of *state intervention* and *professional autonomy*, and the attendant assumption that there is a simple, inverse relationship between the two – the more 'intervention' the less 'autonomy'. The inadequacy of this dualism as a representation of the historical relations between the processes of state formation and occupational development will be illustrated by way of two necessarily brief, but hopefully suggestive, case studies of the developing relations between professions and state in Britain. In stressing the peculiar nature of these relations the paper also indirectly questions misguided attempts in sociology to derive a universal, 'natural history' or professionalisation from the defining 'classical' British experience.

When Durkheim foresaw a moral renaissance of industrial society, rooted in the ethics of corporate occupations, he distinguished the social benefits arising out of such principles of social regulation from the pathological consequences of centralised regulation by the state.[1] A quarter of a century later, when Carr-Saunders and Wilson produced their major work on the professions, they followed Durkheim in viewing state regulation as, in many instances, an undesirable incursion into matters best left to the autonomous professions.[2] The state/profession relationship has, then, from the beginnings of the sociology of the professions been a central, if at times, submerged theme. However, it is a theme which has been too often constrained by analyses dependent upon the intervention/autonomy couple, particularly where they are presented as exclusive processes and, therefore, alternative histories of the state/profession relationship.

186

Interventionist state versus autonomous professions

The recent growth of interest in the theory of the state has given rise to a literature which suggests a variety of answers to our question: what is the relationship between state and professions? However, these variations arise out of the ways in which the broad functions of the state are conceived rather than in their detailed consequences for the professions. For whether we consider the types of Marxist theory of the state characterised by Jessop as parasitic, epiphenomenal, cohesive, instrumental or institutional or non-Marxist theories of the corporatist or mediative state, we find a surprisingly common theme, that of intervention.[3] State intervention, implying as it does the existence of some external, repressive public authority, has the consequence of transforming professionals into functionaries and their associations into outposts of corporatist organisation or branches of the ideological state apparatus. The major variation allowed for in such theory is the location of the professional-functionary in the state hierarchy; are they bureaucratic heads and, therefore, agents of the controlling apparatus or are they subordinated to bureaucratic authority?

In either case the professions are viewed as becoming engulfed by state power and their autonomy conceived only as an aspect of the general and relative autonomy of the state itself. In the context of such theory, intervention is often the given object of study, the unquestioned material of history and, consequently, theoretical debate focusses on the derived problem: why has the state intervened? It is at this point that the distinct accounts of state functions arise. The state intervenes, it is argued, to coordinate the increasing division of labour; to secure the incorporation of the powerless into civil society through such means as an extension of professional services; to mediate between conflicting groups or classes; to ensure the maintenance of class rule; to maintain the necessary conditions of capital accumulation, etc. Whatever the dynamic of history is taken to be, the historical process is accepted as a given – intervention, with the possibility of its opposite, non-intervention. As a result the relationship of state to professions can only be conceived in terms of such a process: intervention leading to loss of autonomy or non-intervention allowing autonomy.

A common feature of the interventionist thesis is the assumption that the history of the process has its origin in an historical moment of separation or non-intervention; that the origins of the modern professions, for example, are to be identified in the heroic age of

Terry Johnson

laissez-faire when free professionals carved out for themselves a market and autonomously regulated its operation. This is, of course, a sub-plot of the general theme that industrial capitalism is marked by the unique separation of economy and polity. However, where capitalism is seen as having its origins in such a defining societal cleavage it also follows that it has a predetermined history. For significant social change is constituted only by the merging of economic and political structures with political institutions increasingly assuming a dominant role through state intervention. Such a model when applied to the state/profession suggests that the relationship has a history in which a free market in professional services becomes increasingly imbued with political criteria and professional practice is increasingly subordinated to state regulation.

The point I wish to emphasise here is that such primitive assumptions of societal cleavage are more representative of *laissez-faire* ideology than they are of the historical relationship between state and professions, and it will be argued in the first of the case studies below that the transition to capitalism in England was not marked by a separation of economic and political institutions but an historically unique articulation which involved the interrelated processes of state formation and professionalisation.

The second case study stresses that the professions have constituted a significant element in the process of state formation. What the state has become includes its relationship with the professions. Aspects of what have become state powers, functions and capacities are an outcome of that developing relationship and not pre-given capacities of the state to intervene in the workings of autonomous occupations.

At this point it may appear that I am excluding the possibility of autonomy for the professions; that the alternative history of the professions, which characterises them as resistant to state intervention, is a non-starter. While it is true that I am rejecting the alternative history of the professions, as a process of resistance to state intervention, this does not commit me to a view that no profession enjoys autonomy. The tendency in the literature to assume a direct link between state intervention and lack of autonomy is in part an outcome of the interventionist thesis and, in part, the product of a confusion in the way in which the concept of autonomy is used.

This confusion has been greatly exacerbated by the recent writings of Poulantzas and others on the state, where the concept is presented as a formula constructed in order to overcome economic reductionism in Marxist theories of the state.[4] The source of confusion is that the problem of autonomy in such writings is characteristically posed at the system level. It is asserted, for example, that in the stage of monopoly capitalism the political system is 'relatively autonomous' from the economic which, nevertheless, retains its effectivity as the 'determinant of the last instance'. Posed at the system level, autonomy remains an empty formula which merely asserts that there are certain structural contexts within which political action is not directly constrained by economic conditions. Autonomy has meaning, then, only when posed at the level of action. The autonomy of a profession consists of a specific structural context where access to organisational, economic, political and technical resources provides the conditions for independent action. Thus, the relationship of a profession to elements of state apparatus may constitute the very conditions within which occupational autonomy is possible.

If we can rid ourselves of the myth of an homogeneous, external, interventionist state, while at the same time rejecting a concept of autonomy which is specified only as a relationship between system parts, we can move toward a view of the state/profession relationship in which, as an historical process, *the professions are emergent as a condition of state formation and state formation is a major condition of professional autonomy* – where such exists.

The alternative history of the state/profession relationship, which stresses the autonomy of the professions, retains a view of the state as interventionist and repressive but seeks the source of occupational autonomy in some *essence* of professionalism which lies beyond the power of the state to control – variously characterised as competence, expertise, knowledge, technique, etc. Thus, the complexity of occupational knowledge and the esoteric nature of occupational expertise or technique is seen as the motor of this alternative history realised as a process of professionalisation. The professionalisation thesis thereby shares with state interventionism a set of historical blinkers. In both cases history has imposed upon it a known outcome – intervention or autonomy. Such predestination is determined by, on the one hand, the 'given' capacities of the state and on the other by the given capacities of an occupation. A common version of the autonomy thesis is where occupational technique is viewed as operating as a universal limitation on state power.[5] Technique stands outside of and determines the outcome of power relations. According to such a thesis the autonomy of an occupation is secured so long as the occupation is free from 'technical evaluation' by the state. However, what goes to make up professional practice, including technique, may itself be an outcome of the state/profession relationship; 'evaluation' is already present in technique as an historical emergent of the relationship between an occupation and the state. If technique has no history of determinations it remains a universal property of the system and autonomy is the necessary outcome – we are back to the systemic definition of autonomy.

In what has been argued there is no rejection of the view that technique and knowledge are important resources of power and conditions of autonomy. Rather, the argument is that within the framework of the theory of professionalisation, knowledge and/or technique are viewed as independent and universal limitations on state power.

What do these brief comments on the theses of state interventionism and professionalisation imply if we are to generate a more adequate view of the history of the profession/state relationship? We can attempt to struggle out of the strait-jacket which the intervention/autonomy couple imposes upon us through the elaboration of an alternative theoretical discourse, but this will prove sterile unless such a discourse generates the alternative history. For what we now have is a sociological history generated by this dualism and what we require is one which transcends it. Bearing this in mind, then, I make no apologies for immediately plunging into all the problems such an historical project implies. There follow two 'cases' which illustrate the general points made in a more positive fashion. First, those processes we have bundled together under the rubric of professionalisation are integral to the process of state formation and vice versa. Second, the history of this relationship is not one of original separation followed by intervention or resistance to intervention. Third, the historical characteristics of the British professions – which, in much of the literature, are regarded as providing a model of the 'classical' features of the professions in general – are in fact specific to the British or English experience.

State and profession in transition

The first case concerns aspects of the relationship between the state and the legal profession in England in the late eighteenth and early nineteenth centuries, focussing on the struggle for the reform of the legal administration for the recovery of small debts. This movement spawned dozens of parliamentary bills, particularly in the 1820s and 1830s, culminating in the Act of 1846 which set up county courts as local tribunals for debt recovery.[6] The subsequent analysis will suggest that to conceive of the modern history of the relationship between the legal profession and the state as having its origin in some form of separation is a distortion of the historical process. Equally, it will be shown that the notion of a state with pre-given capacities for intervention is a further distortion of a process in which it is the *relationship* between state and profession which mediates the transformation of both.

While a number of significant changes in substantive law facilitating credit expansion had been enacted in the course of the eighteenth century, the legal apparatus for its administration was slower to change, despite mounting demands for reform.[7] The immediate impetus for such demands is clear; the growth of manufacture and commerce in the form of small-scale interdependent units of production and distribution had created a rapidly expanding chain of exchange relations which were in turn dependent on systems of credit and effective means of debt recovery for the maintenance of the money–commodity circuit. Thus, the major pressure for reform came from the provincial manufacturing towns and trading centres; from an emergent urban-bourgeoisie and, significantly, from the men who serviced these interests, the provincial attorneys.[8] The context of this pressure for reform was profound changes in the forms of social regulation. Action geared to modifying the system of debt recovery was itself conditioned by a transformation of the social significance of indebtedness. The creation of a novel apparatus for the legal regulation of indebtedness (in which a debt exists as a charge on the property of another) itself arose out of changes in the conception of property, away from one in which landed property, for example, could not be divorced from social identity and the transfer of property was an expression of binding social ties.

The transformation of land into 'a commodity peculiar only by its immobility and limited quantity' involved a transformation of the relationship of indebtedness also.[9] For many estate workers and tenants indebtedness (even in the eighteenth century) was embedded in diffuse social relations of rights and obligation, which constituted a system of social control such that the desire of the creditor to see the debt discharged was, to a large extent, absent from the relationship. As a technique of subordination indebtedness could be a self-generating system leading to varieties of debt bondage. Also, by the eighteenth century the extent of landed-aristocratic indebtedness had reached huge proportions. Debt creation was a natural part of estate management, stimulated by the creation of the mortgage. Indebtedness was a reflection of social power, and the recourse to law, through encumbrance and a centralised system of legal administration, ensured that a successful claim against a large landowner was very unusual.

Terry Johnson

A condition for change in legal relations was the growing significance of a new form of indebtedness, the product of interdependent relations which developed between 'individual producers or producer and merchant . . . relations of purchase and sale of the finished or half-finished product, or else relations of debt incidental to the supply of raw materials or tools of the craft'.[10] The dynamic was an increasing extension of commodity exchange: 'For production to be carried out as production of commodities (for exchange) suitable ways of conceiving social relations and relations of men to their products have to be found.'[11] Such changes in the social significance of property attendant upon the extension of relationships of commodity exchange created problems of legal regulation which, in turn, involved a restructuring of the state/profession relationship. The process of transformation involved the creation of elements of modern state apparatus – the system of county courts – and novel systems of occupational practice and organisation – professionalism.

The pressure from the provincial manufacturers and attorneys for reform came at a time when the legal administration of debt recovery was highly centralised, cumbersome and costly; a situation which secured the interests of a landed class for whom the legal complexities of encumbrance and centralised systems of administration acted as a bulwark to privilege. The oligarchic power of the landed class was the central feature of a state which operated through mechanisms of patronage and personal ties and whose local power was buttressed by highly centralised metropolitan institutions, including the administration of law. The centralisation of judicial business required that all legal actions had to be initiated in London, all pleading drawn up by counsel there, and all arguments of law heard before a London-based judge. Although the trial of issues of fact often took place at an assize court this was no guarantee of a local hearing. Finally, formal judgment had to be delivered in London. Such a system could involve the plaintiff in an action for debt recovery in engaging a local solicitor, who then commmissioned a London agent to initiate action in the high court. A counsel would be required if the issue were also tried at assize, and further counsel might be retained to draft pleadings and to give opinions on questions of law or procedure.[12] In effect the cost of obtaining a judgment in a defended case averaged four times the amount of dispute. Thus, within the overall system of patronage the monopoly enjoyed by the metropolitan profession gave it an abiding interest in the system and secured its social and political reliability, and the result was a concentration of professional power and wealth in London which stood for decades against growing provincial bourgeois demands. The agency houses in particular, which made up one third of London's solicitors and attorneys, at the turn of the century dominated civil proceedings in concert with the senior bar and expressed a consistent opposition to reform. The pressure for reform within the segmented profession came, therefore, from the provinces, and as was the case with other professions such as medicine and architecture, the provinces were also a source of a parallel pressure for reform of the profession. This was the crucible in which the occupational strategy of professionalism was forged. The emergent strategy of professionalism entailed colleague-combination as a means of advancing claims to equality of competence and practice in opposition to the existing hierarchy of patronage. It also entailed an attack on the operation of patronage in stressing occupationally-defined competence as the basis for individual entry and advancement within the profession.

Thus, in the context of this single movement, we can identify provincial attacks on metropolitan power, a struggle internal to the profession centring on access to the control of the emergent apparatus of legal regulation; a struggle, which at the same time involved early steps in the process of professionalisation. These occupational divisions reflected a wider class struggle between an emergent bourgeoisie and landed interest while at the same time the movement was one aspect of a process of state-*trans*formation.

The passing of the County Courts Act in 1846 which decentralised the legal procedures of debt recovery whilst creating a new level of legal administration entailed both a victory and a defeat for the provincial attorneys. The victory gained was in lowering the cost and rationalising the system of debt recovery – in bringing the courts to the people who needed them. The defeat was in the attorneys' failure to obtain equal rights of representation (with the barristers) in the 500 newly constituted courts. They were cut off from any prospect of crowning their careers by way of elevation to the bench. The modern division between barristers and solicitors was thus enshrined in the new act. In effect, the London bar maintained its privileged position but in a reconstructed form. For the context of the reform movement included a bar whose social acceptability to its patrons and political reliability had been the basis of its potential for independent action even in the eighteenth century; only barristers populated the benches of the high court and it was judges' rules that controlled the solicitors and attorneys.[13] This system, at the beginning of the nineteenth century, Harding describes as a 'bewildering multiplicity of expensive

Terry Johnson

and largely medieval courts', which for two centuries had been allowed to develop their own powers and jurisdictions without benefit of legislation.[14] The fact that the bar was tied into the patronage system is merely another way of indicating that the bar was integral to the pre-capitalist state. Yet at the same time it could be said to have enjoyed a level of autonomy. In the sixth report of the Law Commissioners in 1834 it was said of the Inns of Court: 'We cannot think that a power, in the right use of which society is so deeply interested, ought to be left without control in the hands of persons whose functions are not of a public kind.'[15] Such pleas for state regulation never elicited a legislative response, because by this time the oligarchic power of the bar was already in process of transformation as the institutions of the liberal democratic state emerged as dependent on the doctrine of separation of powers and judicial independence. The state was becoming dependent on the independence of the bar. The Law Society, on the other hand, was the creation of a state charter and became an instrument for effecting the enactments of the state. As Carr-Saunders and Wilson pointed out, 'The (Law) Society has not won for solicitors the autonomy and independence which are the cherished privileges of the Bar. It has subjected them instead to the detailed regulation of innumerable Acts of Parliament, while it has only partially freed them from the dominance of judges.'[16] It is not, however, the case that the Bar emerged as autonomous from the state, but that the historical conditions of its involvement in the process of state transformation ensured a continuing high degree of independent action compared with the lower branch. The failure of the provincial attorneys in the reform of 1846 was a failure to share fully with the barristers this favoured relationship with the state. Thus, power of the bar within the patronage system was a significant condition for the emergence of a divided profession, as were the ramifications of the metropolitan/provincial divide which was to be so significant in the general process of professionalisation in the nineteenth century.

A great anomaly which arises in explaining reform of the legal regulations of indebtedness as an aspect of a general transformation of the form of property under conditions of commodity exchange was that the reconstruction of the state/profession relationship was not accompanied by equally radical reforms in the system of land transfer.[17] Why, in short, was the movement for land registration, which followed closely on the heels of the movement for the reform of debt recovery, a failure? Such a failure is anomalous in terms of any interventionist or reductionist thesis.

194

By the nineteenth century the whole kit of legal instruments designed by lawyers to keep the great estates intact was under attack, and their abolition was demanded by the same emergent bourgeois class grouping who successfully engineered the County Courts Act, except, that is, for one important group; the provincial attorneys. The pressure for reform did not build up as rapidly, reaching its peak only after the passing of the County Courts Act. The issue of land registration, then, emerged in an historically changed context and impinged upon class, state and profession in rather different ways.

First, the very success of the reform of debt recovery and the associated changes in the structure of the legal profession – in particular the emergent power of the provincial combination – was transforming the professional context. The relative decline of metropolitan dominance was paralleled by changes in the content of law practice as the role of lawyers in the fields of debt collection, accountancy, estate agency, banking, etc., declined with the emergence of new occupational specialisms and organisational mechanisms. As a result, standard practice had increasingly cohered around the activity of conveyancing, a rapidly expanding field underwritten by the provision of a state granted monopoly as early as 1803.[18] Thus, apart from mercantile lawyers in the provinces and the London agency houses who for a time hoped to halt their declining fortunes by gaining an effective monopoly over access to any future London-based national registry, the legal profession, including the bar (which shared in the monopolistic advantage of the solicitors) presented a unified opposition to reform. Thus, while the success of the County Court reform was associated with the status divisions within the profession, the failure of registration was linked to emergent elements of its homogeneity.

Secondly, the extension of the free trade doctrine to land was never a clear-cut issue of class interest – of bourgeois right versus aristocratic privilege. Despite the legal paraphernalia limiting land transfer, capitalist agriculture had developed and the landed aristocracy had maintained a position of economic and political power within the emergent state which ensured that their fundamental property rights were not easily overturned. Also, the social significance of the land did not entirely evaporate as a result of commodification; it remained an important source of status amplification for the successful bourgeois merchant and manufacturer, and with the emergence of the modern territorial state acquired symbolic properties associated with the rise of nationalist ideology. Finally, the question of reform of land transfer revealed the contradiction inherent in the *laissez-faire*

Terry Johnson

doctrine that market and state were separate. Free trade in land required an administering state agency – a centralised registry.

An understanding of the emergence of the legal profession in its modern divided form – leaving the bar with a controlling access to the state courts and solicitors as the junior branch with a standardised form of practice cohering round the monopoly of conveyancing – is not helped by recourse to the conceptual strait-jacket of intervention and autonomy. The victory of the provincial attorneys in the struggle for the decentralisation of legal administration involved a strengthening of the occupational strategy of professionalism, but at the expense of a divided profession. The old division between metropolitan and provincial practice generated through the operation of a state based on oligarchic patronage gave way to a division justified by occupational criteria such as specialisation. The transformation of the profession was, at the same time, a transformation of state/profession relations, for the victory of provincial interest involved the construction of a particular element of the apparatus of an emergent centralised state – the County Courts – while reinforcing the autonomy of the bar, a feature which was to become integral to the liberal-democratic state. In this sense, the peculiarity of the English legal profession – its divided structure – is not as is sometimes argued a redundant survival, but is a crucial element of the state structure; whereby only a small socially select minority of lawyers enjoy the high level of independent action required by the doctrines of separation of powers and judicial independence. At the same time the failure of land registration, along with a state guaranteed monopoly over conveyancing, provided the solicitors with a means of standardising forms of practice – a significant element in the occupational strategy of professionalisation. The reform movements and their outcomes involved transformative change in which the processes of state formation and professionalisation were integrated. There is no history of 'original separation' nor of intervention versus autonomy.

The professions and the imperial state[19]

A second and significant dimension of the complex interface of state/profession formation was that of empire. The concept of professionalisation is particularly weak as a tool of historical analysis insofar as it conventionally ignores the international dimension of occupational formation. Such neglect has peculiarly damaging consequences for our understanding of the nature of professional development in British society. The expansion and consolidation of the British imperial state was associated with the imperial involvement of emergent professional associations in a form which significantly affected the profession/state relationship in Britain itself. The importance of this relationship was such that certain of the features which have been assumed to characterise professionalisation as a universal process were in fact the outcome of this peculiar articulation of professions and state within the context of the empire.

First, direct institutional links were forged between state and professions in order to facilitate the administration and servicing of the colonies. From the incorporation of professionals into imperial state agencies such as the Indian Medical Service (1764), the West and East African Medical Services (1902 and 1926), and finally the centralised Colonial Medical Service (1934), to the systematic extension of statutes governing registration and recognition, there was created in the imperial arena a complex pattern of dependence and autonomy. This led, for example, to a situation in which the British Medical Association found itself negotiating conditions and pay for those of its salaried members who were subordinated to the requirements of particular colonial bureaucracies, while at the same time, it was enjoying the status of a supra-national organisation beyond the control of any single colonial administration and exercising quasi-official functions as adviser to the Colonial Office.

The BMA in London not only took up the grievances of its colonial members directed against individual colonial governments, it also increasingly conducted a dialogue with the effective employers of large numbers of overseas doctors, namely the India Office and the Colonial Office. This interchange gave the association continuous and increasing access to Whitehall and kept it constantly in the eye of successive governments. While the BMA in London and its overseas branches tended to assess the conditions of colonial doctors in the light of private practice in Britain, this did not stop either from demanding reforms which actually increased the bureaucratic character of colonial medical practice. Such reforms included the struggle for substantive rank in the military medical services,[20] for the inclusion of chief medical officer in the higher echelons of colonial government precedence rankings, and for increased salaries in return for surrendering the right to engage in private practice.[21] Despite the conflicts which characterised the relations between the Colonial Office and the BMA, the medical association related to individual colonial administrations and local interests from the favoured position of a recognised agent of medical organisation and control throughout the empire. At the same time it represented to the Colonial Office significant local interests in the colonies. This intermeshing of state and profession in the empire is not to be dismissed as an early though marginal extension of state control over a particular sector of the profession, but a crucible within which more widely relevant relations of dependence and autonomy were forged.

Second, the conception of the 'true' professions as autonomous qualifying bodies developing universalistic criteria of qualification and entry to practice, is, to a large extent, an invalid extension of the particular circumstances in which the British professions 'universalised' their qualifications in the cause of empire expansion. In this respect a number of the British professions are unique in creating a world-wide system of examining, recognition and reciprocation, which superseded the local and particularistic criteria of entry which continued to characterise professional qualifications and entry in both the United States and in other European countries.

In order to develop these general themes it is necessary to indicate briefly the extent to which the British professions did indeed develop as imperial bodies from the last quarter of the nineteenth century onwards – considering in turn such indicators as association membership, the formation of branches, their role as qualifiers and the developing systems of recognition and registration.

The table clearly shows that the professional associations selected each had a considerable and growing stake in the empire. Imperial membership of the BMA reached a peak of 30% in 1939 (declining thereafter), while the engineering institutions maintained an empire membership of around 20% for the whole period. The Royal Institute of British Architects achieved an empire membership of over 10%, followed by the accountancy associations with 7% (both the RIBA and the accountancy bodies saw a significant expansion of their commonwealth and empire membership after 1950). These figures conceal a great deal: for example, the extent to which in the 1900s empire membership was concentrated in the settler colonies and the extent to which the percentage of British nationals gradually declined in the course of the period under review.[22] What they do not conceal is the extent to which these associations were throughout the first half of the century imperial bodies with imperial interests.

As has already been suggested, increasing numbers of these professionals were officers of the expanding colonial bureaucracies. The relatively large outflows of doctors and engineers at the beginning of the century and before, seeking opportunities in the service of British firms abroad or in practice in the settler communities of

Empire and Commonwealth membership of selected UK professional associations in the first half of the twentieth century

	1900s			1920s			1940s		
	Common-wealth	Total	%	Common-wealth	Total	%	Common-wealth	Total	%
Accountants:[1]	399	7,008	6	1,038	15,307	7	2,580	35,077	7
Medicine:[2] BMA	3,829 (1903)	18,747	18	5,884 (1920)	22,594	26	11,677 (1939)	39,106	30
Architects:[3] RIBA	87 (1900)	1,616	5	517 (1923)	4,712	11	1,225 (1948)	10,892	11
Engineers:[4] ICE	1,299 (1908)	6,815	19	1,558 (1920)	8,039	19	2,099 (1938)	9,642	21
ISE	—	—	—	216 (1923)	1,137	19	821 (1951)	4,154	20

Sources and notes

1. These figures are taken from the membership lists of a number of accountancy bodies: The Institute of Chartered Accountants of Scotland; The Institute of Chartered Accountants in England and Wales; the Society of Incorporated Accountants and Auditors (1885–1957); The London Association of Accountants (later, 1941, the Association of Certified and Corporate Accountants); the Institute of Municipal Treasurers and Accountants; the Institute of Cost and Works Accountants; the Association of International Accountants. For further details of these figures see T. J. Johnson and Marjorie Caygill, *op. cit.* (n. 24)
2. BMA Membership Department Records.
3. Kallendars of the Royal Institute of British Architects. In assessing these figures it must be remembered that at the beginning of the twentieth century RIBA membership comprised only a small fraction of practising architects in Britain and the colonies. Also these figures do not include the overseas membership of the breakaway Association of Architects (1842–1920).
4. Figures compiled from Institution of Civil Engineers Lists of Members and Institution of Structural Engineers Year Books.

Terry Johnson

Australia and South Africa, gave way to colonial service in Africa and the West Indies on a pattern which had already been laid down by the Indian services. Whether facing a chaotic market situation in the settler colonies or the bureaucratic demands of colonial service, these migrant professionals looked to the metropolitan associations for support. One means of ensuring that support was the creation of empire branches.

The level of empire involvement is further identified when we look at the extent of branch formation and affiliation. For example, between 1863 and 1939 sixty-seven BMA branches were formed in the empire (by not means all of these survived until the end of the period).[23] Despite the reluctance of the major British accountancy bodies (the Chartered Institutes) to become involved in imperial affairs, 34 branches and affiliated societies were founded between 1886 and 1967.[24] Another reluctant empire builder, the Royal Institute of British Architects, tolerated alliances with 28 bodies throughout the empire during the period 1892–1960.[25]

The link between provincial interests and the emergence of professionalism as an occupational strategy has already been mentioned with reference to lawyers. The provinces were also an important source of pressure for occupational reform in the case of medicine and architecture, being a source of opposition to the exclusive elitism of the metropolitan-based medical colleges and the Institute of Architects. The significance of such movements for our present concern is that the reforms arising out of provincial pressure, leading to the branch structure of the BMA and the alliance system adopted by the RIBA, laid down the organisational basis for expansion into the empire, rapidly transforming exclusive London 'clubs' into national and imperial organisations. The alliance system, through which the RIBA finally acquiesced to provincial pressure in 1889, opened the door to groups of empire architects who were demanding metropolitan representation and status. In the same way the provincial branch organisation of the BMA was merely extended to the empire, the first overseas branch in Jamaica (1877) adopting the constitution of the Reading branch. Thus, as the British state consolidated its imperial structure, so the emergent professional associations embarked on a parallel and mutually supportive course. The English and Scottish Institutes of Chartered Accountants were more successful than the RIBA in maintaining their elitist character, but in so doing they set into motion a process of continuous fission and amalgamation within the accountancy profession, an important dynamic of which was to be found in the relations with the imperial state. The foundation of the Institute of Chartered Accountants in England and Wales in 1880, which brought together the existing London and provincial bodies, was explicitly an association of public accountants who very rapidly created high barriers to entrance through the costs of obligatory articles and the relative severity of their examinations. More important for present purposes, articles could only be served in England and only British residents could become Fellows. The consequence of such policy was to create the conditions for the emergence of competing associations, notably the Society of Incorporated Accountants and Auditors (founded in 1885) and the London Association of Accountants (founded in 1904).[26] These competing associations not only drew membership from excluded practitioners in Britain, but from their foundations they embarked on a vigorous policy of overseas expansion, such that by 1904 the 'Society' had 14% of its membership in the empire compared with the Institutes' 2%, much of it incorporated into a branch structure. A significant aspect of this movement into the empire was that the struggle for state recognition – particularly that relating to the public audit of companies and friendly societies under the relevant acts – also moved into the imperial arena. From an early date members of the British Chartered Institutes were recognised by the Board of Trade for purposes of company audit, and a Treasury minute secured the same privileges with regard to friendly societies in 1920 ('Society' members were also by that time included among the privileged, but the 'Association' was excluded).[27] Accountants who were by such state action debarred from these lucrative and status-endowing forms of practice fought against the exclusionary effects not only in Britain but throughout the empire.

The significance of empire for the relationships between the various accountancy associations and between the associations and the state can be briefly illustrated by the internecine conflict between 'Society' and the Chartered Institutes during the last decade of the nineteenth and first decade of the twentieth centuries.[28] During this period a dozen or more attempts to pilot private registration bills through the British parliament foundered as a result of both the exclusivist stance of the English Institute and the usurpatory strategies of the 'Society'. The failure of the 'Society' to secure recognition in Britain led to it becoming heavily involved in the struggle for registration in South Africa and Australia. In South Africa the roles of the Institute and Society were to some degree reversed. It was the Institute which opposed registration in a context where the 'Society', as the established empire body, pressed for local legislation guaranteeing its members a monopoly of accountancy work. The Society,

by holding examinations in South Africa and Australia and by forming local branches, was in a position to benefit greatly by the closure
of the profession in these outposts of empire. Through its Transvaal
branch it successfully proposed a bill which transformed the 'Society'
into a statutory body with the task of controlling a register of the
qualified and excluding non-resident practitioners. This was a severe
blow to the English and Scottish Institutes, whose members included
the partners of those large accountancy firms who were in process of
extending their operations throughout the empire in the wake of their
major business clients. The Transvaal ordinance had several major
effects. First, it forced the English Institute to take the 'Society' seriously as an effective competitor, so hastening the process of cooperation, and secondly, it persuaded a number of international London-
based firms of chartered accountants to establish local residential
partners in offices outside London and New York and as such was
an early stimulus to the system of interlocking international partnerships which increasingly dominated public accountancy practice in
the English-speaking world.[29] Finally, the new respectability of the
'Society' paved the way for the London 'Association' to become the
foremost 'outsider' body, feeding on emergent nationalist sentiment
in the empire as a strategy in its opposition to what it called the
'London Trust', which, it claimed, was attempting to control accountancy practices in 'every British possession where it deems it expe-
dient' through the promotion of legislation for the 'exclusive benefit
of its own members'.[30] So, the process of fission was regenerated as
a new outsider group articulated the grievances of the 'unrepre-
sented' in both Britain and the empire. The 'Association' closely followed the 'Society's' tactics in founding overseas branches and
examination centres, and recruiting members throughout the empire.
In this way the 'Association' gradually increased pressure on colonial
governments to recognise its qualification. In India, for example, this
strategy brought the 'Association' into direct confrontation with the
emerging Institute–'Society' axis as well as the government. For while
it was the case in Britain that bills for registration were promoted by
the accountancy bodies in the face of government hostility or scepticism, in many colonies the administration was to develop a positive attitude towards registration as a means of controlling and standardising accountancy practice, particularly as it related to the needs
of international capital. An important aspect of such control was the
practice of officially recognising certain qualifications for the purpose
of public audit within Companies Acts. The Indian Companies Act
of 1913 limited auditing practice to those accountants holding a gov-

ernment certificate, but more important was that the act excluded
from this requirement members of 'recognised' bodies, i.e. the 'London Trust'. The English Institute suppressed its normal distaste for
state involvement, seeing the Act as,

> . . . especially satisfactory because during the past few years . . . unrecognised bodies have been particularly active in India in enrolling natives as
> members . . . This announcement will, it is hoped, not be without its effect
> in this country in as much as it must inevitably tend towards putting a stop
> to the wholesale enrolment . . . of members in India and other places abroad
> (and) . . . compels these unrecognised bodies to rely . . . for their support at
> home.'[31]

The consequences of such legislation was to place the 'Association'
and the unrecognised Indian accountants in the same invidious position, so forging a link between the metropolitan-based body and the
growing nationalist aspirations of Indian professionals. Thus, what
was initiated as a strategy for professional status in Britain was articulated with an attack upon an established imperial combination
comprising the chartered institutes and 'Society', the colonial
bureaucracy and, not least, the international accountancy firms, whose
partners usually took over the leadership of the local 'recognised'
profession. This link between accountancy, capital and the state was
clearly recognised by the English Institute as early as 1908. When
fulminating against the nationalist tendencies in New Zealand and
South Africa, *The Accountant* declared: 'The tendency to deny that it
is reasonable for a qualified British practitioner to practise in all parts
of the British Dominions, must seriously interfere with the flow of
capital from the Mother Country.'[32]

The pattern of the struggle for recognition and registration which
characterised accountancy was repeated in the case of architecture.
The controlling elite of the RIBA were, until well into the twentieth
century, opposed to registration and even protection of the title in
the belief that if the public were not aware of the qualities of a
gentleman-architect, no amount of legislation could overcome such
prejudice. Two events were important in changing this attitude: the
arrival on the scene of a breakaway Society of Architects (1890), which
adopted registration as a policy objective, and the passing of a registration act in Transvaal in 1909. The lack of support by the RIBA for
the South African registration movement was bitterly resented by
local architects, and the breakaway 'Society' was again (as with
accountancy) a vehicle for the campaign for registration in the empire.
In Britain, registration was a bone of contention dividing the London-based elite and the allied provincial associations, and it was this

dual pressure from both the provinces and the empire which led to the change in RIBA policy in 1904. It was this change which symbolised the relative decline of the gentlemanly clique which had throughout the nineteenth century controlled the RIBA. The change in policy also removed the major source of division between the Institute and the Society and an agreement on amalgamation was reached in 1914. Again it was the outsider body which developed an empire strategy as a means of bringing pressure to bear on the established association.

In contrast, in India and the colonies the architect was a late-comer who found himself a subordinate in a bureaucracy controlled by administrators and engineers, the latter monopolising the role of building team coordinator and supervisor.[33] As a result the struggle for architects' registration continued, in many cases for half a century or more, in the face of official resistance and the bitter opposition of engineers. It was an opposition which spilled over into the metropolitan scene, weakening the architects' universalistic claims to be the natural leaders of the building team. Throughout the first half of the twentieth century the imperial state continued to refuse to underwrite architects' claims by excluding engineers and surveyors from architectural practice.

The British professions also fulfilled an imperial role as qualifiers, either through the direct provision of examinations or as accrediting bodies for local courses and systems of training. It was largely in the provision of such facilities that the professions were forced to eliminate local and particularistic criteria from their qualifying procedures. This was achieved through a variety of mechanisms: the creation of a 'colonial list' by the General Medical Council in 1886 and the subsequent system of reciprocal recognition through which the Council accredited overseas medical schools; the extension of the RIBA accreditation system through a scheme which devolved its qualifying functions to allied societies in the empire and commonwealth; and the direct provision and supervision of examination centres by accountancy bodies, which effectively opened up the field of professional education overseas to private correspondence colleges.[34]

The export of British accountancy qualifications became in the course of the twentieth century a large-scale industry. Despite the rules by which the Chartered Institutes restricted membership to British residents, the numbers of candidates sitting British examinations in the empire and commonwealth rose from about 100 annually in 1920, to 400 in 1935, 2,000 in 1950 and 7,000-plus in 1968.

Overseas examinations were instituted by the 'Society', closely followed by the 'Association', which was the major overseas examiner until recently.[35] In Britain the demand for standardised systems of training and examinations was a significant tactic in the armoury of those practitioners who sought to wrest control of their occupations from the London-based oligarchies, and, following the institution of examinations for the Indian and home civil service, the demand became more insistent.

The leaders of the architectural profession, for example, were particularly resistant to the view that entry to the profession should be based on technical competence measured by formal examinations, arguing that architecture was essentially an artistic pursuit involving individual talents which could be neither learned nor effectively examined. The pressure for reform again came from the provincial societies and the Architectural Association, founded in 1842, which called for a qualification that would clearly demarcate the status of trained as against untrained practitioners on the basis of technical competence rather than social standing. The pressure from below forced the RIBA to provide examinations in 1862 and subsequently (1890) to adopt the AA syllabus. Once the RIBA had decided to admit members by examination, the demand for the provision of overseas examination facilities expanded rapidly, the Institute acceding to a demand for a special colonial examination in the 1890s and organising more than twenty examination centres overseas between 1900 and 1938.[36] Once it had imposed a standard for qualification and entry through the provision of examinations, the Institute was content to leave training to the individual efforts of members through a system of pupillage, supplemented by ad hoc lectures and courses. However, entry through formal education was more attractive in the empire, where extensive facilities for pupillage were not available, and as a result the RIBA launched a system of 'recognition' whereby those overseas schools which adhered to its syllabus were allowed certain exemptions from RIBA examinations – on the basis of this scheme 17 architectural schools were recognised between 1921 and 1960. Following on from this, allied societies in the empire and commonwealth were given powers in 1931 to recognise schools on behalf of the RIBA – the devolution scheme was created.[37]

It was this avoidance of direct involvement in the educational process, along with an increasingly firm hold over examination standards, which characterised the development of a number of British professional associations. By limiting control to examinations these associations neither tied their qualifications to specific educational

Terry Johnson

institutions nor to specific local or national training locations. Equally important was the fact that the state, largely as a result of imperial considerations, excluded local, national and ethnic criteria from its registration acts and ordinances. The system of qualification which emerged, then, not only ensured the exportability of qualifications but had the 'peculiar' British consequence of subordinating academic professionals to the authority of practitioner associations and as a commentator on the architectural profession pointed out (which has more general relevance): '. . . the peculiar characteristics of architectural education in the U.K. are due to the fact that examinations preceded education instead of vice versa . . . Consequently architectural training has tended to be governed by the needs of the examinational syllabus rather than the needs of architectural practice.'[38] By ensuring that the focus of control over entry, training and education centred upon the examination, the balance of power shifted toward the professional association and away from the institutions of training and education, and consequently away from an area where state activity has been increasingly directed – educational provision. Thus, the influence of state agencies was less marked in the area of entry and standards than it might otherwise have been, and as it was in other countries. What is suggested here, then, is that the degree of autonomy which a number of the British professions have enjoyed – particularly in the arena of qualification and entry – arise out of their involvement in empire and their relations with the imperial state. The significance of universalistic criteria relating to qualification was not then the 'natural' outcome of professionalisation, but an outcome which had its origins in the imperial role of the British professions.

Conclusion

The primary purpose of these two case studies has been to examine certain limited aspects of the developing relationship between the state and professions in Britain in order to illustrate and underscore the general contention that the conceptual frame of analysis which reduces complex historical processes to the alternative possibilities of state intervention or professional autonomy has been an inadequate and distorting theoretical commitment defining the central issues of the sociology of the professions since its emergence as a specialist field of study.

The analyses presented suggest that both the emergent forms of the liberal-bourgeois state and the later construction of an imperial state apparatus involved the *trans*-formation of professional occupations as processes *integral* to that of state formation; that the formation of a divided legal profession, for example, and the constitution of the various professional associations as imperial bodies were both defining elements in what the state was becoming. The developing relationship of professions to state helped to define the limits and potentialities of state powers, functions and capacities as well as conditioning the possibility of independent action by occupational colleague networks. This latter point, which arises out of our rejection of the position which locates the source of occupational autonomy in some universal essence of professional occupations, was illustrated by reference to an emergent institutional complex at the beginning of the nineteenth century, which created the conditions for independent action on the part of a reconstructed bar as well as the specific conditions associated with formation of the British imperial state whereby a number of professional associations were able to operate as effective gatekeepers to occupational practice throughout the empire.

In rejecting state intervention and professional autonomy as the alternative histories of the state/profession relationship, the case studies also suggest further modifications of conventional analyses of the professions. First, the concept professionalisation can only refer to a process toward *partial* autonomy, being limited to specific areas of independent action which are defined by an occupation's relationship to the state; areas of autonomy which vary from time to time and place to place. Professionalisation, where it occurs, is indicative of a particular form of articulation between the state and those occupations which have been of particular significance in the state's historical formation. As the state and the professions and their relations have been transformed over time, so the areas of partial autonomy enjoyed by the professions themselves change and are refocussed – the process toward professionalisation within the context of an emergent liberal-bourgeois state has institutional characteristics and a focus different from that associated with the emergence of the imperial state. Thus, in any attempt to identify emergent areas of occupational autonomy today it is a mistake merely to measure its extent on the basis of historically derived models of what forms of autonomy were primary. Also, if the focus and location of independent action change over time we can more easily understand why the relationship of state to professions presents itself as one of constant struggle and seeming hostility while at the same time constituting an interdependent structure. The view that professionalisation is not a single process with a given end-state also suggests that the relationship with changing state forms is in flux. This in turn gives rise to constant social ambiguity and ambivalence, a condition which under specific historical conditions may well be of crucial importance in the wider relations of class and state. To claim that the modern professions are a product of state formation does not entail a view of professionals as universally the 'servants of power'.

Finally, both the case studies and this conclusion imply that professionalisation as a necessarily partial development toward autonomy, arising out of the articulation of state and occupation, is likely to vary from society to society. It is a process that has not and will not follow any universal model. The second case study is particularly illuminating in this respect, insofar as the character of the British professions has been significantly affected by the experience of empire which had peculiar consequences for state and professional formation. The fragmenting processes at work within accountancy, for example, cannot be understood other than in an imperial context. More important, the relative power and forms of autonomy of the British professions, particularly relating to qualification and training, are only partially understood if we neglect the imperial dimension.

In Britain, then, the power of the professional colleague association, which gained impetus from the provincial attack upon metropolitan privilege during a process of state transformation, was further reinforced and sustained by the extension of professional activity throughout the empire during the period of imperial state formation. It was the adoption of this imperial role with its quasi-official functions which allowed a number of professional bodies to assume a degree of authority and independence of action which the professions in many other countries have never attained, and which occupations which have only emerged in the twentieth century to claim professional status are unlikely to achieve in a similar form. Equally, the decline of empire foreshadowed further changes in the profession/state relationship, including the erosion of those forms of autonomy which were peculiarly British but which sociologists have mistakenly identified as the classical and potentially universal form.

Divisions within the dominant class and British 'exceptionalism'

GEOFFREY INGHAM

Introduction

In recent years there has been a revival of interest in what is actually a long-standing but heterodox interpretation of the development and structure of British capitalism. Since the early nineteenth century, it has been frequently asserted that the City of London as an international 'financial' centre and domestic industry have been dissociated or 'split' in such a way as to disadvantage the latter. The problem is a complex one and there are important differences between these recent contributions to the debate.[1] I have dealt critically with this work elsewhere; here I wish to consider one of the intellectually 'orthodox' interpretations of British economic development in relation to this issue – the Marxist version.[2]

In the most general terms, the City–industry issue has three inter-related aspects. First, there is the question of the economic and institutional relationships between the two sectors of the economy and the ways in which these have been expressed politically. Secondly, it has been argued that there is an association between the City's economic and political dominance and the structuring of the state system and the ruling class. Thirdly, the possible connection between City hegemony and Britain's secular and increasingly rapid industrial decline is drawn by most writers.

Briefly, then, many writers have attempted to show that the City's control of money-capital has diverted it away from domestic industrial financing and that this has occurred mainly – although not entirely – through overseas investment.[3] Furthermore, successive governments are seen as having pursued policies which have had a detrimental effect on production. On the one hand, it has been argued with some force that several policies have discriminated in favour of City interests – for example, the strenuous attempts to maintain a world role for sterling and the safeguarding of an open economy in order to preserve London as an entrepôt for money. On the other hand, what may be seen as specifically industrially-based strategies designed to strengthen productive capital – most notably, Chamberlain's Tariff Reform Movement, Mondism in the 1920s, and Wilson's National Plan and Department of Economic Affairs in the 1960s – have all suffered defeat at the hands of that section of the ruling class based on the City in its traditional alliance with the Bank of England and the Treasury. In various ways, each strategy has involved threats to the fundamental conditions of existence for the City's activities: namely, the liberal system of free trade in money and other commodities and an unregulated capital market.

Many of these arguments contain the explicit assertion that the industrial bourgeoisie occupies a subordinate position within the ruling class and in relation to the state system. The close relationship between the City, Bank of England and the Treasury, which has endured with few modifications since the eighteenth century, is taken to be the institutional basis for the City's dominance and the means by which part of the aristocracy has maintained its economic and political power.[4]

The general thesis clearly derives much of its significance from political critiques of the British social formation, and the *New Left Review* writers, in particular, hold that the City–industry 'split' and the articulation of the former with the state system have contributed to Britain's decline.

. . . no recovery from industrial 'backwardness' has been possible, precisely because no second industrial revolution of the state has taken place in England; only the state could have engendered such a recovery by revolution from above – but the old patrician structure of England's political system, incapable of such radical action, has also resisted every effort at serious reform to the present day.[5]

In short, we are asked to consider that the 'first industrial nation', the former 'workshop of the world' – that is, the social formation which Marx considered to be the *prototypical* case of the development of the capitalist mode of *production* – possesses a political system in which the traditional elements are more than simple anachronisms. Rather, they are seen as having a materially inhibitive impact on Britain's productive performance. Marx and Engels saw things differently; but rather than spell out their general and familiar position in detail we may simply note one of Marx's typical statements. In *Capital*, he considered that the alliance, which some of the writers referred to above believe has continued to dominate British society, was broken in the mid-nineteenth century. 'In modern English history, the commercial estate proper and the merchant towns are also politically reactionary and in league with the landed and moneyed interest against industrial capital . . . The complete rule of industrial capital was not acknowledged by English merchants' capital until after the abolition of the corn tax.'[6] All the writers referred to above are, in varying degrees, associated with Marxism and are aware of the implications of their arguments for the Marxist analysis of the development of the capitalist mode of production and its impact on the state and politics; but each attempts to reconcile his heterodox substantive analysis with the main strands of Marxist theory. Space precludes a discussion of all these interrelated issues and in what follows I wish to concentrate on what is the basic and preliminary question: that is, the theoretical problem of the economic bases of the City–industry separation.[7]

The City in recent writings

Despite the fact that many of his arguments run counter to Marxist orthodoxy, Nairn believes that 'a generally Marxist model' of Britain's condition is sufficient but it has to be 'a historical and specific model' and that 'the idea that the functioning of British society and state can be explained wholly (or even mainly) in terms of the internal industrial economy and its relations of production (the class struggle)' is an example of the 'overabstraction' which has been the main deficiency of past Marxist analyses of Britain.[8] The historical specificity which Nairn calls for is to be found in Britain's 'external' relations with the rest of the world over the past century which resulted in a 'type of *finance-capital imperialism* [which] rested . . . on a marked division within British capitalism itself'.[9]

Another recent writer, Longstreth, argues that the division within British capitalism cannot be inferred from the 'logic of capital' approach to the state: 'illogic defines the peculiarity of the British state'.[10] In almost exactly the same manner as Nairn, he argues that

. . . while such abstract approaches might be useful in providing a general approach to the analysis of the state, they must be complemented by analyses which are more instrumental not in the sense that the state is depicted as a neutral instrument in the hands of a cohesive dominant class but insofar as they see it as a system penetrated and structured by particular class relations which may vary from society to society and over periods of time.[11]

Although not explicitly acknowledged as such, Longstreth's position is the same as one of Poulantzas's later formulations in which the

211

state is seen as the 'crystallisation' of the power of class 'fractions' or a dominant 'fraction'. In Britain the two 'fractions' are 'the City or banking capital and industry or productive capital'. The coexistence of these two fractions and the pre-eminence of the City are to be explained 'in historical terms' by 'the particular pattern of capitalist development in Britain . . . which meant the coincidence of interests between imperialists and the City'.[12]

Rubinstein's work is not as directly concerned with the separation of forms or fractions of capital – and he is not a Marxist – but his work on the distribution of wealth and Britain's elite structure is valuable, as Nairn acknowledges.[13] Rubinstein draws a careful and detailed picture of the divisions within the nineteenth-century ruling class in which the southern, City-based elite with close aristocratic connections dominated the less wealthy, northern industrialists. Like the other two writers mentioned above, he confronts the general Marxist theory of capitalist development and concludes that: 'Britain is always the exceptional case, and too often its being first has been confused with its being the norm. Marx himself one suspects would have been better employed in the Library of Congress than the British Museum.'[14]

Now, although I am largely in agreement with the general tenor of the case which these writers – Nairn in particular – have put forward, there are three interrelated weaknesses which these accounts share in common. First, they are all to some degree historically inaccurate in a way which obscures the process by which the City gained and maintained its political dominance in British society.[15] Secondly, the nature of the relationship between the historical specificity of British 'exceptionalism' and Marx's general theory of the development of the capitalist mode of production and its impact on the state and the composition of the ruling class is unclear. None of the writers considers that his work constitutes a refutation or drastic revision of Marxism; they merely suggest *ad hoc* modifications to the orthodox analysis. Both these difficulties, I would argue, are the result of a third and major problem: the absence of any clear and coherent conceptualisation of the City's *economic practices* in any of their works. Consequently the analysis of the *basis* for the split or separation between the City and industry remains theoretically undeveloped.

The most explicitly analytical approach is Longstreth's 'fractionalist' account; but even in this account the City is never precisely identified as a 'fraction' of capital. Initially, it is equated with 'banking capital (including here generally the financial sector)', but elsewhere, it is not a 'fraction' of *capital* which exercises power but variously: a 'traditional power bloc'; an 'establishment'; 'the ancien regime'; 'high finance'; and a 'political-economic fraction'. This last designation highlights one of the central problems within Marxist theory – the relationship between the 'economic' and the 'political'. In the first place, is this 'fraction' – that is, the City – to be identified exclusively by the location of its activities at the economic level? Longstreth is obviously not sure – hence the other terms. Moreover, if we assume that this 'fraction' is clearly identifiable and that its relationship with industry is one of conflict and opposition at the political level, to what extent is this inherent in the economic relations as such? In other words, are the relationships between the two 'fractions' in the total circuit of social capital essentially contradictory or only *contingently* conflictual as a result of the particular intrusion of aspects of British 'exceptionalism'? Longstreth does not even pose this question which is central to the 'fractionalist' approach and, of course, could not do so because of his uncertainty about the identity of the City as a 'fraction'. Since the 'fractions' are neither precisely identified, and consequently nor are their economic relationships, the exact nature of the interdependencies between the class 'fractions' and the state is impossible to specify. The conflation of the two levels in the concept of a 'political-economic' fraction merely begs the question.[16] On balance, however, Longstreth implies that, in economic terms, the City is banking or financial capital and that its dislocation from industry stems from its international role – particularly in the export of capital. Similarly, Nairn refers to 'finance-capital imperialism' and, as we have seen, places great emphasis on Britain's external financial relationships in the explanation of the City–industry split. Rubinstein is more decisive: the split between the two sectors of the economy is viewed as a nineteenth-century phenomenon in which the export of capital was largely responsible for the onset of Britain's industrial decline. Later, in the 1920s and '30s, when overseas investment opportunities declined, domestic 'finance-capital' (in Hilferding's sense) emerged. Consequently, British 'exceptionalism' is not a matter of structural idiosyncrasy but merely a matter of timing: 'Britain was the last among the advanced countries to witness a merger of finance and industry.'[17]

Despite their differences, therefore, there is a *general* tendency amongst these writers to see the City as overseas banking or finance-capital and, by implication, the economic split between it and industry as the result of *competition* between domestic and foreign investment opportunities.[18] It is not too difficult to understand the appeal of this line of argument for the Marxist tradition: the City comprises finance-capital which, unlike its counterparts elsewhere, is divorced from domestic industry by *contingent* external relations and, therefore, Marxist theory is not to be refuted but, rather, modified by greater historical sensitivity as the three writers suggest.

There are, however, two overwhelming problems with this conceptualisation of the City. First, the Marxist concept of finance-capital was developed out of a concern to show how bank capital did not simply provide finance for industry – whether at home or abroad, but through the *control* of money-capital was also able to control production and thereby accelerate the movement away from competitive to monopoly capitalism. Moreover, this control was presumed to involve the *organisational fusion* of banks and industry. However, one of the most distinctive and enduring features of the City's financial role has been a marked absence of any interest in the direct control by, say, City merchant banks of the means by which surplus value is produced. Rather, the City institutions have acted almost exclusively as simple *intermediaries* between investors and borrowers, and have traditionally been characterised by an organisational separation from productive enterprise either at home or abroad. British overseas financial involvement was portfolio investment and differed considerably from the direct investment which later was, for example, the hallmark of American international capitalism.[19]

Secondly and relatedly, this emphasis on overseas investment, whilst it highlights an all too obvious connection between the City and domestic industrial decline, directs attention away from the City's other activities. From the 1830s to the present day – with the exception of the period from the late nineteenth century to 1914 – the City's earnings from insurance, the foreign exchange and money markets, the financing of trade, freight and commodity broking, etc. (that is, commercial activity) has *exceeded* the income from interest and dividends from overseas investments.[20] This means, of course, that the City's spectacular revival over the past twenty years cannot be easily explained by the factors adduced by Nairn and Longstreth.

In short, the major deficiency of recent attempts to explain the City–industry split has been the superficial treatment of the City itself. Although the concept of 'finance-capital' is an inappropriate one for the analysis of the City, Marx's own treatment of the various forms of capital and their articulation does, in fact, permit a clearer conceptualisation of the City's economic practices. As we shall see, however, Marx himself did not pursue the possibilities which his own analysis opened up: the main features of his theory of capitalist production, in fact, deflected his attention in another direction. This legacy is, I believe, largely responsible for the failure of later Marxists to grasp the full economic significance of the City.

In the most general terms Marx's enterprise is an attempt to understand capitalist social relations of *production* – that is, the *real* relations of production, as opposed to their mystified representation in bourgeois economics which, in his opinion, focusses erroneously on the phenomenal forms associated with capitalist production as these are expressed in the *circulation* of commodities. Marx constantly argues in his discussion of eighteenth- and nineteenth-century economic theory that: 'The real science of modern economy only begins when the theoretical analysis passes from the process of circulation to the process of production.'[21] In order to establish the primacy of the relations of production in the explanation of the 'laws of motion of modern society', Marx first distinguishes various forms of capital and argues that commercial (merchant) and banking capital operate in a subordinate role within the functionally interrelated production and circulation processes.[22] Secondly, his closely related analysis of money is undertaken from the *point of view of capitalist production* and, in particular, in relation to the problem of how money is able to function as a measure of value. Although Marx attempts to analyse money in all its forms (gold, currency, credit, etc.), he rests his analysis of money as a measure of value on the assumption that, ultimately, money is *commodity money* which embodies labour time in its production. Thus, the mining and minting of gold coin enables it to stand as a signifier of the value of other commodities.[23]

In the remainder of this paper I shall argue that Marx's preoccupation with the productive process – which comprises his distinctive intellectual contribution – is also a source of two weaknesses which impaired his understanding of the British capitalist economic and social formation. First, despite his clear conceptual distinctions between the different forms of *capital*, Marx underestimated the efficacy, under particular but not exceptional circumstances, of the *political* conditions of existence of the non-productive forms – that is, commercial and banking capital. Secondly, the emphasis on money's functional role as an epiphenomenal sign or representation of the movements of the 'real' components of the capitalist mode of production – productive capital, commodities and their underlying social relations – obscures crucially important processes by which *money*, in various forms, is *socially and politically* produced.

Geoffrey Ingham

The City: basic economic practices

As I have suggested, and as Thompson among others has pointed out, finance-capital is not 'simply another term for banking capital' nor does it merely refer to the external provision of money-capital to finance trade, production, state expenditure, etc.[24] As Weber put it: '. . . the term "financing" (*Finanzierungsgeschäften*) will be applied to all business transactions which are oriented to obtaining *control* . . . of favourable opportunities for profit making by business enterprise'.[25] Empirically, the classic cases of 'finance-capital' are those which developed in Germany and the United States in the early twentieth century and Japan some time later. In contrast, the City has been concerned – in Marx's terminology – with the circuits of commercial and banking capital particularly at the international level. Both roles developed in relation to the *pre-industrial* expansion of world *trade* and *state* financing in the eighteenth century.[26]

Trade, money markets and commercial services

In the face of the chronic shortage of an internationally acceptable means of payment (gold currency), the expansion of world trade in the eighteenth century was eased by the use of bills-of-exchange which circulated between merchants. London traders used their surplus money-capital to discount the bills – that is, buy them for cash before they matured – at a rate slightly lower than their face value. Thus, the merchants' liquidity problem was met as they received cash before the delivery of goods and a profit was made by what was now a merchant-banker when the bill was finally redeemed. Eventually, the bills-on-London – as they became known – no longer exclusively represented commodities-in-transit, but became an autonomous form of short-term credit for the world economy. It is essential to note that in these later developments the merchant bankers were acting as middlemen in a long chain of financial intermediation – just as they had in the circulation of physical commodities. Often, they themselves no longer provided the money-capital to discount the bills, but accepted them on commission and in so doing rendered them eligible for discounting by other houses and banks in the London short-term money-market cartel.[27] As the nineteenth century progressed, the cash for discounting came increasingly from the provincial joint-stock banks who were thus drawn into the international money markets.

In essential terms, the modern short-term money markets based upon the major international currencies and the so-called 'Eurocur-

216

rencies' consist of similar practices by the City intermediaries. They act as middlemen or wholesale bankers – that is, as a link between the various types of bank themselves – as opposed to retail or deposit bankers. Thus, I would wish to argue that many of the City's 'banking' activities are fundamentally *commercial* practices insofar as discounting or short-term lending (often overnight) pre-empt any *financial control* of the borrowers by the intermediaries. The City institutions and organisations are part of complex financial *relationships*, but their specific *practices* are commercial. In this particular market structure money exhibits dual characteristics: as a marketable commodity from the merchant banker's or discount house's standpoint, and as finance from that of the lenders and borrowers. The City intermediaries maintain structurally tenuous and discontinuous relationships with lenders and borrowers; their interest is in a high volume and velocity of transactions rather than the ultimate long-term profitability of ventures which are financed in this way.[28]

London's foreign exchange and bullion markets, which were a consequence of Britain's becoming the world's major trading nation and having its domestic currency used globally for the invoicing and settlement of international accounts, are quite unequivocally commercial institutions in which currency and gold are bought and sold.

The recent renewal of interest in the City's historic role in relation to the economy as a whole has focussed one-sidedly on the 'financial' dimension and, in particular, the export of capital. However, before the 1870s and again since the 1960s, the City's direct commercial earnings from the sale of non-life insurance associated with trade and transport, from freight brokerage, from the running of the various commodity markets, and latterly the futures markets, have been more profitable in aggregate terms.[29] Whereas these activities have received scant attention from Marxist historians and social scientists, they have been duly acknowledged by successive governments as crucially important contributors to the balance of payments, and as such have continued to receive support. Furthermore, as Rubinstein has shown, commercial capitalists involved in these activities were amongst the richest men in England during the nineteenth century and there is little to suggest that the situation has changed in any substantial way.[30]

State finance, the stock exchange and the capital markets

The weakness of English Absolutism in the post-feudal period and the relatively equal balance of power between the crown and the mercantile bourgeoisie is widely accepted as one of the nation's most distinctive characteristics which has had a decisive long-term impact on the modern liberal democratic system.[31] A further equally important – but neglected – consequence of the English monarchy's relative weakness was the means by which state expenditure was financed. In England, the existence of a wealthy commercial bourgeoisie was simultaneously the basis both for the resistance to taxation and for the state's use of loans – at a profit to the City – for its finance.[32] Both the Bank of England and the Stock Exchange were the products of England's 'Second Revolution' in the late eighteenth century. The Bank was founded in 1694 as a corporation of over a thousand subscribers which included the City's most prominent merchants and bankers. A charter was granted by the crown in return for a loan of £1.2 m. and through an Act of Parliament in 1708 the Bank gained the privileged status as the country's only joint-stock bank. This jealously guarded monopoly was further strengthened by legislation restricting country banks to partnerships of no more than six which retarded the development of branch banking and encouraged the use of inland bills-of-exchange as the major source of short-term credit. Furthermore, the cartel of the discount houses, merchant banks, etc., for which the Bank acted as lender of last resort, resulted in a split between the powerful metropolitan sector and the weaker provincial banks for which the Bank not only refused to extend rediscount facilities but actively strove to maintain in a subordinate position in the money markets.

By the early eighteenth century, the expanding market in government securities led to the establishment of the Stock Exchange which as early as the 1820s had, more or less, assumed its present form – that is, before *joint-stock* productive industry. Stockbroking had emerged as a specialised role and the distinction between jobber and broker was observed. These roles were based upon the fact that speculative activity and market fluctuations created an active *secondary* market in already issued stock. In this way, the social organisation of the English capital market endowed the stock or share – like money in the short-term market – with dual characteristics: as *finance* for new ventures with an entitlement to a share of surplus value and as a marketable *commercial asset* on the secondary stock market in already issued shares. It is this pronounced structural feature of the Stock Exchange which has been criticised by those who see the capital market as not meeting the needs of productive industry. First, it is argued that the criterion of marketability of shares leads to the neglect of new, unproven, but potentially dynamic companies. Secondly, that London's high volume of trading on the secondary market itself causes share-price fluctuations which may be inimical to industry's long-term strategies. Thirdly, the dominance of the capital market has retarded the development of long-term bank lending and close links between banks and industry – that is, finance-capital which could induce a mutual interest in the profitability of industry.[33]

Even this necessarily very brief survey of the City's basic practices shows that to identify it *simply* in terms of banking or finance-capital is inaccurate. Rather, the practices are predominantly commercial: City institutions are involved in the *buying and selling* of money (in all forms); of stock and shares; of commodities and commercial services such as insurance. Another way of expressing the commercial nature of these operations on the Stock Exchange and in the money markets is to describe them as *wholesale* rather than retail: the exchanges between the financial and commercial intermediaries themselves rather than as a single link between ultimate savers and borrowers or producers and consumers. The merchant banks' management on commission of the pension funds portfolios is one of the most marked examples of these structural arrangements.[34]

It is the existence of these specialised wholesale markets which leads to the attenuation of the financial links between commerce and banking on the one hand and productive capital on the other. The absence of such well-developed secondary markets in, say, Germany and Japan is a commonplace observation and it is, of course, in these countries where finance-capital is most developed. Obviously, the international dimension of London's roles has been a crucially important factor in the City–industry separation and, for example, it is the fact of the incommensurability of different national currencies which requires the existence of specialised wholesale money markets. However, this should not be taken to indicate that simple 'external' relations or Britain's past imperial connections are, *in themselves,* the most important factors in the City–industry split. The actual practices of the pre-industrial institutions in the City were from the outset both oriented to the international economy and commercial, in the sense I have used this term, rather than directly financial in character.

These practices were extended and reinforced by three further conditions which emerged in the nineteenth century. First, Britain's pioneering industrial capitalist role led to the expansion of London's management of the international mercantile and monetary transactions. Britain's trading supremacy saturated the world with sterling which was, in itself, a major reason for the denomination of international transactions in Britain's domestic currency.[35] Secondly,

Geoffrey Ingham

Britain's adoption of the gold standard after the Napoleonic Wars and its legal formalisation in the Bank Charter Act of 1844 provided the guarantee to holders of sterling that their assets were convertible into gold and consequently established the trust in the international gold–sterling standard which the City came to believe was the basis of its prosperity. The constant efforts of successive governments in the twentieth century to secure the position of sterling as a major trading and reserve currency has been stressed by many writers as the source of *political* conflict between the City and industry over exchange rate policy and the level of interest rates.[36] Thirdly, free trade in money, commodities and securities which was introduced gradually in the first part of the nineteenth century came to be defended by the City as tenaciously as the gold standard. Other leading industrial economies such as Germany and the United States introduced protective tariffs in the late nineteenth century, but, in Britain, Chamberlain's Tariff Reform Movement was completely unsuccessful and it was not until after the world monetary crisis of 1931 that a measure of protection was adopted. Any attempt to restrict the volume and velocity of international commercial and monetary transactions through protection, or to curtail the freedom of London to manage them, continues to be vigorously resisted to the present day.

The City–industry separation can be seen, in fundamental terms, as a consequence of a potential contradiction between the commercial and wholesale banking practices of the former and the requirements of industry. The structure of the City's money, securities and other markets is oriented to the rapid turnover of marketable assets, rather than the *direct* involvement with the financing of industrial production. This disjuncture has been continuously manifest in two ways. First, in the low level of long-term external finance for productive industry, and, secondly, the political implementation and defence of policies designed to maintain London as an open, unrestricted market-place with a currency strong enough to be a basis for international mercantile and banking transactions.

Marx, forms of capital and the British economy

Paradoxically, in view of his obvious inability to perceive the continued dominance of commercial and banking capital in Britain, Marx did, in fact, argue in general terms that these forms could stand in an antagonistic relationship with productive industry. In the much neglected volume III of *Capital*, commercial and banking capital –

especially in Britain – are analysed in what he rather confusingly refers to as their *'pre*-capitalist' forms.[37]

Commercial capital belongs to the sphere of circulation and not production and, consequently, the realisation of value can only be achieved by 'the merchant who parasitically inserts himself' between buyers and sellers.[38] Furthermore, although commercial capital – as the basis for the accumulation of money-wealth – may contribute to the development of productive capitalism, '. . . the independent development of merchants' capital stands in inverse proportion to the general economic development of society'.[39] This is because production and circulation remain structurally independent: the merchant has no particularistic interest in production and '. . . it is commerce which here turns products into commodities and not the produced commodity which gives rise to commerce'.[40] However, '. . . within the capitalist mode of production – i.e. as soon as capital has imparted its sway over production and imparted to it a wholly changed and specific form – merchants' capital merely appears as capital with a specific function . . . It functions as an agent of productive capital.'[41] Rather cryptically, Marx continues: 'If merchants' capital *does not overstep its necessary proportions,* it is to be inferred that as a result of the division of labour the capital devoted exclusively to buying and selling . . . is smaller than it would be if the industrialist were constrained to carry on the entire commercial part of his business on his own . . .' (emphasis added).[42] But what guarantees that commercial capital does not overstep its 'necessary proportions'? Marx's answer is exclusively economic: '. . . should merchants' capital yield a higher percentage of average profit than industrial capital, then, a portion of the latter would be transformed into merchants' capital'.[43] This statement lends support to two of the criticisms which have been levelled at Marx's theory from within the Marxist tradition. First, the City has constantly striven to erect *non*-economic barriers to entry since the mid-nineteenth century through the establishment of exclusive associations based upon the discount houses, the accepting houses, the Stock Exchange and Lloyds. As time went by, these cartels assumed a distinctive *social* character based upon the most prestigious public schools and the aristocratically-based 'patrician elite'. In other words, dimensions of 'civil society' have assumed an important independent role in the structuration of the divisions within British capital.[44] Secondly, the *international* division of capital in which Britain monopolised the commercial and banking circuits were originally produced and later maintained through *political* action.[45]

Banking capital is similarly dealt with by Marx in order to demonstrate how 'elemental usurer's capital' is subordinated within the total circuit of productive capital, but his account displays an ambivalence. He is aware that '. . . on the whole interest-bearing capital under the modern credit system is adapted to the conditions of the capitalist mode of production', but also argues that '. . . usury lives in the pores of production' insofar as hoards of commodity-money (gold) remains as the basis for the credit system.[46] 'The universal equivalent' (gold) is necessary as a means of payment in unreciprocated economic transactions or when a debt is finally discharged *and* – most significantly from the point of view of the analysis of the City and sterling's international role – in the demand for 'world money'; that is to say, in the demand for an internationally *acceptable* and *guaranteed* means of payment.

Moreover, this situation is the source of a potential contradiction between 'capital in its money form and capital in its commodity form'.[47] The contradiction derives from the dual nature of money which functions, on the one hand, in its credit form as a sign or symbol of the circulation of commodities and, on the other hand, in its commodity form (gold) as the basis for the means of final payment. In this latter role it is *both* 'world money' and the metallic base for the domestic credit system and, consequently, a demand for commodity-money (gold) for international payments may contract the flow of credit upon which the domestic circulation and production of commodities increasingly depends under conditions of capitalist production:

With a drain on gold its convertibility, i.e. its identity with gold becomes problematic. Hence coercive measures, raising the rate of interest etc., for the purpose of safeguarding the conditions of this convertibility . . . Therefore, the value of commodities is sacrificed for the purpose of safeguarding the fantastic and independent existence of this value of money . . . For a few millions of money, many millions in commodities must, therefore, be sacrificed.[48]

Significantly, Marx commented that this situation could 'be carried more or less to extremes by *mistaken* legislation, based upon false theories of money and enforced upon the nation by the interest of the money-dealers'.[49] The 1844 Bank Charter Act to which Marx refers was based upon the Ricardian quantity theory of money with which it was argued that the issue of currency should be tied directly to the reserves of gold which, in Britain's case, increasingly functioned as the base for international transactions. Marx argued that drains of gold not only disrupted production, but also that the subsequent raising of interest rates in order to induce a return of bullion created fluctuations in the price of money which was a source of speculative profit for money-dealers.

> The credit system, which has its focus in the so-called national banks and the big money lenders and usurers surrounding them, constitutes enormous centralisation, and gives to this class of parasites the fabulous power, not only to periodically interfere in actual production in a most dangerous manner – and this gang knows nothing about production and has nothing to do with it. The Acts of 1844 and 1845 are proof of the growing power of these bandits, who are augmented by the financiers and stock jobbers.[50]

According to Marx, then, the monetary legislation favoured the interests of both commercial capital (money-dealers) and banking capital in their independent 'pre-capitalist' forms and at the expense of productive capital; but he never pursued the theme and consistently refers to the rule of industrial capital which was heralded by the repeal of the Corn Laws.

Marx's inability to perceive the possibility that the 'mistaken legislation' would not be repealed but, on the contrary, persist as the basis for Britain's international commercial and banking roles stems, I would argue, from his general evolutionary assumptions concerning the development, universal dominance and ultimate demise of the capitalist mode of production. The argument that all forms and media of economic activity become subordinated to the requirements of production is clearly apparent in his analysis of *money* which appears to be the proximate cause of his difficulties in comprehending some of the developments in early British industrial capitalism.

Money and the state

Marx's treatment of money is undertaken almost exclusively from the point of view of the *functions* it performs within the capitalist mode of production, and the 'mistakes' in the early Victorian legislation refer to what he considered to be a fundamental intellectual error in Ricardo's economics. Although Ricardo advanced the labour theory of value with respect to commodities in general, he maintained that this was valid for gold (as commodity-money) only if the quantity of gold remained in very close approximation to the quantity and prices of other commodities. In other words, Ricardo argued that commodity-money had an autonomous effect on economic activity and that the production and flow of commodities could be determined by the production and flow of money. At the risk of oversimplification, Marx's argument may be summarised by saying that he firmly located his analysis within the general labour theory of value, but that, in contrast to Ricardo, he maintained that the production and circulation of commodities was determined by forces outside the sphere of circulation. In essence, Marx simply reverses the Ricardian equation:

> It is not money that renders the commodities commensurable. Quite the contrary. Because all commodities, as values, are objectified human labour, and therefore in themselves commensurable, their values can be communally measured in one and the same specific commodity, and this commodity can be converted into the common measure of their values, that is into money. Money as a measure of value is the necessary *form of appearance* of the measure of value which is immanent in commodities, namely, labour time (emphasis added).[51]

Money (mined and minted gold) as a measure of value therefore functions as a sign or symbol of the circulation of other commodities with which it stands in a direct relationship by virtue of their shared status as objectified human labour.

Now, it has been recently observed that the generalisation in Marx's writings that the quantity of money is determined by the quantity of commodities is 'nothing more than a claim'.[52] I would wish to go further and suggest that Marx's theorem is a *prescriptive assertion* as to what ought to be the basis for a monetary system under the capitalist mode of production – that is, the monetary form which would enable capitalism to realise its productive potential was the credit system as the inert representation of *real* commodity-capital. In short, specific *functions* give rise to appropriate *forms* of money.

In this preoccupation with the question of the most suitable form of money for capitalist production, Marx does not appear to have seriously considered the possibility that forms and functions of money can be radically dissociated. In the early nineteenth century, the production of the conditions of existence of the means of circulation (gold currency) was quite independent of the production of commodities. In referring to this period a leading monetary historian has commented: 'At almost every point at which banking and monetary policy might have been used constructively to promote economic growth, the authorities either made the wrong decision or took no action at all.'[53]

Unless all economic activity in a social formation is totally subordinated to the requirements of *production* – and *recognised* as such by state agencies – then there is no guarantee that the monetary system will be so subordinated. Moreover, outside the sphere of production, there exists an *independent* economic relationship which is historically prior to capitalist production and has obvious important effects upon it. The state – as Max Weber among others has pointed out – has assumed the monopoly of regulating the monetary system by legally enforceable statutes. Originally, this monopoly was based upon the fiscal consideration of prohibiting the circulation of foreign coins and safeguarding the profits from seignorage (minting fees). Through the increase in state expenditure required to finance the internal monopolisation of physical force and national political integrity, the state became 'both the largest receiver and largest maker of payments in the society'.[54] This legal discharge of debts, as Weber observed, requires the 'continuity of the nominal unit of money' and refers to this state enforced legal standard as the *formal validity* of money.[55] Furthermore, the *form* of money is neither randomly nor arbitrarily arrived at: 'The public treasury does not make its payments simply by deciding to apply the rules of the monetary system which somehow seems to it ideal, but its acts are determined by *its own financial interests and those of important economic groups*' (emphasis added).[56]

Marx omitted the problem of the political production of money forms from *Capital* because he believed that he had already refuted – in the *Contribution to the Critique of Political Economy* – what he considered to be the most important claim of his adversaries – that the state could manipulate the value of money by controlling the quantity of currency:

The intervention of the state which issues paper money with a legal rate of exchange . . . seems to invalidate the economic law [that the quantity of money] depends on the prices of commodities [but] this power of the state is mere illusion. It may throw any number of paper notes of any denomination into circulation but its control ceases with this mechanical act. As soon as the token of value or paper money enters the sphere of circulation it is subject to the inherent laws of this sphere.[57]

Marx, then, assigns little importance to the state's role in the production of money because it cannot *create* value. But he does not appear to have seriously considered the converse: that the state would wish to knowingly *destroy* value over the long term by the legislative restriction of the money supply.[58] From his perspective, this was inconceivable; the legislation of the 1840s which formalised the gold standard was a temporary mistake which would be rectified with the rule of industrial capital. Of course, it persisted until 1914; was resurrected in 1925 for a further six years; and, subsequently, frantic efforts were made to maintain sterling (without a gold backing) in the role of world money – all with the same restrictive effect on the domestic credit system.

Geoffrey Ingham

Conclusion

Orthodox Marxism has either ignored or misinterpreted the City as a discrete sector of British capitalism. But the more heterodox writings which I looked at in the beginning of this article have failed to identify the specific economic practices which constitute the City. These are not simply 'financial', but commercial and banking activities in which commercial operations are dominant. Marx's own overwhelming preoccupation with the production of value within capitalism is partly responsible for these difficulties which have characterised Marxist treatments of the City and, relatedly, aspects of British 'exceptionalism'. In short, Marx's analysis of the conditions of existence of the independent forms of commercial and banking capital prevented his full recognition of the possibility of their persistent dominance in Britain.

Crucially important aspects of these conditions are to be found in 'political' and 'civil' society. First, characteristics specific to international trade in commodities, money, securities, etc. require conditions which are not typical of trade in general. Most important of these is the need for an acceptable and, preferably, *guaranteed* international means of payment. And, of course, the guarantee is politically generated by the budgetary prudence and the legal enactment of monetary regulations on the part of the nation which undertakes this role. As I have shown elsewhere, the close association between the Bank of England and the Treasury by which the conditions for the City's operations have been maintained cannot be understood simply as a result of the City's instrumental use of the state. For example, the introduction of free trade and the gold standard permitted the *calculability* of international exchanges which Britain's dominant economic position allowed her to exploit.[59] These moves were initially resisted by the City as they threatened their speculative activity which the uncertainties of the international economy encouraged.[60] London is not the centre of what Marx referred to as 'pre-capitalist' activities; or what later Marxists have termed 'finance-capital' but, rather, in Weberian terms, it is the location of *rational forms of commercial capitalism* brought about by initially autonomous political strategies.[61] Furthermore, the City's position has also been reproduced during the twentieth century after the economic bases for its dominance were eroded – through the weakness of sterling and the economy – by what the *New Left Review* writers have correctly observed as the continued hegemony of a traditional 'civil' elite which has monopolised important *cultural* and *political* assets in the educational system and the Civil Service.

All this does not mean that the City will preserve its dominance indefinitely. Its international activities are now based almost exclusively on the absence of regulations on flows of capital, commodities, commercial services, etc. As the Association of British Bankers put it in their evidence to the Wilson Committee: 'Amongst the main advantages which London must seek to maintain is its excellent reputation as the most liberal of major banking centres.'[62] Without the real material base which the British economy provided before 1914, the City's 'liberal' framework is precarious in the sense that it could be destroyed by combined political action on the part of industrial capital and labour almost as easily as it has been supported by the 'civil' elite over the years. In the past, embryonic 'producers' alliances – such as Chamberlain's Tariff Reform Movement, 'Mondism' in the 1920s, and Wilson's industrial strategy in the 1960s – have all failed because they were unable to perceive or were in awe of the fact that a condition of their own success was a thoroughly radical approach to the City. But, of course, even such a realisation is, in itself, insufficient; the dismantling of what is fundamentally a legacy of Britain's *pre-industrial* past would require a far-reaching realignment of British politics in general – so entrenched are the ramifications of the City's hegemony.

Property and control: some remarks on the British propertied class[1]

JOHN SCOTT

A basic problem in studying the capitalist propertied class today is its social and cultural anonymity. Despite its economic distinctiveness from other classes, it is socially and culturally continuous with the 'service class' and so seems to constitute a hierarchically ordered 'middle class'.[2] Whilst the landed class in Britain retained a cultural and social distinctiveness until well into the twentieth century,[3] this was not the case with manufacturing capitalists. From its origins as a 'middle class' in the nineteenth century, the latter group has eschewed the lavish life-style and conspicuous consumption so characteristic of its predecessors.[4] This is not to deny the existence of plutocratic figures at certain times and amongst certain groups; it is to point to the continuing influence of the asceticism recognised by Weber.[5] It can be argued that there is a partial normative convergence in the status dimension between the propertied class itself and the much larger service class. Although the classes remain distinct in economic and relational terms, their partial normative convergence follows from certain important trends in the modern capitalist economy. The transformation of the functions of the individual capitalist entrepreneur into the global function of capital[6] has led to the delegation of operational decision-making to bureaucratic hierarchies of professional managers and to a consequent expansion of the service class. At the same time it has generated important changes in the structure of the propertied class itself.[7] Similarly, the relationship between land and industry as forms of capital and fractions of a propertied class has undergone important transformations in the present century. Together with the changing relationship between 'finance' and 'industry', this has led to considerable complexities in studying the relationship between the anatomy of capital and the anatomy of the propertied class.[8]

The core of the propertied class comprises those who participate in the effective possession of capital, where this is expressed in participation in the strategic control of specific units of capital. The point is commonly made that developments in the modern economy have led to a 'managerial revolution', in which the old capitalist propertied class finally lost power to the professional administrators of the managerial technostructure. To argue in this way, however, is to misread the significance of the economic transformations which capitalism has experienced. Rather than the dissolution of the propertied class we have seen its 'managerial reorganisation': the privileged class of propertied families becomes increasingly autonomous from *particular* proprietary interests, though its members continue to monopolise positions of strategic control in modern capitalist enterprises.[9]

But whilst the propertied class has its basis in the effective possession of capital, it extends beyond this to those members of the professions and other occupations who are linked by kinship and social background to the core of corporate controllers and who enjoy similar privileges and benefits, even though they do not themselves participate in strategic control. We are concerned, that is, with a *social* class, a cluster of market situations between which mobility is frequent. The propertied class is a group of intermarried families enjoying superior advantages deriving from the use of capital and rooted in control over capital. Although the propertied class is not restricted to the smaller group of corporate controllers, the latter play a crucial role in the perpetuation of the propertied class as a whole. It is for this reason that the present paper concerns itself with identifying this controlling group. Some aspects of the debate over the nature of 'control' in the modern business enterprise will be reviewed in order to illustrate the relationship between property and control.

The unit of capital and strategic control

In order to locate the controlling group it is necessary first to identify that which they control. Since the terms 'corporation', 'company', and 'enterprise' are frequently employed in a loose way, it is important to clarify some of the main dimensions of meaning involved. A 'corporation', or joint-stock company, is a business undertaking which is constituted as a distinct legal entity comprising members who provide the share capital for its activities and officers who act in its name.[10] A corporation may draw on additional capital in the form of loans, mortgages, non-participating shares, etc., but its primary legal basis is always its ordinary share capital. Whilst a corporation normally works through one or more plants or establishments, it may at the same time be part of a larger group of corporations. When such a group is tied together through the complete or majority ownership of their shares by another corporation it is normal to speak of the group as an 'enterprise' or 'concern'. Since the whole enterprise generally takes its name and identity from the parent corporation, the enterprise is sometimes confusingly referred to as, for example, a 'large corporation'. It is important to be clear about when reference is intended to a specific legal entity (a corporation) and when reference is intended to a unified group of corporations (an enterprise).

Groups of corporations are not always held together through majority shareholdings, and so reference is often made to 'financial groups' or 'interest groups' where the corporations are linked through minority shareholdings, common directorships, credit relations, and other types of intercorporate relation. Separate companies can draw on various types of intercorporate link in order to weld such a group together, and it is possible to identify three broad types of intercorporate link. *Capital relations* comprise both shareholder relations and creditor relations. Shareholding is tied to the legal concept of ownership, which does not necessarily designate an effective social relation. The latter can be referred to as 'possession' and involves a consideration of the distribution of shareholdings within a company, as well as a consideration of other intercorporate links. It was the recognition of a movement of dispersal in shareholdings which first made the connection between 'ownership' and 'possession' problematic.[11] Thus, possession refers not simply to the fact of share ownership, but to the whole complex of shareholder relations and creditor relations, such as the granting of overdrafts and the holding of loan stock. Having said this, it is important to emphasise that shareholdings are the basis of possession, the foundation upon which all the other relevant factors operate. *Commercial relations*, the second type of intercorporate link, are of two main sub-types: trading relations and service relations. Trading relations are connections which exist between companies as buyers and sellers of one another's products or as participants in joint ventures, whilst service relations comprise the performance of a definite 'professional' service as registrars, management consultants, lawyers, or accountants. Finally, it is possible to recognise *personal relations* whereby any of the above links may be expressed by representation on the board of a company, or where purely 'contingent' ties of friendship, political association, and so on are drawn upon in board recruitment.

There exists, therefore, a complex network of intercorporate links of all types, and it is from within this network that groups of companies are formed. There are various levels and degrees of group formation culminating in the full fusion characteristic of the 'enterprise'. Thus, a group is not itself an enterprise, though it may evolve into an enterprise. A group is normally a looser set of alliances and coalitions which may achieve a certain degree of continuity over time. Apart from simple liaison schemes between companies, involving the exchange of directors and small shareholdings,[12] it is possible to recognise three levels of group formation. The purely personal type of group exists where a particular person, or group of people, sits on the boards of a number of companies. Family links are especially important here and, although this form of organisation is a weak and unstable basis for permanent alliances, it can last for some time when backed up by significant shareholdings. A financial type of group exists where the links between companies go beyond personal shareholdings and board representation to include intercorporate capital relations which are capable of outliving particular individuals and families. This more stable form of group may lead on to the third type of group, which is created through technical or functional organisation. In the latter case, financial links are complemented by links of horizontal or vertical integration such that there is a degree of functional interdependence amongst the various companies. Groups which achieve not simply a financial organisation but also functional links may take the final step from minority holdings to majority holdings and therefore to complete merger. This establishes a legal unity of the group such that all its constituent parts are subordinate to the holding company at the top. At this point it is possible to speak of an 'enterprise' rather than a 'group'. It should finally be pointed out that all the above intercorporate links and types of group formation can apply between enterprises just as much as between corporations.

The effective units of capital in an economy, therefore, may be either enterprises or groups. An enterprise will normally constitute an effective unit of capital, but the group need not. This is because minority shareholdings, common directorships, credit relations, etc., are not necessarily relations of *control* between corporations. The essential characteristic of a unit of capital is the mobilisation of capital through an autonomous corporate strategy. It is, therefore, important to locate the site of control. The institutional locus of possession, the arena of strategic control, is normally the corporate board of directors.[13] In most studies of corporate decision-making, economic 'elites', etc., the board of directors is taken as the basic object of analysis, though this methodological procedure is rarely argued for in any systematic way. I wish to suggest that such a procedure is in fact valid for the identification of the locus of control, but that certain problems inherent in this procedure must be avoided. One reason for caution in using company boards in this way is that not all those top executives who participate in the exercise of strategic control will be members of the board. Today, most boards do in fact include the top executives, but this was far less true in the past. Family firms at the turn of the century, for example, often excluded their chief managers from the board, no matter how important these people may have been. Without a longitudinal study of board composition it is impossible to assess the extent and significance of this practice. This objection, however, is not insuperable so long as the possible limitations of the procedure are recognised; and the objection certainly loses much of its force the nearer to the present that the research is located. A far more important objection makes the converse point and holds that it is invalid to assume that all board members participate equally, or at all, in strategic control. I wish to uphold the validity and force of this objection, but also to defend the methodological procedure of focussing on board membership.

My argument is that the board of directors is an *arena* for control, but not necessarily an *agency* of control. The board is the point at which the various contenders for corporate power are able to come together, and so control over the board is a crucial aspect of business leadership. The actual leadership group, together with its associates and rivals, will treat the board as an arena for the establishment of their power, but the board *as such* should be treated neither as a separate interest nor as a distinct contender for power. It is in this context that we must understand the discussion of company boards given by Pahl and Winkler.[14] These authors distinguish the *'proforma'* board and the 'functioning' board. The *pro forma* board exists where the board is a purely nominal device designed to conform with company law and for purposes of 'window dressing'. This occurs where one person or a clique effectively runs the company, either because they have built up a symbolic or ineffective board or because they have usurped power from the board. The effective controllers may formalise their position as an executive committee or management committee. In such a situation, argue Pahl and Winkler, the majority of the board members will be irrelevant to corporate decision-making. By contrast, a functioning board exists where board meetings are the focus of the time scheduling of the organisation as a whole and are interlinked with a whole series of formal meetings at group and divisional level. The board, therefore, exerts a constraint on the whole managerial hierarchy, and is the supervisory gatekeeper of the managerial process. The main types of functioning board are the non-executive board, where the part-time directors are the crucial gatekeepers, and the 'cabinet' board, where the group and divisional executives play this role.[15] The important point to be drawn from this discussion is not that we should exclude *pro forma* boards from consideration, but that we should be aware of the differential participation of board members in strategic control. Even though it may be valid to assume that all the important decision-makers are represented on the board, we must not make the mistake of assuming that all those on the board are important decision-makers. As Pahl and Winkler put it: 'Many or most of those who are the sought-for economic elites may in fact carry the title "director". But all those who carry the title "director" most certainly are not members of an elite.'[16] Whilst I would not wish to use the notion of 'elite' in this context, I would concur with the general point that the board of directors can be treated as the arena *within* which we should expect to locate business leaders.

So far in this paper I have referred to 'business leadership' and 'strategic control' without specifying their precise meaning, and it is now important to define these concepts. The most concise and acceptable definition of 'business leadership' is that given by Gordon, who argues that it is 'the function of organizing and directing business enterprises, of making the decisions which determine the course of a firm's activities'.[17] Gordon adds that by 'administering individual undertakings, business leaders taken together direct the course of activity in the economic system as a whole'.[18] That is, we may see the general features of the economy as the consequences, frequently unintended, of the actions of business leaders in directing individual enterprises. The question of the control exercised in *particular* enterprises is highly relevant to the question of the distribution of power within the economy as a whole.[19] Within individual enterprises business leadership is expressed in 'strategic control', participation in those decisions which 'establish broad objectives for the business as a whole . . . [and which] help to determine how the composite of economic resources controlled by a firm is to be directed towards productive ends'.[20] To exercise strategic control is to be involved in setting or altering the basic parameters within which the companies forming a particular unit of capital are to act. Typical strategic decisions would include the promotion and initial organisation of companies, determination of its key financial targets and product mix, and the maintenance and reorganisation of the organisation.

Strategic control must be clearly distinguished from 'operational management', which is concerned with lower-level decisions relating to the implementation of corporate strategy and hence with the immediate day-to-day administration of company operations. Bureaucratisation of the large enterprise has involved the delegation of operational decisions so that they are no longer the direct responsibility of the business leaders.[21] Managers and directors of subsidiary companies make operational decisions within the broad financial targets set by the parent firm, and their actions are monitored through divisional executives who are members of the top executive of the parent firm and may sit on its top board as executive directors. Operational decisions, therefore, are the main concern of members of the service class. Strategic control has been little studied by sociologists, most studies of industrial decision-making being concerned with such operational areas as the effort bargain, the price/output equation, and industrial relations. It is also the case that much trade union activity has directed itself to operational rather than to strategic issues: unions have been concerned with wages and with traditional issues of defensive job control in relation to such issues as manning levels, 'de-skilling', etc., and have been relatively unconcerned with control at the strategic level. Worker participation at board level has been built into companies such as J. Lyons, the John Lewis Partnership, and the pre-nationalisation gas companies, but such experiments seem to have had little wider impact. There has certainly been little pressure for co-determination along the lines of that practised in the Federal Republic of Germany, and the lukewarm response to the Bullock Report reinforces this conclusion.

The above discussion of the role of unions brings out the important point that whilst we may legitimately define the board as the locus of strategic control, the enterprise is subject to a number of constraints over and above those inherent in the struggle for dominance on the board. Corporate behaviour follows not only from the strategy formulated by the leadership group, but also from a variety of other constraining factors. Business leaders are constrained by their own workforce, whether formed into unions or not, and the level of such constraint depends upon the market situations of the various types of workers involved. In many areas the activities of the state have become an increasingly important constraint upon business activity. This involves general legislation concerning sex and race discrimination, as well as legislation specifically directed towards business practices: monopolies and mergers regulations, prices and incomes policies, limitation on restrictive practices, and so on. To the extent that the state becomes a shareholder or financier in relation to private enterprise it becomes a possible contender for participation in the leadership group itself. As the state has become important in this respect, so organised labour has for much of the post-war period exercised an influence over business behaviour through its participation in the state apparatus.[22] Perhaps the most important constraint on corporate behaviour is the market situation of the enterprise itself. The market sets definite limits beyond which enterprises are likely to run into serious financial difficulties, and it is only *within* these limits that an effective corporate strategy can be formulated. Business leaders, therefore, are constrained by the power of workers, unions, and the state, and can exercise strategic control within the limits of the market situation of their enterprise. It is for this reason that one major aspect of strategic control has been the attempt to exercise some degree of control over the market itself. The growth of economic concentration has increased the power of enterprises over their markets, and the establishment of interlocking directorships has been seen as an important device for strengthening such power.[23]

I am arguing, therefore, that it is legitimate to treat the board of directors as the institutional locus of strategic control, so long as it is not assumed that all board members are equally important. Similarly, it should not be assumed that business leadership operates in a vacuum: business leaders are constrained by the internal structure of their own enterprises, as well as by such external factors as the market, the state, and the unions. Having said this, it is important not to underestimate the power of business leaders in their own enterprise and in the economy as a whole. The following section will examine the main contenders for membership of that leadership group which I have claimed to be the core of the propertied class.

Contenders for control

The various groups which have an interest in the enterprise will necessarily be interested in the composition of the board. Since the board is the arena of strategic control, the question of recruitment to the board will always involve an overt or latent conflict of interest. This is not, of course, to say that company boards are at the centre of a continuous and deliberate struggle for supremacy; boardroom struggles are a relatively infrequent occurrence. However, the various contenders for control have differing interests and there is always the possibility that this latent conflict of interest will eventuate in overt conflict over the composition of the board. Even the 'normal' processes of orderly recruitment and succession to board positions depend upon the achievement of a balance amongst the various interests concerned. In order to clarify further the bases of this conflict of interest it is necessary to identify the various contenders for power.

The various contenders for control will, perhaps, be apparent from the discussion of the previous section. The major groups involved will be customers, competitors, providers of services, executives, shareholders, and financiers. Customers and suppliers are mainly important as external constraints upon the enterprise, but may sometimes be involved in interlocking directorships aimed at vertical integration. Similarly, competitor relations are external constraints which may occasionally be expressed in the formation of cartels aimed at price and quota controls. Those who provide services to the enterprise are in reality a particular kind of supplier, concerned with the provision of financial and legal advice and services. All these relations – with customers, suppliers, and competitors – involve participation in strategic control only when they are strengthened through a shareholder or creditor relation, and it may therefore be concluded that the major features of the struggle for corporate control can best be seen in terms of three major contenders: executives, who have important organisational responsibilities and are the main 'internal' group;[24] shareholders, who constitute the legal 'members' of the company; and financiers, who are outside groups lending money on a short-term or long-term basis.

(i) Executives and strategic control

The key position in the organisational hierarchy of the modern business enterprise is the chief executive, though the formal title may be General Manager, Managing Director, Chairman, or President. Whatever the job title, there is always one person who heads the full-time executive structure. The chief executive will have various assistants and deputies as well as specialised divisional executives, some or all of whom will be found on the parent company board.[25] Executive functions are not, however, exercised simply through a collection of individuals, but through an executive structure. The executive operates through various committees and sub-committees and is often coordinated through an executive committee of the board, which becomes more important as the number and importance of the sub-committees grows. In enterprises where the central holding company is separate from the central operating company the latter may be constituted as a *de facto* executive committee of the holding company board. In other companies the executive committee may be called the Group Policy Committee, the Management Committee, or the Advisory Board.

The executive managers have been central to the various notions of 'management control' in the large enterprise. It is argued that the full-time, internal executives have various strategies available to them for domination of the board. Although many such strategies are available to the board as a whole (control over board recruitment and over the voting machinery for company meetings), the major strategy available to executives is their control over the information received by board members. Pahl and Winkler have argued that such control is a crucial means through which executives are able to manipulate non-executive directors. They argue that the aim of the executives is 'to get proposals through the board giving only a generalised estimate of the costs involved and a minimum promise of results expected'.[26] The executives seek out generalised approval for courses of action, without detailed scrutiny from the non-executive directors:

> Successful manipulation . . . depends on the skilful structuring of the information which the board has available for assessing proposals. The power which the managers exercise over boards is power based on information control. Essential to such power is the sealing off of any sources of contradictory information. The result is conscious collusion among the management . . . to present a united front to the board.[27]

Executives, according to Pahl and Winkler, aim to pre-empt decisions through non-decision-making procedures: the options and information presented to the board are such that the desired course of action emerges as the only possible course of action. When successful, such strategies make board meetings routine and uneventful matters without argument or substantial discussion. Pahl and Winkler take the predominance of such situations as evidence for the lack of power of non-executive directors in general. However, this may be a misreading of the situation. It can plausibly be argued that non-executive directors do not *want* to be involved in the details of particular decisions and are happy that the boards should operate in this way: if contentious and detailed items are constantly raised at board level, then it is felt that the executives are not doing their job properly. Far from being the manipulated dupe depicted by Pahl and Winkler, the non-executive director actually connives at his own 'manipulation' and sees his job as simply keeping the executives 'on their toes'. [28] Whilst not wishing to resort to the 'elitist' arguments which Pahl and Winkler rightly reject, I want to suggest that the 'power' of non-executive directors rests precisely on the fact that executives have to work extremely hard and very efficiently in order to present the board with a limited set of options. If the non-executive directors were powerless, then such manipulative strategies would hardly be necessary. The need to manipulate is a sign of the relative *weakness* of the executives, not a sign of their power. Having said this, it is important to recognise that boards will vary in their response to such strategies, much depending on the attitudes taken by the other groups represented on the board.

Writers such as Galbraith[29] have drawn on arguments about the expertise of executives and their control over technical information to claim that the board will be dominated by the executives once shareholdings are so widely dispersed that there exists no effective rival to their power. There are, however, few examples of large enterprises in which this has occurred. Where shareholdings do become widely dispersed, outside interests continue to dominate the board and career managers tend to remain in a minority position.

The company which seems, above all, to epitomise the 'managerial' company is Imperial Chemical Industries. This was formed in 1926, and by 1936 the largest shareholder in ICI was the Belgian Solvay firm, which had formerly held an interest in Brunner Mond. By the 1950s this holding had been sold and ICI had a wide spread of share ownership. For a long while the dominant board member had been Lord McGowan, who was indeed a career executive from one of the constituent companies. McGowan had, however, an important economic and political base outside the company and brought onto the board men such as Lord Ashfield and Lord Weir, who had been involved in the Lloyd George experiment of associating businessmen more closely with government, and who were part of an extensive clique of businessmen involved in a number of companies in Britain and abroad. McGowan was able to use the support of Weir and Ashfield to buttress his own position in a boardroom struggle in 1937, where McGowan's power was opposed by the shareholding interests. [30] McGowan was succeeded in the 1950s by other career executives, but the board continued to include directors from other large industrial companies and from the former controlling families, as well as representatives of banks and insurance companies. At the very time that the position of the executives had been consolidated alongside the other interests represented on the board, fundamental changes were occurring in the pattern of share ownership. From a dispersed pattern of shareholding, ICI was evolving towards possession by a constellation of shareholders.

The discussion of ICI brings out not only the continuing importance of struggle in maintaining the board position of a chief executive, but also the fact that executives must not be considered simply as internal, career businessmen. As well as executives having outside interests, they may be people who have moved 'sideways' into the company: both Lord Stamp and Sir Paul Chambers were recruited to ICI from the Inland Revenue. Similarly, McGowan seems to have been instrumental in using his connections with the Lloyd George nexus to defend Nobel Industries' holding in Dunlop: when the latter was in financial trouble in 1922 Sir Eric Geddes was brought in as executive chairman, along with Sir George Beharrel as his assistant. Both men had been involved in Lloyd George's war-time government and both managed to secure positions for their sons at the Dunlop board table. Indeed, it is not uncommon for executives who achieve a position of dominance to bring their sons into the firm: a non-managerial principle of managerial succession.

The 'classical' concept of managerial control involved a view of executives operating in the context of dispersed shareholdings. As was intimated in the discussion of ICI, the 1950s saw a reversal of the trend towards dispersal of shareholdings as insurance companies began to acquire substantial quantities of company shares. The growth of such 'institutional' shareholding – and the consequent re-concentration of share ownership – has meant that executives in the largest companies are once again faced with large, well-informed shareholders. The implications of this will be drawn out in the next part of this paper.

(ii) Shareholders and strategic control

I have argued that 'ownership', a legal category, is distinct from 'possession', an effective social relation. As the 'owners' or 'members' of a company, the shareholders have legal rights and responsibilities in relation to the accounts, the directors, and so on. Where a particular group holds a majority of the shares (or, strictly, of the voting shares), this group of owners will comprise those who have effective possession of the enterprise as a whole. The smaller shareholders have only very limited importance in relation to the question of possession: they may be important as a general constraint, a negative influence which is particularly important when company earnings are depressed, but they are not important as a source of business leaders. The majority shareholder, by contrast, has the powers of possession and may combine these with the powers of the executive. That is, a group may have a majority shareholding *and* fill the top executive positions. This is equally true whether the majority shareholder be a family or another company, though these cases differ in other respects.

Majority ownership by a family is particularly strong where the family shareholding is coordinated through a family trust or family office. Families are able to adopt varying legal arrangements to consolidate and perpetuate their holdings. Prior to its recent acquisition by Allied Breweries, J. Lyons was majority controlled by the Salmon, Gluckstein and Joseph families, who concentrated voting shares in their own hands and issued non-voting shares to the public. The Vestey family, by contrast, has employed numerous international trusts and holding companies so as to minimise their tax payments and so as to finance the expansion of the Union International meat distribution company without the need to bring in outside shareholders. In both cases, the families have filled all the main executive positions in their companies. Where the majority shareholder is not a family but another company, then the pattern of control approximates to the delegated form of authority within the integrated enterprise. That is, the boards of companies which are subsidiaries of other companies, particularly if the parent is a foreign company, tend to be filled with 'middle management' executives concerned mainly with operational decisions. Nationalised companies are those where the government is, in fact or in effect, the majority shareholder, and the main difference between this situation and that of private majority ownership centres upon the fact that the state may not, but generally does, adopt a strict shareholder interest towards its companies. For example, British Steel, British Rail, and the National Coal Board may expect more lenient financial treatment from the government than they would get from private shareholders. However, the state is here important in its dual role of external constraint upon business activity *and* majority shareholder. Indeed, the situation is complicated further by the involvement of the state, directly and indirectly, as a lender of capital to nationalised enterprises.

Shareholdings need involve neither a mass of small holders nor a single majority holder, but a small number of large holders. Such holders may be able to share majority ownership or they may be in a more restricted situation of minority possession. The latter is that situation where a particular interest or group of interests has a minority holding of both the voting shares and the total capital. It is, however, impossible to give an arbitrary cut-off point (such as 20%, 10%, or 5%) below which minority control no longer exists. The size of the minority holding necessary for control depends upon the overall distribution of the capital amongst all the shareholders. Adapting Florence's 'rule' that the twenty largest shareholders have effective possession if they have at least 20% of the capital,[31] it can be argued that a group has a large enough minority stake if the next 20 largest holders do not have sufficient votes collectively to outvote the group.[32] Beyond this quantitative question, however, is the fact that minority holders may be more or less active in company affairs: 'Some of them participate continuously and to an important degree in business leadership; others do so only sporadically; yet others contribute little or not at all to the process of decision-making.'[33] Minority owners will be of least importance in business leadership when they are not represented on the board, and will be of greatest importance when they are not simply represented on the board but occupy executive positions. Gordon has claimed that the most important examples of minority ownership without board representation 'arise out of the transmission of family holdings to succeeding generations'.[34] As I have argued above, the importance of family shareholdings for business leadership depends upon whether a family trust or holding company is used to overcome the centripetal dissolution of inherited family shareholdings. However, Gordon's general point is perhaps pertinent:

family holdings in most very large corporations belong to the second, third, or even later generations. Interest in the business ordinarily tends to decline as holdings are inherited by later generations, and the interests of the original owner's children and grandchildren may well lie in other fields, perhaps outside the sphere of business entirely.[35]

Where such a pattern holds, the minority owners will be relatively unimportant in business leadership and the remaining family representatives on the board may be subjected to the manipulatory strategies of the executives. Nevertheless, there remain a number of important examples of family minority owners who actively participate in business leadership, and active participation is always greater when the minority holder is another company rather than a family.

Family minority holdings, if coordinated adequately, can frequently be as secure a base for control as majority ownership. Thus families are still dominant in companies such as Tesco, W. H. Smith, Inchcape, and S. Pearson, the family holding in each case being between 10% and 30%, and the family being represented on the board and at executive level. Of course, not all personal holdings involve families; individual tycoons and 'entrepreneurs' may also be in positions of minority possession and executive power. Such an individual may be in a stronger position than a family, which may have internal disagreements and fragmented control over its minority holding. To the extent that such individuals attempt to pass on their position to their heirs, they will face the same problems as are involved in the transmission of a family holding. It is, therefore, to be expected that all types of personal minority shareholdings will show similar characteristics.

Minority holdings by other companies are a relatively frequent occurrence and can vary considerably in their significance. Barclays Bank and Lloyds Bank have for a long time held minority holdings in two of the Scottish clearing banks, and whilst the parent banks have board representation the Scottish boards are dominated by Scottish businessmen, together with one or two senior executives.[36] In these cases the minority shareholders have been satisfied with a 'backseat' role and have not attempted to intervene to the extent that they might have done. An even more passive role is taken by the Kuwait Investment Office which has accumulated minority holdings in a number of large companies in the last ten years. In yet other cases, minority holdings can be aggressively used as a means of maximising control at minimum cost. For example, a group of investment trusts managed by Viscount St Davids were welded together through minority holdings in the years leading up to the First World War. These trusts took overlapping minority holdings in many industrial companies which frequently took minority holdings in one another and jointly took stakes in other companies. At its height the group encompassed much of the British passenger road transport network, many electrical supply companies, electrical engineering and ancillary companies, and printing and publishing companies.

The distinction between executives and shareholders is analytical, and does not necessarily refer to distinct social groups. It has already been pointed out that large personal shareholders may be found amongst the top executives of a company, and it is also the case that executives may use shareholdings to buttress their position. Even where they are insignificant as individual shareholders, the executives are able to use the proxy voting machinery to mobilise support for their proposals at company meetings. Similarly, voting trusts can be used to give the executives voting power beyond the extent of their personal shareholdings. Strictly, both the proxy machinery and the voting trust are available to the board as a whole rather than simply to the executives, but they are only likely to be important

issues in the struggle for control when there are no really large shareholders in the company. The British parent of the Unilever enterprise, for example, has only one substantial shareholder – a minority
holding by the Leverhulme trust, set up by the founder of the company. Although the Lever family remain associated with the trust,
the trustees are drawn from Unilever's own board of directors. In this
way the dominant group on the board, which consists mainly of
executives, is able to back up its position with a minority shareholding.

An important trend in company shareholdings has been away from
majority and minority holdings towards a situation where loose constellations of interests have effective possession. These constellations
collectively have minority, or even majority, possession, but they do
not form a cohesive controlling group. However, they do not constitute simply an undifferentiated mass of small shareholders. Their
views and interests must be taken into account and they will often
seek board representation. It is here that we find the main significance of the growth of 'institutional' shareholding – shareholdings
by insurance companies, pension funds, unit trusts, etc. Since these
companies will normally tend to be lenders as well as shareholders,
they will be discussed in the next part of this paper.

(iii) Financiers and strategic control

A number of groups are important in the provision of finance
to enterprises, and many banks and insurance companies combine
the roles of 'institutional investor', trustee for the shareholdings of
others, and provider of loan capital. To this may be added the financial services provided by bankers, stockbrokers, lawyers, and
accountants, all of whom may be important in servicing loan capital
as well as in underwriting share issues and providing financial advice.
Situations which are particularly favourable for the influence of
financial interests over company affairs are when a company is
formed, expanded, or reorganised, whether these are 'internal'
developments or occur through mergers and take-overs. Financial
interests are involved at all these crucial points of strategic decision,
even if this involvement is not always translated into continuous
participation in strategic control.[37]

Merchant banks and investment banks are particularly important
in the mobilisation of long-term loans, and this normally involves
organising underwriting syndicates of investors rather than any
commitment of the banks' own rather limited funds. In cases where
the bank has managerial responsibility for investment trusts and

pension funds which take up company bonds and shares, it is able to use these connections to build up a considerable interest in a company and may become a significant force in its affairs.[38] An important example of this is the merchant bank Hill Samuel. With the backing of Eagle Star Insurance, the Hill group became closely involved with Beecham Pills, the Covent Garden Properties Company, the Timothy Whites chemist chain, Hawker Siddeley, and the Rank family interests. In recent years Hill Samuel consolidated its interests and became heavily involved in Labour and Conservative governments' attempts at industrial reconstruction, using its lending power and financial expertise to play a significant role in the affairs of British Airways, Rolls Royce, and British Leyland, and playing a key role in undermining the National Enterprise Board. Although minority shareholdings have been employed within the Hill Samuel group, the parent company's direct shareholdings have often been very small. Rather, Hill Samuel has utilised its lending and underwriting capacities to weld the group together through a network of financial dependencies and personal connections.

Similar mechanisms were involved when firms of accountants and stockbrokers built up massive interests in electricity supply in the inter-war years. Investment trusts managed by the Touche accountancy firm were involved in the flotation and financing of the Balfour Beatty electrical contracting group and acquired control over a number of local and regional electricity companies. Similarly, stockbrokers such as Foster and Braithwaite, and Greenwells, set up investment trusts for their clients to invest in major electrical holding companies which they had established. The power of such groups rested not so much in their individual financial assets, but in the capital they were able to mobilise from other sources.

Commercial banks such as Barclays, Lloyds, Midland, and National Westminster are likely to be involved in short-term credit rather than long-term credit, though short-term loans may be continuously 'rolled over' to become *de facto* long-term interests. The commercial banks, however, have tended to take a passive role towards their investments and have intervened mainly when this was necessary to protect money lent out as overdrafts. The high point of such bank involvement in Britain has been in the 1920s and 1930s, when the Bank of England coordinated bank intervention on a massive scale in British industry. At this time the commercial banks, and some large insurance companies, were the effective possessors of large enterprises such as Vickers, Armstrong Whitworth, United Steel, and the Royal Mail shipping group. Similarly, the Bank of England has organised clearing bank 'life-boat' rescue operations in the fringe-bank crisis of the 1970s and the recession of 1980–81. The national-isation of the Bank of England in 1946 formalised the close relation-ship between the Bank and the state, and this association of the state with business finance has continued to grow through the provision of loans and supplementary finance to companies whose failure would threaten the perceived national interest. Labour governments estab-lished successively the Industrial Reorganization Corporation and the National Enterprise Board. Both the IRC and the NEB were involved in unresolved party disputes over the question of whether they should operate as ordinary merchant banks or as non-commercial arms of government policy. Although these organisations have often adopted a conventional financier role in relation to the businesses with which they were associated, they were frequently forced to implement gov-ernment policies of support to 'lame-duck' enterprises. The ability of the state to override normal commercial criteria poses a serious chal-lenge to the normal processes of business leadership, though it is true to say that this has been realised more as a support for private business than as a means for its transformation.

The growth of 'institutional' shareholding has been associated with the increasing importance of 'institutions' as providers of loan capi-tal. The constellations of interests which become the dominant ele-ment in possession and finance are increasingly taking an active part in business leadership. In the past there has been a reluctance to intervene on the part of these enterprises, though there has often been direct or indirect board representation. Increasingly, those who sit as non-executive directors take on a watching brief on behalf of the dominant constellation. It is more and more the case that those who are recruited as non-executive directors are drawn from a 'pool' of those associated with the 'institutional' shareholders, whether as bank directors, insurance directors, investment managers, or direc-tors of a bank's client industrial firms. In this sense, non-executive directors come to 'represent' this particular sector of capital rather than any *specific* interest. Such non-executive directors will be recruited as part of the normal procedures of filling board vacancies, with the network of contacts possessed by the existing directors being drawn upon to find a suitable candidate. Non-executive directors may, however, be recruited in a more deliberate way. In promoting or reconstructing an enterprise, financial interests may determine the composition of the board, even if they do not put their own directors and managers on the board. A bank may, for example, insist that the number and calibre of non-executive directors be increased and would use its own contacts and client companies to find suitable people. In this way, the bank would have one or more 'watchdogs' on the board even if there is no direct interlock with the company.

The fact that directors of banks and other financial companies tend to have a large number of non-executive directorships in companies has led writers such as Pahl and Winkler to argue that they are easily subject to manipulation by executives: the director who sits on three, four, five, or more boards has least involvement in any one and so is prone to manipulation. However, I have suggested that such 'manipulation' may be exactly what the non-executive director wants. Whilst it is certainly incorrect to regard non-executive directors as predatory power-seekers involved in a financial rip-off of the various companies with which they are associated, it is equally incorrect to assume that, say, an investment manager who sits on a number of boards is the dupe of managerial strategies. Rather, it should be recognised that both financiers and executives have power, although the way in which that power is exercised and the means which are employed will vary between the two groups. So long as a company is successfully meeting its financial targets, the financial representatives on its board will have no desire to rock the boat by disrupting managerial strategies. Conversely, the absence of such financial representatives as a constraining and inhibiting influence may well lead to a more 'risky' attitude by executives and, therefore, to a greater likelihood of financial failure.

Conclusion

I have argued that the board of directors at the head of the large business enterprise should be seen as an arena for the exercise of business leadership. It is not in itself an agency of power, but is the arena in which executives, shareholders, and financiers come together in order to participate in strategic control. Although there is always the possibility of a conflict of interest between these contenders for power, this is normally latent rather than overt. When a company continues to operate successfully, any competing interests can be subordinated to the smooth exercise of business leadership along the existing lines. It is when a company runs into financial difficulties or enters into risky ventures that conflicts of interest come to the surface and are translated into a struggle over participation in the exercise of strategic control. Such struggles are likely, sooner or later, to eventuate in a re-structuring of the board so as to enable a smooth pattern of business leadership to be re-established.

The various contenders for power – executives, shareholders, and financiers – are not, however, to be considered as totally distinct groups. Executives may be large shareholders, shareholders may also provide finance capital, and so on. The categories are analytical rather than concrete and point to foci of potential differentiation *within* the core of the propertied class. They are not distinct 'fractions' within that class since the intra-generational and inter-generational mobility between the various roles is considerable. It is in this sense that we can understand Zeitlin's claim that enterprises are units in a class-controlled system within which the core of corporate controllers are 'the leading organizers of this class-wide property'.[39] The active participants in strategic control, the business leaders, are the core of the broader class of those who derive benefits and privileges from the results of this business leadership. In this paper I have not been able to look at the structure of this broader class itself, at the patterns of mobility into it, and the ways in which those outside the core are able to maintain their position within the propertied class. Such questions go well beyond the narrower issue of corporate control, and must be deferred to another occasion.

The division of labour, incomes policy and industrial democracy

PAUL HIRST

This essay will contend that a great deal of what is assumed by economists and sociologists to be 'objective' and 'structural' in matters of the division of labour and the system of income distribution is, on the contrary, the result of policies followed by governments, firms and unions, and the result of popular expectations about forms and levels of income and the responsibilities appropriate to non-executive jobs. It will do this by examining attitudes to incomes policies and to industrial democracy, particularly on the part of trade union leaders and activists. Incomes policies are a good example to illustrate this thesis and so is industrial democracy, because both view the economy as a *social organisation*. That is, they treat major macro- and micro-economic factors as being subject to policy and to the orchestration of active consent rather than as resulting from objective economic 'laws'.

The approach to the analysis of wages adopted here follows Barbara Wootton's pioneering *The Social Foundations of Wages Policy*.[1] It will be pointed out that the main obstacles to the implementation of incomes policies stem from the fact that the wages structure is not simply the product of economic necessity or rationality, but is greatly influenced by considerations of status, official attitudes and the results of union activity. Incomes policies have tended to founder on questions of equity between groups of workers, the preservation of differentials, and so on. These forms of hierarchy and difference in the way payments are distributed and jobs organised are intractable and divisive because they have no general economic necessity, workers dispute other groups' claims and yet pursue their own. Hierarchy and difference between groups of workers have been tenaciously defended and promoted by the trade unions. The reason for this is that these forces have played a crucial role in the post-war bargaining system.

248

It will be pointed out that union resistance to the Bullock Report on industrial democracy depended on conceptions of the proper role of trade unions, but that these conceptions are related to the particular way unions and bargaining have been organised in the UK since the last war.[2] The opponents of industrial democracy tend to ignore this and support the existing arrangements as if they are defending the only possible way in which trade unions could be strong and active. Incomes policies have not foundered because of the stupidity and shortsightedness of workers and their leaders, rather they have foundered because of the limitations of the policies themselves. Incomes policies in the UK since 1945 have not seriously addressed themselves to the *social obstacles* to the state regulation and management of wages posed by the wages structure itself, and by the interconnection of pay bargaining with the main representative and defensive capacities of the unions. Incomes policies have been conceived, on both the governments' and the unions' parts, as short-term crises measures to supplement 'normal' Keynesian demand management. Wider questions of social organisation could therefore apparently be ignored. Economic management now depends on a *permanent* incomes policy; that demands a reform of the bargaining system and that in turn demands, if it is not to act against the interest of workers, a radical change in the social organisation of firms and work itself.

Any proposition on which academic and political commentators on the Marxist Left and the free-market Right in Britain whole-heartedly agree must be of considerable interest. One such proposition is the economic futility and political dangerousness of incomes policies. Pro-market commentators like Samuel Brittain contend that incomes policies impede the working of labour markets and, therefore, reduce overall allocative efficiency.[3] Further, in doing this, incomes policies promote reliance on political and administrative expedients to make up for the thwarted action of the market. Thus they provide the trade unions with an access to political power which is unwarranted by their economic contribution and is dangerous in that it undermines the workings of parliamentary democracy. Marxist commentators like Leo Panich argue that incomes policies are part of a 'corporatist' response by Social Democracy to the problems posed for capital by industrial militancy in a full-employment economy.[4] Incomes policies – proposed with the ostensible purpose of combating inflation – are actually an attempt to police and de-mobilise the grassroots militants, thereby cutting back working-class income gains

Paul Hirst

at the expense of profits. Thus the agreement masks a very real political disagreement. On the one hand, incomes policies lead to trade union power, on the other hand, corporatism leads to the conversion of union leaderships into agencies of state control and the crippling of the *real* power base of the unions, the mass movement.

This political disagreement, however, goes along with an agreement about the nature of wage determination in the capitalist economy. Free-marketeers argue that ultimately, despite the imperfections of markets, the demand for particular skills, the marginal productivity of labour and the profitability of firms determine wage levels – unions impede the working of labour markets but in the long run they cannot and do not radically affect the distribution of income. In other words, markets perform their allocative function – in this case the distribution of workers to firms at definite wage rates – better than any other system. The aim should be to make markets work *as well as possible,* rather than further impede their working because they fall short of an abstract concept of perfection. Wages and work organisation are the product of economic necessities, that is, the collective results of subjective decisions and behaviours. Similarly, Panich argues that whilst wage determination is a sphere of class struggle, the form of that struggle is working-class resistance to the consequences of the basic laws of the capitalist system. These laws can only be suspended when the capital–labour relation itself ceases to exist.

This hostility of Marxist and free-market commentators to incomes policies matches the hostility expressed by the majority of the trade union movement. The reason for the latter's hostility is very different from that of the former two, however. It arises from a belief in the benefits of 'free collective bargaining'. Wages in this view are not the product of economic 'laws' but of organised bargaining and a social structure of industrial relations. I would contend that the trade unionists' view is the correct one, but that the inference that incomes policies undercut workers' bargaining strength and therefore their wages by no means follows.

This commitment to collective bargaining has been connected with two widely shared official and mass attitudes about the determination of wages and the place of wage bargaining in the national economy, which have developed since the Second World War.

Firstly, it had come to be assumed that 'Full employment' is the normal state of affairs, that wages and real incomes would rise steadily and that there are no given determinants to the price of 'labour power' or the level of wages. Workers expected to be in work and to receive regular percentage increases in their wage rates from year to year. Wages were conceived as determined by a contest for shares in a growing national income: the shares workers receive depend on their capacity to bargain.

This contrasts markedly with official trade union attitudes before the last war. Neither the Labour Party nor the trade unions had an 'alternative economics'; most of the leaders and the masses in the Labour movement accepted (however ruefully or reluctantly) the prevailing capitalist economic theories about the determinants of economic activity and wages. The syndicalist movement of the early 1900s and the Great War left little in the way of economic ideas, and, like Marxism, was anathema to the largely rightist dominated trade union leaders. Hence the predominant expectations were pessimistic and defensive. A given rate of unemployment (about 10%) was widely accepted as normal. Wages were regarded as industry specific and set by conditions of cost and profitability in that industry. National income was not expected to rise steadily but to fluctuate unpredictably with the cycle of boom and slump. The primary task of most unions in this period was to resist wage *cuts* and a worsening of working conditions; wage reductions were commonplace in the 1920s and early 1930s.

Secondly, union negotiators and the rank and file have stressed take-home pay above all else; all other issues within the enterprise (organisation of work, safety, what is made, investment and company strategy, etc.) have been considered as secondary or ignored. Shopfloor workers have a strong tendency to express such questions as they do raise in terms of bargaining about monetary rewards, questions of safety serving to promote claims for danger bonuses and so on. Many potential issues of struggle in the enterprise cannot be expressed in terms of personal benefits. Short-term material gains commit the workers to little in the way of continuing struggle in the enterprise. Often such claims can only be taken up by transient and organisationally divided workforces (labour turnover and union structure are significant limits on forms of struggle).

With a lessening of opportunities for job mobility and the broadening of the effects of loss of competitiveness, many workers are coming to be more concerned with the nature of the enterprise they are in, its prospects and the future of their jobs. These concerns cannot be settled by pay rises. Often they cannot be effectively raised as issues of struggle because of divisions within the workforce and the different policies of their respective unions. The resolution of differences in union structure is not simply a 'management' issue (simplifying bargaining and the policing of agreements). It also concerns the ability of the working class to struggle about certain issues at a grassroots level.

The commitment to collective bargaining and its past successes, the continued expectations of a steadily rising national income have led the majority of trade union officials and the rank and file to oppose incomes policies. The 'Social Contract', like every other incomes policy the trade unions have agreed to since the war (those of 1948, 1964 and 1966), was conceived as a short-term emergency measure that would be followed by a return to 'normal' collective bargaining. But wage restraint of one kind or another has been an almost permanent feature of the policy of British governments since the 1961 'pay pause'. Mrs Thatcher's government is now practising a *de facto* incomes policy whilst claiming to have left free collective bargaining untouched; for public sector workers this policy has become explicit, and it is evidently inequitable in that it openly and cynically involves surrendering to those whose disruptive power is great whilst penalising the weak.

The point at issue here is that the 'new' trade union attitudes are keyed to the assumptions of economic growth, full employment and relative price-stability. In a period of depression, high unemployment and inflation, they have less relevance. A dogged defence of 'free collective bargaining' may be necessary against the Tories. But as a response to any government committed to reflation and economic growth through positive state action it can only undermine such policies. In all probability a reflationary policy without a system of wage controls would lead to a new wages explosion. The resultant accelerating inflation would then undercut the reflationary programme and lead to new restrictive measures.

The trade union movement should be pushing for a radical and workable incomes policy if it wants the present government-accentuated depression to end. The reason is that there is no 'alternative', no workable policy of government management of macro-economic aggregates that can save us the complex and painful task of radical changes in the social organisation of work and wages.

Trade unionists are clear that the 'monetarist' alternative is neither workable nor acceptable. The present recession has been engineered in large part by government as a means of countering inflation – something an incomes policy is designed to do. Far from being a fiendish and successful capitalist plot, the depth of the British recession is a blunder consequent upon the stubborn persistance in an unworkable policy derived from an irrelevant economic dogma. 'Monetarist' policies have not cured inflation and the Tory government has been forced to resort to an incomes policy after little more than a year in office. This 'policy' is inequitable, does little to control those best placed to bargain, and can only work whilst the economy is kept depressed.

However, for all their vocal opposition, many trade unionists are prepared in practice to live with such policies and would find national income planning far more difficult to countenance. This is explained by the distributional consequences of Tory policy. The principal costs of the recession have so far been borne by the low paid, the unemployed and certain other recipients of state benefits. It is they who have been the main victims of the decline in national income. Wage levels as a whole, however, tend to be resistant to strong downward movement in real terms. Even three million unemployed cannot produce a dramatic fall in wage levels for the employed in general because there is no 'market' in which those without jobs can compete against existing job holders and bid down wage levels. The differentiation of labour markets, unionisation and conditions of service, the preference of firms for workers already trained on the job, and the geographical location of the unemployed all see to that.

Hence those Marxist interpretations which see monetarist strategy as having the covert and rational objective of using unemployment to bring down wage rates and therefore restore profit levels are fallacious. If this *is* the covert aim of the adherents of monetarism then they have made a huge mistake. Negative growth and inflation will tend to act as a brake on real wages – unemployment is a consequence of this general condition of the economy and not in itself a cause of such limitations on wage bargaining as there are. Evidence suggests that until recently *average* earnings have kept pace with inflation. Such averages conceal evident inequalities, but they also show that not all manual workers are victims of inflation and depression. Further, the current depression – far from leading to an increase in profit rates – has in all probability squeezed them further. Short-time working, reduced demand and so on directly reduce productive efficiency, leading to plants working well below capacity and full profitability. Recession tends to be self-reinforcing, reducing both demand for firms' products and their internally generated funds for investment. High interest rates restrict external financing to specially favoured projects and, at least until recently, a strong exchange rate acts against exports. No wonder the CBI has a good deal to complain about to Mrs Thatcher. No attainable level of unemployment will make its members' trading prospects any rosier or their firms more profitable.

It is widely accepted to the point of being conventional wisdom that 'Keynesian' counter-cyclical policies of the traditional kind no longer offer a way of restoring full employment. Such policies were conceived in an era of falling prices and interest rates. 'Keynesianism' is considered ineffective because such instruments as tax cuts and credit creation reinforce inflationary pressures and because a substantial portion of unemployment is now considered to be structural rather than cyclical. A response to this failure of the devices of post-war social democracy has been the proposals from the Left for an 'alternative economic strategy' aiming at the state directed reconstruction of British industry. These proposals (for example, Holland, CSE, and Aaronovitch) all fudge the question of wages policy.[5] Instead they hope to rely on planned trade and price controls. Space prohibits a full discussion of the AES, especially proposals to control imports and plan trade.[6]

Inflation and balance of payments problems really do constrain public policy (independently of the objectives of governments) and also trade union practice. Most of the 'alternative' economic strategies proposed on the Left hardly accept this. The Left as a whole has only recently abandoned arguing strenuously that 'wage rises do not *cause* inflation', and has not started to face up to the consequences of the alternatives. The determinants of inflation are various and situational, and some of them have nothing to do with wage rises, but to argue the irrelevance of wage-fuelled inflation in the middle of the wage–price spiral of the 1970s was little short of madness. An *incomes policy* then became a necessity, and was accepted as such by most unions and workers, precisely because of that spiral. Wage restraint was the only effective means of breaking the spiral relatively quickly. Price controls or controls on incomes other than wages have, on their own, limited effectiveness in controlling inflation. Price controls can be effective within certain conditions: (i) that there are also effective *wage* controls, otherwise company incomes may be unduly squeezed before the measures can have effect, (ii) that they concern prices which can be policed (thousands of price setters are beyond control, from multi-national companies to small traders in the 'black economy'), (iii) for domestic prices, changes in the prices of imported raw materials cannot be controlled without also squeezing company income. Price controls are not an *alternative* to wage restraint. Like subsidies on basic items such as foodstuffs they are an effective *adjunct* and supplement, helping to mitigate the consequences of foregoing rises in money wages and, therefore, to strengthen willingness to accept pay restraint. Controlling personal incomes other than wages cannot control prices, these amount to about a *third* of the total of national personal income (wages and salaries 70%, self-employment 9%, rent interest and dividends 10%, and social security 11%).[7] *Any* incomes policy must therefore work primarily through the control of wages and salaries; there is no easy counter-inflation strategy through price and dividend controls alone.

Inflation and depression are a combination which make *some* form of long-term incomes policy necessary if any sustained economic recovery is to be possible. The current economic crisis has confirmed the relevance of Barbara Wootton's conception of national income planning which was advanced in a period of full employment. National income planning is more than wage controls, it is a new system of wage determination linked to economic and social policy objectives. The Left and the trade union movement have shunned any prospect of this, preferring to insist on the autonomy of free collective bargaining. The reasons for this response are not hard to find. Effective incomes planning would make most of the present trade union practices redundant. It would remove one of the major sources of Left influence with the organised working class: support for militant wage claims and struggles. A national incomes policy, it is argued, would strengthen the state, the TUC and a handful of union officials, and through them the employers, against the mass of organised labour. The spectacle of socialists opposing incomes policy and supporting 'free collective bargaining' is not as bizarre and irrational as it might appear. 'Corporatism' and 'tripartism' are feared because it is supposed that whatever 'influence' they give the TUC in directing national policy and control over state apparatuses (MSC, ACAS, etc.), an 'influence' always subject to political reversal, will be bought at the price of demobilisation and policing of the mass movement.

What stagflation prevents is a general process of 'bidding-up' wage levels by claim and counter-claim between different occupations, industries and regions which characterised the 1950s and 1960s. To attempt to continue such a process would produce a wages–prices spiral in which only a small minority of organised workers could keep ahead of the game. Those workers who were poorly organised, lacked appropriate industrial bargaining power and did not benefit from 'status' lost out in the 1950s and 1960s. However, the breakdown of the 'ladder' of claims will sharpen the distributional consequences of wage rises. A minority of workers will benefit under any

255

Paul Hirst

implicit or explicit incomes policy which exists simply to police wage rises. The end of the 'ladder' of claims makes questions of the present distribution of income between groups of workers explosive. The present wage structure is not the product of some uniformly acting general economic laws. It is primarily the result of decades of collective bargaining, of differential capacities to bargain, on the one hand, and of notions by governments, managements and unions about 'statuses', forms of payment and the organisation of work hierarchies. Those most able and organised to bargain, irrespective of official and popular notions about 'status', have benefited most.

'Free collective bargaining' is increasingly an effective option only for workers in certain enterprises and trades. As the conditions have become tougher more organised workers now find themselves in positions analogous to the 'low paid' in the 1950s and 1960s. In conditions of semi-stagnation, increased foreign competition in the home market and low returns on capital, more industrial firms will tend to resist wage rises in a way they did not in the 'go' periods of the 1950s and 1960s domestic demand. Most public employees, many private-sector organised workers, and the bulk of the 50% of the labour force which is not unionised will have few opportunities to strike favourable bargains. Their living standards will be eroded by the general level of inflation and by the transferred wage costs of some of their more favoured brethren.

Given the fundamental changes in expectations about income since the 1930s outlined above, differential capacities to bargain could become an explosive question. To see a minority enjoying a constant or increasing standard of living whilst one's own is declining or stagnant, and simply because of the accident of the trade, firm or place where they work, will be generally unacceptable. This is what the ending of a 'ladder' of claims will produce. The irrationalities of the wages structure, differentials, regional differences, etc., have been accepted and defended precisely *because* they offered pretexts to bargain and the prospect of 'moving up' the ladder. The minority who can maintain or increase their living standards could become increasingly isolated and vulnerable to political pressure through the ballot box. Pensioners, the unemployed, recipients of social security have votes too. Unless the Labour Party can provide a credible alternative to either a wage freeze or a 'free-for-some', it could well find itself excluded from power.

Stagflation may have made an incomes policy of some kind necessary but one which consists *only* of prolonged wage restraint is practically and politically unworkable. The only condition in which

256

such negative state controls could work is the suspension of many basic political rights and the destruction of the unions and of the workers' capacity to bargain. Even the current Tory regime has shown little inclination to move in this direction. The trade union movement has reluctantly accepted 'wage freezes' as emergency measures in the past but only on the assumption that they would be short-lived. The 1966 wage freeze was effective because it was temporary – the Labour Government could discover no effective incomes policy to replace it. Its 'controls' became a laughing stock. Incomes policy has come to *mean* wage-freeze or restraint for most trade unionists. But this attitude, that incomes policy is temporary and can be forgotten about as a mere setback in earnings, is intelligible only on the assumption that self-sustained economic growth is the norm. On any other assumption this attitude becomes deeply problematic. In conditions of stagnation *and* inflation 'free collective bargaining' *is also* practically and politically unworkable in the long run.

Only a policy which attempts to break open the reliquary of our wages structure can hope to succeed and achieve a sufficient measure of consent and compliance. Such a policy cannot be *imposed* on the trade union movement by any national government, however enlightened. The reason is that the recognition and resolution of differences between groups of workers is the main stumbling block to any incomes policy. Only a mass commitment to the objectives of such a policy could make such a process of recognition and resolution possible. Something 'as limited' as a policy of wage restraint will only work for more than a couple of years if it is capable of becoming something more, a policy to reshape income distribution. In order to do this it must involve the active participation of a significant number of trade unions and masses of trade unionists.

Without national income planning 'incomes policies' can only amount to an arbitrary and uneven 'wage freeze'. Such policies produce both the intractable problems of those who can bargain and break the 'freeze' and of the disturbed differentials which are the results of the point at which the last round of 'bidding-up' was terminated. In the 'Social Contract' all the trade union movement did agree to was a *measure* of wage restraint, the *norms* of that policy were a matter of continuous dispute. But even if a percentage limit were agreed to pay rises, this could not settle the mass of distributional questions which remain from an entirely different system of setting wage and earnings levels. The problems incomes policies have faced in Britain since the war can only be resolved by turning them into something broader. The difficulties of wage limitation show that an incomes policy which persists for any period of more than a year or so requires a set of 'ideological' objectives which can secure the commitment of the mass of the workers and which can serve as criteria or bases of principle in settling hard cases. Fear of inflation or other pragmatic economic policy goals cannot secure this commitment in the long run, for such pragmatic commitment is weakened to the extent that economic conditions improve. Such 'ideological' objectives must necessarily transcend immediate economic policy objectives and must involve commitments to broad principles. Without such principles disputes are insoluble. Such principles must provide the framework of 'national income planning', it cannot be a mere economic technique directed by civil servants. National policy can only be secured by the elaboration of commitments and objectives at a mass level. This is only possible if the trade union movement *itself* adopts an incomes policy as an objective and actively assists in organising its application.

Such an objective could only be the planned re-organisation of the wages structure, attainment of national minimum wage, reduction of regional inequalities, arbitrary differentials, etc. Trade union involvement in setting and realising the objectives is the key to the success of any non-authoritarian incomes policy. The only progressive basis for such involvement is an egalitarian and socialist commitment towards the equalisation of the distribution of income and wealth. The trade union movement has argued that the 'price' of consent to temporary wage limitation is government control of profits and high incomes. It must also be accepted, however, and it has not hitherto been, that the main problem of perceived inequality and the main cause of the breakdown of incomes policies has been differentials between *wage earners* themselves.

To resolve the chaos of our wages structure and to redistribute income between classes of wage and salary earners involves a protracted programme and practice of negotiation and struggle *between* unions and groups of workers. The most intelligent Labour oriented arguments for an incomes policy, Wootton and Clegg, both recognise the need to resolve and rationalise differentials.[8] Both, however, despite many acute observations and proposals on other matters rely almost wholly on 'job-evaluation' to resolve this question. Differentials cannot be resolved merely by calling in management trained experts or by ranking people's 'feelings' about the merits of a variety of jobs (pilot studies cited by Wootton reveal the notorious fact that people tend to 'over-rate' their own job in the general scale of merit).[9] To change differentials also involves changes in the organisation of work and in the composition of tasks. It requires *means* whereby workers in particular industries and companies can discuss and resolve these issues, *objectives* for them to follow in doing so, and *powers* to get managements to accept the results. This can only begin from the bottom up within definite enterprises between workers involved in particular divisions of labour. The same is true of the related question of rationalising methods of payment. On this basis *unions* can begin to negotiate changes of rules, procedures and scales, exchanges of membership and amalgamations.

These changes are not something which take a matter of a couple of years, nor are they something that workers will do merely to support the working of an incomes policy. They must relate to other basic objectives and practices in the enterprise itself that workers can see to be bringing them real benefits (greater job security, more control over work, etc.). As differentials will tend to be erased *upwards* this way of securing compliance with an incomes policy would work against one of its major objectives and would need to be phased over some time to counter inflationary effects. Workers will not accept regrading, loss of 'status' and relative benefits unless other people's work is changing too and they can see personal advantages in reorganisation. It is for this reason that we have linked questions of incomes policy to Bullock. Differentials can best be tackled within a strategy of progressive increase in workers' control.

If such a 'socialist-egalitarian' incomes policy were to be adopted and implemented by the trade unions and the state this would necessarily weaken the role of local wage bargaining. Many Left commentators argue that this must involve a massive strengthening of the TUC and the state and a reduction in the power of the shop stewards' movement. But the conditions of *general* shop stewards' power in wage bargaining are conditions of economic growth and relatively full employment. Wage bargaining has tended to monopolise trade union struggle, virtually excluding all other issues. But closures, investment policy, what is produced, health and safety, the organisation of work and the level of employment are all factors which *can* be struggled over at enterprise level. The idea that there are inherent limits to the content of trade union politics rests on an essentialistic notion of organisations and their location ('economic' level, 'political' level). It is true that the powers workers have within enterprises originated through wage bargaining, but the capacity to control the enterprise now depends on the strength of the workers' organisation itself. This strength could be extended if the scope of collective bargaining were widened and workers sought the power to determine enterprise policy on these other issues. These issues have been neglected in the past but will, given the present economic conditions, become far more important in the future.

There is no reason why the powers of shop stewards need be weakened by a successful incomes policy. What is needed is the development of new objectives and new forms of struggle at enterprise level. The scope of bargaining must be extended from questions of immediate personal benefits to questions of enterprise policy and operation. This change in the issues involved in bargaining means radical changes in the information and skills required in the struggle for those objectives and the forums through which the struggles can be conducted. It requires forms of cooperation between unions and commitments *to* management of a scope and timescale hitherto rare in collective bargaining. Many union leaders are now arguing the need for 'extended collective bargaining' as an addition to the wages struggle, both in order to cope with questions of redundancies and levels of investment, and to offer some alternative to Bullock or other participation schemes. Most trade unionists rightly welcomed the Employment Protection Act 1975 precisely because it does provide them with certain of the means to engage in 'extended collective bargaining'. The hostility to Bullock in the Labour movement from Left and Right is intelligible and has the same sources of opposition as to income policies: it is the fear that 'traditional' trade union forms and issues of struggle will be confused, displaced and subverted by formal participation in management. If an incomes policy becomes necessary then something far stronger and more radical than experiments in 'extended collective bargaining' is needed to preserve workers' capacities to defend themselves and to extend their capacities for control in their enterprises. The opposition by organised Labour to Bullock was an untimely error. It will be infinitely more difficult to get as close to legislative proposals satisfactory to trade union interests in the near future.

Bullock was defeated by default. Organised management and the Right mounted an unprecedented campaign against the report. The Minority Report indicated very clearly why a scheme of single channel representation through trade unions on a unitary management board was unacceptable to representatives of management: it gives 'sectional interests' direct access to policy formation in companies. The scheme would extend the information and capacities to bargain of the trade unions, whilst preserving their existing structures and capacities of struggle. As John Elliot has demonstrated, Bullock became possible because elements of the leadership and officials of the TUC, notably Jack Jones and David Lea, were able to exercise a disproportionate influence in formulating the overall policy of the movement and then after the 1974 election pursue it at the highest level with the Labour government.[10] Management, civil servants and the Right were kicking an open door. Jones and a few other TUC leaders were isolated with an advanced policy which was only nominally that of the movement and lacked any kind of mass support. The question of how 'feasible' the Bullock proposals would have been as legislation is therefore open; they were never fought for.

In this context, before discussing how something like the Bullock proposals would complement an incomes policy, it is necessary to consider in detail the grounds of the opposition to them in the Labour movement. A common theme, uniting Right and Left, is that board representation would conflict with the traditional structures and forms of accountability to the membership. The primary task of a union is wage bargaining and the defence of its members which requires it to stay clear of any involvements in managerial responsibility. The EETPU argued this in its submission to Bullock.[11]

The more conservative trade union leaders are by no means 'corporatist' in orientation, on the contrary, many want union struggles and organisation to be limited to questions of personal and material benefit to the members. To take up other issues forces the introduction of 'politics', because it involves proposing alternative policies and forms of organisation for enterprises, and this requires higher levels of discussion and political knowledge among members than do questions of take-home pay. It is not easy to see where such a process might go: it might not stop with the issues, forms of member organisation and skill differentiation with which traditional trade union officials would feel comfortable. The trade union Right has a clear and very limited conception of the scope of union issues and action. Others take a broader view of the issues capable of being taken up in collective bargaining, for example the British Communist Party argued in its submission to Bullock that 'extended collective bargaining' should include questions of investment, manpower planning and redundancies, plant location, etc.

A union like the EETPU, given the position it takes, is quite right to oppose Bullock. For traditional collective bargaining on wages and shopfloor conditions it adds nothing and is a diversion of effort. The proponents of 'extended collective bargaining' have a tougher time. Consider the EETPU's arguments against Bullock:

(1) that wage bargaining issues and general company policy cannot be easily separated;
(2) that the existence of two channels of representation, worker directors and shop stewards, creates a conflict of loyalties which must make the directors' position impossible in any conflict of interests.

Both these points take on special sharpness if wages are determined at enterprise level and if the worker representatives on the Board are not following any strategy agreed with their union colleagues in the enterprise. These objections have much less force under an incomes policy. Wages cannot be the primary question in union struggle at enterprise level in this case, and it is wage bargaining that has provided the pertinent examples of a conflict of interests in the opposition case. Under national income planning, on the other hand, bargaining and general company policy would indeed be difficult to separate, the unions in an enterprise would require a company strategy, and they would need to use access to management discussions as a means of its pursuit. In any clash with the rest of the board, the union members could vote against, report back and expect their position to be reinforced by industrial action.

'Extended collective bargaining' is possible but it is not something different in nature from workers' representation on the board. Firstly, in order to work it requires new levels of disclosure of company information. Whilst the Employment Protection Act does make this possible, the information gleaned tends to be about past performance rather than future policy, and the provisions in the Act are sufficiently general to be evaded. Whether other detailed information is given on the plans or position of the company this will be given to negotiating officials and senior shop stewards at the discretion of the management and in confidence. The membership are as much dependent on officials reporting and recommending policies on the basis of confidential information as they are with worker directors. Further, the information given is what the board has decided to make available; conflicting views on policy and so on will not be communicated (whereas a worker director will be aware of these in reporting back and advising on policy). In respect of the problems of coping with information and monitoring performance, shop stewards under 'extended collective bargaining' and worker directors will face common problems.

Secondly, 'extended collective bargaining' is *bargaining*, it involves commitments on both sides. Complex bargaining on *wage questions*, like the Fawley Productivity agreements, commits workers on issues like the right to strike and work organisation to long-term policies. It involves cooperation with the enterprise and a restriction of the scope of struggle (as certain issues become subject to agreed procedures). If bargaining is extended to questions of company policy then the commitments demanded in return for guarantees on employment, investment, etc., will be no less extensive or binding. 'Extended' bargaining, by the nature of the issues at stake and the bargains struck, must limit the scope of trade union struggle and involve cooperation with the management. In itself it does not extend the forms of or the means of struggle; bargains will limit the right to strike, involve reorganisation of jobs, etc. Otherwise managements will not strike them. Bullock offered an extension of the means of struggle which parallels the commitments of 'extended collective bargaining'. Bullock was not some form of cooptation to which 'extended collective bargaining' is an alternative. Extending the *scope* of issues for negotiation and agreement must commit the organised workers to the enterprise in a way that limited wage negotiations never did. To limit struggle to wage questions is to limit what needs to be fought over and what can be won. 'Extended collective bargaining' is a sign that the unions recognise that changed economic conditions and their own strength necessitate and make possible an extension of the scope of bargaining. It is a pity that they have not recognised that new forms and methods of struggle are made possible by industrial democracy.

The Bullock proposals would have complemented an incomes policy of the type suggested above in three main ways. First, it would provide for the first time in many companies a forum, the Joint Representation Committee, where union members could get together to discuss policy and resolve differences at enterprise level. This is an essential precondition for considering methods of payment, differentials, demarcation, work organisation, etc. It has the advantage of being able to press proposals developed in this forum as company policy through board representation. Second, it provides a means of monitoring management commitments on issues such as investment, employment levels, and (potentially) of the formation of union personnel at enterprise level with the knowledge and skills to press for alternatives to those proposed by management. Thirdly, it would force at least some unions, through contacts at the base between members and demands for information and guidance, to consider in some depth the economic policies their members should pursue in definite companies and industries. Hopefully, this would lead to changes in the nature of political/policy discussions in the unions concerned. Unions also might start placing less reliance on merely urging governments to remedy unemployment, under-investment and so on by changes in economic management – pressures a hostile government can all too easily evade.

Legislation could have served as a catalyst to the unions entering into this process and as a means of compelling managements to accept union representation. As we have seen, workers' representation on company boards need not contradict 'extended collective bargaining'; indeed, such representation is one of the means by which it can be made effective. It will be infinitely more difficult for unions to group together to bargain without Bullock, and the scope of the issues entering into bargaining without such cooperation will be severely restricted (since one union's commitments cannot bind another). It will be much more difficult to get managements to concede what Bullock would have compelled them to do. Bullock and incomes policies together represent a great lost opportunity for the trade unions and the Labour Party. It is a failure of political thinking and response which will have to be overcome if democratic socialism in Britain is to succeed in its objectives.

This essay might be considered an uneasy mixture of political advocacy and social science. I would prefer to consider it as an example of an engaged and pragmatic social science which offers alternatives to conventional political analysis on questions of social organisation.[12] This is the kind of approach stimulated by Barbara Wootton among others, and one which is increasingly necessary to fill the gaps and break up the rigidities in thinking in the Labour movement.

The political role of the working class in Western Europe

TOM BOTTOMORE

In an earlier paper[1] I discussed, in the context of the revival of radical thought and radical social movements in the late 1960s, some of the changes in working-class and middle-class political orientations, and various sociological interpretations of them. My general conclusion was that a turning point had perhaps been reached '. . . when the established class parties have attained a peak in their development, while new political forces are beginning to challenge their dominance', and I suggested that new styles of politics had become apparent in four main directions: the rise of new elites committed to technological progress and economic growth; the emergence of a radical movement, critical of the technocratic and bureaucratic character of advanced industrial societies, in opposition to these elites; the growth of the regional and nationalist movements, and finally the attempts – exemplified by the European Community – to create supra-national associations. But I added that it was extremely difficult to evaluate one factor of vital importance for the future development of classes and political movements: namely, the likelihood that economic growth would continue in the rapid and uninterrupted manner which had so far characterised the post-war period.

A decade later the conditions have indeed changed substantially. The radical movements declined during the 1970s and a conservative mood, reminiscent of the 1950s, came to prevail again (although this has been more pronounced in Britain than elsewhere). At the same time, however, an increasingly severe economic recession has developed, with low growth rates and mass unemployment, and there has been a renewal of the nuclear arms race, which now appears to be accelerating. These events may well give rise to a new radicalism, of which there are already some indications; and in this situation it seems appropriate to reconsider the political trends in Western Europe over a longer period, with particular attention to the historical experience and the prospects of the working-class movement.

There are, of course, important differences between the countries of Western Europe to which I shall refer in the relevant contexts (and Britain is in many respects an exceptional case), but for the most part I intend to concentrate upon the common features to be found in party doctrines and policies, the extent of public support for such policies (including voting support), party membership and broad class allegiance. Let us consider first the membership of working-class parties as an indicator of political commitment to broadly socialist policies (either 'reformist' or 'revolutionary'). With very few exceptions the membership of working-class parties has either grown, or has been maintained, in the post-war period. In West Germany the Social Democratic Party (SPD) has increased its membership steadily to over 1 million (higher than it was in Germany as a whole in 1931); the Austrian Socialist Party (SPÖ) has grown ever since 1945, and with some 700,000 members is probably larger than at any time in its history; and the Swedish Social Democratic Party (SAP), which has grown regularly and rapidly since the 1930s, now has over a million members. In France, the Socialist Party (PS) experienced a sharp decline in membership from 1946 to 1950, but it has been growing steadily again since 1970, while the membership of the Communist Party (PCF) after declining from its post-war peak remained more or less stable until the last few years, though with some fluctuations resulting from political crises in Eastern Europe; and in Italy the Socialist Party (PSI) maintained its membership at around 500,000 from the early 1960s to the mid-1970s, while the Communist Party (PCI) increased its membership.[2] Only the British Labour Party provides a notable exception to this trend, its individual membership having declined steadily, and in the past decade quite sharply, from over 1 million members in 1952 to about 300,000 in 1979.

Voting support shows broadly the same trend as do membership figures. In Germany the SPD increased its votes from 29.7% of the total in 1949 to 42.6% in 1976 and it has been the governing party, in a coalition with the small Liberal Party (FDP), since 1969; in Austria, the SPÖ, which has had a substantial share of the vote since 1945 increased this to 50.4% in 1975 and has been the governing party since 1970; in Sweden the SAP has regularly obtained 45%–50% of the popular vote and was the governing party (or the main party in a coalition) for 44 years from 1932 to 1976; while in France and Italy the socialist and communist parties together have gradually increased their share of the vote. In Italy the total Left vote rose from 39.9% in

1953 to 47.4% in 1976; in France the Left vote for the 'common programme' in 1978 almost reached 50% and the Left might well have
achieved a majority had it not been for the disagreement between
the PCF and the PS which emerged at a late stage in the election.
And in May 1981 the Socialist candidate, François Mitterand, won
the Presidential election; shortly afterwards the PS won a large
majority in the National Assembly.

Again the British Labour Party provides something of an exception, with its share of the vote reaching a peak of 48.3% in 1951 and
then declining fairly steadily to 36.9% in 1979. What is still more
striking in Britain is the general decline of electoral support for either
of the two main parties (Conservative and Labour). As Crewe *et al.*
have noted:

In the general election of 1951 almost nine out of ten eligible electors turned
up at the polls, the vast majority (96 per cent) to vote Labour or Conservative,
thereby giving them all but twelve seats in the House of Commons. In the
quarter century that has since elapsed, the absolute and relative fortunes of
the two parties have fluctuated, albeit with increasing volatility. But one
electoral change has been unrelenting: the growing, in fact accelerating,
refusal of the electorate to cast a ballot for either of the two governing parties.[3]

In fact, the share of the two parties in the total electorate fell from
80.3% (Conservative 39.5%, Labour 40.8%) in 1951 to 56.1% (Conservative 26.8%, Labour 29.3%) in October 1974, although there was
a modest increase in the 1979 election when it rose to 61.3% (Conservative 33.3%, Labour 28.0%). Crewe and his colleagues go on to
discuss the reasons for the loss of support by the two 'class based'
parties, and suggest that it indicates a decline in class alignment:
'. . . only half of the electorate (51%) held an enduring allegiance to
the party of their occupational class by the time of the last election'
(October 1974).[4] They observe further that '. . . in no group of Labour
partisans have Labour principles lost more ground over the decade
(1964–1974) than the post-1950 generation of working class trade
unionists';[5] and there was a further loss of support among trade
unionists, especially skilled workers, in the 1979 election.

This is very different from the situation in Western Europe as a
whole, where the traditional left-wing parties have generally succeeded in retaining working-class support,[6] although this support is
divided, in several countries, between rival parties;[7] and it will be
necessary to examine the peculiarities of the British case more closely
in due course. But even if many of the West European parties of the
Left are solidly based upon working-class support, it may still be

asked whether they are any longer socialist; that is to say, whether they express a distinctive, clearly defined class outlook which has been historically associated with the idea of socialism. This question itself has two related aspects: first, whether there is a working-class 'outlook', 'conception of the social world', or 'consciousness', which is fundamentally socialist, or at least anti-capitalist; and second, whether such an outlook is expressed in the doctrines, and above all in the policies, of working-class parties.

The first aspect poses what Hilferding called 'the most difficult problem' of the relation between *class interests* and *class consciousness*.[8] This is too large an issue to be fully examined here, but some of its basic elements need to be briefly considered. The idea of class interests underlies the whole historical development of the modern labour movement, and has been more or less clearly expressed in the constitutions and programmes of working-class parties. Its most precise and vigorous expression is to be found, of course, in Marxist social theory, and the whole conception of a *class* party, with socialism as its objective, has been profoundly shaped by Marxism in almost all the European parties of the Left (though not in the British Labour Party). Marx's theory, as it has generally been interpreted, asserts the existence of *objective* class interests, determined by the position occupied by a group in the social process of production; and further, in the specific case of the working class in a capitalist, commodity-producing society, a *necessary* development of revolutionary class consciousness which will manifest itself in a political struggle to bring about a radical transformation of society.

This conception raises a number of problems. In the first place it may be questioned whether such a strict separation between 'interests' and 'consciousness' can be sustained; for human interests are always consciously formulated in some way and are matters for reflection and debate (except, perhaps, in the case of the most primitive interest in sheer physical survival). Some recent Marxists have strongly contested such a separation; notably Poulantzas, who argues that 'ideological and political relations . . . are themselves part of the structural determination of class', and hence rejects what he calls 'the Hegelian schema' (though it was clearly set out by Marx) of the distinction between 'class in itself' and 'class for itself'.[9] Unfortunately, like many other recent theorists, he does not go on to analyse the notion of 'class interest' itself. Such an analysis, setting out from Marx (and perhaps reflecting more closely the general tenor of his thought),[10] would begin with a conception, not of objective *interests*, but of objective *conditions* for the emergence of interests in a complex social interaction which involves the practical experiences of the everyday labour process, the confrontations between diverse theoretical and ideological views, and the activities of trade unions, political parties, and other organisations and movements. One possible outcome of the development of interests conceived in this way is the emergence of the working class as a class which – to use Marx's own admirable formulation of its role – arouses

. . . in itself and in the masses, a moment of enthusiasm in which it associates and mingles with society at large, identifies itself with it, and is felt and recognized as the *general representative* of this society. Its aims and interests must genuinely be the aims and interests of society itself, of which it becomes in reality the social head and heart. It is only in the name of general interests that a particular class can claim general supremacy.[11]

It is in this sense – as the bearer of a new civilisation – that the working-class movement has had a historical importance in the development of modern European society.

But this is not the *only* possible outcome. It may also be the case that, in the later development of capitalist society, ideological debate, political action, and changes in the process of social production bring about a redefinition and reconstruction of the interests of the working class such that these interests can be accommodated within a modified form of capitalism (which could be described as a 'mixed economy' and/or a 'welfare state'). This means, positively, that working-class interests would now require only a limited control over the labour process (regulation of working conditions, hours of work, etc.), an assurance of levels of living which for most workers are not very far below the average level in a prosperous society, and hence a certain degree of social equality, all of which can be attained by a combination of trade union action and welfare policies; and negatively, that these interests do not require a transition to a socialist society, in the sense of a 'classless' society where the use of major productive resources and the distribution of the social product would be collectively determined.

Such a conception of working-class interests, which now seems to be held by many trade union and party leaders, is open to several objections, however. In the first place, it may be argued that it is only relevant to a particular historical period, now drawing to a close, which was characterised by newly-won affluence, sustained economic growth, and full employment. The present economic crisis, and still more the longer-term prospect of stagnation (determined in part by environmental limits to growth), high unemployment, static or declining material levels of living, intensified attacks on trade union

Tom Bottomore

power, and deliberate attempts to reallocate the social product in favour of the owners of capital, make the notion of working-class interests which can be adequately satisfied within a capitalist system much less plausible. Second, a more general argument can be advanced to the effect that there is a universal human 'emancipatory interest' (implied in Marx's theory of history) which is embodied, in the capitalist era, in the struggle of the working class to end its subordination to the 'masters of production' by achieving the transition to a classless 'society of associated producers'. From this standpoint, the interests of the working class could never be conceived as being restricted, in a final and definitive way, to the improvements in its economic and social situation gained under a regime of welfare capitalism, even if there were any certainty that such improvements could be maintained.

On the other side, however, it has to be recognised that this notion of the emancipatory interest of the working class, expressed in the ideal aim of a 'society of associated producers', has itself been brought into question by the historical experience of socialist societies. As Touraine has written recently,

Socialism is dead. The word appears everywhere . . . but it is meaningless. Except when it refers to a vast family of authoritarian states. . . . Socialism was the theory of the labour movement; in a large part of the world it has become the name of the state power [while] in other countries it amounts only to a defence of particular sectional interests which are less and less the bearers of a general project of human progress.[12]

Undoubtedly, the idea of socialism as the goal of the labour movement loses much of its appeal when it is set against the reality of socialism as a system of centralised planning and one-party rule; and the ideological defence of a capitalist 'free market economy' – and by association, of a 'free society' – has thereby been made much easier and more effective. It seems probable, indeed, that the example of authoritarian socialist states has been a major factor in promoting that transformation of socialism in Western Europe into the defence of sectional interests, or at most a moderate reformist doctrine of the trade unions, to which Touraine refers. More generally, it may be argued that the labour movement, if it pursues the socialist aim, always runs the risk of bringing into existence a new, and perhaps harsher, form of domination, which Konrád and Szelényi, in their study of Eastern European societies, see as the outcome of the intellectuals' rise to class power. They suggest that rational-redistributive society

270

. . . can best be described as a dichotomous class structure in which the classical antagonism of capitalist and proletarian is replaced by a new one between an intellectual class being formed around the position of the redistributors, and a working class deprived of any right to participate in redistribution.[13]

Nevertheless, this stark contrast between 'free market' capitalist societies and authoritarian socialist states, which is nowadays so widely current and so readily accepted, leaves out of account the existence of other forms of society which are either socialist or seem to be developing from an advanced kind of welfare state towards democratic socialism, or what Robson called a 'welfare society'.[14] One example, for all its limitations and imperfections, is the system of socialist self-management in Yugoslavia; others are the growth of a more clearly defined socialist political outlook in the Swedish working class, which Korpi has described in a recent study,[15] and the achievements of the SPÖ in Austria, building upon the experience of the Austro-Marxists in their government of Vienna in the 1920s. Hence, in evaluating the significance of socialism as an expression of working-class interests, we should not concentrate our attention exclusively upon the extreme cases of authoritarian rule, but take account also of the continuing vigour and effectiveness of the democratic socialist movement, which is also not without some influence in Eastern Europe as a succession of working-class rebellions there indicates.

But in addition to the general question of the nature of 'class interests' in relation to 'class consciousness' which I have so far discussed, there is a second, more specific and empirical, problem which needs at least briefly to be considered here. The notion of working-class interests assumes or embodies, in much Marxist theory, the idea of the homogeneity of the class itself, which would be progressively realised as capitalism developed, so that eventually the 'two great classes' of bourgeoisie and proletariat would confront each other as two wholly different and incompatible worlds. This model of two 'pure classes'[16] may well seem inappropriate, or at any rate inadequate, in the light of the actual historical development of capitalist societies, which has resulted in a more complex social differentiation, a substantial growth in numbers of the 'intermediate strata', massive state intervention and the creation of a large category of public employees, and generally rising levels of living. These and other factors have produced, or in some cases perpetuated, many differences within the working class – between workers in different regions or different housing situations, in older and newer indus-

271

tries, in the state, monopolistic, and competitive sectors of the economy, between men and women workers, between groups of immigrant workers and others – and they may also have brought about a greater blurring of the lines of class division in some countries. Hence, the 'interests' of the working class as a whole have to be conceived, in my view, as only *possible* or *potential* interests, which have certainly been clearly expressed in some historical circumstances, but are always a relatively fragile construction, continually challenged, modified, and sometimes dissolved, by the assertion of more limited sectional interests, which may be more easily apprehended and, in some plausible sense, more 'real'.

If, therefore, as I have suggested, interests are not simply 'given' but are constructed through reflection and discussion – although they *are* related to real, objective conditions – the problem of the relation between working-class interests and the representation of those interests by political parties becomes a great deal more complex. We cannot, on this view, simply assert the existence of quite definite 'class interests' and then go on to show that one or other party either promotes or betrays these interests. Rather, we have to say that there are diverse tendencies towards the constitution of class interests in various forms, and that political parties themselves participate in this process by elaborating, giving a more definite shape to, and diffusing, a particular conception of what the 'real interests' are (not overlooking the phenomenon that there is also a process of construction of the interests of parties themselves).

Two examples will illustrate the way in which such a model can be used in the interpretation of political events. One study of the British Labour Party in the post-war era suggests that in the early 1950s, following the victory of 1945 in which it gained its largest ever working-class support, but also its largest share of middle-class support, the party was faced with a choice between two possible strategies: 'Should it seek to maximise the manual working class vote, or should it seek to pursue more strongly a broader social appeal?'[17] In fact, the party chose to follow the second course, and to become what was called a 'people's party' (whatever that may mean), but this did not prove conspicuously successful from an electoral point of view. As the authors of the study just cited observe: 'Certainly on the basis of the evidence of generational displacement and working class fertility it may well have been the case that Labour's movement away from its working class base in the 1950s was a major error of strategy and one whose consequences cannot easily be undone.'[18] Of this particular course of events we might say that the party did misconstrue (for whatever reasons) the interests of the working class, and that this misunderstanding then helped to reconstitute the interests themselves in such a way that they were less and less able to find adequate expression in the policies of the Labour Party. At the present time, however, the party seems to be embarking on a new course, as a more distinctively socialist party, and it may be that as a result of another reshaping of class interests it will be possible to overcome the consequences of the 1950s strategy and to achieve much greater electoral success in the future. In Germany, the SPD also transformed itself, though in a more formal way, by adopting at the Bad Godesberg conference of 1959 a new programme which declared that: 'From the party of the working class the Social Democratic Party has become a party of the people.' But unlike the British Labour Party it has not lost working-class support, and it has been relatively successful in elections since 1969. In this case it might be argued that the party has construed correctly a change in working-class interests, and at the same time reinforces that change by its own reformulation of interests as those of the 'people' rather than of a 'class'. Undoubtedly, the negative effect of East European socialism, and more specifically that of the German Democratic Republic, has been particularly important in leading the SPD to distance itself from its Marxist past; nevertheless, Marxism in its non-Stalinist Western forms is far from having been eliminated as a significant current of thought in German socialism, especially among the Young Socialists, and it seems probable that working-class support for the party is still based to some extent upon its traditional image as a socialist party.

Comparisons of this kind between working-class parties in the West European countries need to be undertaken in a much more comprehensive and systematic way than has yet been attempted. This is obviously beyond the scope of the present essay, but one feature which I have mentioned at various points – namely, the peculiar situation in Britain – does merit a separate brief comment. The British Labour Party has become one of the weakest and least successful of the West European parties, and it has always been one of the least socialist. The reasons for this are complex, and I can do no more here than sketch a possible framework of explanation by drawing attention to some of the most important elements in the situation. In the first place, capitalism itself, in Britain, has developed in a very idiosyncratic and incomplete way. Not only have many feudal elements – both structural and cultural – retained an important influence in British society, but the dominant capitalist groups themselves have been those associated with mercantile and agrarian capital; that is to say, with pre-industrial forms of capitalism.[19] And since there has not been a dominant *modern* capitalist class, so there has been no modern working-class movement, given coherence and direction by its own alternative social theory, to combat capitalism; the fundamental issues and the nature of the social conflict have remained permanently blurred. Furthermore, the same factor that helped to ensure the continued dominance of mercantile and financial capital – namely, Britain's position as the leading colonial power – also facilitated in various ways the incorporation of the working class into a national and imperial community. This, in turn, helps to explain why Marxism had so little influence in Britain in the last two decades of the nineteenth century,[20] whereas it became firmly established as the theory of the labour movement in much of continental Europe; and why the Labour Party came to be formed eventually, not as a socialist party, but as a party of the trade unions. As a result the 'class interests' of British workers have almost always been expressed as reformist and sectional interests, and this tendency, far from being counteracted, has been reinforced by the prevalent ideology in the Labour Party, characterised by a persistent, stubborn rejection of the idea of 'class politics'.

However, this situation now appears to be changing. Not only is Marxist thought more widely diffused and more influential than ever before in Britain, but in a much broader sense there is a notable revival of socialist ideas in the Labour Party. This owes much, no doubt, to a growing recognition of the peculiar incompetence of the dominant groups in British capitalism, demonstrated in the protracted, and now accelerating, decline of the economy; but it is also a consequence of more general changes affecting Western Europe as a whole. During the past decade, two of the styles of politics which I considered in my earlier essay have declined substantially in influence. The European Community no longer arouses any enthusiasm, its policies are in disorder, and its character as an elaborate form of customs union which is supported only so long as it serves specific national interests has become increasingly evident. Its survival in its present form is a matter of doubt, and it will perhaps only become viable if it develops eventually as a community of socialist states. At the opposite pole, the various nationalist movements within existing states (except for the Basque movement in Spain) have also suffered a decline.

The style of politics which has shown the greatest vitality, in spite of an apparent eclipse at the beginning of the decade, is in fact that of the radical movements of the late 1960s. Not only have these

274

movements brought into existence new parties which have acquired a significant political influence in some countries (the Green Party in Germany, the Ecology Party in France), and contributed greatly to reanimating the nuclear disarmament movement in Europe which is now growing rapidly; they have also played an important part in the revival of socialist ideas and policies within the traditional working-class parties of Western Europe. In Britain especially it is noteworthy that the new generation of Labour Party activists – those in their early or mid-thirties – who are increasingly socialist in outlook, are in many cases people who were either participants in, or were strongly influenced by, the movements of the 1960s.

In this sense, it is certainly possible to subscribe to Touraine's view of the political importance of the new social movements. What seems to me much more questionable is the idea that new political organisations based upon these movements are likely to take the place of working-class parties, and to become the principal embodiment of a new radicalism. The indications at present are that there is a renewal of socialist ideas in the labour movement; that class politics will continue to dominate political life in Western Europe, and may become even more prominent in the course of this decade; and that the crucial political opposition remains that between a capitalist and a socialist organisation of society.

Notes

Foreword

1 I. Neustadt, *Le problème de l'organisation internationale en Europe centrale 1919–1939* (Paris, 1939).
2 I. Neustadt, 'Some Aspects of the Social Structure of Belgium' (unpublished PhD dissertation, University of London, 1944).
3 I. Neustadt, *Teaching Sociology – an Inaugural Lecture* (Leicester, 1965).
4 N. Elias, 'Problems of Involvement and Detachment', *British Journal of Sociology* vol. 7 (September 1956), p. 229.
5 *Teaching Sociology*, p. 15.
6 *Ibid.* pp. 19–20.
7 Walter Birmingham, Ilya Neustadt and E. N. Omaboe (eds.), *A Study of Contemporary Ghana* vol. 1, *The Economy of Ghana* (London, 1966), vol. II, *Some Aspects of Social Structure* (1967).

Marx and the abolition of the division of labour

1 See, for example, R. Tucker, *Philosophy and Myth in Karl Marx* (Cambridge, 1961), p. 222 and *passim*; S. Avineri, *The Social and Political Thought of Karl Marx* (Cambridge, 1968), p. 250.
2 *The German Ideology* (London, 1965), p. 45. It is worth remarking at this point that 'abolition' as in 'abolition of the division of labour' is often rendered by the (Hegelian) term *Aufhebung* in the original Marx and Engels texts. *Aufhebung* implies 'transcendence' rather than simple 'eradication'. But no amount of play on the term actually reveals its implications for the division of labour, which can only be grasped by analysing the more concrete proposals – few though they are – which appear at various points in their writings, and by placing these proposals in the context of the overall structure of their theorisation. Besides, as Evans has pointed out, both Marx and Engels use several other terms in such contexts, none of which is simply reducible to *Aufhebung:* M. Evans, 'Marx Studies', *Political Studies* vol. 18 (1970). This is an appropriate point at which to indicate that in the context of the present discussion it is unnecessary to separate off Marx's writings from those of Engels.
3 *The German Ideology*, p. 224.
4 *Capital* vol. III (London, 1960), pp. 799–800.

5 Of those commentators who have had access to both the early and later writings of Marx, by far the largest number have seen little contradiction in his views on the abolition of the division of labour. Some of these authors explicitly discuss the issue: cf. Tucker, *op.cit.* (n.1); Avineri, *op. cit.* (n.1); E. Kamenka, *The Ethical Foundations of Marxism* (revised ed., London, 1972); E. Mandel, *The Formation of the Economic Thought of Karl Marx* (London, 1971); T. Bottomore, 'Socialism and the Division of Labour', in B. Parekh (ed.), *The Concept of Socialism* (London, 1975); K. Axelos, *Alienation, Praxis and Techné in the Thought of Karl Marx* (Austin, Texas, 1976). Others remain silent on this particular question, but emphasise the unity of the earlier and later works, especially as expressed through the concept of alienation, and so can be said to support implicitly the interpretation that Marx did not alter his views on the abolition of the division of labour: cf. I. Mészáros, *Marx's Theory of Alienation* (London, 1970); R. Garaudy, *Karl Marx: The Evolution of His Thought* (London, 1967); B. Ollman, *Alienation* (Cambridge, 1971); *idem,* 'Marx's Vision of Communism: A Reconstruction', *Critique* no. 3 (1977). Some interpreters of Marx, however, have emphasised the discontinuity that seems apparent between the two passages, without providing convincing or elaborate explanations for the transformation in Marx's discourse: cf. M. Evans, *Karl Marx* (London, 1975); A. Schmidt, *The Concept of Nature in Marx* (London, 1971); D. McLellan, 'Marx and the Whole Man', in Parekh, *op.cit.* (The list of authors in each school of interpretation is not meant to be exhaustive.)

6 See my *Marx and the Division of Labour* (London, 1981). The present essay does not resolve the complex issues arising out of Marx and Engels's commitment to the abolition of the sexual division of labour. However, it is necessary to register here a profound dissatisfaction with their characteristically class-reductionist forms of explanation of women's subordination as well as their consequent complacency in relation to the transformation of the sexual division of labour under socialism. For an excellent general discussion, which includes a critique of Marx and Engels's typical views, see M. Barrett, *Women's Oppression Today: Problems in Marxist Feminist Analysis* (London, 1980).

7 *The German Ideology,* p. 33. Cf. p. 44: 'Division of labour and private property are, moreover, identical expressions: in the one the same thing is affirmed with reference to activity as is affirmed in the other with reference to the product of the activity.'

8 *Ibid.* pp. 45–6.

9 *Ibid.* p. 49.

10 *Economic and Philosophic Manuscripts of 1844,* ed. D. Struik (London, 1970), p. 111.

11 *Ibid.* p. 68.

12 *Ibid.* p. 65.

13 *Ibid.* p. 156.

14 Marx's intellectual formation prior to 1844 is examined in much greater detail than is possible here in my *Marx and the Division of Labour, op.cit.* (n.6). The forms of connection between property, division of labour and exchange established by Hegel, classical political economy and early socialism are also explored in this text.

15 L. Easton and K. Guddat (eds.), *Writings of the Young Marx on Philosophy and Society* (Garden City, N.Y., 1967), pp. 236–7.
16 *Ibid*. p. 246.
17 *Ibid*. p. 263.
18 *Economic and Philosophic Manuscripts of 1844*, p. 118 (emphasis added).
19 *The Poverty of Philosophy* (New York, 1963), p. 135. Both Charles Babbage (1792–1871) and Andrew Ure (1778–1857) were instrumental in underlining to their contemporaries the distinctiveness of the organisation of labour under conditions of factory production: see further, *Marx and the Division of Labour, op.cit.* (n.6), Part I.
20 *The Poverty of Philosophy*, p. 128.
21 *Ibid*. p. 183.
22 *Ibid*. p. 154 (emphasis added).
23 In between, of course, Marx wrote other works, including *The Communist Manifesto:* see further, *Marx and the Division of Labour, op.cit.* (n.6), Part III.
24 Cf. 'The Eighteenth Brumaire of Louis Bonaparte', in Marx and Engels, *Selected Works* vol. I (London, 1968), p. 477. For more detailed commentaries on the political writings of this period and which underline Marx's new conception of the political level, see *Marx and the Division of Labour*, and also the excellent essay by Stuart Hall, 'The "Political" and the "Economic" in Marx's Theory of Classes', in A. Hunt (ed.), *Class and Class Structure* (London, 1977).
25 *Capital* vol. I, pp. 175–6 (emphasis added). That the contrast between the levels of exchange and production is of crucial significance in Marx's intellectual formation is particularly forcefully argued in M. Nicolaus, 'The Unknown Marx', in R. Blackburn (ed.), *Ideology in Social Science* (London, 1972). Nicolaus, however, exaggerates the significance of the *Grundrisse*: cf. K. Tribe, 'Remarks on the Theoretical Significance of the "Grundrisse" ', *Economy and Society* vol. 3 (1974); J. Mepham, 'The *Grundrisse*: Method or Metaphysics?', *Economy and Society* vol. 7 (1978).
26 Cf. *Capital* vol. I, p. 217; *Capital* vol. III, p. 772. The discursive significance of these passages has been especially emphasised by L. Althusser and E. Balibar: cf. *Reading Capital* (London, 1970). See further, *Marx and the Division of Labour, op.cit.* (n.6), Part III.
27 *Grundrisse*, ed. M. Nicolaus (London, 1973), p. 85.
28 *Ibid*.
29 *Ibid*. p. 86.
30 *Ibid*. p. 38.
31 *Capital* vol. I, p. 177.
32 *Ibid*. pp. 324–5. Cf. p. 328.
33 *Ibid*. p. 386.
34 *Ibid*. pp. 383–4.
35 *Ibid*. pp. 444–5.
36 *Ibid*. p. 351.
37 Marx and Engels, *Selected Correspondence* (Moscow, 1965), p. 209 (emphasis in original).
38 *Capital* vol. I, pp. 330–1. Cf. p. 332.
39 *Capital* vol. III, p. 379. Cf. p. 376. More recent Marxist discussions of class

relations and the capitalist labour process have attempted to incorporate this form of argument into their analyses: see, for example, G. Carchedi, *On the Economic Identification of Classes* (London, 1977); M. Burawoy, *Manufacturing Consent: Changes in the Labour Process Under Monopoly Capitalism* (Chicago, 1979); R. Edwards, *Contested Terrain: The Transformation of the Workplace in the Twentieth Century* (London, 1980).

40 *Capital* vol. II, p. 135.
41 *Capital* vol. I, pp. 513–14.
42 *Ibid.* p. 513.
43 A. Schmidt, *The Concept of Nature in Marx* (London, 1971), p. 139. For a more detailed discussion of the argument from 'natural necessity', see *Marx and the Division of Labour, op.cit.* (n.6), Part V.
44 Cf. *Capital* vol. I, pp. 376, 402.
45 *Ibid.* p. 349. However, it is important to recognise that this general form of reasoning also led Marx to make highly dubious 'naturalist' assumptions about the physical capacities of women in the process of production: cf. V. Beechey, 'Women and Production: A Critical Analysis of Some Sociological Theories of Women's Work', in A. Kuhn and A. Wolpe (eds.), *Feminism and Materialism* (London, 1978).
46 *Selected Works* vol. III, p. 18.
47 Cf. *Capital* vol. I, p. 488; *Anti-Dühring* (London, 1969), pp. 348, 349, 353, 355.
48 *The German Ideology,* pp. 474–7.
49 *Ibid.* p. 40.
50 *Capital* vol. I, p. 171. Cf. p. 512.
51 *Ibid.* pp. 42–3 (emphasis added).
52 *Ibid.* p. 530. Although the mature Engels also abandons the idea of the complete abolition of the division of labour, he appears not to have changed his mind about the complete abolition of scarcity. And it must be pointed out that the mature Marx continues to espouse a belief in the complete abolition of exchange relations, despite the fact that this presupposes the abolition of scarcity. Both sets of issues are explored in detail in my *Marx and the Division of Labour* (n.6), Part V.
53 See *Capital* vol. I, pp. 361, 386 and *passim.*
54 *Ibid.* pp. 487–8.
55 *Ibid.* p. 419.
56 *Ibid.* pp. 483–4.
57 *Ibid.* p. 488. Cf. S. Castles and W. Wüstenberg, *The Education of the Future: An Introduction to the Theory and Practice of Socialist Education* (London, 1979).
58 *Ibid.* p. 424. Engels's *On Authority,* authoritarian though it might appear, also calls for an elective system of representation in the socialist factory: *Selected Works* vol. II, pp. 377–8. This strand in Marxian thought goes hand in hand with an emphasis on the self-emancipation of the working class: cf. H. Draper, 'The Principle of Self-Emancipation in Marx and Engels', in R. Miliband and J. Saville (eds.), *The Socialist Register 1971* (London, 1971).
59 Marx and Engels, *On the Paris Commune* (Moscow, 1971). Cf. M. Evans, 'Karl Marx and the Concept of Political Participation', in G. Parry (ed.),

Participation in Politics (Manchester, 1972); H. Draper, 'The Death of the State in Marx and Engels', in R. Miliband and J. Saville (eds.), *The Socialist Register 1970* (London, 1970).

60 *Marx and the Division of Labour, op.cit.* (n.6), Part V. It is worth indicating that in this text I also show that Marx's mature analysis of the impact of capitalism on the division of labour also differs quite significantly from the analysis in the early writings. Limitations of space have prevented me from setting out the relevant considerations in this paper.

Power, the dialectic of control and class structuration

1 See *New Rules of Sociological Method* (London, 1976); *Studies in Social and Political Theory* (London, 1977); *Central Problems in Social Theory* (London, 1979).
2 *Central Problems in Social Theory, op.cit.* (n.1).
3 *Ibid.*
4 *Ibid.* pp. 145ff.
5 See *New Rules of Sociological Method, op.cit.* (n.1).
6 Harry Braverman, *Labor and Monopoly Capital* (New York, 1974.)
7 Max Weber, *Economy and Society* vol. I (California, 1978), p. 223.
8 *Idem, The Methodology of the Social Sciences* (Glencoe, Ill., 1949).
9 Wolfgang Mommsen, *The Age of Bureaucracy* (Oxford, 1974).
10 Cf. Arthur Mitzman, *The Iron Cage: An Historical Interpretation of Max Weber* (New York, 1970).
11 Emile Durkheim, *The Division of Labour in Society* (New York, 1968).
12 Peter M. Blau, *The Dynamics of Bureaucracy* (Chicago, 1955); see also the important discussion in Martin Albrow, *Bureaucracy* (London, 1970).
13 Michel Crozier, *The Bureaucratic Phenomenon* (London, 1964).
14 *Central Problems in Social Theory, op.cit.* (n.1), pp. 147ff.
15 Cf. Reinhard Bendix: *Work and Authority in Industry* (New York, 1963).
16 Braverman, *op.cit.* (n.6), p. 27.
17 See Russell Jacoby's review of *Labor and Monopoly Capital*, in *Telos* no. 29 (1976); and Gavin Mackenzie, 'The Political Economy of the American Working Class', *British Journal of Sociology* vol. 28 (1977).
18 *The Class Structure of the Advanced Societies* (London, 1973), p. 111.
19 Cf. Bryan Palmer, 'Class, Conception and Conflict; the Thrust for Efficiency, Managerial Views of Labour and Working Class Rebellion, 1903–22', *Review of Radical Political Economy* vol. 7 (1975); H. G. J. Aitken, *Taylorism at Watertown Arsenal* (Cambridge, Mass., 1960); Stanley Aronowitz, *False Promises* (New York, 1973), and 'Marx, Braverman, and the Logic of Capital', *Insurgent Sociologist* vol. 8 (1978).
20 Andrew L. Friedman, *Industry and Labour* (London, 1977).
21 Cf. Michael Burawoy, *The Manufacture of Consent* (Chicago, 1979).
22 Friedman, *op.cit.* (n.20), p. 7.
23 C. B. Macpherson, *The Real World of Democracy* (Oxford, 1966).
24 For a critique of functionalism, in the light of the conception of structuration, see 'Functionalism: après la lutte', in my *Studies in Social and Political Theory, op.cit.* (n.1).
25 Wolfgang Müller and Christel Neusüss, 'The "Welfare-state Illusion" and the Contradiction between Wage-labour and Capital', in John Holloway

and Sol Piciotto (eds.), *State and Capital, a Marxist Debate* (London, 1978), p. 34.

26 For the elements of such analysis, see my *A Contemporary Critique of Historical Materialism* (London, 1981).

27 T. B. Bottomore, *Karl Marx: Early Writings* (New York, 1964), p. 125.

Managing the frontier of control

1 This essay is based upon work made possible by a research grant from the Social Sciences Faculty at the Open University. My collaborator in this research, Craig Littler, has not only contributed to the project overall, but has made numerous valuable comments on this essay.

2 We will regard as management that level of organisational employee which is conventionally described as 'middle' management, i.e. between supervision and board members. Management includes both line managers whose main responsibilities consist of organising and monitoring the work of others, and applying board directives and targets; and experts whose responsibilities, while they may include the management of research teams, or other, subordinate experts in marketing, accounts, or personnel, concern primarily the production of specialist procedures or techniques.

3 C. Kerr, J. T. Dunlop, F. Harbison and C. A. Myers, *Industrialism and Industrial Man* (Cambridge, Mass., 1960).

4 S. R. Parker, R. Brown, J. Child and M. Smith, *The Sociology of Industry* (London, 1977), p. 113.

5 *Ibid.*

6 H. Braverman, *Labor and Monopoly Capital: The Degradation of Work in the Twentieth Century* (New York, 1974), p. 125.

7 A. Chandler, *The Visible Hand: The Managerial Revolution in American Business* (Cambridge, Mass., 1977).

8 H. Braverman, *Labor and Monopoly Capital*, p. 267.

9 A. Giddens, *Central Problems in Social Theory* (London, 1979), p. 112.

10 F. Parkin, 'Social Stratification', in T. Bottomore and R. Nisbet (eds.), *A History of Sociological Analysis* (London, 1978).

11 N. Poulantzas, *Classes in Contemporary Capitalism* (London, 1975); E. O. Wright, *Class, Crisis and the State* (London, 1978).

12 H. Braverman, *Labor and Monopoly Capital*, p. 258.

13 *Ibid.* p. 260.

14 *Ibid.* p. 405.

15 D. J. Lee, 'Skin, Craft and Class: A Theoretical Critique and a Critical Case', *Sociology* vol. 15 (1981), p. 57.

16 A. Giddens, *The Class Structure of the Advanced Societies* (London, 1973).

17 E. O. Wright, 'Class Boundaries in Advanced Capitalist Societies', *New Left Review* no. 98 (1976), p. 20.

18 J. Stephens, 'Class Formation and Class Consciousness', *British Journal of Sociology* vol. 30 (1979), p. 391.

19 *Ibid.* p. 389.

20 Braverman, *Labor and Monopoly Capital*, pp. 405–6.

21 M. Burawoy, 'Towards a Marxist Theory of the Labour Process', *Politics and Society* vol. 8 (1978), pp. 256–7.

22 A. Levine, *Industrial Retardation in Britain* (London, 1967); A. Francis, 'Families, Firms and Finance Capital', *Sociology* vol. 14 (1980).

23 A. Francis, 'Families, Firms and Finance Capital', p. 12.

24 Nicos Poulantzas and R. Miliband, 'The Problem of the Capitalist State', in R. Blackburn (ed.), *Ideology in Social Science* (London, 1972).

25 *Ibid.* pp. 258–9.

26 M. Nadworny, *Scientific Management and the Unions, 1900–1932* (Cambridge, Mass., 1955).

27 R. Edwards, *Contested Terrain: The Transformation of the Workplace in the Twentieth Century* (New York, 1979), p. 130.

28 E. Cadbury, 'Some Principles of Industrial Organisation: The Case for and against Scientific Management', *Sociological Review* vol. 8 (1914), p. 106. Of course this was not the only, possibly not the major reason for British employers' resistance to scientific management. As Littler points out (C. Littler, *Control and Conflict* (London, 1981), ch. 7), British employers failed to install scientific management systems because of fewer opportunities for standardisation, diversified product markets, rejection of a high wage Taylorite policy, and a failure to see a profit in scientific management. Some of these factors – economic, organisational and attitudinal – still survive. Loveridge, in a recent survey of forms of organisation, remarks: 'In the U.K. for example, the engineering industry is dominated by a few large companies but their approach to labour management hardly relates to that described in the prescriptive or normative literature. The manpower policies of these corporations may be seen as typical of an industry in which the bulk of the establishments have less than 1000 employees. Their procedures are highly localised and based on "custom and practice" within the district or plant. Their reward structures are based on the concept of hourly paid labour working to short term incentives. In many ways they are illustrative of the commodity view of labour that Marx ascribed to "primitive capitalism". The organisation of the workplace owes as much to earlier practices of craft administration and sub-contracting in these establishments as to newer forms of long-term techniques of employee career development' (R. Loveridge, 'Business Strategy and Community Culture', in D. Dunkerley and G. Salaman (eds.), *The International Yearbook of Organisational Studies* (London, 1982)).

29 C. Littler and G. Salaman, 'Bravermania and Beyond' (forthcoming).

30 See also J. Child, 'Organisation Structure, Environment and Performance: The Role of Strategic Choice', in Graeme Salaman and Kenneth Thompson (eds.), *People and Organizations* (London, 1973); M. Dalton, *Men who Manage* (New York, 1959).

31 A. Pettigrew, 'Occupational Specialization as an Emergent Process', and P. Elliott, 'Professional Ideology and Social Situation', in Geoff Esland, Graeme Salaman and Mary-Anne Speakman (eds.), *People and Work* (Edinburgh, 1975).

32 See L. Reisman, 'A Study in Role Conceptions in Bureaucracy', *Social Forces* vol. 27 (1949); A. Gouldner, 'Cosmopolitans and Locals', *Admin. Sci. Q.* vol. 2 (1957).

33 T. Watson, *The Personnel Managers* (London, 1978).

34 R. Bendix, *Work and Authority in Industry* (New York, 1963).

35 J. Child, *British Management Thought* (London, 1969), pp. 234–5; R. Bendix, *Work and Authority in Industry*, p. 619.
36 M. Burawoy, 'Towards a Marxist Theory of the Labour Process', *op.cit.* (n.21); C. Littler and G. Salaman, 'Bravermania and Beyond', *op.cit.* (n.29).
37 H. Braverman, *Labor and Monopoly Capital*, p. 27.
38 A. Giddens, *Central Problems in Social Theory*.
39 D. Stark, 'Class Struggle and the Transformation of the Labour Process', *Theory and Society* vol. 9 (1980).
40 Magali Sarfatti Larson, 'Proletarianization and Educated Labour', *Theory and Society* vol. 9 (1980).
41 C. Littler and G. Salaman, 'Bravermania and Beyond', *op.cit.* (n.29).
42 D. Stark, 'Class Struggle and the Transformation of the Labour Process', p. 89.
43 M. de Vroey, 'Managers and Class Relations: A Marxist View of Ownership and Control', in T. Nichols (ed.), *Capital and Labour* (London, 1980), p. 229.

Class boundaries and the labour process

1 Quoted in T. B. Bottomore and M. Rubel, *Karl Marx: Selected Writings in Sociology and Social Philosophy* (London, 1956), p. 201.
2 Stuart Hall, 'The "Political" and the "Economic" in Marx's Theory of Classes', in Alan Hunt (ed.), *Class and Class Structure* (London, 1977), p. 26.
3 *Ibid.* p. 55.
4 For a fuller discussion of Marx's analysis of intermediate classes see, e.g., Gavin Mackenzie, 'Class and Class Consciousness: Marx Re-examined', *Marxism Today* (March, 1976); D. C. Hodges, 'The "Intermediate Classes" in Marxian Theory', *Social Research* vol. 28 (1961).
5 Karl Marx and Friedrich Engels, *Manifesto of the Communist Party* (Moscow, 1959), p. 56.
6 *Capital* (London, 1960).
7 Charles H. Page, *Class and American Sociology* (New York, 1969), p. xvi.
8 Amongst contemporary writers the work of Westergaard and Resler springs most readily to mind. See John Westergaard and Henrietta Resler, *Class in a Capitalist Society* (London, 1975).
9 Of this genre Parkin is at present without equal. See most recently: Frank Parkin, *Marxism and Class Theory* (London, 1979).
10 Nicos Poulantzas, *Classes in Contemporary Capitalism* (London, 1975), p. 14.
11 *Ibid.* p. 18.
12 *Ibid.* p. 19.
13 *Ibid.* p. 14.
14 For a discussion of other, more detailed, criticisms see Erik Olin Wright, 'Class Boundaries in Advanced Capitalist Societies', *New Left Review* vol. 98 (July–August, 1976).
15 *Ibid.* p. 21.
16 *Ibid.* p. 26.
17 *Ibid.* p. 35.
18 *Ibid.* p. 36.

19 *Ibid.* pp. 39–40.
20 *Ibid.* p. 41.
21 G. Carchedi, 'On the Economic Identification of the New Middle Class', *Economy and Society* vol. 4 (1975); 'The Reproduction of Social Classes at the Level of Production Relations', *Economy and Society* vol. 4 (1975).
22 For a more detailed comparison of Wright and Carchedi see Erik Olin Wright, Class Structure and Income Inequality unpublished PhD dissertation, (Berkeley, California), pp. 72–8. My own analysis of Carchedi has been significantly influenced by that comparison.
23 David M. Gordon, 'Capitalist Efficiency and Socialist Efficiency', *Monthly Review* vol. 28 (July–August, 1976), p. 20.
24 Harry Braverman, *Labor and Monopoly Capital* (New York, 1974), p. 53.
25 *Ibid.* p. 58.
26 Stephen Marglin, 'What do Bosses do?', in André Gorz (ed.), *The Division of Labour* (Hassocks, Sussex, 1976).
27 Braverman, *op.cit.* (n.24), p. 301.
28 See, *inter alia,* Douglas F. Dowd, book review, *Contemporary Sociology* vol. 6 (November, 1976); Russell Jacoby, book review, *Telos* no. 29 (1976); Gavin Mackenzie, 'The Political Economy of the American Working Class', *British Journal of Sociology* vol. 28 (1977); David Stark, 'Class Struggle and the Transformation of the Labour Process', *Theory and Society* vol. 9 (1980).
29 Braverman, *op.cit.* (n.24), pp. ix–x.
30 Mackenzie, *op.cit.* (n.28).
31 Gordon, *op.cit.* (n.23).
32 *Ibid.* p. 22.
33 *Ibid.* p. 23.
34 *Ibid.* p. 24.
35 *Ibid.* p. 26.
36 *Ibid.* p. 25.
37 Richard Edwards, *Contested Terrain: The Transformation of the Workplace in the Twentieth Century* (New York, 1980), p. 16.
38 Edwards's primary concern is, of course, with class-based capitalist societies. But he is also quick to recognise that the term is equally appropriate '. . . in socialist societies like the U.S.S.R. where democratic control over the labour process has not been established', *ibid.* p. 17. Furthermore, while the *development* of the three forms of control can be traced clearly over the last hundred years or so, since capitalism develops unevenly with certain sectors of production pushing far in advance of other sectors, all three forms of control can of course be found in present-day society.
39 *Ibid.* p. 19.
40 *Ibid.* p. 118.
41 J. W. Kuhn, *Bargaining in Grievance Settlement* (New York, 1961).
42 Edwards, *op.cit.* (n.37), p. 124. See also Stanley Aronowitz, *False Promises* (New York, 1973), ch. 1.
43 Edwards, *op.cit.* (n.37), p. 131.
44 *Ibid.* p. 145.
45 *Ibid.* p. 157.
46 *Ibid.* p. 154. Edwards's argument regarding this consequence has much in common with the thesis of the 'New Working Class', at least in the

form put forward by Mallet and Touraine and, subsequently, several others.
47 *Ibid.* p. 159.
48 *Ibid.* p. 73. Limitations of space prevent full discussion of this continual
experimentation which began with 'simple control', moving through
'hierarchical control', 'welfare capitalism', scientific management and
company unions on the way to 'technical' and 'bureaucratic' forms of
workplace organisation.
49 *Ibid.* pp. 167–8.
50 *Ibid.* p. 173.
51 *Ibid.* p. 177.
52 It should not be necessary to point out that by regarding the accumulation process as the starting point for the analysis of class boundaries I am
in no sense advocating an economically *determining* approach. I am only
too aware of ideological and political factors. And I interpret the latter
two terms more widely than do Poulantzas or Wright as I am well aware
that classes are *social* collectivities. A complete theoretical approach to the
siting of class boundaries would clearly have to include reference to the
media, to the State, to patterns of social, ethnic and gender inequality,
the structure of family *and* education systems, to name but a few. I am
also not unaware that many positions in the social division of labour are
far removed from the production or appropriation of surplus value. This
is a daunting task: the problems are, I recognise, formidable. But we
must, at least, start in the right place.
53 See in particular Andrew L. Friedman, *Industry and Labour* (London, 1977),
and Michael Burawoy, *Manufacturing Consent* (Chicago, 1979), which
focusses on the importance of internal labour markets. The limitation of
space prevents discussion of these highly pertinent studies in the present
essay.

Control and resistance on the assembly line

1 William Serrin, *The Company and the Union* (New York, 1974), p. 236.
2 Quoted in Allan Nevins, *Ford: The Times, the Man, the Company* (New
York, 1954), p. 282.
3 Quoted in *ibid.* p. 475.
4 The term is taken from Richard Edwards, *Contested Terrain* (London, 1980).
5 Louis E. Davis, 'Pacing Effects on Manned Assembly Lines', *International
Journal of Production Research* vol. 4 (1966), p. 171.
6 *The Times,* London, 8 July 1973.
7 Quoted in Robert W. Dunn, *Labor and Automobiles* (New York, 1929), p.
85. In 1927 the playwright Paul Sifton focussed attention upon the exploitativeness of the assembly line in a play entitled *The Belt;* the setting was
unmistakably the Ford plant, one of the leading – and unsympathetic –
characters was clearly Henry Ford.
   During the 1930s, the assembly line gained almost universal currency
as the symbol of human exploitation in industry in two very successful
films that are still widely shown. René Clair's *A Nous la Liberté* made in
France in 1931 drew a graphic parallel between the factory and assembly

line, which subjected workers to the iron domination of both machine and management, and the prison in which men marched, ate, and worked in lockstep. Charles Chaplin's *Modern Times*, which appeared in 1936, offered a picture of the assembly line that has since been widely taken as archetypal. Embodied in a comic yet sympathetic figure familiar to moviegoers the world over, the assembly-line worker was pictured as an automaton, stupefied by his endlessly repeated simple task, unable even to cease the motions required by the job when he leaves the line. The image of Charlie Chaplin in overalls, a wrench in each hand, mechanically tightening bolts became the epitome of assembly-line work. So identified with that image has the assembly line become that in her recent critical analysis of the automobile industry Emma Rothschild entitled the chapter on work simply 'Modern Times'.

8 For the debate over Lordstown, see Barbara Garson, 'Luddites in Lordstown', *Harper's Magazine* (June, 1972), pp. 68–73; Stanley Aronowitz, *False Promises* (New York, 1973), ch. 1; Jon Lowell, 'Lowdown on Lordstown – GMAD: Jekyll or Hyde', *Ward's Auto World* (April, 1972), pp. 27–31; Emma Rothschild, *Paradise Lost* (New York, 1973), ch. 4; Russell W. Gibbons, 'Showdown at Lordstown', *Commonweal* vol. 95 (3 March 1972), pp. 523–4; and coverage in the *New York Times, Newsweek, Time*, and *Business Week*.

9 Judson Gooding, 'Blue-Collar Blues on the Assembly Line', *Fortune* vol. 82 (July 1970), p. 70.

10 Lack of space precludes discussion of the uniqueness of the Japanese economy in general and the 'successful' control of the assembly line in particular. An excellent analysis of Japanese industrial relations is Kazuo Okochi, Bernard Karsh and Solomon Lervine (eds.), *Workers and Employers in Japan* (Princeton, New Jersey, 1974).

11 Report of a Special Task Force to the Secretary of Health, Education and Welfare, *Work in America* (Cambridge, Mass., 1973), p. 19.

12 While this essay has focussed on the operation of the assembly line in Western capitalist societies, focussing primarily on the United States, this must in no way be taken to mean that I draw a naïve and simplistic distinction between 'state socialism' and 'capitalism'. Rather I am in agreement with Braverman when he says 'Whatever view one takes of Soviet industrialisation, one cannot conscientiously interpret its history . . . as an attempt to organise labour processes in a way fundamentally different from those of capitalism.' Harry Braverman, *Labor and Monopoly Capital* (New York, 1974), p. 22.

13 Ely Chinoy, *Automobile Workers and the American Dream* (Boston, 1965), p. 133. (Originally published in 1955.)

Fatalism: Durkheim's hidden theory of order

1 Emile Durkheim, *Suicide* (London, 1952), p. 276 n.25. For subsequent discussion see Barclay D. Johnson, 'Durkheim's One Cause of Suicide', *American Sociological Review* vol. 30 (1965), and Bruce Dohrenwend, 'Egoism, Altruism, Anomie and Fatalism', *American Sociological Review* vol. 24 (1959). A notable exception to the tendency to confine discussion of fatalism to the study of suicide is the paper by Sakari Sariola, 'Fatalism

and Anomie: Components of Rural–Urban Differences', *Kansas Journal of Sociology* vol. 1 (1965).

2 Percy S. Cohen, *Modern Social Theory* (London, 1968), pp. 21–5. And it should be noted that, even in the case of what are considered to be purely coercive institutions, order depends in no small degree on informal exchange relationships between custodians and inmates. See, for example, Gresham Sykes, *The Society of Captives* (Princeton, 1958).

3 Talcott Parsons, *The Structure of Social Action* (New York, 1937), pp. 378ff.

4 See, for example, the summary of research in this field by Herbert J. Gans, 'Poverty and Culture: Some Basic Questions about Methods of Studying Life-Styles of the Poor', in Peter Townsend (ed.), *The Concept of Poverty* (London, 1970).

5 It seems unlikely that moral despotism can be equated with the loss of autonomy that occurs when individuals are 'over-attached' to social groups, since Durkheim identifies this state of 'excessive' social subordination as 'altruism' in contrast with 'egoism', and quite deliberately places fatalism at the opposite pole to anomie. Moreover, there is no reason to suppose that simply because individuals are strongly attached to a social group their wants and aspirations will be fatalistic in the sense that they present no challenge to the existing social order. Revolutionary sects (of the political as well as the religious kind) are a case in point: in Durkheimian terms their internal bonds are in a high degree altruistic, but their ends are plainly anomic.

6 *Socialism,* ed. and with an introduction by Alvin W. Gouldner (New York, 1962), p. 243.

7 Or for that matter of anomie. The closest Durkheim comes to a consideration of the way in which specific belief systems exacerbate social conflict is in his discussion of the 'forced division of labour' and again, on the same theme, in *Professional Ethics and Civic Morals* (London, 1957), ch. 18. But in general, there is nothing in his work that suggests any systematic connection between the content of the collective conscience and the level of social integration. The subject is first rigorously attended to by Robert K. Merton in his celebrated essay on 'Social Structure and Anomie', in his book, *Social Theory and Social Structure* (Glencoe, 1957).

8 For example, Parsons: 'There is a range of possible modes of orientation in the motivational sense to a value standard. Perhaps the most important distinction is between the attitude of "expediency" at one pole, where conformity or non-conformity is a function of the instrumental interests of the actor, and at the other pole the "introjection" or internalization of the standard so that to act in conformity with it becomes a need-disposition in the actor's own personality structure, relatively independently of any instrumentally significant consequences of that conformity. The latter is to be treated here as the basic type of integration of motivation with a normative pattern-structure of values.' *The Social System* (Glencoe, 1952), p. 37.

9 S. M. Tumin, *Social Class and Social Change in Puerto Rico* (Princeton, 1961), p. 478. See also Gerald D. Berreman, 'Caste in India and the United States', *American Journal of Sociology* vol. 65 (1960). Compare the distinction made by Mann between 'pragmatic acceptance, where the individual complies because he perceives no realistic alternative, and normative acceptance,

where the individual internalizes the moral expectations of the ruling class and views his own inferior position as legitimate'. M. Mann, 'The Social Cohesion of Liberal Democracy', *American Sociological Review* vol. 35 (1970), p. 425.

10 See, for example, Parsons, *The Social System, op.cit.* (n.8), especially pp. 349ff. 'Since there must be relative consistency in the value orientation patterns of a collectivity – though perfect consistency is not possible – this consistency must extend to the system of beliefs which give cognitive meaning to these value-orientations, again imperfectly to be sure. If ideological beliefs and value-patterns are, as assumed, interdependent, relative stability and consistency of the belief system has the same order of functional significance as do stability and consistency of the value-orientation patterns. Hence there must be a set of beliefs, subscription to which is in some sense an obligation of collectivity membership roles, where the cognitive conviction of truth and the "moral" conviction of rightness are merged' (p. 351).

11 W. Robertson Smith, *The Religion of the Semites* (New York, 1956), pp. 20–1. See also 'The Importance of Religious Practice', in Louis Schneider (ed.), *Religion, Culture and Society* (New York, 1964), Part II.

12 This point is made very well by Rajni Kothari, *Politics in India* (Boston, 1970), pp. 259–60. 'Any system that is wide open and flexible develops rigidities in some sphere, which imparts a sense of confidence and manoeuverability. In India we find this in the social and institutional sphere. Ideologically, Indian society has faced many challenges and this has produced a high degree of ideological tolerance and flexibility. Institutionally, however, Indian society has been traditionally very rigid, working out a precise and clearly identifiable hierarchy, formalized rules, and conventions, conformity with which was mandatory and defined by birth, and a system of substantive and symbolic distances which articulated the hierarchy in a definitive and predictable manner. Thus developed a peculiar combination of a high tolerance of ambiguity and diversity in thought and value patterns on the one hand and a deep concern with formal rituals and compliance with "rules of the system" on the other.'

13 For a thorough consideration of this issue, see Christel Lane, *The Rites of the Rulers: Ritual in Industrial Society, the Soviet Case* (Cambridge, 1981). See also Martin King Whyte, *Small Groups and Political Rituals in China* (Berkeley, 1974).

14 John Plamenatz, *Man and Society* vol. II (London, 1969), p. 341. The emphasis on literacy is perhaps exaggerated, since religious teachings can be transmitted orally; for example, for many centuries the *Vedas* were handed down by recitation alone. What is fundamental is the division of sacred from profane labour and the formation of a class of religious specialists.

15 On these points, see, for example, Keith Thomas, *Religion and the Decline of Magic* (London, 1971), ch. 2.

16 *The Religion of India*, transl. and ed. H. H. Gerth and D. Martindale (Illinois, 1958), p. 17; 'Rebellions by lower castes undoubtedly occurred. The question is: why were there not more of them, and most important, why did the great, historically significant, religious revolutions against the

Hindu order stem from altogether different, relatively privileged strata and retain their roots in these?'

17 *The Sociology of Religion,* transl. E. Fischoff (Boston, 1963), p. 113.
18 *The Religion of India, op.cit.* (n.16), pp. 122–3.
19 'All Hindus accept two basic principles: the *samsara* belief in the transmigration of souls and the related *karma* doctrine of compensation. These alone are the truly "dogmatic" doctrines of all Hinduism.' *Ibid.* p. 118. See, however, M. N. Srinivas, *Social Change in Modern India* (Berkeley, 1966), p. 3: 'Certain Hindu theological ideas such as *samsara, karma* and *dharma* are woven into the caste system, but it is not known whether awareness of these concepts is universal or confined only to certain sections of the hierarchy. This depends on the degree to which an area is Sanskritized.'
20 *The Religion of India, op.cit.* (n.16), p. 167.
21 Kenelm Burridge, *New Heaven, New Earth* (Oxford, 1971), pp. 86–95, provides a succint and cogent account of the socio-economic context of the development of Jainism. Another noteworthy analysis of the process of innovation is to be found in Gananath Obeyesekere, 'Theodicy, Sin and Salvation in a Sociology of Buddhism', in E. R. Leach, ed., *Dialectic in Practical Religion* (Cambridge, 1968). See also K. Malalgoda, 'Millennialism in Relation to Buddhism', *Comparative Studies in Society and History* vol. 12 (1970).
22 Weber probably underestimated the mass appeal of the *bhakti* movements. See Scrinivas, *op.cit.* (n.19), pp. 25–6, and especially p. 76; R. C. Zaehner, *Hinduism* (London, 1972), ch. 6 and pp. 147–8; *Speaking of Siva,* transl. and with an introduction by A. K. Ramanujan (London, 1973).
23 Sinclair Stevenson, *The Heart of Jainism* (New Delhi, 1970; first published 1915), p. 1.
24 Louis Dumont, *Homo Hierarchicus: The Caste System and its Implications* (London, 1970), ch. 9.
25 *The Religion of India, op.cit.* (n.16), pp. 23 and 326.
26 'Allowance must always be made for the thinness, past and present, of the Indian intellectual strata proper and, in general the strata interested in "salvation" in some sort of rational sense. The masses, at least, of the contemporary Hindus know nothing about "salvation" (*moksha, mukti*). They hardly know the expression, let alone its meaning. Except for short periods, it must always have been so. Quite crude and purely this-worldly interest, gross magic, along with the betterment of rebirth chances were the values for which they did and do strive' (*ibid.* p. 326). L. S. S. O'Malley, *Popular Hinduism: The Religion of the Masses* (Cambridge, 1935), is still the best general work on the subject.
27 See especially the review of Weber's *Religion of India* by Milton Singer in *American Anthropologist* vol. 63 (1961), pp. 143–50. Also M. S. A. Rao, who, in his *Tradition, Rationality and Change* (Bombay, 1972), provides a useful summary of the principal objections to Weber's thesis. Many of these are misdirected, namely that he ignored reformatory sects within Hinduism, that he believed that it was possible to deduce concrete motives from the study of sacred texts, and that he was unaware of the variety of interpretations of such notions as *karma* and *moksha*. The empirical study

of fatalism in contemporary India is sparse. See, for example, Joseph W. Elder, 'Fatalism in India', *Anthropological Quarterly* vol. 39 (1966), and 'Religious Beliefs and Political Attitudes', in D. E. Smith (ed.), *South Asian Politics and Religion* (Princeton, 1966), and Everett M. Rogers, *Modernization among Peasants* (New York, 1969), ch. 12.

28 See Srinivas, *op.cit.* (n.19), ch. 1, and James Silverberg (ed.), *Social Mobility in the Caste System in India* (The Hague, 1968). These writings, together with Andre Béteille, *Caste, Class and Power* (Berkeley, 1965); F. G. Bailey, *Caste and the Economic Frontier* (Manchester, 1957), and *Caste and Race: Comparative Approaches,* ed. Anthony de and Julie Knight (London, 1967), seriously weaken the claim made, above all, by Dumont, that the Indian caste system cannot be analysed in terms applicable to other forms of social stratification.

29 Srinivas, *op.cit.* (n.19), p. 30. See also Weber, *The Religion of India, op.cit.* (n.16), vol. III, ch. 2, 'Caste Schism'.

30 *Ibid.* p. 305. On this sect, see R. E. Enthoven, 'Lingayat', in *Encyclopedia of Religion and Ethics* vol. VIII, p. 75; William McCormack, 'Lingayats as a sect', *Journal of the Royal Anthropological Institute* vol. 93 (1963); and Dumont, *op.cit.* (n.24).

31 *The Religion of India, op.cit.* (n.16), p. 19.

32 Moreover, the extent to which objective conditions were in themselves conducive to fatalism should not be ignored. The tremendous economic burden imposed on the mass of the population by the governing and landowning classes, which is demonstrated by I. Habib, *The Agrarian Structure of the Mughal State* (Bombay, 1963), meant, as Lannoy has noted, that the lack of a 'stimulus to cultivate a surplus' was due to 'the certainty of its appropriation by landlords' rather than to 'any sense of religious fatalism'. See Richard Lannoy, *The Speaking Tree* (Oxford, 1971), p. 223.

33 *The Religion of India, op.cit.* (n.16), p. 24: 'Hinduism is primarily ritualism, a fact implied when modern authors state that *mata* (doctrine) and *marga* (holy end) are transitory and "ephemeral" – they mean freely elected – while *dharma* is "eternal" – that is, unconditionally valid.'

34 His argument on this score is well summarised by Reinhard Bendix, *Max Weber: An Intellectual Portrait* (New York, 1960), pp. 207–8: 'Certain common denominators of Indian religion – the belief in reincarnation, the idea of retribution (*karma*), and the identification of virtue with ritual observance – influenced the masses through the social pressures of the caste system. Caste was the "transmission belt" between the speculative ideas of an intellectual elite and the mundane orientation of religious observance among the people at large.'

35 The untouchables do not appear in Weber's depiction of the system which appears to be based on the *varna* model, which Srinivas, among many modern authorities, holds to be a quite inadequate representation of the historical reality in that it does not take account of the innumerable *jatis* who were for the most part difficult to locate with an exactitude within the *varna* scheme, and who were engaged in constant local rivalry with one another over ritual precedence. 'One wonders,' he writes, 'how many dominant peasant castes in rural India had even heard of the rules governing different *varnas,* or, having heard of them, paid heed to them. One is also at a loss to understand how people living in villages were

made to obey the rules, or punished for violating them. Even today, with all the facilities and resources at the disposal of the Government of India, it has been found very difficult to ensure that the rights which the Indian consititution confers on the Harijans are actually translated into practice in India's 560,000 villages. The situation in ancient or medieval India can be left to the reader's own inferences.' Srinivas, *op.cit.* (n.19), pp. 6–7. Others who emphasise the role of relative power between castes as the stabilising factor in the caste system include Gerald D. Berreman, 'Caste in India and the United States', *American Journal of Sociology* vol. 65 (1960), pp. 120–7, and McKim Marriott, 'Little Communities in an Indigenous Civilization', in *Village India,* ed. McKim Marriott (Chicago, 1955), p. 131.

36 It is believed that a caste system existed in Southern India before the infiltration of Vedic culture from the North; moreover caste remained stronger in the south, even though it has been claimed that, in certain regions at any rate, belief in *karma* was not prevalent among lower castes. On caste, see J. H. Hutton, *Caste in India* (Cambridge, 1946), pp. 136, 144 and 152; and on beliefs, O'Malley, *op.cit.* (n.26), p. 31. On the other hand, contemporary anthropological studies of caste tend to support Weber's portrayal of popular Hinduism, and suggest that the masses have a better understanding of Sanskritic Hinduism than he allowed for. See Singer, *op.cit.* (n.27), p. 149.

37 The Jains, Buddhists, Lingayats and Sikhs, not to mention Islam, all attracted many recruits from the lower castes. See Romila Thapar, *A History of India* vol. I (London, 1974), pp. 67, 216 and 311, and André Béteille, *Castes Old and New* (Bombay, 1969), p. 96.

38 On the more radical, less easily containable, movements that were influenced by Islamic doctrine – of which the Sikhs are the most notable – see Thapar, *op.cit.* (n.37), pp. 305–12.

39 Max Weber, *The Religion of China,* transl. and ed. Hans Gerth (Glencoe, 1951), p. 219.

40 Joseph R. Levenson, *Confucian China and its Modern Fate* vol. II (London, 1964).

41 *The Religion of India, op.cit.* (n.16), p. 330.

42 *The Sociology of Religion, op.cit.* (n.17), p. 269.

43 A useful summary of the literature is to be found in Chalmers Johnson, *Revolutionary Change* (Boston, 1966), ch. 7.

44 Robert M. Marsh, *The Mandarins* (New York, 1961), p. 43. For similar characterisations of the traditional pattern of rebellion, see Victor Purcell, *The Boxer Uprising* (Cambridge, 1963), ch. 7; E. Balazs, *Chinese Civilization and Bureaucracy* (New Haven, 1964), ch. 2, and C. K. Yang, *Religion in Chinese Society* (Berkeley, 1961), ch. 9.

45 Levenson, *op.cit.* (n.40), p. 86. In *The Taiping Rebellion and the Western Powers* (Oxford, 1971), p. 6, S. Y. Teng agrees that 'the movement had a clear-cut revolutionary and anti-traditional character', but then argues that it should nonetheless be classed as a rebellion on the rather weak ground that 'the Taipings did not make any "permanent change of a good kind" or "progress" '

46 Levenson, *op.cit.* (n.40), ch. 7, section 2.

47 Levenson, *op.cit.* (n.40), chs. 7 and 8. See also Eugene P. Boardman, 'Millenary Aspects of the Taiping Rebellion, 1851–64', *Comparative Studies in*

Society and History Supplement 2 (The Hague, 1962). The most detailed account of the movement's ideology is to be found in Vincent Y. C. Shih, *The Taiping Ideology: its Sources, Interpretations and Influences* (Seattle, 1972). Although Shih stresses the inability of the Taipings to adopt Christian beliefs except by anchoring them in traditional Chinese thought, he acknowledges the 'catalystic influence' of the former and argues that 'without this new ideology, it would have been nearly impossible to break the hold that orthodoxy had on the mind of the people' (xviii), and that these ideas 'held a genuine possibility of bringing about a real revolution' (xv). Moreover, he explicitly contrasts the revolutionary potential of Christian beliefs with 'the traditional attitude of fatalism' (xiii and 472).

48 See Franz Michael, *The Taiping Rebellion* (Seattle, 1966). 'If the Taiping Rebellion was a new beginning in Chinese history, it arose in a setting that still contained the familiar elements characteristic of periods of dynastic decline and rebellious uprisings in the past. Grave corruption in government, heavy over-taxation of the farmers, high rent, desertion of the land by the peasants, the increase in a roaming population, banditry and general insecurity, the increasing importance of secret societies, the formation of local self-defence units that took matters into their own hands, and frequent small-scale warfare which led to uprisings against government authority – these had been the conditions for dynastic changes by rebellion or foreign conquest throughout imperial history . . . While the setting was similar to that of earlier rebellions, the Taiping Rebellion itself and its goal were basically different from former dynastic upheavals. The Taipings attacked not only the ruling dynasty – they attacked the traditional order itself. And this wider attack gave their rebellion a character totally different from that of rebellious movements of the past' (p. 4). It is undeniable that the Western military and economic impact on China was a new element in the setting of the rebellion. But, since China had been subject to foreign conquest before without its having had any marked effect on the nature of rebellion, it would seem unlikely that the distinctive ideological character of the Taiping movement is attributable to the military and economic effects of the Western encroachment.

49 See, for example, Owen Lattimore, *Inner Asian Frontiers of China* (New York, 1940), ch. 17, and Jean Chesneaux, *Peasant Revolts in China 1840–1949* (London, 1973).

50 *The Religion of China, op.cit.* (n.39), p. 219.

51 At the same time, Weber's hypotheses do raise problems of the weighting of causal factors which historical evidence seems unlikely to provide unequivocal answers to. On this, see his parting shot at the critics of his protestant ethic thesis: 'Dass es "ziffernmaessige" Tei-lungsschluessel bei der historischen Zurechnung nicht gibt, liegt nicht an mir.' 'Antikritisches Schlusswort,' *Archiv für Sozialwissenschaft und Sozialpolitik* vol. 31 (1910), p. 598. The difficulties encountered in testing Weber's thesis against historical data are clearly demonstrated by Gordon Marshall's admirable study, *Presbyteries and Profits* (Oxford, 1981).

52 It is arguable that the only formulation of fatalistic order Durkheim could possibly have arrived at would have been what has been called 'conditional' fatalism. This has to do with the fact that his explanation of anomic

disorder finally has recourse to very vaguely defined structural factors of a non-normative kind that are entirely residual elements of his conceptual scheme. This fault is remarkably the reverse of his failure to incorporate into his explanation of order any systematic consideration of the structure of values and beliefs; and both would appear to be due to his very pronounced tendency to conceive of social forces, whether sacred or profane, in quantitative rather than qualitative terms. At any rate, the systematic form of anomie, which involves a deregulation of a society's social or moral 'classification of men and things', has its ultimate cause in what Durkheim refers to cryptically as an 'abrupt' change in 'power and wealth'. This is just one of the terms he uses to describe those socially disruptive forces which he generally sees as originating in the 'economic' or 'utilitarian' sphere of society, that dark and threatening Hobbesian realm existing only on the periphery of his analytical vision. It must be concluded then that, since anomie results from sudden changes in material conditions, fatalism must somehow be explained by reference to the extraordinary stability of this selfsame class of social facts. The form that such an explanation might take has been indicated in the first section of this paper.

Work histories, career strategies and the class structure

1 The importance of the division of labour was fully acknowledged in Ilya Neustadt's own work from the time of his early work on Belgian social structure for his (second) doctoral thesis, to studies of social change in Ghana, and an unfortunately never published collection of readings from classic social theory on the division of labour.

2 The term 'occupation' is, of course, ambiguous. Housewives and students are both 'occupied', as are many retired people, but not 'employed' or 'self-employed'. In this discussion I shall use 'occupation' to refer to 'gainful occupation'. The difficulties of consistently maintaining any other usage are reflected in S. R. Parker, 'Occupation', in P. Barker (ed.), *A Sociological Portrait* (Harmondsworth, 1972), pp. 23–38, where a careful initial distinction between 'occupation' and 'job' is followed by a discussion concerned entirely with gainful occupations. See also F. Bechhofer, 'Occupations', in M. Stacey (ed.), *Comparability in Social Research* (London, 1969), esp. p. 99.

3 See D. Lockwood, 'Sources of Variation in Working Class Images of Society, *Sociological Review* vol. 14 no. 3 (November, 1966), esp. pp. 249–50; the papers contained in M. Bulmer (ed.), *Working Class Images of Society* (London, 1975); and H. H. Davis, *Beyond Class Images* (London, 1979).

4 The Oxford Social Mobility Group: J. H. Goldthorpe and K. Hope, *The Social Grading of Occupations: A New Approach and Scale* (Oxford, 1974), and J. H. Goldthorpe *et al.*, *Social Mobility and Class Structure in Modern Britain* (Oxford, 1980); the sociology group in the Department of Applied Economics, University of Cambridge: A. Stewart, K. Prandy and R. M. Blackburn, *Social Stratification and Occupations* (London, 1980); the University of Edinburgh occupational cognition project: A. P. M. Coxon and C. L. Jones, *Class and Hierarchy: the Social Meaning of Occupations* (London, 1979); and fourthly, the Scottish Mobility Study: G. Payne, G. Ford

and C. Robertson, 'Changes in Occupational Mobility in Scotland', *The Scottish Journal of Sociology* vol. 1, no. 1, (1976), pp. 57–79.

5 Bechhofer, 'Occupations', pp. 104–5.

6 The project entitled 'Employment in the Inner City – Attitudes, Aspirations and Opportunities', is supported by a grant from the Department of the Environment as part of their inner cities research programme, and is being carried out by Mr J. M. Cousins, Mrs M. M. Curran and the author.

7 Goldthorpe, *Social Mobility and Class Structure*, p. 140.

8 *Ibid.* p. 141.

9 A. Stewart *et al.*, *Social Stratification and Occupations*, pp. 74–5, 148–9, 113. This line of argument is developed further in a most interesting way in the final section of the book, see pp. 203–7.

10 W. H. Form and D. C. Miller, 'Occupational Career Patterns as a Sociological Instrument', *American Journal of Sociology* vol. 54, no. 4 (1949), pp. 317–29; see also D. C. Miller and W. H. Form, *Industrial Sociology* (New York, 1964), esp. ch. 13.

11 H. L. Wilensky, 'Work, Careers and Social Integration', in T. Burns (ed.), *Industrial Man* (Harmondsworth, 1969; first published 1960) pp. 125–6.

12 Indeed for much longer than that! W. I. Thomas and F. Znaniecki, in *The Polish Peasant in Europe and America* (first published 1918–20), asserted 'life records, as complete as possible, constitute the *perfect* type of sociological material'.

13 See, for example, the discussion of 'the 1974 follow-up inquiry' in Goldthorpe, *Social Mobility and Class Structure* pp. 291–5, and in B. H. S. Lienard and C. M. Llewellyn, 'The Analysis of Life History Data using Graphical Devices' (unpublished – I am grateful to Catriona Llewellyn for making a copy of this paper available). In our study (see n.7), we also feel confident that data collection and coding problems have been satisfactorily overcome for work history data extending over 10 years for nearly 900 respondents. Re-interviews with certain respondents have allowed us to check the reliability of such data with overall satisfactory results.

14. G. M. Norris, 'Unemployment, Subemployment and Personal Characteristics', *Sociological Review* vol. 26, nos. 1 and 2 (1978), pp. 89–123 and 327–47.

15 R. A. Carr-Hill and K. I. Macdonald, *Problems in the Analysis of Life Histories*, Sociological Review Monograph, no. 19 (July 1973), pp. 57–95. See also the work of Form and Miller (n.10), Lienhard and Llewellyn (n.13), and R. Bland, B. Elliott and F. Bechhofer, 'Social Mobility in the Petite Bourgeoisie', *Acta Sociologica* vol. 21, no. 3 (1978), pp. 229–48.

16 E. Goffman, 'The Moral Career of the Mental Patient', in *Asylums* (New York, 1961), esp. p. 127. Goffman uses 'career' to refer to 'any social strand of any person's course through life'. I have preferred to use the term 'work history' in this more general sense, and, following Wilensky (n.11), to restrict 'career' to 'a succession of related jobs arranged in a hierarchy of prestige, through which persons move in an ordered, predictable sequence'.

17 See, for example, H. H. Gerth and C. Wright Mills, *From Max Weber* (London, 1948), ch. 7.; and A. Giddens, *The Class Structure of the Advanced Societies* (London, 1973), esp. ch. 6.

18 This literature is discussed in R. K. Brown, 'Sources of Objectives in Work and Employment', in J. Child (ed.), *Man and Organization* (London, 1973), esp. ch. 4; and in T. J. Watson, *Sociology, Work and Industry* (London, 1980), esp. ch. 4.

19 D. N. Ashton, 'The Transition from School to Work: Notes on the Development of Different Frames of Reference among Young Male Workers', *Sociological Review* vol. 21, no. 1 (1973), pp. 107–25; and 'From School to Work: Some Problems of Adjustment Experienced by Young Male Workers', in P. Brannen (ed.), *Entering the World of Work: Some Sociological Perspectives* (London, 1975), pp. 53–69.

20 Ashton, 'From School to Work', pp. 58, 60, 61.

21 Ashton, 'The Transition from School to Work', p. 121 n.10.

22 Some 'opportunities', of course, perhaps especially for those seeking an occupationally oriented career, result from the collective actions and strategies of those with a particular skill or qualification operating through trade unions or professional associations. It is not possible to pursue this occupational structuring of labour markets here.

23 For further discussion of this distinction see P. B. Doeringer and M. J. Piore, *Internal Labor Markets and Manpower Analysis* (Lexington, Mass., 1971), and R. M. Blackburn and M. Mann, *The Working Class in the Labour Market* (London, 1979), esp. ch. 1.

24 M. Mann, *Workers on the Move* (London, 1973).

25 Norris, 'Unemployment, Subemployment and Personal Characteristics'.

26 This is difficult to avoid but particularly regrettable. It is clear that women's position in the labour market in our society differs markedly from that of men, and tends to be distorted if considered using the same categories and frames of reference as for men. Comparative analysis of work history data for men and women could, I suspect, be particularly helpful in illuminating the nature of the differences, and it is to be hoped that such work will be undertaken. In the case of our own research, work history information was obtained from women respondents on exactly the same basis as from men, but it has not so far been analysed in any detail.

27 R. Bendix, *Work and Authority in Industry* (New York, 1963), esp. pp. 228–36.

28 C. Erikson, *British Industrialists: Steel and Hosiery, 1850–1950* (Cambridge, 1959), esp. p. 50.

29 See, for example, the very varied career paths of those who became small shopkeepers, in Bland *et al.*, 'Social Mobility in the Petite Bourgeousie'.

30 A. W. Gouldner, 'Cosmopolitans and Locals: Toward an Analysis of Latent Social Roles', *Administrative Science Quarterly* vol. 2, nos. 2 and 3 (December 1957 and March 1958).

31 See, for example, M. Dalton, *Men who Manage* (New York, 1959), and T. Burns and G. M. Stalker, *The Management of Innovation* (London, 1961).

32 A. L. Stinchcombe, 'Social Structure and the Invention of Organizational Forms', in T. Burns (ed.), *Industrial Man* (Harmondsworth, 1969), p. 188.

33 S. Cotgrove and S. Box, *Science, Industry and Society* (London, 1970); and J. Ford and S. Box, 'Sociological Theory and Occupational Choice', *Sociological Review* vol. 15, no. 3 (1967), pp. 287–99.

34 See the discussions in T. Nichols, *Ownership, Control and Ideology* (Lon-

don, 1969), and J. Child, *The Business Enterprise in Modern Industrial Society* (London, 1969), esp. ch. 3.

35. Gouldner, 'Cosmopolitans and Locals'; C. Fletcher, 'On Replication: Notes on the Notions of a Replicability Quotient and a Generalizability Quotient', *Sociology* vol. 4, no. 1 (1970), pp. 51–69.

36 See, for example, A. Heath, *Social Mobility* (London, 1981), esp. pp. 236–7.

37 A. Stewart *et al.*, *Social Stratification and Occupations*, pp. 148–52.

38 Norris, 'Unemployment, Subemployment and Personal Characteristics'.

39 *Ibid.* p. 341.

40 The project entitled 'Transmitted Deprivation and the Local Labour Market' was carried out by Mr J. M. Cousins and the author and was supported by funds from the DHSS/SSRC Joint Working Party on Transmitted Deprivation.

41 For a review and discussion of cluster analysis, see B. Everitt, *Cluster Analysis* (London, 1974). The technique used was the Relocation programme in D. Wishart's Clustan 1A package. Each record consisted of a large number of items including educational qualifications, occupation and industry of first job, average length of job, indices of the range of industrial and occupational experience, and experience of unemployment and redundancy.

Gender inequality and class formation

1 I. Neustadt, *Teaching Sociology* (Leicester, 1965).

2 E. A. Westermarck, 'Sociology as a University Study', *Inauguration of the Martin White Professorships of Sociology, University of London, 17 December 1907*, quoted in I. Neustadt, *Teaching Sociology*, p. 19.

3 See, for example, Robert Bocock, Peter Hamilton, Kenneth Thompson, Alan Waton (eds.), *An Introduction to Sociology* (London, 1980); David J. Smith, *Unemployment and Racial Minorities* (London, 1981); Frank Parkin, 'Social Stratification', in Tom Bottomore and Robert Nisbet (eds.), *A History of Sociological Analysis* (London, 1978).

4 Dorothy E. Smith, 'A Peculiar Eclipsing: Women's Exclusion from Man's Culture', *Women's Studies International Quarterly* vol. 1 (1978).

5 Joan Acker, 'Women and Social Stratification: A Case of Intellectual Sexism', *American Journal of Sociology* vol. 78 (1973); Jackie West, 'Women, Sex and Class', in Annette Kuhn and Ann Marie Wolpe (eds.), *Feminism and Materialism* (London, 1978); Ann Oakley and Robin Oakley, 'Sexism in Official Statistics', in John Irvine, Ian Miles and Jeff Evans (eds.), *Demystifying Social Statistics* (London, 1979).

6 Michael Anderson, 'The Relevance of Family History', in Chris Harris (ed.), *The Sociology of the Family: New Directions for Britain*, Sociological Review Monograph no. 28 (Keele, 1979).

7 Rayna Rapp, Ellen Ross and Renate Bridenthal, 'Examining Family History', *Feminist Studies* vol. 5 (1979), contains a useful bibliography.

8 Margaret Stacey, 'Family and Household', in Margaret Stacey (ed.), *Comparability in Social Research* (London, 1969).

9 *Social Trends* (Government Statistical Service, London, 1980).

10 Oakley and Oakley, 'Sexism in Official Statistics', p. 179.

11 Hilary Land, 'Women: Supporters or Supported', in Diana Barker and Sheila Allen (eds.), *Sexual Divisions and Society: Process and Change* (London, 1976), p. 119.
12 Anthony Heath, *Social Mobility* (London, 1981).
13 *Ibid.* p. 114.
14 Jan Pahl, 'Patterns of Money Management within Marriage', *Journal of Social Policy* vol. 9 (1980); Laura Oren, 'The Welfare of Women in Labouring Families: England 1860–1950', *Feminist Studies* vol. 1 (1973); Joanna Bornat, 'Home and Work. A New Context for Trade Union History', *Radical America* vol. 12 (1978).
15 Christine Delphy, 'Continuities and Discontinuities in Marriage and Divorce', in Diana Barker and Sheila Allen (eds.), *Sexual Divisions and Society: Process and Change* (London, 1976), p. 81.
16 Anderson, 'The Relevance of Family History'.
17 Delphy, 'Women in Stratification Studies', in Helen Roberts (ed.), *Doing Feminist Research* (London, 1981), pp. 126–7.
18 Parkin, 'Social Stratification', p. 606.
19 David Lockwood, *The Blackcoated Worker* (London, 1958).
20 'Female Activity Rates: Annex', *Department of Employment Gazette* (January, 1974), p. 18.
21 Oakley and Oakley, 'Sexism in Official Statistics'.
22 Lois Scharf, *To Work and to Wed* (London, 1980); Sheila Allen, 'Invisible Threads', *Institute of Development Studies Bulletin* no. 12 (1981).
23 Heath, *Social Mobility*, p. 108.

The petty bourgeoisie and modern capitalism

1 This is the common characteristic identified by the contributors to Bechhofer and Elliott's volume, in which there are discussions of, for example, Canadian and English farmers, French bakers and small-scale producers in Third World countries. F. Bechhofer and B. Elliott (eds.), *The Petite Bourgeoisie: Comparative Studies of the Uneasy Stratum* (London, 1981).
2 'Other labour' tends to be either 'unpaid' family labour or wage-labour on such a small scale that it does not contribute significantly to the production of surplus value. See, for example, N. Poulantzas, *Classes in Contemporary Capitalism* (London, 1975).
3 F. Bechhofer and B. Elliott, 'Persistence and Change: The Petite Bourgeoisie in the Industrial Society', *European Journal of Sociology* vol. 17, (1976), p. 77.
4 F. Bechhofer, B. Elliott, M. Rushforth and R. Bland, 'The Petits Bourgeois in the Class Structure: The Case of the Small Shopkeepers', in F. Parkin (ed.), *The Social Analysis of Class Structure* (London, 1974), p. 123; F. Bechhofer and B. Elliott, 'Petty Property: The Survival of a Moral Economy', in F. Bechhofer and B. Elliott *op.cit.* (n.1), p. 183.
5 F. Bechhofer *et al.*, in F. Parkin, *op. cit.* (n.4), p. 123.
6 F. Bechhofer, B. Elliott, M. Rushforth and R. Bland 'Small Shopkeepers: Matters of Money and Meaning', *Sociological Review* vol. 22 (1974), p. 479.
7 *Ibid.;* F. Bechhofer *et al.*, in F. Parkin, *op.cit.* (n.4).
8 *Ibid.* p. 124.

9 F. Bechhofer and B. Elliott, *op.cit.* (n.4), pp. 183, 184, 187.
10 This argument is summarised in J. Boissevain, 'Small Entrepreneurs in Changing Europe: Towards a Research Agenda', unpublished paper presented to the European Centre for Work and Society (Utrecht, 1980).
11 See, for example, E. F. Schumacher, *Small is Beautiful* (London, 1973); D. Dickson, *Alternative Technology* (London, 1974).
12 J. Boissevain, *op.cit.* (n.10), pp. 21–2.
13 J. Martin and A. Norman, *The Computerized Society* (Englewood Cliffs, N.J., 1970), p. 32.
14 For empirical evidence of this decline, see F. Blackaby (ed.), *De-Industrialisation* (London, 1979).
15 R. E. Pahl, 'Employment, Work and the Domestic Division of Labour', *Int. Jour. of Urban and Regional Research* vol. 4, no. 1 (1980), p. 4.
16 *Ibid.* p. 5.
17 R. Scase and R. Goffee, *The Real World of the Small Business Owner* (London, 1980).
18 J. Boissevain, *op.cit.* (n. 10), p. 11.
19 See, for example, N. Poulantzas, *op.cit* (n.2); E. O. Wright, *Class, Crisis and the State* (London, 1978); and G. Carchedi, 'On the Economic Identification of the New Middle Class', *Economy and Society* vol. 4, no. 1 (1975).
20 K. Marx and F. Engels, *The Manifesto of the Communist Party* (*1848*), in K. Marx and F. Engels, *Selected Works* (London, 1968), p. 42.
21 See K. Marx, *Capital* vol. I (London, 1960).
22 *Ibid.* p. 320.
23 *Ibid.* p. 364.
24 *Ibid.* p. 478.
25 *Ibid.* pp. 586–7.
26 N. Poulantzas, *op.cit.* (n.2), p. 151.
27 *Ibid.* p. 286.
28 *Ibid.* pp. 285–6.
29 E. O. Wright, *op.cit.* (n.19), ch. 2.
30 *Ibid.* pp. 79–80.
31 The criteria employed by Wright to define class position are derived from an historical analysis of three major changes in capitalist relations of production. The first concerns the loss of control by direct producers over the labour process as a result of the division of labour and technological changes associated with the stage of 'modern industry'. The second involves the separation of 'legal' and 'real' economic ownership, as stocks are dispensed and propertyless managers hired, in large corporations during the stage of monopoly capitalism. Consequently, economic 'possession' (control over the immediate labour process) is separated from economic 'ownership' (control over investments and resource allocation). Third, the functions of economic 'possession' are further differentiated in terms of 'control over the physical means of production' and 'control over labour power'; there is, then, the emergence of specialist managers and supervisory hierarchies. Class relations and class locations may, therefore, be defined according to control over (1) the physical means of production; (2) labour power and (3) investment and resources. See E. O. Wright, *op.cit.* (n.19), pp. 61–83.
32 N. Poulantzas, *op.cit.* (n.2), p. 143.

33 *Ibid.*
34 *Ibid.* p. 147.
35 *Ibid.* p. 140.
36 *Ibid.*
37 E. O. Wright, *op.cit.* (n.19), pp. 79–80.
38 J. Westergaard, 'Class, Inequality and "Corporatism" ', in A. Hunt (ed.), *Class and Class Structure* (London, 1977), p. 168.
39 N. Poulantzas, *op.cit.* (n.2), p. 17.
40 E. O. Wright, *op.cit.* (n.19), p. 10.
41 *Ibid.* pp. 74–5, n. 67.
42 *Ibid.*
43 F. Parkin, 'Social Stratification', in T. Bottomore and R. Nisbet (eds.), *A History of Sociological Analysis* (London, 1978), p. 625.
44 For recent discussions of this distinction and the implications for research into social mobility and class structure, see R. M. Blackburn, 'Social Stratification', unpublished paper presented to the Annual Conference of the British Sociological Association (Lancaster, 1980), and A. Stewart, K. Prandy and R. M. Blackburn, *Social Stratification and Occupations* (London, 1980).
45 N. Poulantzas, *op.cit.* (n.2), p. 329.
46 K. Marx, *op.cit.* (n.21), p. 586.
47 V. I. Lenin, *Collected Works* vol. XXII (London, 1949), p. 70.
48 *Ibid.* vol. XV, p. 39.
49 The few exceptions are the works of A. Friedman, *Industry and Labour* (London, 1977); S. Berger, 'The Uses of the Traditional Sector in Italy', in F. Bechhofer and B. Elliott, *op.cit.* (n.1), and C. Gerry and C. Birkbeck, 'The Petty Commodity Producer in Third World Cities', in F. Bechhofer and B. Elliott *op.cit.* (n.1)
50 S. M. Miller, 'Notes on Neo-Capitalism', *Theory and Society* vol. 2 (1975), p. 15.
51 A. J. Mayer, 'The Lower Middle Class as Historical Problem', *Journal of Modern History* vol. 47 (1975), p. 417.
52 V. I. Lenin, *The Development of Capitalism in Russia* (Moscow, 1956).
53 Most studies of social mobility assume that the main channel for upward mobility is through occupational positions within large-scale bureaucracies on the basis of various kinds of meritocratic criteria. For a recent review of this work see A. Heath, *Social Mobility* (London, 1981).
54 A. J. Mayer, *op.cit.* (n.51), p. 432.
55 For a review of this literature, see J. Boissevain, *op.cit.* (n.10).
56 A recent empirical investigation is reported in H. Aldrich, 'Asian Shopkeepers as a Middleman Minority', in A. Evans and D. Eversley (eds.), *The Inner City: Employment and Industry* (London, 1980).
57 The extension of *real* managerial control over the work process has been of considerable interest to Marxists during the 1970s. Much of this has been stimulated by H. Braverman, *Labor and Monopoly Capital* (New York, 1974).
58 For evidence and a discussion of these attitudes, see R. Scase and R. Goffee ' "Traditional" Petty Bourgeois Attitudes: The Case of Self-Employed Craftsmen', *Sociological Review* vol. 29, no. 4 (1981).
59 See, for example, the *Report of the Committee of Inquiry on Small Firms,*

(The Bolton Report), Cmnd. 4811 (London, H.M.S.O., 1971); and R. Scase and R. Goffee, *The Real World of the Small Business Owner, op.cit.* (n.17).

60 These are discussed in some detail in R. Scase and R. Goffee, *ibid.*

61 Many managers quit corporations because of curtailment of their work autonomy and start their own small businesses. See, R. Scase and R. Goffee, *The Real World of the Small Business Owner, op.cit.* (n.17).

62 See, R. Goffee and R. Scase, 'Fraternalism and Paternalism as Employers' Strategies in Small Firms', paper presented at the Annual Conference of the British Sociological Association (Aberystwyth, 1981).

63 For a discussion of 'high' and 'low trust' work relationships, see A. Fox, *Beyond Contract: Work, Power and Trust Relations* (London, 1974).

64 In the personal services sector, and especially in the general building industry, there has been the rapid growth of labour-only sub-contracting.

65 For a discussion of a typology of self-employed, small employers, owner-controllers and owner-directors see, R. Scase and R. Goffee, *The Real World of the Small Business Owner, op.cit.* (n.17); and more particularly *The Entrepreneurial Middle Class* (London, 1982).

66 Owner-controllers and owner-directors cease to be direct producers and are, instead, solely capitalists and supervisors of labour. According to Marx it is only after this transition that small employers become 'pure' capitalists. To quote, 'Capitalist production only then really begins . . . when each individual capital employs simultaneously a comparatively large number of labourers; when consequently the labour process is carried on an extensive scale and yields, relatively, large quantities of products. A greater number of labourers working together at the same time, in one place (or, if you will, in the same field of labour), in order to produce the same sort of commodity under the mastership of one capitalist, constitutes, both historically and logically, the starting-point of capitalist production . . . the amount of surplus value (thus) produced might suffice to liberate the employer himself from manual labour, to convert him from a small master into a capitalist, and thus formally to establish capitalist production' (K. Marx, *Capital* vol. I (London, 1960), pp. 303, 312).

67 Evidence on these attitudes is to be found in R. King and N. Nugent (eds.), *Respectable Rebels* (Dunton Green, 1979).

68 The self-employed in particular, can be 'agnostic' on some of these issues. See, R. Scase and R. Goffee, ' "Traditional" Petty Bourgeois Attitudes', *op.cit.* (n. 58).

69 F. Bechhofer and B. Elliott, 'The Voice of Small Business and the Politics of Survival', *Sociological Review* vol. 26, no. 1 (1978).

On the service class, its formation and future

1 See Pierre Belleville, *Une Nouvelle Classe Ouvrière* (Paris, 1963); Serge Mallet, *The New Working Class* (Nottingham, 1975); André Gorz, *Strategy for Labor: A Radical Proposal* (Boston, 1967).

2 One of its proponents, Gorz, has clearly changed his own position – cf. 'Technical Intelligence and the Capitalist Division of Labour', *Telos* vol.

12 (1972); and it seems that shortly before his death Mallet was also revising his views.

3 The Ehrenreichs first advanced their thesis in 'The Professional-Managerial Class', *Radical America* vol. 11 (1977), but see also their contributions, including their response to critiques from other left-wing positions, in Pat Walker (ed.), *Between Capital and Labour* (Hassocks, 1979).

4 See G. Carchedi, 'On the Economic Identification of the New Middle Class', *Economy and Society* vol. 4 (1975); E. O. Wright, 'Class Boundaries in Advanced Capitalist Societies', *New Left Review* no. 8 (1976).

5 In a further structuralist Marxist view, that of Nicos Poulantzas, *Classes in Contemporary Capitalism* (London, 1975), professional, administrative and managerial employees are seen as a newly emerging 'fraction' of the petty bourgeoisie – i.e. as having an unproblematic class location; but as exhibiting in their socio-political orientation a basic conflict between their productive and their non-productive (political and ideological) functions within the division of labour. The difficulties involved in linking all such structuralist analyses to the explanation of class action is nowhere more clearly revealed than in the embarrassments of British expositors. See, for example, Terence Johnson, 'What is to be Known: The Structural Determination of Social Class', *Economy and Society* vol. 6 (1977), pp. 199–200 esp. (which would seem to make the remainder of the article redundant), and Rosemary Crompton and Jon Gubbay, *Economy and Class Structure* (London, 1977), pp. 97, 171, 196ff.

6 Cf. Talcott Parsons, 'The Professions', in *International Encyclopaedia of the Social Sciences* (New York, 1968); Clark Kerr, John T. Dunlop, Frederick Harbison and Charles A. Myers, *Industrialism and Industrial Man* (Cambridge, Mass., 1960).

7 Early contributions of major influence appear to have been D. P. Moynihan, 'Equalising Education: In whose Benefit?', *The Public Interest* (Fall, 1972), and Irving Kristol, 'About Equality', *Commentary* (November, 1972). See also, however, the papers collected in B. Bruce-Briggs (ed.), *The New Class?* (New Brunswick, 1979). On the 'new class project' which led to this publication, see the interesting observations in Peter Steinfels, *The Neoconservatives* (New York, 1979).

8 Alvin W. Gouldner, *The Future of Intellectuals and the Rise of the New Class* (London, 1979). Cf. the similar, though more modestly presented, arguments in Michael Harrington, 'The New Class and the Left', in Bruce-Briggs, *op.cit.* (n.7), and also the earlier work of Alain Touraine (which would appear to anticipate a number of Gouldner's arguments), *The Post-Industrial Society* (London, 1974).

9 The difficulties in question have been well brought out by Daniel Bell, who has himself been regarded, rather unfairly, as one of the originators of 'new class' theory. See 'The New Class: A Muddled Concept', in Bruce-Briggs, *op.cit.* (n.7).

10 See Karl Renner, *Wandlungen der modernen Gesellschaft: Zwei Abhandlungen über die Probleme der Nachkriegszeit* (Vienna, 1953). For a translation of the most relevant passage from these essays and useful commentary, see Tom Bottomore and Patrick Goode (eds.), *Austro-Marxism* (Oxford, 1978).

11 The idea of the service class might also, *mutatis mutandis*, prove of value in analysis of present-day communist societies. Cf. Russell Hardin, 'Stability of Statist Regimes: Industrialisation and Institutionalisation', in Tom R. Burns and Walter Buckley (eds.), *Power and Control* (London, 1976).

12 Cf. the discussion of 'discretionary' as distinct from 'prescribed' work and of the 'dynamics of high-trust relations' associated with the former in Alan Fox, *Beyond Contract: Work, Power and Trust Relations* (London, 1974). Attempts by Marxist authors such as Harry Braverman (*Labor and Monopoly Capital* (New York, 1974) to argue that professional, administrative and managerial employees are, in the same way as other grades, having their autonomy and discretion progressively eliminated by the inexorable logic of the capitalist labour process find no consistent support in empirical research. For example, a recent report on a major cross-national study of engineers concludes: 'For the engineer . . . the daily experience of work is one of autonomy.' Allan Silver, Robert Zussman, Peter Whalley and Stephen Crawford, 'Work and Ideology among Engineers: An International Comparison of the "New Working Class" ', paper presented to the Annual Meeting of the American Sociological Association, 1979.

13 Ralf Dahrendorf, 'Recent Changes in the Class Structure of European Societies', *Daedalus* (Winter, 1964).

14 Anthony Giddens, *The Class Structure of the Advanced Societies* (London, 1973), pp. 187–8.

15 As Gouldner has pertinently observed, such internal differentiation of classes is usual and can in no way be seen as precluding the possibility of class-based political action, especially when the nature of this is properly understood: 'For the most part, classes themselves do not enter into active political struggle; the active participants in political struggle are usually organisations, parties, associations, vanguards. Classes are cache areas in which these organisations mobilise, recruit, and conscript support and in whose name they legitimate their struggle' (*op.cit.* (n.8), p. 31).

16 The most important borderline grouping in modern Western societies could be regarded as that made up of those working directors and senior executives of companies who also have a non-negligible ownership interest in their firms, and in whose case it is hard to say how far their positions of control derive from their ownership – as in the case of the classic capitalist entrepreneur – or how far their ownership is the result, and reward, of a successful bureaucratic career.

17 For further discussion of these intermediate groupings, see John H. Goldthorpe (with Catriona Llewellyn and Clive Payne), *Social Mobility and Class Structure in Modern Britain* (Oxford, 1980), pp. 40–1, esp.

18 In other words, while the expansion of the service class must be seen as a response to organisational exigencies and at the same time as being made possible by economic growth, this does not mean that it can be understood as resulting simply from a 'natural' development of the division of labour in the course of economic growth – for example, as following automatically from a sectoral redistribution of the active population according to such mechanisms as those suggested by Clark, Fourastié, Kuznets and other development economists. Rather, the size and the

detailed occupational composition of the service class will, in any particular society, to an important extent reflect organisational and political choices, and in turn thus the structure of organisational and political power and the character of dominant values and ideologies.

19 Comparable data for women, available for France and Sweden, are currently being analysed by Lucienne Portocarero, and show a high level of mobility. So do data for English women (although organised on a somewhat different basis) presented in Anthony Heath, *Social Mobility* (London, 1981), Table 4.2 (after recalculation from outflow to inflow percentages).

20 These analyses are to be presented in a forthcoming paper by Robert Erikson, Lucienne Portocarero and the present author; but cf. also Goldthorpe, *op.cit.* (n.17), ch. 3.

21 Two further points are also brought out here: first, that the exercise of delegated authority can be undertaken with little specialised knowledge or expertise (and, one may add, in a style that suggests little familiarity with 'the culture of critical discourse'); and second, that the extent to which the application of such knowledge and expertise requires a theoretical basis can still be easily exaggerated so far as present-day industry, commerce and administration is concerned.

22 See, for example, Goldthorpe, *op.cit.* (n.17), ch. 5 esp.; Max Haller and Robert W. Hodge, 'Class Structure and Career Mobility of Men and Women', paper presented to the 9th World Congress of Sociology (Uppsala, 1978).

23 In this respect, a major contrast may be noted with the mobility patterns associated with the routine clerical and sales, technical and supervisory occupations which were earlier seen as giving their incumbents an 'intermediate' location between service class and working class. Data from national mobility surveys and monographic studies alike reveal that these are occupations of generally low 'retentiveness': i.e. individuals have a high propensity to be mobile from them to a wide range of other positions.

24 The same result is obtained for French and Swedish women.

25 See, for example, Braverman, *op.cit.* (n.12), and, more specifically, Rosemary Crompton, 'Class Mobility in Modern Britain', *Sociology* vol. 14 (1980) (and also the 'Reply to Crompton' by the present author, *ibid.*).

26 See Goldthorpe, *op.cit.* (n.17), Table 7.9.

27 Cf. *ibid.* pp. 55–7.

28 For example, the data of the Oxford national occupational Mobility Survey reveal (i) that among men found in service-class positions in 1972, around a fifth of *all* those who had entered work in a professional occupation were by 1972 in an administrative or managerial one; and (ii) that of all sons of professionals, 55% were themselves found in professional occupations and 28% in administrative and managerial ones, while for the sons of administrators and managers the corresponding percentages were 49 and 35.

29 Most notably, groupings of professional, administrative and managerial employees come generally close to each other on the 'life-style' scale recently reported by Stewart *et al.*, which is in fact derived from the patterning of friendship choices (see A. Stewart, K. Prandy and R. M. Black-

burn, *Social Stratification and Occupations* (London, 1980), Part I, and very similar results so far emerge from work currently being undertaken on data from the Oxford Mobility Survey by Clyde Mitchell and the present author in which the main relationship analysed is that of 'spare-time associate'.

30 The paradigm case here might be taken as that of the class basis of party political support. The results of careful analysis do however suggest that the 'partisan realignment' now evident in many Western democracies – and in particular greater white-collar support for left-wing parties – is to a significant extent the result of class mobility. For the British case, see Phyllis Thorburn, 'Class, Mobility and Party: the Political Preferences of Englishmen' (unpublished University of Michigan PhD thesis, 1979).

31 In this respect, the present analysis reaches the same conclusion as that of Dahrendorf, although via a rather different line of argument. Cf. *op.cit.* (n.13), pp. 249, 250–1.

32 Frank Parkin, *Marxism and Class Theory: a Bourgeois Critique* (London, 1979), pp. 54–60.

33 Cf. *ibid.* pp. 110–11, and for a recent case-study, Michael P. Kelly, *White-Collar Proletariat: The Industrial Behaviour of British Civil Servants* (London, 1980). While the present analysis does not follow Parkin's recommendation 'that social classes be defined by reference to their mode of collective action rather than to their place in the productive process or the division of labour' (p. 113), it does however strongly underwrite his argument that the tendency of recent Marxist theorists to minimise the importance of distributive aspects of class inequality as a source of division and conflict is a major sociological error.

34 See, for example, in the collection edited by Bruce-Briggs already cited (n.7), the contributions by Peter L. Berger, 'The Worldview of the New Class: Secularity and its Discontents', pp. 52–4 esp., and by Aaron Wildavsky, 'Using Public Funds to serve Private Interests: The Politics of the New Class,' pp. 147–9 esp.; also Gouldner, *op.cit.* (n.8), pp. 58ff. To a large extent, in fact, the arguments in question are a re-run of those used in the 1950s and 1960s by writers such as Bell and Lipset to try to explain periodic upsurges of *right-wing* extremism. Cf., for example, Daniel Bell (ed.), *The New American Right* (New York, 1963).

35 It might also be anticipated that a good deal of the radicalism that does occur will be channelled into 'single issue' movements or into forms – e.g. environmentalism – which avoid direct involvement in questions of class inequalities in distribution or production.

36 See, for example, in the British case Roy Lewis and Angus Maude, *The English Middle Classes* (London, 1949), and *Professional People* (London, 1952).

37 See, for example, Gouldner, *op.cit.* (n.8), pp. 66–70; Harrington, *op.cit.* (n.8), pp. 135–6.

38 For interesting empirical results, see Charles Derber, 'Underemployment and the American Dream – "Underemployment Consciousness" and Radicalism among Young Workers', *Sociological Inquiry* vol. 49 (1979).

The state and the professions: peculiarities of the British

1 Emile Durkheim, *Professional Ethics and Civic Morals* (London, 1957).
2 A. M. Carr-Saunders and P. A. Wilson, *The Professions* (London, 1933).
3 Bob Jessop, 'Remarks on Some Recent Theories of the Capitalist State', *Cambridge Journal of Economics* vol. 1 (1977).
4 Nicos Poulantzas, *Political Power and Social Classes* (London, 1973).
5 Terence Johnson, 'Imperialism and the Professions: Notes on the Development of Professional Occupations in Britain's Colonies and the New States; in Paul Halmos (ed.), *Professionalization and Social Change, Sociological Review Monograph* no. 20 (Keele, 1973).
6 A short discussion of this movement is to be found in Brian Abel-Smith and Robert Stevens, *Lawyers and the Courts* (London, 1967), pp. 32–7, but I am particularly indebted to Derek Crothal who has kindly allowed me to draw upon his unpublished work on the legal profession during this period.
7 See A. Harding, *A Social History of English Law* (London, 1965), pp. 307 – 29.
8 *Fifth Report of the Commissioners Appointed to Inquire into the Practice and Proceedings of the Superior Courts of Common Law,* 3 May 1833, House of Commons, p. 17.
9 Eric Hobsbawm, *Industry and Empire* (London, 1968).
10 Maurice Dobb, *Studies in the Development of Capitalism* (London, 1963).
11 Evgeny Pashukanis, *Law and Marxism: A General Theory* (London, 1978).
12 See G. R. Y. Radcliffe and Rupert Cross in C. J. Hand and D. J. Bentley (eds.), *The English Legal System*[6] (London, 1977), p. 279.
13 The legal journals united in suggesting that the exclusion of attorneys was due to the large number of barristers in the House of Commons, *Law Times* vol. 7 (5 August 1846), p. 442, and *The Legal Observer* vol. 32 (29 August 1846), p. 402.
14 Harding, *op.cit.* (n.7).
15 *House of Commons Sixth Report* vol. 26 (2 May 1934), p. 8.
16 Carr-Saunders and Wilson, *op.cit.* (n.2).
17 Abel-Smith and Stevens, *op.cit.* (n.6), pp. 59–61.
18 The significance of conveyancing is suggested by the *Law Times* vol. 7 (2 May 1846), p. 100, claiming that it was the most profitable branch of lawyers' work, while by 1957 the same journal estimated that conveyancing had become the largest part of most solicitors' practices. *Law Times* vol. 30 (28 November 1857), p. 133.
19 This section is based on material deriving from a S.S.R.C. funded project on the professions in Commonwealth countries.
20 See Paul Vaughan, *Doctors' Commons* (London, 1959), pp. 56–88, and E. J. Muirhead Little, *A History of the British Medical Association, 1832–1936* (London, 1937), pp. 141–59.
21 The right to private practice was established in 1773. The Act XIII, Geo. III, Cap 63, provided that no person holding civil or military office under the Crown should accept any gratuity, but section 25 made an exception of persons '. . . who shall carry on or exercise the profession of a counsellor at law, a physician, or a surgeon, or being a chaplain'. Those colo-

nial doctors who had no access to private patients were, however, willing to surrender this statutory right in lieu of salary increase.

22 These variations are considered in some detail in T. J. Johnson and Marjorie Caygill, *Community in the Making: Aspects of Britain's Role in the Development of Professional Education in the Commonwealth* (Institute of Commonwealth Studies, University of London, 1972), pp. 132–46.

23 See T. J. Johnson and Marjorie Caygill, 'The British Medical Association and its Overseas Branches: A Short History', *Journal of Imperial and Commonwealth History* vol. 1 (1973), pp. 308–9.

24 See T. J. Johnson and Marjorie Caygill, 'The Development of Accountancy Links in the Commonwealth', in R. H. Parker (ed.), *Readings in Accounting and Business Research, 1970–77* (London, 1978), pp. 156–62.

25 See T. J. Johnson and Marjorie Caygill, 'The Royal Institute of British Architects and the Commonwealth Profession', *Working Paper* no. 5 (Institute of Commonwealth Studies, London, 1972), pp. 30–1.

26 These bodies will be referred to as the 'Society' and 'Association'.

27 The movements for recognition and registration in Britain are outlined by N. A. H. Stacey, *English Accountancy: A Study in Social and Economic History* (London, 1954).

28 A detailed examination of the empire involvement of these accountancy associations is to be found in Johnson and Caygill, *op.cit.* (n.24).

29 For an indication of the extent of the overseas operations of British accountancy firms see Johnson and Caygill, *op.cit.* (n.22), pp. 147–66.

30 Letter to the *Cape Times* quoted in the *Certified Accountant's Journal* vol. 16 (1924), p. 197.

31 *The Accountant* vol. 1 (1914), pp. 403–5.

32 *Ibid.* vol. 39 (1908), p. 602.

33 For a more detailed discussion of the development of the architectural and other professions in the colonies see Johnson, *op.cit.* (n.5).

34 For a full account of examination centres see Johnson and Caygill, *op.cit.* (n.24), pp. 159–62.

35 *Ibid.* pp. 162–6.

36 Johnson and Caygill, *op.cit.* (n.25), pp. 38–40.

37 *Ibid.* pp. 36–47.

38 Quoted in B. L. Barrington Kaye, *The Development of the Architectural Profession in Britain: A Sociological Study* (London, 1960), p. 157.

Divisions within the dominant class and British 'exceptionalism'

1 For the most important and recent contributions to the debate, see: Perry Anderson, 'Origins of the Present Crisis', in *Towards Socialism* (London, 1965); Tom Nairn, 'The Decline of the British State', *New Left Review* nos. 101–102 (Feb/April 1977), and 'Britain's Perennial Crisis', *New Left Review* nos. 113–14 (Jan/April 1979); W. D. Rubinstein, 'Wealth, Elites and the Class Structure of Modern Britain', *Past and Present*, vol. 76 (August 1977); Frank Longstreth, 'The City, Industry and the State', in C. Crouch (ed.), *State, Economy and Contemporary Capitalism* (London, 1979).

2 See Geoffrey K. Ingham, *Capitalism Divided* (London, forthcoming).

3 For a summary of the relevant data, see P. L. Cottrell, *British Overseas*

Investment in the Nineteenth Century (London, 1975). The issue is discussed fully in Ingham, *Capitalism Divided*, ch. 2.

4 Anderson, *op.cit.* (n.1), has referred to the 'aristocratic coloration of the City' which has survived since the pre-industrial era and Rubinstein, *op.cit.* (n.1), sees the emergence in the late nineteenth century of an elite 'dominated by the South of England and finance, with its London-based associates of great influence'. In Nairn's recent essays, *op.cit.* (n.1), the association of the aristocracy with the City's spectacularly successful profit-making activities provides the 'material' underpinning for the *New Left Review* thesis that part of British 'exceptionalism' consists in the persistence of traditional pre-industrial political and cultural forms. The argument that English culture is inimical to dynamic industrial capitalism is a familiar one (see Martin J. Wiener, *English Culture and the Decline of the Industrial Spirit* (Cambridge, 1981), for the latest contribution). The significance of the City is that it provided the wealth for aristocratic culture in a way which enabled it to remain isolated from industry. The view that the late nineteenth century witnessed a fusion of 'traditional' and industrial elites – for example in P. Stanworth and A. Giddens, *Elites and the British Class Structure* (Cambridge, 1974), pp. 99–101 – is vastly overdrawn. For a critique of this position, see Ingham, *Capitalism Divided*.

5 Nairn, 'The Decline', pp. 11–12.

6 Karl Marx, *Capital* vol. III (London, 1960), p. 327. See also 'The Elections – Tories and Whigs', *New York Daily Tribune*, 21 August 1852; 'The Chartists', *New York Daily Tribune*, 25 August 1852, in T. B. Bottomore and Maximillien Rubel, *Karl Marx: Selected Writings in Sociology and Social Philosophy* (London, 1956), pp. 191–200. In referring to the Whig landed oligarchy, Marx wrote: 'After 1688 we find them united with the Bankocracy, just then rising into importance, as we find them in 1846, united with the Millocracy' (p. 194). In the second article, Marx argues that the industrial bourgeoisie compromised with the aristocracy through their need of an ally against the emerging working class; that is, whatever aristocratic power remains is, as it were, by permission of the manufacturers. This view is, I believe, largely erroneous and has diverted successive historians and social scientists away from forming a more accurate picture of the distribution and exercise of political power in Britain.

7 See Ingham, *Capitalism Divided*, ch. 5, for an analysis of the political reproduction and manifestation of the City–industry separation.

8 Nairn, 'Perennial Crisis', p. 52. At what point, one might ask, does the historically specific model Nairn has in mind part company with the Marxist concept of the capitalist mode of production? Surely, this concept is definitively central to Marx's social theory in the sense that the constitutive class relations of the C.M.P. – that is, those between productive capital and exploited labour – comprise the human agency through and by which social and economic transformation takes place.

9 Nairn, 'The Decline', p. 12.

10 Longstreth, *op.cit.* (n.1), p. 184.

11 *Ibid.* p. 159.

12 *Ibid.* p. 186.

13 See W. D. Rubinstein, *Men of Property* (London, 1981).

14 Rubinstein, *op.cit.* (n.1), p. 126. Earlier in the same passage Rubinstein

attempts the following theoretical modification of Marxism: 'It is a logical fallacy to infer from the central importance of industrial capitalism in the dialectical process the central importance of industrial capitalism for the bourgeoisie.' If this statement means anything it is that the 'dialectical process' may proceed *independently* of the actions of that class which has supposedly revolutionised the forces and relations of production and whose removal is a pre-condition for the transition to socialism. To distort Marx's writings in this way merely betrays the seriousness of Britain's so-called 'exceptionalism' for his theory of social development.

15 To take one example, Nairn, 'The Decline', believes that the aristocracy simply moved into the City when the opportunity arose, in the late nineteenth century, and ignores the wholesale ennobling of City bankers and merchants in the early part of this century; the connection between the aristocracy and the City's speculative commercial and financial ventures in the eighteenth century; and the fact that the vast majority of the brokers' clients for government stock during this early period were the landed governing classes.

16 As Clarke, among others, has argued, unless political conflict between the so-called 'fractions' of capital can be reduced to their inherent and general economic relations which exist independently of their particular or temporary expression in concrete circumstances, then a 'fraction' is simply a misleading *descriptive* term for a 'pressure group', or the like, whose existence is determined by other conditions – the narrowly political or ideological – and whose relations are the product of contingency. Clarke has, in fact, argued – by means of an exegesis of Marx's treatment of the forms of capital – that the 'fractionalist' enterprise is inherently misconceived as total social capital comprises an *integration* of the circuits of the various forms of capital. However, as we shall see, this conclusion is reached by smoothing over the ambivalence and uncertainty in Marx's treatment of the problem which is particularly evident in volume III of *Capital*. See Simon Clarke, 'Capital, Fractions of Capital and the State: "Neo-Marxist" Analyses of the South African State,' *Capital and Class* no. 5 (Summer, 1978) 32–77.

17 Rubinstein quite uncritically accepts William M. Clarke's argument (*The City in the World Economy* (London, 1967) that the City became heavily involved in domestic industry during the 1930s. A closer inspection of the period shows how the world recession forced the City to look to British industry but that this was only a temporary flirtation. The banks and finance companies were only concerned to nurse industry to health in order that its equity could find willing buyers on the Stock Exchange. No finance-capital along German or American lines emerged or has done since. Clarke's book was written when he was editor of *The Banker* and he subsequently became Deputy Chairman of the City Communications Centre. For an account of these developments in the 1930s which generally defends the British financial system but points out the absence of close finance–industry links, see: W. A. Thomas, *The Finance of British Industry, 1914–1976* (London, 1978).

18 Ironically, this diagnosis is similar to the City's own neo-classical defence of its activities – but with the direction of causation reversed. City apol-

ogists and official enquiries – the majority Wilson Report, for example – have argued that the low productivity of industry is not attractive to investors.

19 See Robert Gilpin, *U.S. Power and the Multinational Corporation: The Political Economy of Foreign Direct Investment* (London, 1976), especially ch. 3, 'The British Strategy of Portfolio Investment', for an explicit contrast of the two modes of overseas investment. Furthermore, one of the major problems in conceptualising British overseas investment as part of a finance-capital imperialism is the fact that there was virtually no correlation between the areas which received the capital and those which were formally part of the Empire. See D. K. Fieldhouse, *Economics and Empire, 1830–1914* (London, 1973), p. 54.

20 See the data in Peter Mathias, *The First Industrial Nation* (London, 1969), p. 305.

21 *Capital* vol. III (London, 1960), p. 337.

22 *Capital* vol. I (London, 1960), p. 266. Marx refers to *merchant* capital, in general, and distinguishes commercial and *money-dealing* capital within this form. In my treatment of the structure of British capitalism, I have used *commercial* capital as the general form of profit-making through the repeated and continuous buying and selling of commodities (including money), and have therefore continued to use this term in the present analysis rather than the archaic *merchant* capital of Marx's work. See *Capital* vol. I (London, 1960), ch. 4; and vol. III (London, 1960), p. 267, for Marx's distinctions.

23 For two general accounts of Marx's analysis of money – the first exegetical and the second critical – see: Suzanne de Brunhof, *Marx on Money* (New York, 1976), and Anthony Cutler *et al.*, *Marx's Capital and Capitalism Today* vol. II, 1 (London, 1971).

24 Grahame Thompson, 'Financial and Industrial Sector in the United Kingdom Economy', *Economy and Society* vol. 6 (1977), p. 250.

25 Max Weber, *Economy and Society* vol. I (New York, 1968), p. 161.

26 The following account is of necessity brief and illustrative rather than exhaustive. For a fuller treatment see Ingham, *Capitalism Divided.*

27 The London houses were greatly helped in this activity by having the Bank of England act as lender of last resort in times of crisis for themselves but not their provincial competitors.

28 In Thompson's terminology, *op.cit.* (n.24), commercial capitalists possess a *realisationist* ideology – i.e. they are oriented to rapid turnover of commodities – as opposed to the *consolidationist* ideology of bankers which refers to their concern with maintaining the value of money wealth and the accumulationist ideology of industrial capital. Strictly speaking, Thompson is not referring to *ideologies* but *practices*. Furthermore, he concludes that the ideology of banking capital is dominant in the British economy whereas, as I would wish to argue, *commercial* practices are dominant in the City banking and financial sectors.

29 For the post-1945 period see, for example: J. R. Sargent, 'U.K. Performance in Services', in Frank Blackaby (ed.), *De-industrialisation* (London, 1979), pp. 102–23. Of course, the recent abolition of exchange controls has once again led to a rapid and marked increase in the export of capital.

30 W. D. Rubinstein, *op.cit.* (n.13).
31 Barrington Moore, Jr, *Social Origins of Dictatorship and Democracy* (London, 1966).
32 It is significant that the only other country to possess a central bank at this time was Sweden which similarly had a relatively weak aristocracy, a constitutional monarchy and, if not a powerful mercantile bourgeoisie, then a politically and economically strong freeholding peasantry.
33 See Ingham, *Capitalism Divided*. These and the counter-arguments are briefly presented in the Wilson Report (1980), chs. 13, 15, 19 and 20.
34 See Richard Minns, *Pension Funds and British Capitalism* (London, 1980). The orientation of this practice is clearly realisationist: the making of rapid profits through buying and selling of securities.
35 As many writers have recently pointed out the gold standard was in reality a gold-based sterling standard. See David Williams, 'The Evolution of the Sterling System', in C. R. Whittlesey and J. S. G. Williams, *Essays in Money and Banking: in Honour of R. S. Sayers* (Oxford, 1968), 266–97.
36 For a survey of the events see Longstreth (1979).
37 See *Capital*, vol.III ch. 36, 'Pre-Capitalist Relationships'. Marx clearly means pre-*productive* capital or pre-industrial; but this terminological confusion is symptomatic of his inability to grasp the extent to which, under conditions which prevailed after the mid-nineteenth century – in his own words: 'Usury, like commerce, exploits a given mode of production,' (vol.III, p. 609).
38 *Capital* vol.I, p. 267.
39 *Capital* vol.III, p. 327.
40 *Capital* vol.III, p. 328.
41 *Capital* vol.III, pp. 326–7.
42 *Capital* vol.III, p. 275.
43 *Capital* vol.III, p. 286.
44 See John Urry, *The Anatomy of Capitalist Societies* (London, 1981).
45 See, for example, Cutler *et al.*, *op.cit.* (n.23). 'Marxism has consistently neglected "national" economies as units of analysis, rejecting the economic-policy standpoint of mercantilism and classical political economy. Marxists argue that phenomenon at this level merely create the basis for theoretical illusions and obscure the reality of capitalism as a general phenomenon. Thus, while nations may obtain wealth through merchants' capitalist trade they merely redistribute the values produced and in no way add to that totality' (p. 244). It need scarcely be mentioned that I entirely endorse this view.
46 *Capital* vol.III, p. 598.
47 *Capital* vol.III, p. 460.
48 *Capital* vol.I, p. 243.
49 *Capital* vol.III, p. 516.
50 *Capital* vol.III, p. 545.
51 *Capital* vol.I, p. 188.
52 Cutler *et al.*, *op.cit.* (n.23), p. 86.
53 Rondo Cameron's conclusion to his chapter on England in *Banking in the Early Stages of Industrialisation: A Comparative Study* (Oxford, 1967), pp. 15–59.
54 Max Weber, *Economy and Society*, p. 166.

55 *Ibid.* p. 168.
56 *Ibid.* p. 172.
57 Karl Marx, *A Contribution to the Critique of Political Economy* (Moscow, 1970), p. 119.
58 Space does not permit a full analysis of the political determination of the domestic gold standard in nineteenth-century Britain and I shall restrict myself to two brief comments. First, all the evidence points to the fact that the requirements of production were scarcely considered and when Midlands' industrialists objected to the deflationary consequences of the monetary restrictions caused by the rigid gold standard they were completely ignored. Secondly, although the City was later to defend the gold standard as the pivot of their international activities, the major impetus for the monetary legislation came from within the state itself. The main intention was to free the state from the 'moneyed powers' in the City by removing the inflation and massive National Debt which the Napoleonic Wars had spawned. It was argued that a supposedly automatic or 'natural' monetary system based on gold could not be easily manipulated by the operators of the London money markets. Moreover, the solution was also an effective compromise as the money-dealers and financiers were similarly satisfied that the gold standard would prevent the discretionary printing of money by the state to meet its own financial requirements and, therefore, pre-empt the administrative fiscalisation of free market relations. In many ways, the policies of the radical Tories in the 1820s are remarkably similar to the ones pursued by the present Conservatives (1979–   ).
59 Marx may not have been aware of the continued expansion of Britain's commercial roles but others who were closer to the City's activities and in a position to encourage these obviously were. For example, during the proceedings of the 1832 committee on the Bank of England Charter, Nathan Rothschild observed that bills-of-exchange on London were being used to finance trade which never passed through England and that 'this country in general is the Bank for the whole world . . . all transactions in India, China, in Germany, in Russia, and in the whole world are guided here and settled through this country'. (Quoted in Wilfred King, *History of the London Discount Market* (London, 1936), p. 264.) Fourteen years earlier, Huskisson – President of the Board of Trade – whose economic reforms and pursuit of free trade are generally and misleadingly considered to be primarily in the interests of northern industrialists, argued that Britain had only to restore and strengthen the domestic gold standard, repeal 'those universally exploded laws' forbidding free trade in bullion and, then, 'the extent of our commercial dealings and operations of exchange, which make this country the Emporium not only of Europe but of America, North and South, . . . would make London the chief Bullion market of the world'. (Quoted in Boyd Hilton, *Cash, Corn and Commerce: The Economic Policies of Tory Governments, 1815–1830* (Oxford, 1977).)
60 See Boyd Hilton, *op.cit.* (n.59), on the speculative nature of the City's activities in the eighteenth and early nineteenth centuries.
61 See Max Weber, *Economy and Society* p. 159, for the distinction between 'rational' and 'speculative' commerce and p. 164 for his definitions of the

'Principal Modes of Capitalistic Orientation of Profit-Making'. The use-fulness of Weber's classification for the understanding of the City in the British economy is discussed in Ingham, *Capitalism Divided.*

62 *London as an International Banking Centre.* Evidence from the British Bank-ers' Association for the Committee to Review the Functioning of Finan-cial Institutions (London, 1977), p. 3.

Property and control: some remarks on the British propertied class

1 This paper draws upon research supported by the Social Science Research Council under grant number HR 6992. The research is part of a broader international project sponsored by the European Consortium for Political Research. I am grateful to Charlotte Kitson and Catherine Griff for research assistance and to my colleagues in the ECPR group and Catherine Griff for their help in the clarification of some of the ideas in this paper. Infor-mation is drawn from project files as well as from the specific sources given below.

2 On the notion of a 'service class' see Goldthorpe in this volume.

3 J. A. Rex, 'Capitalism, Elites, and the Ruling Class', in P. Stanworth and A. Giddens (eds.), *Elites and Power in British Society* (Cambridge, 1974).

4 T. Veblen, *The Theory of the Leisure Class* (New York, 1953; originally published 1899).

5 M. Weber, *The Protestant Ethic and the Spirit of Capitalism* (London, 1971; originally 1905).

6 G. Carchedi, *On the Economic Identification of Social Classes* (London, 1977).

7 Some of these features of capitalist production are discussed further in J. Scott, *Corporations, Classes and Capitalism* (London, 1979). The general characteristics of the British propertied class are taken up in my forth-coming book on this subject.

8 D. B. Massey and A. Catalano, *Capital and Land* (London, 1978). W. D. Rubinstein, 'Wealth, Elites, and the Class Structure of Modern Britain', *Past and Present* vol. 70 (1976). See also Ingham in this volume.

9 This is elaborated more fully in Scott, *op.cit.* (n.7), especially ch. 5.

10 P. S. Florence, *The Logic of British and American Industry* (London, 1972; originally published 1953), pp. 203–11. In this paper the terms corpora-tion and company will be used interchangeably.

11 Florence, *op.cit.* (n.10), pp. 213ff.

12 Tube Investments and Stewarts and Lloyds entered into such a liaison scheme to coordinate their steel tube businesses in 1930. Similarly, Brad-ford Dyers and British Cotton and Wool Dyers entered into a liaison scheme in the textile industry.

13 The exception would be, for example, a private foundation separate from the corporation. Such exceptions are rare and are normally associated directly with a particular corporate board.

14 R. E. Pahl and J. T. Winkler, 'The Economic Elite: Theory and Practice', in Stanworth and Giddens, *op.cit.* (n.3).

15 *Ibid.* pp. 105–8.

16 *Ibid.* pp. 113–14.

17 R. A. Gordon, *Business Leadership in the Large Corporation* (Berkeley, 1961; originally published 1945), p. 5.

18 *Ibid*. Gordon tends to use 'business leaders' and 'management' inter-changeably. I prefer to use the latter term in the more restricted sense of the executives and their subordinates. The degree of overlap between 'management' and the leadership group therefore becomes an empirical question.

19 Scott, *op.cit.* (n.7), p. 137.

20 Gordon, *op.cit.* (n.17), pp. 50–1; Scott, *op.cit.* (n.7), pp. 36–7.

21 Gordon, *op.cit.*(n.17), p. 79. A. D. Chandler, *Strategy and Structure* (Cambridge, Mass., 1962).

22 See a particularly strong statement of this view in J. Winkler, 'The Corporatist Economy: Theory and Administration', in R. Scase (ed.), *Industrial Society* (London, 1977). Some of the general issues in the debate over corporatism can be found in P. C. Schmitter and G. Lehmbruch, *Trends Towards Corporatist Intermediation* (London, 1979).

23 J. Pennings, *Interlocking Directorates* (San Francisco, 1980).

24 Gordon includes 'minor executives' alongside the top executives. As I have argued, the former are not normally involved in strategic decisions and they will, therefore, be disregarded here.

25 In recent years, British companies have begun to call this post 'Chief Executive', but this is by no means universal. In the USA the designation 'President' is still most common. The board may also include Chairmen and Vice-Chairmen who have part-time executive positions.

26 Pahl and Winkler, *loc. cit.* (n.14), p. 109.

27 *Ibid*. See also Florence, *op.cit.* (n.10), pp. 241ff.

28 In some companies the division of function between executive and non-executive directors is being formalised by constituting the latter as an audit committee or finance committee, which meets as a sub-committee of the board and aims to scrutinise executive actions.

29 J. K. Galbraith, *The New Industrial State* (Harmondsworth, 1974; originally published 1967).

30 W. J. Reader, *Imperial Chemical Industries* (Oxford, 1970).

31 Florence, *op. cit.* (n.10), pp. 221ff.

32 Ideally, such an analysis would refer not only to both voting and non-voting capital, but also to loans and bonds. However, this information is not generally available and there are no accepted procedures for handling such information as is available. In this discussion, therefore, I concentrate on ordinary shareholdings.

33 Gordon, *op.cit.* (n.17), p. 167.

34 *Ibid*. p. 180.

35 *Ibid*. p. 185.

36 See J. Scott and M. Hughes, *The Anatomy of Scottish Capital* (London, 1980).

37 Gordon, *op.cit.* (n.17), p. 191.

38 R. Minns, *Pension Funds and British Capitalism* (London, 1980).

39 M. Zeitlin, 'On Class Theory of the Large Corporation', *American Journal of Sociology* vol. 81 (1976).

The division of labour, incomes policy and industrial democracy

1 Barbara Wootton, *The Social Foundations of Wages Policy* (London, 1955).
2 Lord Bullock, *Report of the Committee of Inquiry on Industrial Democracy* Cmnd 6706 (London, 1977).
3 Samuel Brittain, 'The Futility of British Incomes Policy', *Challenge* (May–June 1979), pp. 5–13; Samuel Brittain and Peter Lilley, *The Delusion of Incomes Policy* (London, 1977).
4 Leo Panich, *Social Democracy and Industrial Militancy* (Cambridge, 1976); 'Trade Unions and the Capitalist State', *New Left Review* no. 123 (1981).
5 Stuart Holland, *The Socialist Challenge* (London, 1975); CSE, *The Alternative Economic Strategy* (London, 1980); Sam Aaronovitch, *The Road from Thatcherism* (London, 1981).
6 See David Purdy, 'The Left's Alternative Economic Strategy', *Politics and Power*, vol. 1 (1980).
7 Barbara Wootton, *Incomes Policy* (London, 1974).
8 *Ibid.*; Hugh Clegg, *How to Run an Incomes Policy* (London, 1971).
9 Barbara Wootton, *Incomes Policy*.
10 John Elliot, *Conflict or Co-operation* (London, 1978).
11 Bullock Report, p. 39.
12 This essay is a revised version of a much longer discussion of the same issues – 'On Struggle in the Enterprise', published in Mike Prior (ed.), *The Popular and the Political* (London, 1981).

The political role of the working class in Western Europe

1 Tom Bottomore, 'Class and Politics in Western Europe' (1971). Reprinted in Tom Bottomore, *Sociology as Social Criticism* (London, 1975).
2 Many of the data on party membership (and subsequently on voting support) are taken from the summaries of party publications and of election statistics given in William E. Paterson and Alastair H. Thomas (eds.), *Social Democratic Parties in Western Europe* (London, 1975).
3 Ivor Crewe, Bo Särlvik and James Alt, 'Partisan Dealignment in Britain 1964–1974', *British Journal of Political Science* vol.7 (1977), p. 129.
4 *Ibid.* p. 136.
5 *Ibid.* p. 181.
6 See the essays in Paterson and Thomas, *op.cit.* (n.2), especially those on Sweden and Austria. In the case of Sweden, Richard Scase remarks that '. . . since 1956 the Social Democratic Party has never failed to obtain at least 69 per cent of the votes of industrial manual workers (and) in elections during the 1960s the level of support . . . was around 80 per cent' (p. 327). This illustrates a more general point made by Erik Allardt, and cited in my earlier essay (Bottomore, *op.cit.* (n.1), p. 119), that in the Scandinavian countries since the war class membership has become increasingly important in voting and working-class voters have been more apt to vote for workers' parties.
7 This situation, as is most evident in France, may be a major factor in keeping the left out of power.
8 Rudolf Hilferding, *Das historische Problem.* Unfinished manuscript (1941) first published, with an introduction by Benedikt Kautsky, in *Zeitschrift*

für Politik (new series) vol.1 (1954); part translation in Tom Bottomore (ed.), *Modern Interpretations of Marx* (Oxford, 1981).

9 Nicos Poulantzas, *Classes in Contemporary Capitalism* (London, 1975), pp. 14ff.

10 Though this would need to be argued more fully. For an illuminating analysis of the concept of 'interest' in relation to Marxist theory, see Ted Benton, ' "Objective" Interests and the Sociology of Power', *Sociology* vol. 15, 2 (1981), pp. 161–84.

11 Karl Marx, 'Contribution to the Critique of Hegel's Philosophy of Right. Introduction' (1844). English trans. in Tom Bottomore (ed.), *Karl Marx: Early Writings* (London, 1963), pp. 55–6.

12 Alain Touraine, *L'Après-Socialisme* (Paris, 1980), pp. 11–12. Touraine seems to conceive a new radicalism based upon the social movements of the 1960s as taking the place of socialism, but this radicalism – as a doctrine and a programme – has not yet assumed a very precise shape.

13 George Konrád and Ivan Szelényi, *The Intellectuals on the Road to Class Power* (Brighton, 1979), p. 222.

14 See William Robson, *Welfare State and Welfare Society* (London, 1976).

15 Walter Korpi, *The Working Class in Welfare Capitalism* (London, 1978).

16 See the excellent discussion of this question in Stanislaw Ossowski, *Class Structure in the Social Consciousness* (London, 1963), ch.5, especially pp. 73–4, 82–3.

17 Lewis Minkin and Patrick Seyd, in Paterson and Thomas, *op.cit.* (n.2), pp. 111–12.

18 *Ibid.* p. 135.

19 As long ago as 1910 Hilferding, in *Finance Capital* (1910), English trans. (London, 1981), drew attention to the backwardness of British capitalism, which is widely recognised today as a long process of deindustrialisation. There is a good account of the pre-eminent position of the commercial and landed elites well into the 20th century, and the eventual emergence of a single elite 'dominated by the South of England and finance', in W. D. Rubinstein, 'Wealth, Elites and the Class Structure of Modern Britain', *Past and Present* vol.76 (1977); and an interesting analysis of cultural and political anti-industrialism in Britain in Martin J. Wiener, *English Culture and the Decline of the Industrial Spirit* (Cambridge, 1981).

20 This question, however, needs to be studied much more fully. Few scholars, so far as I am aware, have tried to provide a rigorous explanation; and one attempt, by Stanley Pierson, *Marxism and the Origins of British Socialism* (Ithaca, N.Y., 1973), seems to me to misinterpret the situation completely, because of its erroneous view of the development of Marxism in general.

Bibliography

Aaronovitch, S., *The Road from Thatcherism* (London, 1981).

Abel-Smith, B. & Stevens, R., *Lawyers and the Courts* (London, 1967).

Accountant, vol. 1 (1914) and vol. 39 (1908).

Acker, J., 'Women and Social Stratification: A Case of Intellectual Sexism', *American Journal of Sociology* vol. 78 (1973).

Aitken, H. G. J., *Taylorism at Watertown Arsenal* (Cambridge, Mass., 1960).

Albrow, M., *Bureaucracy* (London, 1970).

Aldrich, H., 'Asian Shopkeepers as a Middleman Minority', in A. Evans and D. Eversley (eds.), *The Inner City: Employment and Industry* (London, 1980).

Allen, S., 'Invisible Threads', *Institute of Development Studies Bulletin* vol. 12 (1981).

Althusser, L. & Balibar, E., *Reading Capital* (London, 1970).

Anderson, M., 'The Relevance of Family History', in C. Harris (ed.), *The Sociology of the Family: New Directions for Britain*, Sociological Review Monograph no. 28 (Keele, 1979).

Anderson, P., 'Origins of the Present Crisis', in *Towards Socialism* (London, 1965).

Aronowitz, S., *False Promises* (New York, 1973).

Aronowitz, S., 'Marx, Braverman, and the Logic of Capital', *Insurgent Sociologist* vol. 8 (1978).

Ashton, D. N., 'The Transition from School to Work: Notes on the Development of Different Frames of Reference among Young Male Workers', *Sociological Review* vol. 21 (1973).

Ashton, D. N., 'From School to Work: Some Problems of Adjustment Experienced by Young Male Workers', in P. Brannen (ed.), *Entering the World of Work: Some Sociological Perspectives* (London, 1975).

Avineri, S., *The Social and Political Thought of Karl Marx* (Cambridge, 1968).

Axelos, K., *Alienation, Praxis and Techné in the Thought of Karl Marx* (Austin, Texas, 1976).

Bailey, F. G., *Caste and the Economic Frontier* (Manchester, 1957).

Balazs, E., *Chinese Civilization and Bureaucracy* (New Haven, 1964).

Barrett, M., *Women's Oppression Today: Problems in Marxist Feminist Analysis* (London, 1980).

Bechhofer, F., 'Occupations', in M. Stacey (ed.), *Comparability in Social Research* (London, 1969).

316

Bechhofer, F. & Elliott, B., 'Persistence and Change: The Petite Bourgeoisie in the Industrial Society', *European Journal of Sociology* vol. 17 (1976).

Bechhofer, F. & Elliott, B., 'The Voice of Small Business and the Politics of Survival', *Sociological Review* vol. 26 (1978).

Bechhofer, F. & Elliott, B., 'Petty Property: The Survival of a Moral Economy', in F. Bechhofer and B. Elliott (eds.), *The Petite Bourgeoisie: Comparative Studies of the Uneasy Stratum* (London, 1981).

Bechhofer, F. & Elliott, B. (eds.), *The Petite Bourgeoisie: Comparative Studies of the Uneasy Stratum* (London, 1981).

Bechhofer, B., Elliott, B., Rushforth, M. & Bland, R., 'The Petite Bourgeoisie in the Class Structure: The Case of the Small Shopkeepers', in F. Parkin (ed.), *The Social Analysis of Class Structure* (London, 1974).

Bechhofer, F., Elliott, B., Rushforth, M. & Bland, R., 'Small Shopkeepers: Matters of Money and Meaning', *Sociological Review* vol. 22 (1974).

Beechey, V., 'Women and Production: A Critical Analysis of Some Sociological Theories of Women's Work', in A. Kuhn and A. Wolpe (eds.), *Feminism and Materialism* (London, 1978).

Bell, D. (ed.), *The New American Right* (New York, 1963).

Bell, D., 'The New Class: A Muddled Concept', in B. Bruce-Briggs (ed.), *The New Class?* (New Brunswick, 1979).

Belleville, P., *Une Nouvelle Classe Ouvrière* (Paris, 1963).

Bendix, R., *Max Weber: An Intellectual Portrait* (New York, 1960).

Bendix, R., *Work and Authority in Industry* (New York, 1963).

Berger, P. L., 'The Worldview of the New Class: Secularity and its Discontents', in B. Bruce-Briggs (ed.), *The New Class?* (New Brunswick, 1979).

Berger, S., 'The Uses of the Traditional Sector in Italy', in F. Bechhofer and B. Elliott (eds.), *The Petite Bourgeoisie: Comparative Studies of the Uneasy Stratum* (London, 1981).

Berreman, G. D., 'Caste in India and the United States', *American Journal of Sociology* vol. 65 (1960).

Béteille, A., *Caste, Class and Power* (Berkeley, 1965).

Béteille, A., *Castes Old and New* (Bombay, 1969).

Birmingham, W., Neustadt, I. & Omaboe, E. N. (eds.), *A Study of Contemporary Ghana*, vol. I, *The Economy of Ghana* (London, 1966).

Birmingham, W., Neustadt, I. & Omaboe, E. N. (eds.), *A Study of Contemporary Ghana*, vol. II, *Some Aspects of Social Structure* (London, 1967).

Blackaby, F. (ed.), *De-Industrialisation* (London, 1979).

Blackburn, R. M., 'Social Stratification', unpublished paper presented to the Annual Conference of the British Sociological Association (Lancaster, 1980).

Blackburn, R. M. & Mann, M., *The Working Class in the Labour Market* (London, 1979).

Bland, R., Elliott, B. & Bechhofer, F., 'Social Mobility in the Petite Bourgeoisie', *Acta Sociologica* vol. 21 (1978).

Blau, P. M., *The Dynamics of Bureaucracy* (Chicago, 1955).

Boardman, E. P., 'Millenary Aspects of the Taiping Rebellion 1851–64', *Comparative Studies in Society and History* Suppl. 2 (The Hague, 1962).

Bocock, R., Hamilton, P., Thompson, K. & Waton, A. (eds.), *An Introduction to Sociology* (London, 1980).

Boissevain, J., 'Small Entrepreneurs in Changing Europe: Towards a Research

Agenda', unpublished paper presented to the European Centre for Work and Society (Utrecht, 1980).

Bornat, J., 'Home and Work. A New Context for Trade Union History', *Radical America* vol. 12 (1978).

Bottomore, T. B., *Karl Marx: Early Writings* (New York, 1964).

Bottomore, T. B., 'Socialism and the Division of Labour', in B. Parekh (ed.), *The Concept of Socialism* (London, 1975).

Bottomore, T. B., *Sociology as Social Criticism* (London, 1975).

Bottomore, T. B. & Goode, P. (eds.), *Austro-Marxism* (Oxford, 1978).

Bottomore, T. B. & Rubel, M., *Karl Marx: Selected Writings in Sociology and Social Philosophy* (London, 1956).

Braverman, H., *Labor and Monopoly Capital: The Degradation of Work in the Twentieth Century* (New York, 1974).

British Bankers' Association, *London as an International Banking Centre* (London, 1977).

Brittain, S., 'The Futility of British Incomes Policy', *Challenge* (May–June 1979).

Brittain, S. & Lilley, P., *The Delusion of Incomes Policy* (London, 1977).

Brown, R. K., 'Sources of Objectives in Work and Employment', in J. Child (ed.), *Man and Organization* (London, 1973).

Bruce-Briggs, B. (ed.), *The New Class?* (New Brunswick, 1979).

Bulmer, M. (ed.), *Working Class Images of Society* (London, 1975).

Burawoy, M., 'Towards a Marxist Theory of the Labor Process', *Politics and Society* vol. 8 (1978).

Burawoy, M., *Manufacturing Consent: Changes in the Labor Process under Monopoly Capitalism* (Chicago, 1979).

Burns, T. & Stalker, G. M., *The Management of Innovation* (London, 1961).

Burridge, K., *New Heaven, New Earth* (Oxford, 1971).

Cadbury, E., 'Some Principles of Industrial Organisation: The Case for and against Scientific Management', *Sociological Review* vol. 8 (1914).

Cameron, R., *Banking in the Early Stages of Industrialisation: A Comparative Study* (Oxford, 1967).

Carchedi, G., 'The Reproduction of Social Classes at the Level of Production Relations', *Economy and Society* vol. 4 (1975).

Carchedi, G., 'On the Economic Identification of the New Middle Class', *Economy and Society* vol. 4 (1975).

Carchedi, G., *On the Economic Identification of Social Classes* (London, 1977).

Carr-Hill, R. A. & Macdonald, K. I., *Problems in the Analysis of Life Histories*, Sociological Review Monograph no. 19 (1973).

Carr-Saunders, A. M. & Wilson, P. A., *The Professions* (London, 1933).

Castles, S. & Wüstenberg, W., *The Education of the Future: An Introduction to the Theory and Practice of Socialist Education* (London, 1979).

Chandler, A. D., *Strategy and Structure* (Cambridge, Mass., 1962).

Chandler, A. D., *The Visible Hand: The Managerial Revolution in American Business* (Cambridge, Mass., 1977).

Chesneaux, J., *Peasant Revolts in China, 1840–1949* (London, 1973).

Child, J., *The Business Enterprise in Modern Industrial Society* (London, 1969).

Child, J., *British Management Thought* (London, 1969).

Child, J., 'Organisation Structure, Environment and Performance: The Role of Strategic Choice', in G. Salaman and K. Thompson (eds.), *People and Organizations* (London, 1973).

Chinoy, E., *Automobile Workers and the American Dream* (Boston, 1965).

Clarke, S., 'Capital, Fractions of Capital and the State: "Neo-Marxist" Analyses of the South African State', *Capital and Class* no. 5 (Summer, 1978).

Clarke, W. M., *The City in the World Economy* (London, 1967).

Clegg, H., *How to Run an Incomes Policy* (London, 1971).

Cohen, P. S., *Modern Social Theory* (London, 1968).

Cotgrove, S. & Box, S., *Science, Industry and Society* (London, 1970).

Cottrell, P. L., *British Overseas Investment in the Nineteenth Century* (London, 1975).

Coxon, A. P. M. & Jones, C. L., *Class and Hierarchy: The Social Meaning of Occupations* (London, 1979).

Crewe, I., Särlvik, B. & Alt, J., 'Partisan Dealignment in Britain 1964–1974', *British Journal of Political Science* vol. 7 (1977).

Crompton, R., 'Class Mobility in Modern Britain', *Sociology* vol. 14 (1980).

Crompton, R. & Gubbay, J., *Economy and Class Structure* (London, 1977).

Crozier, M., *The Bureaucratic Phenomenon* (London, 1964).

CSE, *The Alternative Economic Strategy* (London, 1980).

Cutler, A. et al., *Marx's Capital and Capitalism Today* vol. II (London, 1971).

Dahrendorf, R., 'Recent Changes in the Class Structure of European Societies', *Daedalus* (Winter, 1964).

Dalton, M., *Men who Manage* (New York, 1959).

Davis, H. H., Beyond Class Images (London, 1979).

Davis, L. E., 'Pacing Effects on Manned Assembly Lines', *International Journal of Production Research* vol. 4 (1966).

de Brunhof, S., *Marx on Money* (New York, 1976).

de Vroey, M., 'Managers and Class Relations: A Marxist View of Ownership and Control', in T. Nichols (ed.), *Capital and Labour* (London, 1980).

Delphy, C., 'Continuities and Discontinuities in Marriage and Divorce', in D. Barker and S. Allen (eds.), *Sexual Divisions and Society: Process and Change* (London, 1976).

Delphy, C., 'Women in Stratification Studies', in H. Roberts (ed.), *Doing Feminist Research* (London, 1981).

Department of Employment Gazette, 'Female Activity Rates: Annex', (January, 1974).

Derber, C., 'Underemployment and the American Dream – "Underemployment Consciousness" and Radicalism among Young Workers', *Sociological Inquiry* vol. 49 (1979).

Dickson, D., *Alternative Technology* (London, 1974).

Dobb, M., *Studies in the Development of Capitalism* (London, 1963).

Doeringer, P. B. & Piore, M. J., *Internal Labor Markets and Manpower Analysis* (Lexington, Mass., 1971).

Dohrenwend, B., 'Egoism, Altruism, Anomie and Fatalism', *American Sociological Review* vol. 24 (1959).

Dowd, D. F., book review, *Contemporary Sociology* vol. 6 (1976).

Draper, H., 'The Death of the State in Marx and Engels', in R. Miliband and J. Saville (eds.), *The Socialist Register 1970* (London, 1970).

Draper, H., 'The Principle of Self-Emancipation in Marx and Engels', in R. Miliband and J. Saville (eds.), *The Socialist Register 1971* (London, 1971).

Dumont, L., *Homo Hierarchicus: The Caste System and its Implications* (London, 1970).

Bibliography

Dunn, R. W., *Labor and Automobiles* (New York, 1929).

Durkheim, E., *Suicide: A Study in Sociology* (London, 1952).

Durkheim, E., *Professional Ethics and Civic Morals* (London, 1957).

Durkheim, E., *Socialism* (New York, 1962).

Durkheim, E., The Division of Labour in Society (New York, 1968).

Easton, L. & Guddat, K. (eds.), *Writings of the Young Marx on Philosophy and Society* (New York, 1967).

Edwards, R., *Contested Terrain: The Transformation of the Workplace in the Twentieth Century* (London, 1980).

Ehrenreich, J. & Ehrenreich, B., 'The Professional-Managerial Class', *Radical America* vol. 11 (1977).

Elder, J. W., 'Fatalism in India', *Anthropological Quarterly* vol. 39 (1966).

Elder, J. W., 'Religious Beliefs and Political Attitudes', in D. E. Smith (ed.), *South Asian Politics and Religion* (Princeton, 1966).

Elias, N., 'Problems of Involvement and Detachment', *British Journal of Sociology* vol. 7 (1956).

Elliot, J., *Conflict or Co-operation* (London, 1978).

Elliott, P., 'Professional Ideology and Social Situation', in G. Esland, G. Salaman and M. A. Speakman (eds.), *People and Work* (Edinburgh, 1975).

Engels, F., 'On Authority', in Karl Marx and Frederick Engels, *Selected Works* vol. II (Moscow, 1950).

Engels, F., *Anti-Dühring* (London, 1969).

Enthoven, R. E., 'Lingayat', in *Encyclopedia of Religion and Ethics* vol. VIII.

Erikson, C., *British Industrialists: Steel and Hosiery, 1850–1950* (Cambridge, 1959).

Erikson, R., Goldthorpe, J. H. & Portocarero, L., 'Intergenerational Class Mobility in Three Western European Societies', *British Journal of Sociology* vol. 30 (1979).

Evans, M., 'Marx Studies', *Political Studies* vol. 18 (1970).

Evans, M., 'Karl Marx and the Concept of Political Participation', in G. Parry (ed.), *Participation in Politics* (Manchester, 1972).

Evans, M., *Karl Marx* (London, 1975).

Everitt, B., *Cluster Analysis* (London, 1974).

Fieldhouse, D. K., *Economics and Empire, 1830–1914* (London, 1973).

Fifth Report of the Commissioners appointed to inquire into the Practice and Proceedings of the Superior Courts of Common Law, 3 May 1833, House of Commons.

Fletcher, C., 'On Replication: Notes on the Notions of a Replicability Quotient and a Generalizability Quotient', *Sociology* vol. 4 (1970).

Florence, P. S., *The Logic of British and American Industry* (London, 1972; originally published 1953).

Ford, J. & Box, S., 'Sociological Theory and Occupational Choice', *Sociological Review* vol. 15 (1967).

Form, W. H. & Miller, D. C., 'Occupational Career Patterns as a Sociological Instrument', *American Journal of Sociology* vol. 54 (1949).

Fox, A., *Beyond Contract: Work, Power and Trust Relations* (London, 1974).

Francis, A., 'Families, Firms and Finance Capital', *Sociology* vol. 14 (1980).

Friedman, A. L., *Industry and Labour: Class Struggle at Work and Monopoly Capitalism* (London, 1977).

Galbraith, J. K., *The New Industrial State* (Harmondsworth, 1974).

Gans, H. J., 'Poverty and Culture: Some Basic Questions about Methods of Studying Life-Styles of the Poor', in P. Townsend (ed.), *The Concept of Poverty* (London, 1970).

Garaudy, R., *Karl Marx: The Evolution of His Thought* (London, 1967).

Garson, B., 'Luddites in Lordstown', *Harper's Magazine* (June, 1972).

Gerry, C. & Birkbeck, C., 'The Petty Commodity Producer in Third World Cities', in F. Bechhofer and B. Elliott (eds.), *The Petite Bourgeoisie: Comparative Studies of the Uneasy Stratum* (London, 1981).

Gerth, H. H. & Wright Mills, C., *From Max Weber* (London, 1948).

Gibbons, R. W., 'Showdown at Lordstown', *Commonweal* vol. 95 (3 March 1972).

Giddens, A., *The Class Structure of the Advanced Societies* (London, 1973).

Giddens, A., *New Rules of Sociological Method* (London, 1976).

Giddens, A., *Studies in Social and Political Theory* (London, 1977).

Giddens, A., *Central Problems in Social Theory* (London, 1979).

Giddens, A., *A Contemporary Critique of Historical Materialism* (London, 1981).

Gilpin, R., *U.S. Power and the Multinational Corporation: The Political Economy of Foreign Direct Investment* (London, 1976).

Goffee, R. & Scase, R., 'Fraternalism and Paternalism as Employers' Strategies in Small Firms', paper presented at the Annual Conference of the British Sociological Association (Aberystwyth, 1981).

Goffman, E., *Asylums* (New York, 1961).

Goldthorpe, J. H., 'Reply to Crompton', *Sociology* vol. 14 (1980).

Goldthorpe, J. H. & Hope, K., *The Social Grading of Occupations: A New Approach and Scale* (Oxford, 1974).

Goldthorpe, J. H., Llewellyn, C. & Payne, C., *Social Mobility and Class Structure in Modern Britain* (Oxford, 1980).

Gooding, J., 'Blue-Collar Blues on the Assembly Line', *Fortune* vol. 82 (July, 1970).

Gordon, D. M., 'Capitalist Efficiency and Socialist Efficiency', *Monthly Review* vol. 28 (1976).

Gordon, R. A., *Business Leadership in the Large Corporation* (Berkeley, 1961).

Gorz, A., *Strategy for Labor: A Radical Proposal* (Boston, 1967).

Gorz, A., 'Technical Intelligence and the Capitalist Division of Labour', *Telos* vol. 12 (1972).

Gouldner, A. W., 'Cosmopolitans and Locals: Toward an Analysis of Latent Social Roles, I, II', *Administrative Science Quarterly* vol. 2 (1957, 1958).

Gouldner, A. W., *The Future of Intellectuals and the Rise of the New Class* (London, 1979).

Habib, I., *The Agrarian Structure of the Mughal State* (Bombay, 1963).

Hall, S., 'The "Political" and the "Economic" in Marx's Theory of Classes', in A. Hunt (ed.), *Class and Class Structure* (London, 1977).

Haller, M. & Hodge, R. W., 'Class Structure and Career Mobility of Men and Women', paper presented to the 9th World Congress of Sociology (Uppsala, 1978).

Hardin, R., 'Stability of Statist Regimes: Industrialisation and Institutionalisation', in T. R. Burns and W. Buckley (eds.), *Power and Control* (London, 1976).

Bibliography

Harding, A., *A Social History of English Law* (London, 1965).
Harrington, M., 'The New Class and the Left', in B. Bruce-Briggs (ed.), *The New Class?* (New Brunswick, 1979).
Heath, A., *Social Mobility* (London, 1981).
Hilferding, R., *Finance Capital* (1910). English trans. (London, 1981).
Hilferding, R., *Das historische Problem*. In *Zeitschrift für Politik* (new series) vol. 1 (1954); part translation in T. Bottomore (ed.), *Modern Interpretations of Marx* (Oxford, 1981).
Hilton, B., *Cash, Corn and Commerce: The Economic Policies of Tory Governments, 1815–1830* (Oxford, 1977).
Hirst, P., 'On Struggle in the Enterprise', in M. Prior (ed.), *The Popular and the Political* (London, 1981).
Hobsbawm, E., *Industry and Empire* (London, 1968).
Hodges, D. C., 'The "Intermediate Classes" in Marxian Theory', *Social Research* vol. 28 (1961).
Holland, S., *The Socialist Challenge* (London, 1975).
House of Commons Sixth Report vol. xxvi (2 May, 1934).
Hutton, J. H., *Caste in India* (Cambridge, 1946).
Ingham, G. K., *Capitalism Divided* (London, forthcoming).
Jacoby, R., review of Harry Braverman, *Labor and Monopoly Capital*, *Telos* no. 29 (1976).
Jessop, B., 'Remarks on Some Recent Theories of the Capitalist State', *Cambridge Journal of Economics* vol. 1 (1977).
Johnson, B. D., 'Durkheim's One Cause of Suicide', *American Sociological Review* vol. 30 (1965).
Johnson, C., *Revolutionary Change* (Boston, 1966).
Johnson, T. J., 'Imperialism and the Professions: Notes on the Development of Professional Occupations in Britain's Colonies and the New States', in P. Halmos (ed.), *Professionalization and Social Change*, Sociological Review Monograph no. 20 (Keele, 1973).
Johnson, T. J., 'What is to be Known: The Structural Determination of Social Class', *Economy and Society* vol. 6 (1977).
Johnson, T. J. & Caygill, M., *Community in the Making: Aspects of Britain's Role in the Development of Professional Education in the Commonwealth* (Institute of Commonwealth Studies, University of London, 1972).
Johnson, T. J. & Caygill, M., 'The Royal Institute of British Architects and the Commonwealth Profession', *Working Paper* no. 5 (Institute of Commonwealth Studies, London, 1972).
Johnson, T. J. & Caygill, M., 'The British Medical Association and its Overseas Branches: A Short History', *Journal of Imperial and Commonwealth History* vol. 1 (1973).
Johnson, T. J. & Caygill, M., 'The Development of Accountancy Links in the Commonwealth', in R. H. Parker (ed.), *Readings in Accounting and Business Research, 1970–77* (London, 1978).
Kamenka, E., *The Ethical Foundations of Marxism* (revised edition, London, 1972).
Kaye, B. L. B., *The Development of the Architectural Profession in Britain: A Sociological Study* (London, 1960).
Kelly, M. P., *White-Collar Proletariat: The Industrial Behaviour of British Civil Servants* (London, 1980).

Kerr, C., Dunlop, J. T., Habison, F. & Myers, C. A., *Industrialism and Industrial Man* (Cambridge, Mass., 1960).

King, R. & Nugent, N. (eds.), *Respectable Rebels* (Dunton Green, 1979).

King, W., *History of the London Discount Market* (London, 1936).

Knight, A. de & J., *Caste and Race: Comparative Approaches* (London, 1967).

Konrád, G. & Szelényi, I., *The Intellectuals on the Road to Class Power* (Brighton, 1979).

Korpi, W., *The Working Class in Welfare Capitalism* (London, 1978).

Kothari, R., *Politics in India* (Boston, 1970).

Kristol, I., 'About Equality', *Commentary* (November, 1972).

Kuhn, J. W., *Bargaining in Grievance Settlement* (New York, 1961).

Land, H., 'Women: Supporters or Supported', in D. Barker and S. Allen (eds.), *Sexual Divisions and Society: Process and Change* (London, 1976).

Lane, C., *The Rites of the Rulers: Ritual in Industrial Society, the Soviet Case* (Cambridge, 1981).

Lannoy, R., *The Speaking Tree* (Oxford, 1971).

Lattimore, O., *Inner Asian Frontiers of China* (New York, 1940).

Law Times vol. 7 (2 May 1846).

Law Times vol. 7 (5 August 1846).

Law Times vol. 30 (28 November 1857).

Lee, D. J., 'Skin, Craft and Class: A Theoretical Critique and a Critical Case', *Sociology* vol. 15 (1981).

Legal Observer vol. 32 (29 August 1846).

Lenin, V. I., *Collected Works* vol. xv and xxii (London, 1949).

Lenin, V. I., *The Development of Capitalism in Russia* (Moscow, 1956).

Levenson, J. R., *Confucian China and its Modern Fate* vol. II (London, 1964).

Levine, A., *Industrial Revolution in Britain* (London, 1967).

Lewis, R. & Maude, A., *The English Middle Classes* (London, 1949).

Lewis, R. & Maude, A., *Professional People* (London, 1952).

Lienard, B. H. S. & Llewellyn, C. M., 'The Analysis of Life History Data using Graphical Devices' (unpublished paper).

Littler, C., *Control and Conflict* (London, 1981).

Littler, C. & Salaman, G., 'Bravermania and Beyond' (forthcoming).

Lockwood, D., *The Blackcoated Worker* (London, 1958).

Lockwood, D., 'Sources of Variation in Working Class Images of Society', *Sociological Review* vol. 14 (1966).

Longstreth, F., 'The City, Industry and the State', in C. Crouch (ed.), *State, Economy and Contemporary Capitalism* (London, 1979).

Loveridge, R., 'Business Strategy and Community Culture', in D. Dunkerley and G. Salaman (eds.), *The International Yearbook of Organisational Studies* (London, 1982).

Lowell, J., 'Lowdown on Lordstown – GMAD: Jekyll or Hyde', *Ward's Auto World* (April, 1972).

McCormack, W., 'Lingayats as a Sect', *Journal of the Royal Anthropological Institute* vol. 93 (1963).

Mackenzie, G., 'Class and Class Consciousness: Marx Re-examined', *Marxism Today* (March, 1976).

Mackenzie, G., 'The Political Economy of the American Working Class', *British Journal of Sociology* vol. 28 (1977).

McLellan, D., 'Marx and the Whole Man', in B. Parekh (ed.), *The Concept of Socialism* (London, 1975).

Macpherson, C. B., *The Real World of Democracy* (Oxford, 1966).

Malalgoda, K., 'Millennialism in Relation to Buddhism', *Comparative Studies in Society and History* vol. 12 (1970).

Mallet, S., *The New Working Class* (Nottingham, 1975).

Mandel, E., *The Formation of the Economic Thought of Karl Marx* (London, 1971).

Mann, M., 'The Social Cohesion of Liberal Democracy', *American Sociological Review* vol. 35 (1970).

Mann, M., *Workers on the Move* (London, 1973).

Mannheim, K., *Ideology and Utopia* (London, 1952).

Marglin, S., 'What do Bosses do?', in A. Gorz (ed.), *The Division of Labour* (Hassocks, Sussex, 1976).

Marriott, McK., *Village India* (Chicago, 1955).

Marsh, R. M., *The Mandarins* (New York, 1961).

Marshall, G., *Presbyteries and Profits* (Oxford, 1981).

Martin, J. & Norman, A., *The Computerized Society* (Englewood Cliffs, N.J., 1970).

Marx, K., *Capital* vols. I–III (London, 1960).

Marx, K., 'Contribution to the Critique of Hegel's Philosophy of Right. Introduction' (1844). English translation in T. Bottomore (ed.), *Karl Marx: Early Writings* (London, 1963).

Marx, K., *The Poverty of Philosophy* (New York, 1963).

Marx, K., *The German Ideology* (London, 1965).

Marx, K., *A Contribution to the Critique of Political Economy* (Moscow, 1970).

Marx, K. & Engels, F., *Manifesto of the Communist Party (1848)* (Moscow, 1959).

Marx, K. & Engels, F., *Selected Correspondence* (Moscow, 1965).

Marx, K. & Engels, F., 'The Eighteenth Brumaire of Louis Bonaparte', in *Selected Works* Vol. I (London, 1968).

Marx, K. & Engels, F., *On the Paris Commune* (Moscow, 1971).

Massey, D. B. & Catalano, A., *Capital and Land* (London, 1978).

Mathias, P., *The First Industrial Nation* (London, 1969).

Mayer, A. J., 'The Lower Middle Class as Historical Problem', *Journal of Modern History* vol. 47 (1975).

Mepham, J., 'The *Grundrisse:* Method or Metaphysics?', *Economy and Society* vol. 7 (1978).

Merton, R. K., 'Social Structure and Anomie', in *idem, Social Theory and Social Structure* (Glencoe, Ill., 1957).

Mészáros, I., *Marx's Theory of Alienation* (London, 1970).

Michael, F., *The Taiping Rebellion* (Seattle, 1966).

Miller, D. C. & Form, W. H., *Industrial Sociology* (New York, 1964).

Miller, S. M., 'Notes on Neo-Capitalism', *Theory and Society* vol. 2 (1975).

Minkin, L. & Seyd, P., 'The British Labour Party', in W. E. Paterson and A. H. Thomas (eds.), *Social Democratic Parties in Western Europe* (London, 1975).

Minns, R., *Pension Funds and British Capitalism* (London, 1980).

Mitzman, A., *The Iron Cage: An Historical Interpretation of Max Weber* (New York, 1970).

Mommsen, W., *The Age of Bureaucracy* (Oxford, 1974).

Moore, Jr, B., *Social Origins of Dictatorship and Democracy* (London, 1966).

Moynihan, D. P., 'Equalising Education: In whose Benefit?', *The Public Interest* (Fall, 1972).

Muirhead Little, E. J., *A History of the British Medical Association, 1832–1936* (London, 1937).

Müller, W. & Neusüss, C., 'The "Welfare-state Illusion" and the Contradiction between Wage-labour and Capital', in J. Holloway and S. Piciotto (eds.), *State and Capital, a Marxist Debate* (London, 1978).

Nadworny, M., *Scientific Management and the Unions, 1900–1932* (Cambridge, Mass., 1955).

Nairn, T., 'The Decline of the British State', *New Left Review* nos. 101–102 (1977).

Nairn, T., 'Britain's Perennial Crisis', *New Left Review* nos. 113–114 (1979).

Neustadt, I., *Le problème de l'organisation internationale en Europe centrale 1919–1939* (Paris, 1939).

Neustadt, I., 'Some Aspects of the Social Structure of Belgium' (unpublished PhD dissertation, University of London, 1944).

Neustadt, I., *Teaching Sociology* (Leicester, 1965).

Nevins, A., *Ford: The Times, the Man, the Company* (New York, 1954).

Nichols, T., *Ownership, Control and Ideology* (London, 1969).

Nicolaus, M., 'The Unknown Marx', in R. Blackburn (ed.), *Ideology in Social Science* (London, 1972).

Nicolaus, M. (ed.), *Grundrisse* (London, 1973).

Norris, G. M., 'Unemployment, Subemployment and Personal Characteristics', *Sociological Review* vol. 26 (1978).

Oakley, A. & Oakley, R., 'Sexism in Official Statistics', in J. Irvine, I. Miles and J. Evans (eds.), *Demystifying Social Statistics* (London, 1979).

Obeyesekere, G., 'Theodicy, Sin and Salvation in a Sociology of Buddism', in E. R. Leach (ed.), *Dialectic in Practical Religion* (Cambridge, 1968).

Okochi, K., Karsh, B. & Lervine, S. (eds.), *Workers and Employers in Japan* (Princeton, 1974).

Ollman, B., *Alienation* (Cambridge, 1971).

Ollman, B., 'Marx's Vision of Communism: A Reconstruction', *Critique* no. 3 (1977).

O'Malley, L. S. S., *Popular Hinduism: The Religion of the Masses* (Cambridge, 1935).

Oren, L., 'The Welfare of Women in Labouring Families: England 1860–1950', *Feminist Studies* vol. 1 (1973).

Ossowski, S., *Class Structure in the Social Consciousness* (London, 1963).

Page, C. H., *Class and American Sociology* (New York, 1969).

Pahl, J., 'Patterns of Money Management within Marriage', *Journal of Social Policy* vol. 9 (1980).

Pahl, R. E., 'Employment, Work and the Domestic Division of Labour', *International Journal of Urban and Regional Research* vol. 4 (1980).

Pahl, R. E. & Winkler, J. T., 'The Economic Elite: Theory and Practice', in P. Stanworth and A. Giddens (eds.), *Elites and Power in British Society* (Cambridge, 1974).

Palmer, B., 'Class, Conception and Conflict; the Thrust for Efficiency, Managerial Views of Labour and Working Class Rebellion, 1903–22', *Review of Radical Political Economy* vol. 7 (1975).

Panich, L., *Social Democracy and Industrial Militancy* (Cambridge, 1976).

Panich, L., 'Trade Unions and the Capitalist State', *New Left Review* no. 123 (1981).

Parker, S. R., 'Occupation', in P. Barker (ed.), *A Sociological Portrait* (Harmondsworth, 1972).

Parker, S. R., Brown, R., Child, J. & Smith, M., *The Sociology of Industry* (London, 1977).

Parkin, F., 'Social Stratification', in T. Bottomore and R. Nisbet (eds.), *A History of Sociological Analysis* (London, 1978).

Parkin, F., *Marxism and Class Theory* (London, 1979).

Parsons, T., *The Structure of Social Action* (New York, 1937).

Parsons, T., *The Social System* (Glencoe, Ill., 1952).

Parsons, T., 'The Professions', in *International Encyclopaedia of the Social Sciences* (New York, 1968).

Pashukanis, E., *Law and Marxism: A General Theory* (London, 1978).

Paterson, W. E. & Thomas, A. H. (eds.), *Social Democratic Parties in Western Europe* (London, 1975).

Payne, G., Ford, G. & Robertson, C., 'Changes in Occupational Mobility in Scotland', *The Scottish Journal of Sociology* vol. 1 (1976).

Pennings, J., *Interlocking Directorates* (San Francisco, 1980).

Pettigrew, A., 'Occupational Specialization as an Emergent Process', in G. Esland, G. Salaman and M. A. Speakman (eds.), *People and Work* (Edinburgh, 1975).

Pierson, S., *Marxism and the Origins of British Socialism* (Ithaca, N.Y., 1973).

Plamenatz, J., *Man and Society* vol. II (London, 1969).

Poulantzas, N., *Political Power and Social Classes* (London, 1973).

Poulantzas, N., *Classes in Contemporary Capitalism* (London, 1975).

Poulantzas, N. & Miliband, R., 'The Problem of the Capitalist State', in R. Blackburn (ed.), *Ideology in Social Science* (London, 1972).

Purcell, V., *The Boxer Uprising* (Cambridge, 1963).

Purdy, D., 'The Left's Alternative Economic Strategy', *Politics and Power* vol. 1 (1980).

Radcliffe, G. R. Y. & Cross, G. in G. J. Hand and D. J. Bentley (eds.), *The English Legal System* (London, 1977).

Ramanujan, A. K. (translator), *Speaking of Siva* (London, 1973).

Rao, M. S. A., *Tradition, Rationality and Change* (Bombay, 1972).

Rapp, R., Ross, E. & Bridenthal, R., 'Examining Family History', *Feminist Studies* vol. 5 (1979).

Rattansi, A., *Marx and the Division of Labour* (London, 1981).

Reader, W. J., *Imperial Chemical Industries* (Oxford, 1970).

Reisman, L., 'A Study in Role Conceptions in Bureaucracy', *Social Forces* vol. 27 (1949).

Renner, K., *Wandlungen der modernen Gesellschaft: Zwei Abhandlungen über die Probleme der Nachkriegszeit* (Vienna, 1953).

Report of the Committee of Inquiry on Small Firms (The Bolton Report), Cmnd. 4811 (London, 1971).

Report of the Committee of Inquiry on Industrial Democracy (The Bullock Report), Cmnd. 6706 (London, 1977).

Rex, J. A., 'Capitalism, Elites, and the Ruling Class', in P. Stanworth and A. Giddens (eds.), *Elites and Power in British Society* (Cambridge, 1974).

Robertson Smith, W., *The Religion of the Semites* (New York, 1956).

Robertson Smith, W., 'The Importance of Religious Practice', in L. Schneider (ed.), *Religion, Culture and Society* (New York, 1964).

Robson, W. A., *Welfare State and Welfare Society* (London, 1976).

Rogers, E. M., *Modernization among Peasants* (New York, 1969).

Rothschild, E., *Paradise Lost* (New York, 1973).

Rubinstein, W. D., 'Wealth, Elites and the Class Structure of Modern Britain', *Past and Present* vol. 76 (1977).

Rubinstein, W. D., *Men of Property* (London, 1981).

Sarfatti Larson, M., 'Proletarianization and Educated Labour', *Theory and Society* vol. 9 (1980).

Sargent, J. R., 'U.K. Performance in Services', in F. Blackaby (ed.), *De-Industrialisation* (London, 1979).

Sariola, S., 'Fatalism and Anomie: Components of Rural–Urban Differences', *Kansas Journal of Sociology* vol. 1 (1965).

Scase, R. & Goffee, R., *The Real World of the Small Business Owner* (London, 1980).

Scase, R. & Goffee, R., ' "Traditional" Petty Bourgeois Attitudes: The Case of Self-Employed Craftsmen', *Sociological Review* vol. 29 (1981).

Scase, R. & Goffee, R., *The Entrepreneurial Middle Class* (London, 1982).

Scharf, L., *To Work and to Wed* (London, 1980).

Schmidt, A., *The Concept of Nature in Marx* (London, 1971).

Schmitter, P. C. & Lehmbruch, G., *Trends towards Corporatist Intermediation* (London, 1979).

Schumacher, E. F., *Small is Beautiful* (London, 1973).

Scott, J., *Corporations, Classes and Capitalism* (London, 1979).

Scott, J. & Hughes, M., *The Anatomy of Scottish Capital* (London, 1980).

Serrin, W, *The Company and the Union* (New York, 1974).

Shih, V. Y. C., *The Taiping Ideology: its Sources, Interpretations and Influences* (Seattle, 1972).

Sifton, P., *The Belt* (New York, 1927).

Silver, A., Zussman, R., Whalley, P. & Crawford, S., 'Work and Ideology among Engineers: An International Comparison of the "New Working Class" ', paper presented to the Annual Meeting of the American Sociological Association (1979).

Silverberg, J. (ed.), *Social Mobility in the Caste System in India* (The Hague, 1968).

Singer, M., review of M. Weber's *Religion of India*, *American Anthropologist* vol. 63 (1961).

Smith, D. E., 'A Peculiar Eclipsing: Women's Exclusion from Man's Culture', *Women's Studies International Quarterly* vol. 1 (1978).

Smith, D. J., *Unemployment and Racial Minorities* (London, 1981).

Social Trends (Government Statistical Service, London, 1980).

Srinivas, M. N., *Social Change in Modern India* (Berkeley, 1966).

Stacey, M., 'Family and Household', in Margaret Stacey (ed.), *Comparability in Social Research* (London, 1969).

Stacey, N. A. H., *English Accountancy: A Study in Social and Economic History* (London, 1954).

Stanworth, P. & Giddens, A., *Elites and the British Class Structure* (Cambridge, 1974).

Stark, D., 'Class Struggle and the Transformation of the Labour Process', *Theory and Society* vol. 9 (1980).

Steinfels, P., *The Neoconservatives* (New York, 1979).

Stephens, J., 'Class Formation and Class Consciousness', *British Journal of Sociology* vol. 30 (1979).

Stevenson, S., *The Heart of Jainism* (New Delhi, 1970; first published 1915).

Stewart, A., Prandy, K. & Blackburn, R. M., *Social Stratification and Occupations* (London, 1980).

Stinchcombe, A. L., 'Social Structure and the Invention of Organizational Forms', in T. Burns (ed.), *Industrial Man* (Harmondsworth, 1969).

Struik, D. (ed.), [Karl Marx], *Economic and Philosophic Manuscripts of 1844* (London, 1970).

Sykes, G., *The Society of Captives* (Princeton, 1958).

Teng, S. Y., *The Taiping Rebellion and the Western Powers* (Oxford, 1971).

Thapar, R., *A History of India* vol. I (London, 1974).

The Times (London, 8 July 1973).

Thomas, K., *Religion and the Decline of Magic* (London, 1971).

Thomas, W. A., *The Finance of British Industry, 1914–1976* (London, 1978).

Thomas, W. I. & Znaniecki, F., *The Polish Peasant in Europe and America* (1918–20).

Thompson, G., 'Financial and Industrial Sector in the United Kingdom Economy', *Economy and Society* vol. 6 (1977).

Thorburn, P., 'Class, Mobility and Party: the Political Preferences of Englishmen' (unpublished University of Michigan PhD thesis, 1979).

Touraine, A., *La Conscience Ouvrière* (Paris, 1966).

Touraine, A., *The Post-Industrial Society* (London, 1974).

Touraine, A., *L'Après-Socialisme* (Paris, 1980).

Tribe, K., 'Remarks on the Theoretical Significance of the "Grundrisse" ', *Economy and Society* vol. 3 (1974).

Tucker, R., *Philosophy and Myth in Karl Marx* (Cambridge, 1961).

Tumin, S. M., *Social Class and Social Change in Puerto Rico* (Princeton, 1961).

Urry, J., *The Anatomy of Capitalist Societies* (London, 1981).

Vaughan, P., *Doctors' Commons* (London, 1959).

Veblen, T., *The Theory of the Leisure Class* (New York, 1953; originally published 1899).

Walker, P. (ed.), *Between Capital and Labour* (Hassocks, 1979).

Watson, T., *The Personnel Managers* (London, 1978).

Watson, T. J., *Sociology, Work and Industry* (London, 1980).

Weber, M., 'Antikritisches Schlusswort', *Archiv für Sozialwissenschaft und Sozialpolitik* vol. 31 (1910).

Weber, M., *The Methodology of the Social Sciences* (Glencoe, Ill., 1949).

Weber, M., *The Religion of China*, translated and edited by H. Gerth (Glencoe, Ill., 1951).

Weber, M., *The Religion of India* (Illinois, 1958).

Weber, M., *The Sociology of Religion* (Boston, 1963).

Weber, M., *Economy and Society*, 3 vols. (New York, 1968).

Weber, M., *The Protestant Ethic and the Spirit of Capitalism* (London, 1971; originally published 1905).

West, J., 'Women, Sex and Class', in A. Kuhn and A. M. Wolpe (eds.), *Feminism and Materialism* (London, 1978).

Westergaard, J., 'Class, Inequality and "Corporatism" ', in A. Hunt (ed.), *Class and Class Structure* (London, 1977).

Westergaard, J. & Resler, H., *Class in a Capitalist Society* (London, 1975).

Westermarck, E. A., 'Sociology as a University Study' (University of London, 1907).

Whyte, M. K., *Small Groups and Political Rituals in China* (Berkeley, 1974).

Wiener, M. J., *English Culture and the Decline of the Industrial Spirit* (Cambridge, 1981).

Wildavsky, A., 'Using Public Funds to serve Private Interests: The Politics of the New Class', in B. Bruce-Briggs (ed.), *The New Class?* (New Brunswick, 1979).

Wilensky, H. L., 'Work, Careers and Social Integration', in T. Burns (ed.), *Industrial Man* (Harmondsworth, 1969).

Williams, D., 'The Evolution of the Sterling System', in C. R. Whittlesey and J. S. G. Williams, *Essays in Money and Banking: in Honour of R. S. Sayers* (Oxford, 1968).

Winkler, J., 'The Corporatist Economy: Theory and Administration', in R. Scase (ed.), *Industrial Society* (London, 1977).

Wootton, B., *The Social Foundations of Wages Policy* (London, 1955).

Wootton, B., *Incomes Policy* (London, 1974).

Work in America, Report of a Special Task Force to the Secretary of Health, Education and Welfare (Cambridge, Mass., 1973).

Wright, E. O., 'Class Structure and Income Inequality' (unpublished PhD dissertation, Berkeley, California, 1976).

Wright, E. O., 'Class Boundaries in Advanced Capitalist Societies', *New Left Review* no. 98 (1976).

Wright, E. O., *Class, Crisis and the State* (London, 1978).

Yang, C. K., *Religion in Chinese Society* (Berkeley, 1961).

Zaehner, R. C., *Hinduism* (London, 1972).

Zeitlin, M., 'On Class Theory of the Large Corporation', *American Journal of Sociology* vol. 81 (1976).

Index